WORLD GNOSIS

Mark Amaru Pinkham

To Michele
Peace & blessings
to you
Mark Amaru

ADVENTURES UNLIMITED PRESS

World Gnosis:
The Coming Gnostic Civilization

Published by
Adventures Unlimited Press
Kempton, Illinois 60946 USA

www.adventuresunlimitedpress.com

Cover art by Onnie Kahlenberg Gutierrez
www.onnieart.com

Illustrations by
Chadwick St. John
www.inkshadows.com
William Brooks
Don Swanson

ISBN: 978-1-935487-08-1

Printed in the United States of America

10 9 8 7 6 5 4 3 2 1

World Gnosis
The Coming Gnostic Civilization

by
Mark Amaru Pinkham

Dedicated to the
World's Gnostics
Past, Present and Future

Acknowledgments

A huge thank you goes to Onnie Gutierrez for taking the time to design and create the cover. An amazing piece of work! And to Chadwick St. John for his wonderful and exotic line drawings. And to my patient wife, Andrea, who once again was forced to deal with an absent husband held hostage by his computer.

Table of Contents

Introduction

Part I: The Origin and Dispersal of the Gnostics

Chapter I: The Origin of the Gnostic Path….. ....pg 2
The Garden of Eden; the Serpent on the Tree; the Goddess Sophia; Lemuria; The First Instructor; Enki; Skanda-Murugan; Thoth-Hermes; The Peacock Angel; Neptune-Volcan; Ptah-Sokar-Osiris; Dionysus; Quetzlcoatl

Chapter 2 The Sons (and Daughters) of Seth…..................pg 50
The Sons and Daughters of Seth; of Enki; of Thoth-Hermes; of Quetzlcoatl; of Shiva; of Dionysus. Alexandrian Gnostic sects: The Sethains; The Cainites; The Carpocratians; The Barborites; The Ophites and Nasseni.

Chapter 3: The Daughters and Sons of Sophia………pg 86
The Amazons; Witchcraft of the Middle Ages; The Dianics; The Goddess is the Doer; The Goddess is our Inner Guidance; The Goddess takes us to Gnosis.

Chapter 4: The Johannite Gnostics……………………pg 100
The Mandeans; Nasoreans, Nazarenes; Essenes; John the Baptist; Simon Magus; Nag Hammadi texts; Pistis Sophia; Mary Magdalene; John the Apostle; the Lineage of Johns; The Johannite Knights Templar

Chapter 5 The Gnostic Knight Templars……....................pg 140
Origin of the Knights Templar; Rosslyn Chapel; Baphomet: The Head of John the Baptist; the Templars and the Sufis; The Templars and Essenes; The Knights Templar: Emissaries of the Left Hand Path; Templar alchemical initiations; Fall of the Templars

Chapter 6 The Sub-Rosa Gnostics……………pg 170
The Sub-Rosa Secret Societies; The Knights of the Rosy Cross; The Rosicrucians; Royal Order of Scotland; Strict Observance; St. Germain; Paris Congress of the Lodge of Philalethes

Chapter 7: The Gnostic Conspiracy………….pg 202
The Rose Cross Confederacy; the Illuminati; Rashiyana, the Illumined Ones

Chapter 8: Star Missionaries of a Gnostic Civilization ……pg 220
Extraterrestrial Missionaries from Sirius, the Pleiades, Orion, Dogon, the Hopi

Part II: The Coming Gnostic Civilization

Chapter 9: Gnostic Civilizations..pg 230
The Gnostic Civilization of Lemuria, of Shambhala, of Tibet, of Peru, of Egypt, of the Druids, of the Yezidi, of the Mandaeans, of Manichaeism, of the Cathars

Chapter 10: The Coming Gnostic Civilization..................................pg 298
The Components of the Coming World Gnostic Civilization

Part III: The Coming Gnostic Spirituality

Chapter 11: The Path of Alchemy..pg 314
The Complete Theory and History of Alchemy

Chapter 12: Safe and Easy Alchemical Practices...........................pg 372
Alchemical Meditation; Yoga; Elixirs; Alchemical Stones; Pyramids; Sweat Lodges, Alchemical Mantras

Chapter 13: Living Gnosis..pg 392
The Three Stages of Gnosis; Attitudes & Life Styles that support Gnosis

Footnotes: ....pg 402

Author pages:...pg 408
Author Biography; The International Order for Gnostic Templars; The IOGT Five Point Plan for a One-World Spirituality; Sacred Sites Journeys; The Khemit School of Ancient Mysticism; Yezidi Genocide

Introduction

Since the dawn of history ideological wars have raged around our planet regarding the purpose of human existence. Two predominant camps with opposing viewpoints have arisen in this war known as the Right and Left Hand Paths which have continually sought the destruction of each other. By another name the Right Hand Path is patriarchy; and its intellectual theology posits that human existence is about coming in alignment with the will of a vengeful and strict God that dwells in a heaven world above. By contrast, the matriarchal Left Hand Path contends that God, the Infinite Spirit, exists right within every human's heart, and the goal of life is to realize this truth while learning to live in harmony with God's power and wisdom, the Goddess, which has created the phenomenal universe out of Herself and governs it. This book is about the battle between the Right and Left Hand Paths and the divergent ideologies they have spread around the globe throughout history. It is not meant a treatise meant to denigrate either path; on the contrary, it recounts the passage of history since the Garden of Eden while ultimately seeking to show why the existence of both paths have been necessary for human evolution and its fulfillment. The reconciliation of the Left and Right Hand Paths is both necessary if we are to survive as a planetary humanity; and if prophesy serves us correctly, their peaceful truce is destine to occur soon during what has been called the Third Era and Fourth World of human history.

The Left Hand Path and its Gnostics

This book is primarily a recounting of the Left Hand Path and its gnostic ideology, practices and sects. This is because the history of the Right Hand Path and its orthodox, fundamentalist belief systems are well known by most people, as well as because the principle movers and shakers in the creation of a one-world gnostic civilization will be principally those affiliated with the Left Hand Path. Since the dawn of civilization the votaries of the Left Hand Path have experimented with cultures that had a gnostic emphasis, so their guiding influence will be indispensible in guiding us all to the Coming Gnostic Civilization.

This book will cover the initial appearance of the Left Hand Path during the fabled Garden of Eden scenario, and then move forward to its manifestations around the globe and its continual battle with the Right Hand Path. The later chapters will outline the coming reconcilliation of the two paths and their equal involvement in the gnostic civilization of the Third Era. Finally, the book will conclude with a treatise on the history and theory of the new spirituality of the Third Era, the gnostic-alchemical path, and how you can start living as a gnostic now!

Part I

The Origin and Dispersal of the Gnostics

The Origin of the Gnostics

Who are the Gnostics?

The gnostics have come from every race, color, creed, nationality and strata of society. They are simply those humans involved in the timeless quest of realizing the universal admonition of "Know Thyself." They have contacted an inner fount of intuitive knowledge through which all wisdom can be known, including the highest truth that all persons are physical embodiments of the same Infinite Spirit.

When the gnostics achieve their final and most sought-after revelation of I AM SPIRIT, the veils of social programming and lifetimes of illusion naturally fall away. Like a "thief in the night," their revelation spontaneously emerges as an unassailable knowingness. The clouds of illusion part, and the gnostic finally recognizes himself or herself to be the unlimited and eternal consciousness that transcends all concepts and phenomenon in the physical universe. Finally, as the gnostic authors of the *Gospel of Truth* clearly states, the enlightened human finally knows from "whence he has come and whither he is going."

To achieve their goal, gnostics worldwide have followed the ideology and alchemical practices of the Left Hand Path which were first taught to Adam and Eve by the gnostic Goddess Sophia or her Son as the Serpent on the Tree. Following Eden, the rites and practices of the Left Hand Path were passed down to gnostics the world over, who collectively have been referred to by their peers as venerators of the Goddess and "Adepts of the Mother."[1] The Left Hand Path practices activate a manifestation of the Goddess within the human body, which is an alchemical power that leads an aspirant to the gnostic wisdom lying dormant within certain gnostic centers and inside the human heart. Various gnostic traditions worldwide have acknowledged the existence of this force, referring to it variously as the Holy Spirit, the power of the Dark Goddess, Baraka, as well as Kundalini or the Serpent Power.

Since this power culminates in complete alchemical purification, the gnostic path of the Goddess is a "serpent" path that can lead to many deaths and rebirths, like a snake that is constantly shedding its own skin. It will, however, eventually culminate in the eternally unchanging state that accompany both physical and spiritual immortality.

Where was the Garden of Eden of the Gnostics?

If we use both the legends of the ancients and the academically accepted tool of Continental Drift Theory for locating Eden, we must accept that the Garden existed in the region of what is now the Pacific Ocean. Continental Drift Theory posits that the earliest continents on Earth were initially joined as a primal land mass known as Pangea. When this incipient continent split apart it gave rise to Gondwanaland, a smaller but still colossal continent that covered the entire southern hemisphere. When Gondwanaland subsequently split it gave rise to the still smaller land mass known as Lemuria, a continent best known for extending across the Pacific Ocean and into the neighboring Indian Ocean. The indigenous myths of the pan-Pacific people, as well as a multitude of legends worldwide, agree that it was here, on Lemuria, that human evolution was initiated.

The legends of Lemuria held by the pan-Pacific peoples all identify Lemuria as the "Motherland;" it was both the Land of the Goddess and the cradle of humanity. The legends of the Easter Islanders allude to this continent as Hiva, the "Motherland," which once swallowed up their current, tiny island and connected it with many other islands. The Hawaiian legends recollect the Pacific Motherland with numerous titles, including the Land of Goddess Rua. This was a name for the Pacific Motherland found in their creation myth, *Tumuripo*, that first brought forth humans. The Hawaiians also remember their early Motherland as Havai'i, which means "the streaming terrain over which moisture rained," as well as Havai'i-ti-Havai'i, meaning "the land where life sprang into existence and developed growth."[2] In their legends, the Samoans allude to the Pacific continent as Talua or Tahua, the "mother country," where the wise men or Tahunas appeared (Tahuna later evolved into Kahuna). The Tahitian wise men can still be found alluding to an earlier and much larger continent called "Tahiti," which was a name of the Motherland when the Gods came down to Earth and established divine lineages of kings to teach the first humans. They also speak of modern Tahiti as having anciently been part of the "Islands of the Mu," perhaps alluding to a time in Lemurian history when the continent was divided up into hundreds or even thousands of islands. The Hindus, who are anciently related to the

Polynesians, fondly remember the Pacific Motherland as Rutas, a name that ostensibly reveals a common ancient origin with "Rua." The Tamils of south India remember Lemuria as Kumari Nadu or Kumari Kandam, meaning the "Land of the Goddess Kumari" or the "Land of the Kumara Immortals." Most of these Pacific legends of Lemuria also agree that the Motherland harbored one of the most spiritual civilizations that ever existed on Earth, and that the patroness and founder of this civilization was the Goddess herself. Her teachers were Her Sons, who took physical form as the Sons of God/Goddess from other dimensions and star systems to teach the various components of the Goddess spiritual tradition. These emmisaries of the Goddess taught and exemplified the highest respect and veneration for the female principle in all thought, word, and deed, and initially their favored and principal students were female. They taught that the Goddess was the pure, cosmic energy that had crystallized into all life forms on Earth, as well as the all pervasive nurturing presence that tends to the needs of all Her "children." Each living thing on Earth was a child or progeny of the Goddess; and they had been created out of the same substratum, the Goddess' universal body of dynamic energy, thus making them completely equal. When any of the Goddess' children were ready to truly know themselves, She was also the uplifting power that could reveal their identity as a divine incarnation of Spirit.

Not only the pan-Pacific peoples, but the Right Hand Path religion of Islam has also indentified Lemuria with the ancient Garden of Eden, albeit solely that part of the continent now known as the Island of Sri Lanka. Moslems claim that it was on Sri Lanka that God placed Adam, and the first man's footprint on the top of Adam's Peak, the island's second highest mountain, remains a timeless symbol of his arrival on the island. When Adam hiked down from this peak the Eden scenario of legend ensued.

The Moslems also maintain that although Sir Lanka as the Garden of Eden, the island was not the first Eden but a terrestrial mirror of a more etheric Paradise. Adam and Eve's original sin occurred in an upper astral Paradise, and they were then tossed down to mirror image garden on Earth for their crime. Adam landed on Sri Lanka and Eve's descent brought her to a location in the Middle East, but Adam soon located her and transported her to the island so they could begin the evolution of the human race.

Thus, the Moslem legend points to two Edens: a celestial Garden of Eden and its terrestrial mirror image on Earth, Sri Lanka. Their enigmatic history of two Edens was also embraced by the gnostic Ophites of Alexandria and the Mandaeans, a gnostic sect of southern Iraq, whose legends trace their roots back to Sri Lanka. In alluding to the celestial Eden as the site of the First Fall of humanity, the Ophite historians stated:

"It was the Serpent, who by tempting (Adam and Eve), brought them Gnosis...That is why Ildabaoth, mad with fury, cast it down from the heavens."[3]

The Mandaeans' myth of two Edens is perhaps the most unique. It states that the celestial Adam and Eve, whom they call Adam Kasia and Hawa (Eve) Kasia, remained in the etheric paradise even after the orignal sin while their physical counterparts, Adam Paghra and Hawa Paghra, were subsequently created in an Eden on Sri Lanka. This Mandaean creation legend was disclosed to Lady Ethel Stefana Drower of Britain, who was allowed to live and study with the Mandeans in the 1920s. The rest of the myth is as follows:

"The story of our nation is this. Two hundred and fifty (thousand) years ago the Subba (a name for the Mandeans, meaning "Baptizers"), who are the true children of Adam Paghra and Hawa Paghra, lived in Serandib (Sri Lanka). They were all cut off by plague except one pair, whose names were Ram and Rud. These had children who in turn multiplied until at last there were many of them, a race of mankind. But, after 150,000 years, by the command of Hiwel Ziwa (the Creator), the whole earth broke into flames and only two escaped. These were Shurbey and Shurhabiel. These children multiplied and increased and became a people again. All this was in Serendib."[4]

According to some maps from south India, as recently 30,000 BCE the island of Sir Lanka was joined with the tip of India as the ancient "Pandyan Kingdom," and both countries were united to a western section of Lemuria that extended into the Indian Ocean. Therefore, the ancient legend of Eden recounted by both the Moslems and Mandaeans apparently refers to a period when Sri Lanka was part of the continent of Lemuria, the collosal land mass that was the true Motherland and Garden of Eden.

The Gnostics' "First Instructor"

According to the Alexandrian gnostics, once Adam and Eve were settled in their terrestrial Eden they encountered the Serpent on the Tree and were taught by it the wisdom of gnosis. Depending on the gnostic sect, the legendary snake was identified by them as either a manifestation of the Son of the Goddess Sophia, or Sophia herself, who had spiraled into the fabled Garden to serve as the First Instructor and Savior of humanity. Taken together, the collection of Alexandrian legends maintain that the First Instructor appeared in order to save humanity from one of Sophia's other Seven Sons, Ildabaoth, who had created the physical bodies of the first couple but refused to reveal to them the divinity that existed within their own hearts as

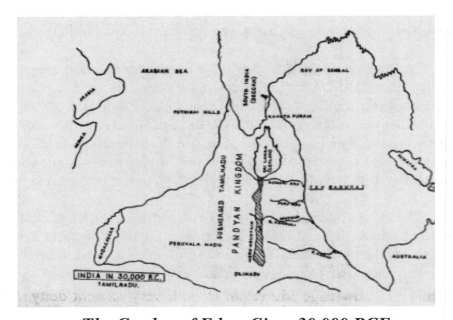

The Garden of Eden, Circa 30,000 BCE
*South India and Sri Lanka are joined together as the Pandyan Kingdom,
which is itself joined to the Pacific Continent of Lemuria.*

7362 foot Adam's Peak in the Garden of Eden of Sri Lanka
Courtesy of Martin Gray, www.SacredSites.com

The Temple of Sri Pada, "The Holy Footprint"
Photo by Mark Amaru Pinkham

A Buddhist monk venerating the Holy Footprint on Adam's Peak
Courtesy of Martin Gray, www.SacredSites.com

the Infinite Spirit. Instead, he kept them ignorant of their divinity and forced them to obey his oppressive laws. It was for this reason that the compassionate Sophia (or her Son) descended to lift the veil of false identification from humanity and the suffering that accompanies it.

The Descent of the Serpent into the Garden

To truly understand the Serpent on the Tree the sequence of events leading up to its descent into the Garden of Eden must first be reviewed. Before its manifestation in the fabled Garden, the Serpent on the Tree had been born as the Primal Serpent that precipitated out of the Infinite Spirit at the beginning of time. It was pure energy and the first finite form of God, through which the Infinite Spirit was able to create the physical universe out of itself. From a scientific perspective, the Primal Serpent represents the primal mass of fiery energy that spiraled through the universe like innumerable serpents following the Big Bang, and then eventually cooled to take on definitive, solid forms.

The Primal Serpent and the fiery energy it embodied was conceived within the minds of the early cosmologists to be a spiraling snake that slithered down a colossal cosmic tree. As it descended, the energy of the snake became increasingly dense until it crystallized into solid matter at the base of the tree. The gnostic teachers of the Kabbala represented this progressive contraction of primal energy in their original diagrams of the Tree of Life. The serpent was depicted as slithering down from the top of the tree and around its 10 globes or Sephiroth from Kether to Malkuth (see image on following page). This version of the Tree of Life was meant to reveal that the serpent began as a life force emanation from Kether, the creator, and ended as the density of matter at Malkuth.

The Two Edens

Since *Genesis* has the Serpent in Eden slithering upon the upper branches of the Tree, the drama of Eden must occurred before the primal energy had crystallized into dense matter. Only at the base of the tree does the Serpent life force become completely solid. So if the dense Earth had not yet been created when the Eden scenario occured, the Garden must have existed on another level or dimension of the multi-layered universe. This conclusion is consistent with the Moslem, Ophite, and Mandaean interpretations of the Eden myth.

Thus, when we first meet Adam and Eve they apparently occupy a celestial Eden of a high dimensional frequency. They are enjoying an etheric Paradise until attraction to some fruit on a tree catalyzes their descent to a terrestrial Eden of a physical world of a lower frequency. Such fruit could have only triggered such a fall into physicality if it was somehow incongruent with Paradise, since its enjoyment precipitated the eviction of Adam and Eve. Most probably the density of the "fruit" was inconsistent with the high frequencies and the consciousness of oneness that pervaded the etheric Paradise, and its delightful sensual indulgence was part of (and a doorway into) a denser and dualistic world. The "fruit" may therefore have represented both the sensual pleasures found on the physical plane, as well as the "fruits" of understanding that accrue through capricious, earthplane experience, where judgement is made between right and wrong, good and evil. This interpretation would explain why the tree was associated with the knowledge of good and evil, and why Adam, Eve and the Serpent garnered the curses they did for their abominable "sin." Their principal "curse" was to be sent down to live and die upon the physical Earth. Adam and Eve's "curse" of old age and death, as well as the pains of childbirth, are the natural consequences of descending into the temporal bodies of the physical world. And the Serpent's "curse," to descend to the base of the tree and crawl on its stomach, can similarly be explained as the primal, serpentine energy needing to contract into dense matter so that Adam and Eve would have a physical world upon which to live, as well as abundant physical fruits to enjoy. After it had become the solid Earth, the Serpent would then become "bruised" by the heels of Eve's descendants who walked upon it, and it, in turn, would bruise their heels with its hardness.

How did the Serpent teach Adam and Eve?

Because there were two Edens the primal instruction from the Serpent on the Tree could theoretically have occurred in two places and on two different dimensions. Apparently the teaching occurred in both an upper and lower Eden because the gnostics tell us that the Serpent transmitted its wisdom to Adam and Eve both in Paradise and after the dark lord Ildabaoth had created their physical bodies on Earth but left them in ignorance of their divine nature. Thus, at least some of the gnostic teachings that were passed down must have originated on the physical Eden that was Lemuria.

Of course the intriguing question that begs to be answered is: "how did the Serpent teach Adam and Eve the secrets of gnosis?" As the Divine Power and Wisdom of the Infinite Spirit itself, the Serpent *is* gnosis, so somehow it manifested within the bodies of the first couple. According to the gnostics of the East, a version of the Serpent was implanted within the bodies of Adam and Eve during their creation, and it then taught them gnostic

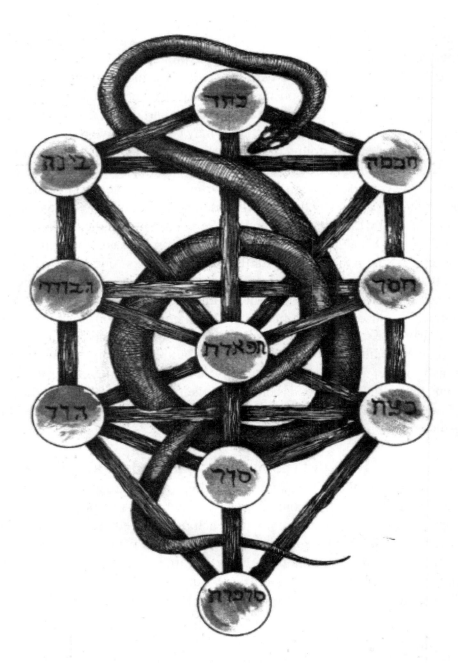

The Serpent on the Tree of Life
by Chadwick St. John
www.inkshadows.com

The Spiralling Serpent on the Tree
by Chadwick St. John
www.inkshadows.com

wisdom from within. They base this rationale on the theorem of "as above, so below," or what is in the macrocosm is mirrored in the microcosm.

For many ages the gnostics of India and China, as well as the Kabbalists and Occultists of the West, have maintained that the human body is a microcosm of the universe. The Kabbalists have asserted that the human is a microsmic reflection of the Adam Kadmon, the divine man whose body is the universe. The Chinese contend that all levels of the cosmos, as well as its 72,000 gods, reside within the human form Thus, if everything in the universe has its reflection in the human form, they collectively maintain, then Eden and the Serpent on the Tree must also have their reflection in the physical body. The inner "Tree of Life," claim these gnostics and esotericists, is manifest as the spinal cord, whose neurons extend outward like branches, and the Serpent manifests within as life force and alchemical power that slithers along the spine to the head. The gnostics claim that the inner serpentine force, which they have designated the Serpent Power, normally functions in a lower frequency within an unenlightened person and fuels their intellect and discriminatory faculty, but when a seeker is ready to know his or her true identity a higher freqency of it awakens at the base of the spine and ascends the inner Tree of Life. The person's infinite and divine nature is gradually revealed to them as the rising serpent awakens the centers of gnostic awareness along the spine known by the Hindu gnostics as chakras. The most important chakras associated with gnostic awareness are the Ajna Chakra between the eyes, and the Anahata or Heart Chakra, the central seat of the inner Spirit. Activation of the Third Eye Chakra by the ascending Serpent corresponds to a dramatic awakening of the three-quarters of the brain which are not normally active, as well as the inner antennae that receive psychic information, while the Heart Chakra, the last to fully open, aligns a person with his or her true Self and their identity as the Infinite Spirit. When the chakras are all activated they collectively work to endow a person with perfect gnostic awareness regarding both the secrets of the universe and their true identity. Awakening these chakras, say the gnostic yogis of India, is how the serpent teaches its students gnosis. It does not transmit its wisdom as audible facts or information, it does so by activating the inner gnostic centers within a person so that he or she can know the wisdom directly and intuitively. In short, the Serpent reveals the gnostic wisdom that is always there by simply opening those inner centers that can access it.

The Many Faces of the First Instructor

Since the beginning of human civilization gnostic historians around the world have attached their own indigenous names and personalities to the First Instructor and Serpent on the Tree. They have referred to it as the Goddess, or Her primal Son, as well as Guru and Savior. It has been venerated as both the "female" Goddess or Her "male" Son because, technically, it is an embodiment of pure energy and consciousness and therefore genderless. Its gender specific names and titles are unimportant and simply denote a philosophical preference. Within the following pages you will find many titles and personalities ascribed to the neutral and genderless First Instructor by the world's gnostics

The Serpent on the Tree was the Goddess

The most consistent identification of the First Instructor and Primal Serpent among the world's gnostics has been the Goddess Herself. This association initially arose in response to the need to differentiate the Infinite Spirit and its finite manifestation of serpentine energy. So the Infinite became labeled the "male" God while the Primal Serpent became the "female" Goddess. The "female" Serpent Goddess, explained the philosophers of the Left Hand Path, was the embodiment of the Divine Wisdom and Divine Power of the "male" God, and it was through Her that He had created the universe. However, while the proponents of the Left Hand Path also maintained that God and Goddess could not be separated - you cannot separate the sun from its rays or an individual from its thoughts and personal power - the promulgators of the Right Hand Path have contended that God and Goddess are eternally separate, and the latter is inferior to the former.

In light of these associations, within many of the countries where the gnostics of the Left Hand Path have flourished the Goddess has been portrated with a serpentine form and revered as the embodiment of the Divine Wisdom and Divine Power of God. Among the Alexandrian Gnostics, forexample, the Goddess was venerated by the names of Barbela and Sophia and conceived of as the incipient primal serpentine emanation of the Infinite and "Un-nameable." The name Barbela denotes the Serpent's Divine Power while Sophia, meaning "wisdom," is an epithet denoting Divine Wisdom. It was she as the Serpent on the Tree that Michelangelo painted on the ceiling of the Sistine Chapel in the Vatican during the great revival of gnostism in the Renaissance Age. Among the Hindus the primal Goddess has been venerated as Shakti, the serpent who emanates from the Infinite Spirit, Shiva. In iconography she drapes herself as multiple serpents around the neck of docile Shiva who sits in rapt stillness as a yogi lost in contemplative union with himself, the Infinite Spirit. The ancient Egyptians knew the Goddess as the Serpent Uadjet, which was the Divine Wisdom and Power that had emanated as multiple serpentine rays from the Eye of Infinite Ra. The Sumerians and Babylonians knew the Goddess as Inanna or Ishtar, "the Serpent that emanated from the Heaven God Anu."

The Goddess and Her Universal Tree

Often, wherever gnostics have venerated the Goddess they have also revered images of her as a serpent slithering upon a tree or cross, which is another manifestation of Her. Gnostics have understood that the Goddess is the great serpent of energy that crystallized into dense matter as it descended along Her alternate form of a tree or cross. The branches of the tree that the serpent encoils upon are an important part of this motif since they delineate the various levels and dimensions of the universe that the serpent descends through on its way to physicality.

The Goddess, tree-cross and serpent are all interconnected, a truth understood by the Alexandrian Gnostics who worshipped Goddess Sophia as both the serpent and the tree-cross it coiled upon. All three are different names for the primal emanation from Spirit that gradually condenses to become the levels of the universe. Motifs of the Goddess as a female, a tree-cross, or a serpent have been venerated by gnostics in India, China, Persia, Central America and the Middle East. Within these countries the tree representing the Goddess is often endowed with bountiful fruit to emphasize Her nurturing nature.

Both the cosmic tree and cross symbol of the Goddess symbolize Her as the union of Spirit and matter, Heaven and Earth. The cross embodies the polarity union intrinsic to the Goddess as a horizontal beam (female principle, matter) that is bisected and inseminated by a vertical shaft (male principle, Spirit). An interesting Masonic legend illustrates the relationship between the tree and cross, and how one can "magically" evolve into the other. The myth states that at one point following the Eden drama Adam sent his son Seth back to the Garden to obtain the Oil of Mercy which God had promised humankind. When Seth arrived at the Garden he found the tree at its center had magically transformed into a huge cross that extended from Earth to Heaven. This tree/cross was subsequently cut down and later used as wood for the cross that Jesus was crucified upon.

The Goddess and Her Twins

It is said that in the course of creating the universe the Goddess divides into Her polarity and the Primal Serpent becomes Twin Serpents. The motif of this division is the caduceus. The Twin Serpents are the male/female polarity of the Serpent and represent its Divine Wisdom (male) and its Divine Power (female). They also represent every other manifestation of the Serpent's polarity as they manifest in the cosmos following its creation, including night and day, darkness and light, proton and electron, and the male and female genders. Only through the continued interplay of the polarity can balance and stability be achieved throughout the universe.

The dual nature that is inherent to the Primal Serpent Goddess is a common motif among Left Hand Path cultures worldwide. A perfect example of the Goddess's dual nature is depicted as Goddess Coatlicue of the Mexican gnostic tradition (see image on following page). Other cultures have represented the dual aspects of the Goddess as the twin serpents of the caduesus, as well as twin boys who embody her Divine Mind and Divine Power and her two powers of creation and destruction. As both snakes and twin boys, the dual aspects of the Goddess have been known variously as the Kaberoi Twins, the Dioscouri, the Poyang of the Hopis, the Ahayuta of the Zunis, Monster Slayer and Child of the Waters, and Hunapu and Xbalenque.

Within the human body the caduceus and its twin serpents have long been identified by the Hindu, Kabbalistic, and Chinese gnostics as the two etheric serpents or energy vessels that emerge out of the Third Eye, the upper seat of the Serpent Goddess. After leaving the Third Eye these two serpentine vessels spiral down along the spine and intersect five times to produce the five chakras, each of which is associated with one of the five elements. When these twin snakes reach the lowest chakra, which corresponds to the Earth plane and the base of the inner Tree of Life, their journey is complete. They then oversee the balance of male/female and hot/cold energies in the body. When a gnostic is ready to know his or her divinity, the twins reunite as the androgynous Serpent Goddess that rises up the center spine or shaft to completely open the chakras and release their power and wisdom to the inner arsonal of the evolving gnostic.

The Serpent Goddess and Her Seven Rays

In some traditions it is recognized that the Serpent Goddess also divides into seven parts when creating the universe. These are the Goddess's seven serpent sons or seven twin boys. The seven serpent sons represent the Goddess's septenary nature that is also brought into manifestation during the creation process. As she condenses to become physical matter, the Goddess's

The Serpent Goddess Sophia on the Tree

A Tree Goddess of India

The Serpent Goddess on Her Foliated Tree-Cross

The Serpent Goddess Coatlicue
She is divided into Twin Serpents

septenary nature manifests as the seven colors and tones that characterize all the physical forms of the three dimensional world.

The seven serpents have also been conceived by the ancients as Seven Rays and venerated as the Rainbow Goddess, or as seven heads or seven tails joined to the singular Primal Serpent. In our local Milky Way Galaxy the septenary manifestation of the Goddess was associated with the seven stars of Pleiades. The Seven Sisters, which collectively are the one Goddess, was percieved to be the Primal Serpent that was coiled upon the highest branches of the cosmic tree and preparing to descend to become dense matter. The Pleiades was also the cosmic manifestation of the Primal Dragon that "moved upon the face of the waters" (i.e., the cosmic "waters") during the shadowy epoch preceding the creation of the cosmos. The Australian Aborigines knew the Pleiades as Makara, the crocodile that floated upon the cosmic sea; the Greek Gnostics referred to the asterism as the Seven Pillars of Goddess Sophia; and the Maya venerated her as Tzab, the seven rattles of the great cosmic rattlesnake.

The Serpent on the Tree was the Son of the Goddess

In some traditions it is said that the Primal Serpent that became the Serpent on the Tree was not the Goddess; it was Her Serpent Son that She sent down to the Garden of Eden as Her representative to teach Adam and Eve. As the Serpent Son, the Serpent on the Tree was looked upon as the progeny of the primal union of God and Goddess which occurred at the beginning of time. From this perspective it was the cosmic serpentine life force that was created when God and Goddess, Spirit (God) and matter (Goddess), sexually united. But although the Primal Serpent was denominated the Son of the Goddess by some worshippers, the true initiates of the Left Hand Path knew that the Serpent on the Tree was pure energy and androgynous. Technically it was neither gender, and could, therefore, be identified as either Goddess or Son...or both. This truth was reflected in the Sumerian texts where both the Goddess and her Son were both denominated "the Serpent who emanated from the Heaven God Anu."

In iconography, the Serpent of the Tree as the Son of the Goddess has been represented as a bisexual snake or dragon, an androgynous young boy, and even a peacock whose duality is manifest in its angelic beauty that contrasts with its demonic cry. Moreover, as a reflection of his mother, the Serpent Goddess, the Serpent Son has also been split into 2-7 snakes or identical twin boys.

Skanda-Murugan: Lemurian Serpent on the Tree

Perhaps the most important name of the Serpent Son in the present context is Skanda-Murugan. This is the name of the Serpent on the Tree in the best known Eden drama, the one that occurred on the island of Sri Lanka when it was part of Lemuria. Thus, from one perspective, the Serpent of Sri Lanka never left Eden, and today he resides in a shrine city that is just miles away from Adam's Peak, the legendary mountain when God set Adam down in the Garden of Eden.

Skanda-Murugan's current home on Sri Lanka is Kataragama, the "Place of Karttikeya," where he is worshipped by many names and forms, including a forever-young boy, a snake and a peacock. His votaries know him variously Skanda, Murugan, Karttikeya, Subramaniam, and Sanat Kumara. The name Skanda pivots around "kan," the universal sound-syllable-name of the serpent, and denotes the serpentine nature of the First Son. The title Murugan carries a meaning that refers to the radiant beauty of the eternally young boy, and his immortal and holy nature is intrinsic to the title of Sanat Kumara. Sanat denotes "eternal" and Kumara denotes the one who is the union of God and Goddess (Ra and Ma) manifesting as energy (Ku).

The epithet Karttikeya is the Son's name in his role as Commander-in-Chief of the Angelic Host of Heaven, and it also affiliates him intimately with the Pleiades. Karttikeya, meaning "He of the Pleiades," is a name derived from the Sanscrit term for the Pleiades, "Krittika." Thus, the Pleiades are the cosmic manifestation of both the Serpent Goddess and Her Serpent Son.

As a manifestation of the Pleiades, Karttikeya is venerated by his devotees as a boy with six heads. Just as the Pleiades consists of six bright stars and one invisible one, the priests of Kataragama claim that Karttikeya was born with seven heads, but one was removed soon after birth (they offer various reasons why). According to the Shaivites who worship Karttikeya's father, Shiva, both the six stars of the Pleiades and the corresponding six heads of the Divine Son have their origin as six rays of spiritual light that emanated from the Third Eye and Divine Mind of Shiva, the Infinite Spirit, at the beginning of time. At the same primal moment Shiva also emitted his scolding hot seminal fluid, his Divine Power, which became the vehicle for his Divine Mind and the life force body of his Serpent Son. Scientifically, this fiery primal emanation from the Infinite refers to the earliest moments of the "Big Bang," when the spiralling energy body of the Primal Serpent Son manifested as cosmic fire. In reference to Karttikeya's incipient fiery nature, the Divine Son is intimately associated with Agni, the Lord of Fire, and his iconography often portrays him as Seyon, the "Red One," with red skin.

The Peacock Entrance to Kataragama
Photo by Mark Amaru Pinkham

At the front gate Skanda-Murgan greets his devotees in his forms of a peacock and snake

Photo by Mark Amaru Pinkham

Inside the Temple of Six-Headed Karttikeya
Photo by Mark Amaru Pinkham

The Three Forms of Skanda-Murugan:
The Six-Headed Karttikeya, the Snake & the Peacock

Karttikeya's Yantra

Karttikeya with his Vel,
Symbol of the Human Spine and Third Eye
Karttikeya is surrounded by his six holy places

22

Skanda-Murugan is the Lord of Gnosis and Alchemy

As Karttikeya, the commander of Shiva's celstial army, Skanda-Murugan is the Protector and Savior of his devotees. He is also Savior for another reason. As the First Instructor, he is venerated as the Jnana Pandita, the "Teacher of Gnosis," who saves his disciples by helping them achieve gnosis. Skanda-Murugan saves his devotees by entering them as alchemical power, or Kundalini, and then fully awakens their chakra centers of gnostic wisdom to reveal their true identities.

One image of Skanda-Murugan at Kataragama, and perhaps his most venerated, is his "yantra" or geometrical form body that represents his alchemical power. Engraved upon a golden disc and kept hidden from public view for all but one day in a calendar year, Karttikeya's yantra has the shape of a six pointed star, the universal symbol of God/Goddess united as the Primal Serpent Son, or the male and female polarities that unite as the alchemical force. In addition, the two interlacing triangles of the yantra also denote the Divine Mind and Divine Power that unite as the primal Serpent Son. This sacred image of Karttikeya was engraved on alchemical gold by one of ancient India's premier alchemists, Bogarnath, who received invaluable assistance from Skanda-Murugan on his path to gnosis.

Karttikeya's principal weapon that he uses to protect and enlighten his devotees is his spear or "Vel." With his Vel, Karttikeya destroys both the harmful threats against his devotees, as well as the inner obstructions that keep them from attaining self-knowledge or gnosis. Esoterically, the shaft of the Vel represents the human spine that Karttikeya as the alchemical power rises up within, and the blade that surmounts the Vel denotes the Third Eye of gnostic awareness at the summit of the spine that the rising Serpent Son fully awakens. In ancient Sri Lanka, Karttikeya's Vel was inserted in the ground and worshipped by itself as the truest form of the Jnana Pandita, the Teacher of Gnosis. Through his symbollic Vel, Karttikeya revealed both the inner path of gnosis, as well as an important universal truth, that the best weapon against any adversary is one's inner, gnostic wisdom and guidance.

Karttikeya is the St. Michael of the East

In his function as the Commander-in-Chief of the Celestial Army of Shiva, Karttikeya is synonymous with his western counterpart, St. Michael, who also carries a spear as the Judeo-Christian Commander-in-Chief of the Celestial Army of Yahweh. St. Michael is, actually, a direct evolution of Karttikeya, who was taken west to become in succession the Persian Mithras and then Michael. The latter evolution corresponded to the final days of the Jewish exile in Babylonia, when the Persian Magi accompanied Cyrus the

Karttikeya and his Peacock
The Same Warrior, Solor God, and Divine Mind
manifests within the Hindu (Karttikeya),
Jewish (St. Michael) and Persian (Mithras) Traditions

St. Michael and his Dragon

Mithras and his Bull

Great into the Middle East and then taught the Jewish rabbis their dualistic legend of the solar god and warrior, Mithra, and his archenemy, Ahriman. When the Jews returned to their homeland they simply changed the name of the characters but kept the Persian plot. Thus, Mithra became known as St. Michael, and Ahriman's name was changed to Belial.

Because they are the same deity, Karttikeya and St. Michael naturally share many characteristics, including their association with the universal male principle and the Sun and the fiery, red color they possess. They are both recognized to be the Lord of the Blue Ray, which is the first of the seven rays and their synthesis, and each is identified as being the first of the Goddess's seven sons. St. Michael is the first of the Seven Archangels, and Karttikeya, as Sanat Kumara, is the first of the Seven Kumaras.

The meaning behind the icons of Karttikeya and St. Michael is also the same. The dual human and animal components of their icons, i.e., Karttikeya and his peacock, and St. Michael and his dragon, represent the two aspects of the Primal Serpent Son, its male/female polarity manifest as its Divine Mind and Divine Power. Spear-wielding Karttikeya and St. Michael are embodiments of the male principle and Divine Mind of the Serpent, and the blue-green dragon or blue-green peacock represent the female principle and Divine Power of the Serpent that the Divine Mind harnesses and shapes. This is the original and true understanding of Michael's victory over the dragon, and Karttikeya's taming of his wild peacock. Both were taming and shaping, not killing or destroying. St. Michael inserted his iconic spear, the symbol the Divine Mind he embodies, into the body of the struggling dragon in order to transmit into chaotic matter a well-defined code or blueprint that would determine the shapes that emerged out of it when it crystallized.

When the theologians of the Right Hand Path eternally separated Spirit from matter, the interpretation of St. Michael's battle with the dragon was concurrently distorted. St. Michael then became the Right Hand Path's representative of the pure, uncorrupted will of God, while the unwieldy dragon was identified as the embodiment of everything dark and evil, including the sensual appetites that keep a person from aligning with the will of God. This biased interpretation became the foundation of various patriarchal theologies, including those of Persia and Babylonia, where tales were told of the battle between Mithras and his bull, and Marduk and the unruly dragoness Tiamat. This eternal battle of polar opposite adversaries was also projected into the heavens by the early priest astrologers as the warrior Orion, the "Hunter" and representative of the Spiritual, Divine Mind, who with spear and arrows in hand is forever in pursuit of the Seven Doves or Bull of the Pleiades, the cosmic representative of the Material, Divine Power.

The Peacock Angel: The Serpent on the Tree of the Yezidis

When one group of Lemurians left India for the west they brought with them the image of Skanda-Murugan's peacock, albeit without its for-ever-young male passenger. This is how the First Instructor manifested to the Yezidis in the Garden of Eden, when he introduced himself to them as Tawsi Melek, the "Peacock Angel" and "Peacock King." Ever since the dawn of humanity, the Yezidis, who refer to themselves as the "first people of the Earth," have venerated their deity as a peacock, which is the Divine Power of the Primal Serpent that invisibly incorporates its informing Divine Mind.

The Yezidis maintain that Tawsi Melek was, like his counterparts Michael and Karttikeya, the first and greatest of the angels made by Spirit. He was the first limited form of Spirit, Lord of the Blue Ray, and the synthe-sis of all the seven rays. Because of his seven-rayed "rainbow" nature, when-ever the Yezidis see a seven-colored rainbow in the sky they worship it as a manifestation of Tawsi Melek. The Peacock Angel, they say, produced the other six archangels from out of itself and then proceeded to create all the material forms of the universe. He then ruled over his completed cosmic empire as its Peacock King.

Yezidi legend states that when the Earth was molten hot and still shaking with continual earthquakes, Spirit sent Tawsi Melek to Earth as his envoy to endow our planet with flora and fauna, and all the seven colors of the rainbow. The Peacock Angel landed in the center of the world, a place now known as Lalish in northern Iraq, and then covered the planet with his peacock colors and plumes. Although his plumes eventually crystallized into the multi-colored physical flora that covers our planet, they still have an etheric manifestation that can be viewed by those whom Tawsi Melek blesses with a vision of himself. The plumes initially present themselves as millions of eyes, which on closer examination are found to be the "eyes" that embel-lish peacock feathers. When the peacock feathers are then studied they are found to unite as actual peacocks, and then everything, including the moun-tains, is found to take on the radiant form of a peacock. The vision of Tawsi Melek's millions of eyes do indeed give the impression that he is everywhere on our planet, and according to the Yezidis he is. He is the Peacock King of the world and his will reigns supreme. In relation to the Jewish legends, Tawsi Melek is the eternal "Watcher" who continually studies humanity from a transcendental plane. Nature worshippers know him as the Green Man, and Theosophists allude to him as the Planetary Logos and Planetary Mind.

After greening the Earth, Tawsi Melek traveled to the Garden of Eden and breathed life into the lifeless physical forms of Adam and Eve that the other six angels had previously struggled to produce. He then created the

The Peacock Angel by Larry Welker

***The Peacock Angel creates the Universe in 3, 7, & 12 stages.
These stages are represented as the 3 head feathers and
the 7 and 12 layers of peacock feathers behind them.
The Peacock Angel sits upon the circular Earth it endows with color.***

**A Yezidi kisses a brass image of the Peacock Angel
which is identical to the lamps used in honoring the Hindu Karttikeya**
Courtesy of Eszter Spat, author of *The Yezidis*

first people, the Yezidis, from a drop of Adam's sperm which he placed in a special jar. Following a period of gestation, Shehid bin Jar, "Son of Jar," emerged from the container, and after rapidly maturing he took as his wife a "Houri," or angelic spirit, who had been a resident of Paradise. Together they became the matriarch and patriarch of the Yezidi people, who have ever since been known as the chosen people of Tawsi Melek. Soon after their creation Adam and Eve produced the 72 sons and daughters who mated to become the other 72 tribes of people of Earth.

Tawsi Melek taught Adam and Eve many chants and rituals to observe daily in their worship of Spirit, and to awaken their inner, gnostic wisdom. He turned them towards the Sun, the physical form of Spirit, thus revealing to them that there was something much greater than their physical embodiments....and it could be found right within their own hearts. Following the dissemination of this teaching, it is said that the Peacock Angel flew around the Earth to spread his special religious observances in the 72 languages of the 72 people who had dispersed around the globe. Returning to his chosen people, he presented the Yezidis with a special "Black Book" containing pages of gold leaf wherein he laid out the daily spiritual observances that would keep them in alignment with the Divine Will and ultimately lead them to redemption and enlightenment. This book was later lost during the 72 persecutions directed against the Yezidis in the Middle East.

Dionysus: The Serpent on the Tree in Greece

The Greek Serpent on the Tree was Dionysus, the counterpart of Skanda-Murugan who similarly manifested as a snake and forever-young boy. The link between Dionysus and Skanda-Murugan was discovered by the early Greek soldiers of Alexander the Great when they briefly visited Sri Lanka. Arriving in the area now known as Kataragama, they looked around and studied the temples and images. Pointing to an image of Kartikeya, they exclaimed with great excitement to the residing priests, "We know him, he is our Dionysus, our Bacchus!" Later, when the returning soldiers recounted their discovery to their Greek brethren, the first historical Greek cartographer, Ptolemy, incorporated their knowledge into his world map and identified the area of Kataragama as Bachi Oppidum, the "Place of Bacchus."

Some of the first Greeks to recognized Dionysus as the Primal Serpent and Serpent on the Tree were the Orphics, the followers of the sage Orpheus. Their myths stated that he had originally hatched out of the cosmic egg his father/mother had laid upon the vast cosmic sea. As a great serpent Dionysus arose out of his shattered shell and proceeded to create the physical universe and planet Earth. On Earth he manifested as the Green Man, and

Ptolomy's Map of Sri Lanka

Ptolomy's Bachi Oppidum, the "Place of Bacchus,"
is currently known as Kataragama, the "Place of Karttikeya"

his Greek legends later maintained that Dionysus would annually be born and resurrected each spring with the new shoots of vegetation and then die each autumn with the falling leaves.

As the Greek Serpent on the Tree, Dionysus became the patron of all trees and hailed as their "protector." He was the life force power that moved within them and around them. In ceremony, the favored "tree" and symbol of Dionysus was the Thrysus, a fennel stalk encoiled by his sacred serpentine ivy vines and surmounted by a pine cone that corresponded to the human Third Eye of Wisdom (the pine cone represented the underlying pine-al gland of the Third Eye). Like its counterparts, the Vel of Skanda-Murugan and the Caduseus of Thoth-Hermes, the Thrysus was the "weapon" of Dionysus and was used by the Greek Son to induce within his followers the "madness" of gnosis. It also symbolized his path up the spine as the inner fire serpent.

During ceremony when a seeker's inner Dionysian serpent was activated, the Thrysus was held against the candidate's back while a live, golden serpent representing Dionysus was let loose inside their clothing. The synnergy of the Thrysus and snake would awaken the inner fire serpent and initiate the process of alchemical unfoldment. Dionysus's form of a live snake was also on display during the fertility festivals dedicated to him, the Bacchanalias, when great torturous snakes representing Dionysus' Primal Serpent form were paraded through Grecian cities with great fanfare.

Like Skanda-Murugan, Dionysus was a divine androgyny who had been given birth to from the union of God and Goddess, Spirit and matter. His father was Zeus, counterpart of Shiva, and his mother had been Semele, the Goddess of matter, or the Earth, and the counterpart of Shakti. And similar to his eastern counterpart, Dionysus was also the principal inhabitant and teacher of a paradisiacal Eden. This was Arcadia, the Garden of Eden of the Greeks, where the gnostic teachings of Dionysus were first transmitted. The wisdom of Dionysus later became assimilated into the Underground Stream of secrets that moved clandestinely throughout Europe. Like Karttikeya, Dionysus was not only the primal teacher of gnosis, but also the alchemical fire that awakens gnosis. In his manifestation of Iaachos, the Lord of Fire, Dionysus carried the special symbol that represented him, a fiery torch, during processions that marked the beginning of the alchemical initiation rites of the Greek mystery schools. His fiery and destructive nature was also embodied by his sacred animal, the black goat, which was ceremonially slaughtered in rituals that reenacted the dismemberment of Dionysus by the Titans.

With so many similarities, it is not surprising that Skanda and Bacchus also shared the same name. Skanda's name of Jnana, which is John in English, is identical to Dionysus' title of Iaachos, which is Greek for Jack/John.

Dionysus and his Spear or Thrysus
His "weapon" to enduce the "madness" of Gnosis

Dionysus and his Thrysus,
Symbol of the human spine and Third Eye

A Contemporary Bacchanalia
by
Chadwick St. John

Enki: The Serpent on the Tree in Sumeria

The Serpent on the Tree and First Instructor of gnosis among the Sumerians was known as Enki. The personailty of Enki, and the components of Enki's cult, may have arrived in the Middle East from both East and West. His eclectic form and personna possessed multiple similarities with Skanda-Murugan as well as with the image of the First Instructor brought east by the Atlanteans, Neptune-Volcan (see following section on Neptune-Volcan). Enki's Serpent on the Tree manifestation is most famous for having been the Sumerian model for the Hebrew Serpent on the Tree in *Genesis.*

The eastern influence on the personality and cult of Enki most likely arrived via the Mandaeans, the modern gnostics of southern Iraq who claim to have originated on Sri Lanka and bear a striking resemblance to modern East Indians. The occurance of an early westward migration of Skanda-Murugan by the Mandeans to Sumeria can be deduced at least partly by the characteristics shared by Enki and Skanda. Both were venerated within their respective cultures as the Serpent on the Tree and the Lord of Wisdom who taught humanity both alchemy and gnosis, and they also shared the same "Lord of Wisdom" name. Skanda's Sanscrit name of Jnana, meaning "gnosis" and "wisdom," becomes Ioannes (John) in Greek which is nearly identical to Enki's Greek "wisdom" name of Oannes. Enki's link to Ioannes and John can also be discerned from another perspective. Enki rules the month of January as the goat-fish of the Zodical sign of Capricorn, and the name "January" was adopted from the name of the Roman God of wisdom, Janus, whose name is a Latin counterpart of Jnana, Ioannes, and John. Thus, Ioannes, Oannes, John, Janus and Jnana are all interrelated. They are all Indo-European names for "Lord of Wisdom."

According to the Sumerian creation myths, Enki was born as a goat-fish styled dragon in the primal cosmic sea, the Apzu. Finding no other entity than himself in the nascent cosmos, he formally proclaimed himself the "first born" of Anu, the Infinite Spirit. Enki then created the physical universe out of himself by uttering his cosmic word, Mummu, and by quickly expanding his life force body to fill out the universe. He then completed the process of becoming physical by slithering down the Gish Gana, the foliated tree that separated the heavenly "waters" that were above from the terrestrial "waters" that were below. The lower waters included the fresh water springs that covered the Earth, as well as the Apzu that flowed underneath it. These became Enki's favorite abodes.

Like all Primal Serpents, Enki was dual natured. His androgyny is revealed by his goat-fish image that unites fire (the goat) and water (the fish). His dual nature, as well as that of his son, Ningishzida, was also portrayed by

Enki, the Goat-fish

Enki, the Serpent Lord of Wisdom

Enki, the Lord of the Two Rivers

the Sumerians as two snakes slithering down a caduceus, as well as by twin boys known as the Kerabu. When the twin Kerabu were later assimilated into the Hebrew tradition where they became known as the twin Kerubs or Cherubs that stretched over the Ark of the Convenant. The Kerabu were also intimately related to the Kaberoi Twins from Atlantis, as can be easily be gleened from their related names.

Similar to all septenary Primal Serpents, Enki also had seven parts ascribed to him. His seven corresponding parts were often referred to as the seven Anunnaki, with Enki as both the first Anunnaki as well as their synthesis. Enki's Divine Mind and profound wisdom was divided equally among the Anunnaki, who served principally as underworld judges for newly departed souls.

When Enki had completed his descent down the Gish Gana and became the solid Earth he was accorded his new title of EN.KI, meaning "Lord of the Earth." His first residence was a paradisiacal land mass at the center of the Earth, the Sumerian Garden of Eden known as E.DIN, where he assisted in the creation of the first humans. It is said that he initially made seven men and seven women out of his seven component parts and they became the progenitors of humankind. When Enki then attempted to teach humanity the secrets of gnosis and immortality he was opposed by the demi-god Enlil of the Right Hand Path, who had hatched a plan to destroy all humanity for its perceived transgression against the "law." Always the Savior and protector of humanity, Enki was quick to instruct the Sumerian Noah, Ziusandra, in the art of building an ark that would save himself, his family and as many animals and plants as possible. After the flood had receded, Enki showed his appreciation to Ziusandra be bestowing upon him the greatest of all possible gifts, that of gnosis and immortality. As his last act of service to humanity, Ziusandra led the few remaining survivors of the flood to a cache of books on alchemy and gnosis that Enki had instructed him to bury in the city of Sippur preceding the deluge. It is said that one of these texts eventually found its way to the later Assyrian King Assurbanipal, who then placed it within his extensive library alongside many other antiquated scrolls and documents.

Since Enki's principle abode was the Earth's rivers, many of the Sumerian temples built along the Tigris and Euphrates waters were dedicated to him. As ruler of the two principal Mesopotamian arteries, Enki became known to the Sumerians as the "Lord of the Two Rivers." The dual rivers were Enki's homes and repesented his dual nature. One of the famous Sumerian drawings of Enki as Lord of the Two Riviers have two streams of water, or rivers, emanating from him, one from each of his shoulders.

Enki lived in the Tigris and Euphrates as the subtle life force that moved through their physical water. His invisible current, which was potent with life-giving and alchemical properties, was honored by the Sumerians with the epithet "Water of Life." To commune with Enki and his subtle power, the priests of Sumeria's riverside temples performed most of their rites in pools of slow moving water that had been diverted from the main rivers. As the subtle power of Enki washed over a worshipper immersed in one of these pools it would cleanse and transform him or her on all levels, thus transporting them closer to gnosis and immortality. The baptismal rites of the Sumerians are today continued by the Mandeans of south Iraq, who conduct their ceremonies in the Tigris and Eurphrates nearly identically to their ancestors.

Neptune-Volcan: The Serpent on the Tree in Atlantis

The influence on the Sumerian Enki and his cult may have also come from the east via missionaries from Atlantis, where according to legend the Serpent on the Tree manifested variously as Ladon, the guardian of the sacred golden apples of wisdom and immortality, as well as King Neptune or Poseidon, whose sacred animals included the fiery billy goat. It has been suggested that when Atlantean ships arrived in the Middle East their prows were decorated with the head of their goat diety, one of which may have been discovered in the Egyptian desert and later put on display in the Berlin Museum[5] (see image on facing page). The addition of a goat head to the prow of any ship would make it a "goat-fish," so perhaps it was a fleet of Atlantean goat-fishes that landed in Sumeria and transplanted the cult of Enki there. This would explain how Enki acquired his enigmatic goat-fish image and why it was said that his amphibian missionaries spent half their time in the water and the other half on land. They were going to and from their ships.

On Atlantis, the fiery goat was chosen as a symbol of the Serpent on the Tree because it reflected the serpent's fiery and destructive nature as it ambled as molten fire within a network of subterranean caverns and precipitated volcanoes and earthquakes upon the continent's surface. At those times the Serpent on the Tree was also placated on other parts of the island by Atlanteans beseeching Neptune by his moniker Poseidon, meaning the "Earthshaker," or as Volcan, the volatile spirit of the volcanoes.

Neptune, whom the occultist Madam Blavatsky refers to as a "dragon," was simply the Sumerian Enki by another name and form. Both were born within the universal cosmic sea and created the universe out of life force. Neptune's mastership over his own primal energy and the three powers of creation, preservation, and destruction, is symbolized by the three prongs of his trident. Both Neptune and Enki ruled the world's waters, and each was

A Goat Head once attached to an Atlantean Ship?
From: *The Ancient Atlantic*

The Symbolic Crown of the Atlantean Kings

Neptune-Volcan
by Chadwick St. John

identified as the Lord of the Earth who could make the planet shake and convulse, or erupt in explosive fire. Neptune's title on Atlantis that specifically associated him with the volcanic explosions on the island was Volcan, the volcanic fire serpent. A description of Neptune as Volcan is recounted in the legends of the Mescalero Apaches, who as Atlantean descendants remember him as the fire god and fire serpent. The Apache legends state:

"...the fire god (Neptune-Volcan) himself took this form sometimes (the dragon) and lived in the swamps. At other times he crawled through our (underground) galleries, for we had miles of painted galleries. He shook the land with his anger and left the galleries burned with his anger."[5]

The Mescalero also recall that Neptune-Volcan was intimately involved with the final destruction of Atlantis. According to their records of the Motherland's concluding drama:

"...the sacred mountain began to spurt fire like a giant fountain, and the fire god crawled through the caverns, roaring and thrashing the land about like a wolf shakes the rabbit."[6]

Fortunately, during much of their history the Atlanteans were protected from the thrashings of Neptune-Volcan by their rulers, who were embodiments of the deity. To represent themselves as such, the Atlantean monarchs adorned in ceremonial regalia that included motifs associated to both Neptune and the explosive Volcan. Their volcanic power was represented by their regal, ceremonial crowns which had tuffs of white feathers representing billowing smoke emerging from their apexes. According to some Native American legends, one lineage of Atlantean Kings, the Votans, further revealed themselves as incarnations of the fire god Volcan by walking with a limp and acquiring the reputations of Master Craftsmen! According to a later Roman legend, Volcan as Vulcan was a Master Craftsman who received his characteristic limp when he was throne out of heaven and broke his legs.

Other symbols covering the crown worn by the Atlantean monarchs affiliated them with Neptune, especially in his role as the Lord of Venus. Eight triangles displayed across its bottom, and the thirteen triangles along the sides of the crown, were associated with Venus's sacred eight-year cycle, during which the planet encircles the Sun thirteen times while constructing a perfect five-pointed star in the heavens. Neptune's association with Venus was cryptically conveyed by Plato when he stated that Neptune had fathered five pairs of twin sons, thereby incorporating five and two in his legend, which are the two sacred numbers of Venus.[7]

Two reflecting shields associated with the Morning and Eveing Star positions of Venus also covered the breast of the Atlantean monarch's regalia. These twin discs also revealed the kings to be the incarnation of the twin serpent sons, as well as the wielders of the Divine Wisdom and Power of the Primal Serpent.

Neptune-Volcan became Ptah-Sokar-Osiris

When Neptune-Volcan was eventually taken to mainland Europe he was transformed into the Roman deity Vulcan, but before that he arrived in Egypt with Atlantean and renamed Ptah or Ptah-Sokar-Osiris. Ptah was the lord of creation; Osiris was the lord of preservation; and Sokar was the lord of death and destruction. Since he was the Primal Dragon that wielded the three powers of creation, preservation, and destruction as represented by his trident, Neptune was the synthesis of all three Egyptian gods.

Ptah-Sokar-Osiris, whom the Alexandrian record keeper Manetho priest referred to later as the most ancient of the Egyptian gods, became one manifestation of the Serpent on the Tree in Egypt. When Egypt first evolved into a huge, united empire, Ptah was chosen to be the patron deity of its capital city, Memphis, which was originally built on a mound that represented the primeval form of Primal Serpent Ptah when he emerged from the cosmic sea at the beginning of time. Known as Hi-Ku-Ptah, the "mansion of the Ka of Ptah," the name of this mound city later evolved into the Greek name for the entire country. Hi-Ku-Ptah thus became E-gu-ptah, or Egypt.

Ptah's consort at Memphis, Sekhmet, embodied the destructive-transformative component of Ptah's fire. Fierce Sekhmet was venerated as a snake, a flame, as well as a ferocious red lioness. She was patroness of the alchemists, who identified her with the inner fire serpent on the Tree of Life, and summoned by the practitioners of medicine who used her destructive-transformative power to help them heal and transform their patients.

One of Ptah's appelations was the Master Craftsman of the Universe, which he had created out of his own fire. The artisans and craftsmen of Egypt invoked the power of the Master Craftsman for success in all their creations, and later, when they banded together in fraternities and Masonic lodges, Ptah became their patron. When Ptah-Sokar-Osiris was subsequently taken by Egyptian merchants to Tyre, he merged with the Phoenicians' Tautus or Thoth-Hermes to produce the figure of Hiram Abiff or Chiram, the Master Builder of Freemasony. Thus, the legend of the Master Builder Chiram that has been passed down to through generations is a synthesis of the legends and characteristics of Ptah, Osiris and Thoth-Hermes.

The Kaberoi: Twin Serpents of the Caduceus

The twin sons of the Primal Serpent Ptah were given a temple of their own behind their "father" in Memphis and therein worshipped as twin snakes or twin boys known as the Kaberoi. Among the esoterically informed, they were identified as the two snakes that spiral down the Egyptian "tree," the caduceus.

The cult of the Kaberoi Twins was eventually taken to many locations in and around the Mediterranean and Aegean Seas. At their new homes they were venerated as the Sons of Ptah-Vulcan and the teachers of their father's alchemical mysteries. Their temples were principally built upon volcanic islands, such as Samothrace and Rhodes, where the fiery currents of their father's volcanic energy naturally supported the observance of the transformative practices of alchemy and the acquisition of gnosis.

The principal Aegean headquarters of the Kaberoi Twins was Samothrace, "the Holy Island" where all Greek seekers of wisdom flocked to receive initiation into their alchemical tradition. Images of the Kaberoi snakes upon the caduceus could be found on all parts of the island, and as twin boys they were worshipped for protection and spiritual advancement. When a candidate for initiation would be led into their temple he would find the "Twin Flames" elevated high above him as two naked boys with hands and erect phalluses raised in blessing. Their vertical erections symbolized the heating of the seminar fluids and its transformation into ascending spiritual power that the candidate would soon experience when Ptah-Volcan, the inner Primal Serpent, began its journey up the inner Tree of Life to the crown of the head. At the conclusion of the initiation on Samothrace a new initiate would be placed upon a throne. Having awakened to the gnostic revelation of "I am Spirit," he would now look upon the world as his own creation and kingdom.

Thoth-Hermes: The Serpent on the Tree in Egypt

A close relative of Ptah-Sokar-Osiris was Thoth-Hermes, a deity with an abundance of titles and functions who gained prominence as the Serpent on the Tree especially during the Ptolemaic period of Egypt. His most popular of titles, Thoth, Djehuti, and Hermes, reveal his nature as the Primal Serpent and union of Divine Mind and Power. The name Thoth, which is close in sound and meaning to the English word thought, was his title as the embodiment of the Divine Mind, and his denominations of Djehuti and Hermes revealed him to be the embodiment of the Serpent Power that created the universe. The Dj of Djehuti was an ancient Egyptian word for "serpent," and the title of Hermes refered to his nature as an embodiment of the

43

serpent fire. A clear and precise definition of the name Hermes is offered by the famous esotericist Manly Palmer Hall in his *The Secret Teachings of All Ages,* wherein he states that Hermes is derived from Chiram, an occult term denoting both the creative and transformative properties of Cosmic Fire. Hall reveals that Chiram is a synthetic word that unites Cheth, Resh, and Mem, which are the three radical consonants associated with the elements of fire, water and air that unite as Cosmic Fire. In the foundational Masonic legend, Chiram is the Master Builder Hiram Abiff, whose esoteric function is to alchemically re-build a pure body for each initiate of Freemasonry through the fire of purification.

In his manifestation of the Serpent on the Tree, Thoth-Hermes' Garden of Eden was Khemenu, the capital city of the fifteenth nome or province of Upper Egypt that became known during the later Greek era as Hermopolis, the "City of Hermes." The early artistic renderings of this city by the Egyptian scribes portray it as the primal mound surrounded by the protective coils of the Primal Serpent Thoth. The legends of Hermopolis stated that at the beginning of creation the Primal Serpent Thoth-Hermes divided his body into four serpent progeny known as Nothing, Inertness, Infinity, and Invisibility, which then divided into their own male and female halves to bring the total number of serpents to eight. It was for this reason that Hermopolis was also known as "Eight Town." When these serpent progeny swam away to create their own "Eden," one of the eight, Ammon, founded a city known as No-Ammon, meaning "the Town of Ammon," which later acquired the name of Thebes.

Hermopolis became one of the great centers of learning in ancient Egypt and was recognized as headquarters of the Divine Mind of Thoth-Hermes. Among other intellectual accomplishments, the city distinguished itself as an important center of theology where one of the four main cosmological systems of Egypt was promulgated. Many Egyptian priests and priestesses in training spent time at Hermopolis imbibing the full spectrum of both mundane and spiritual subjects ascribed to Thoth-Hermes. All told, 36,000 texts or scrolls were attributed to him, with the most important of these being 42 books that were carried in sacred procession by the Egyptian priesthood.

During the reign of the Greek Ptolomies, Thoth-Hermes was venerated as the Primal Serpent and invoked by the Greeks as the Agathodeamon, the "Good Spirit." He was depicted on Alexandrian coins as a huge serpent carrying within its coils the distinctive Egyptian "tree," the caduceus, or as two twin serpents known as the male Agathodeamon and the female Agathotyche. As the Agathodeamon, Thoth-Hermes was typically invoked

The Agathodeamon
Inscribed on an Alexandrian Coin

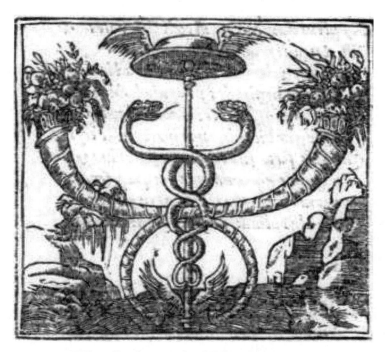

The Caduceus of Thoth-Hermes
The Tree of Life

by the masses for his creative and fertilizing power, and by the gnostics for his inner, alchemical influence.

It was also during the heyday of the Ptolomies that the followers of Thoth-Hermes residing in the great city of spiritual light, Alexandria, compiled their deity's wisdom into lengthy scrolls full of esoteric, astrological and alchemical information. Seventeen of these scrolls were eventually brought together as the *Corpus Hermeticum*, which later served as the essential guide book of Hermes' teachings for the gnostics and alchemists of Renascence Europe. Each of these texts referred to their author as Hermes Trismegistus, meaning "Thrice Great," thus referring to both the triune nature of Thoth-Hermes, the serpentine deity who was the union of air, water and fire, as well as to his three powers of creation, preservation and destruction. The most important text that portrays Thoth-Hermes in his Primal Serpent form in the *Corpus Hermeticum* is the *Divine Pymander*, a document that contains a conversation between Hermes the seeker and Hermes the Primal Dragon Pymander. At the beginning of the text when Pymander is invoked by Hermes the seeker, the mammoth dragon form of Hermes quickly arrives and a dialogue ensues between them. After introducing himself as "...the Light and the Mind which were before substance was divided from spirit and darkness from Light," Pymander implants a series of visions in the mind of the seeker Hermes that revealed the entire sequence of events that had been orchestrated by the Primal Serpent at the beginning of time. Pymander concluded his presentation with the secrets of alchemy that culminate in the highest gnosis and complete the universal drama.

Another esoteric text attributed to Thoth-Hermes with special alchemical wisdom was the *Book of Thoth*. This was a precious book during Dynastic Egypt said to have been kept in the "Secret Chambers of Thoth." It contained the highest alchemical wisdom of Thoth-Hermes that his missionaries had brought from the Motherland of Atlantis. An icon attached to the text, Thoth's eternal symbol of the caduceus, was a map of the inner tree that Hermes climbs as the transformative serpent fire. During special initiations by the Egyptian priesthood, a caduceus made of solid gold was laid upon a person to awaken the inner power of Thoth-Hermes and commence the process of alchemical transformation.

It is also speculated that kept within the "Secret Chambers of Thoth" was the *Tabula Smaragdina*, the "Emerald Tablet" of Hermes, upon which were inscribed the 13 stages of alchemy as 13 precepts. These 13 precepts were a guide and map for all serious alchemists both in Egypt and later in Europe, where determined alchemists used its guidance to try and create the Philosophers Stone and the Elixir of Immortality. The Emerald Tablet emanated the vibration of Thoth-Hermes, the Primal Serpent, so theoretically just by sitting in front of it alchemy could have been induced within an aspirant. The gem's green color, the color of polarity union, was amplified by the stone's crystalline matrix, and could thus have easily entered within a person to unite the polar opposite energies as the serpent fire.

Quetzlcoatl: The Serpent on the Tree in Mexico

The Serpent on the Tree in Mexico and Middle America was also anciently influenced by Atlantean missionaries. This was Quetzlcoatl, the "Plumed" or "Feathered" Serpent, which Mesoamerican legends maintain colonists from the east brought with them to Mexico. The Feathered Serpent possessed an androgynous or "dual" body of a snake with attached wings, thus making it the union of Heaven and Earth. Its wings and feathers gave it an avian component and associated it with Heaven, and its snake body associated it with Earth. When Heaven and Earth, or Spirit and matter unite, pure energy results. This is the true understanding of the Feathered Serpent; it is the symbol of the serpentine primal force or cosmic fire at the beginning of time before it slithered down the Cosmic Tree and became dense matter. In some traditions, such as the Maya and Toltec, following its completed descent the Primal Serpent has its wings "clipped" or removed and assumes the form of a thick snake, the symbol of matter. The Maya then send the beast's wings back to the top of the tree in the form of a bird and then create a world tree motif with a bird at the top and a snake at its lower extremity.

In their codices or records, the various tribes of the Maya and Toltec portrayed the world tree with the two parts of the Plumed Serpent, the quetzal bird and the snake, at its upper and lower extremities respectively, and the rest of the tree they covered in vegetation. The famous Foliated Cross at Palenque depicts this final evolution and split of Quetzlcoatl. According to author Willian Irwin Thompson, both exoteric and esoteric implications reside in this motif. He states:

"In the Temple of the Foliated Cross at Palenque, Mexico, the Maya relief shows two men beside a tree, a beast (serpent) at the base of the tree, and a quetzal bird on top. I believe that the spinal column is esoterically represented in all these iconographic traditions, be they Sumerian, Hebrew, Hindu, Hopi or Maya. To raise the serpent of Kundalini until it touches the brain and causes the 'Thousand-petalled lotus' to flower is, in Mexican terms, to teach the serpent to fly."[8]

Other depictions of the Primal Serpent within the codices of the Maya and Toltecs allude to the era when the newborn Primal Serpent floated upon the vast ocean of consciousness and had yet to create the universe. At the beginning of their creation myth known as the *Popul Vuh,* the Quiche Maya allude to the incipient form of Quetzlcoatl. The passage reads:

"All was immobility and silence in the darkness, only the creator, the maker, the denominator, the serpent covered with feathers, they who engender, they who create, were on the waters as an ever increasing light. They were surrounded by green and blue."

This passage suggests that the Primal Serpent was the creator of the universe, while also identifying it as not one but a collection of entities. When cross-referencing with other similar legends worldwide, it becomes evident that the seven entities are the rays and sons of the Primal Serpent.

A nearly identical passage to the one in the *Popul Vuh* can be found at the beginning of *Genesis*:

"In the beginning the earth was without form, and void; and darkness was upon the face of the deep. And the Elohim Creators moved upon the face of the waters. And the Elohim said, Let there be light: and there was light."

The original name of Elohim, which was replaced with "Spirit of God" in the later versions of the *Holy Bible,* has been reinserted in this passage. Like the passage in the *Popul Vuh*, it also refers to a collection of creators who "floated upon the face of the waters." If the interpretation of the Biblical passage is to be consistent with most other creation legends worldwide, including those of India, Egypt, and Mesopotamia, then the Biblical primal creators must also be part of a great Primal Serpent.

The "Elohim" Feathered Serpent moved upon the "Face of the Waters"

Quetzlcoatl, The "Feathered Serpent"

"Serpent Plumage"
by Chadwick St. John

The Sons (and Daughters) of Seth

When the Garden of Eden drama came to its predestined conclusion, many gnostics dispersed around the globe and subsequently established a planetary network of Left Hand Path sects whose members venerated and sought to embody the Serpent on the Tree. The Gnostics of Alexandria, Egypt referred to these times as the dispersion of the "Sons of Seth," with "Seth" referring both to Setheus, the First Instructor, as well as Seth, the Son of Adam, who acted as a guardian and disseminator of the teachings his father received from the Serpent on the Tree. In whatever areas of the globe they colonized, the Sons of Seth founded gnostic sects wherein aspirants could achieve gnosis and fully embody both the power and wisdom of the Primal Serpent. In Egypt, the Sons of Seth aspired to embody the power and wisdom of the Primal Serpent Thoth-Hermes and hence became known historically as the Djedhi, the "Serpents," and the Thoth-Hermes Masters. In Greece, the Sons of Seth sought to wield the serpentine power and wisdom of Dionysus or Bacchus and went down in history as the Bacchae; and in India, the Sons of Seth merged with the transcendental witness consciousness of Shiva and wielded the power and wisdom of the Primal Serpent, known both as the wife of Shiva, the Goddess Shakti, or as Shiva's Son, Skanda-Murugan. In Sumeria, the Sons of Seth covered themselves in fish regalia in order to fully identify with and embody the power and wisdom of the Primal Serpent Enki; and in Mesoamerica, the Sons of Seth sought union with Queztlcoatl, the Feathered or Plumed Serpent, and historically became masters in the lineage of the Quetzlcoatls. In this chapter the history and unique practices of all these various sects of the "Sons of Seth" will be presented in detail.

Dispersion of the Right and Left Hand Paths

Wherever the sects and communities founded by the Sons of Seth proliferated, missionaries of the Right Hand Path often established headquarters for their orthodox religions right alongside them while making it clear that they expected all people, including the Sons of Seth, to observe the iron-clad religious sanctions of their male God. The Sons of Seth were gnostics of the Left Hand Path who perceived the male God as a manifestation of the oppressive Ildabaoth and therefore firmly opposed the stringent mandates imposed upon them by the votaries of the Right Hand Path, believing such mandates to be strategically designed by the First Son to keep humanity ignorant of its divinity. Thus, the gnostics reasoned that to achieve gnosis they needed to adopt a lifestyle that was diametrically opposed to such rigid, religious edicts. Many gnostic sects proceeded to adopt unorthodox and heretical rites while displaying rebellious and aberrant behavior that was thoroughly disparaged by the Right Hand Path. The gnostics refused to obey most of the mandates of the Right Hand Path, including "be fruitful and multiply," and took careful precautions to avoid any pregnancy so as not to bring more souls into the First Son's tortuous kingdom. In time, the rebellious gnostics became known as contraries and labeled "heretics," sinners, and even psychopathic lunatics by the Right Hand Path hierarchy.

Because of the persecution suffered at the hands of the militia of the Right Hand Path, many gnostic branches of the Sons of Seth were eventually compelled to become clandestine and completely remove themselves from the world's stage. Some gnostics developed the ability to astral travel, so at least for awhile they could escape Ildabaoth's oppressive kingdom and soar to their true celestial home in the upper heavens, known as the Pleroma, the "fullness" of Spirit. Their life on Earth eventually became nearly untenable when observance of their ancient rites, including worship of the Goddess and the Serpent on the Tree, became illegal. As they watched helplessly from the sidelines, the gnostics witnessed many of their most beloved deities become assimilated into the Right Hand Path's symbol of ultimate evil, Satan, Lucifer, or the Devil, and it was not long before all their gnostic worship would become a guarantee of torture and possibly even death. Many gnostics managed to survive these times, even in the face of a genocidal movement directed against them, by establishing hidden mystery schools or by living their lives in complete seclusion. Other gnostic sects survived by compromising many of their beliefs and ostensibly embracing the tenants of the Right Hand Path.

Time has a way of healing wounds, and eventually many gnostics became more accepting of the adversarial Right Hand Path, and vice versa. They ultimately acknowledged that most evolving souls needed to immerse themselves in the rigid rites and dualistic theology of the Right Hand Path before they were ready to fully embrace alchemy and transcend into the gnostic awareness offered by the Left Hand Path. They needed to place God outside themselves for a time before they could accept that the Infinite Spirit exists right within their own hearts. And they also needed to develop the discernment that comes through developing the dualistic intellect before transcending the mind and intellect and moving into superconsciousness.These conclusions led to the development of spiritual paths that were a synthesis of the Right and Left Hand Paths, such as the Kuala Path of India. Such amalgamated traditions were structured so that they began with the observance of the rites and theology of the Right Hand Path and then progressed to the practices of the Left Hand Path in their latter and final stages.

The Sons and Daughters of Seth-Cain

The Sethians

During the heyday of Alexandria, Egypt, one group of gnostics arose that maintained it was the direct descendant of the earliest Sons of Seth. This sect, the Sethians, was composed of gnostics who identified Seth as both the Son of Adam and the Primal Serpent. Their goal was to embody both the Christed consciousness of the Divine Son, as well as the Divine Power of Set or Setheus, which was their name for the Primal Serpent.

The Sethians maintained that Adam had transmitted his gnostic wisdom to his son Seth, who had then passed it down to them. They equated Seth with the Christed spirit or Divine Mind that had overshadowed Jesus during the time of his ministry and had in earlier times also manifested as King Melchizedek. Seth was "the great saviour" of the Sethians, who would protect and bestow gnosis on them during the "three ages or "aeons" following the Garden of Eden.[1] Under his guidance they would eventually acquire Christ Consciousness, the Divine Mind which the Sethian gnostics referred to as "the Second Logos of the great Seth."[2]

The Sethains also acknowledged that Seth took the form of the Primal Serpent Setheus, which they identified as the first form of the Infinite and the Creator of the Universe. After spiraling down the world tree Seth as Setheus had become ruler of the Earth and the "Earth-Shaker."[3] Setheus of the Sethians would eventually become synonymous with the destructive deity known in the Egyptian pantheon as Set.

Once the Sethians had identified the Divine Mind of Seth with the Christ Consciousness and the Divine Power of Seth with the Egyptian Set, these gnostics cobbled together an amalgamated deity that was the union of both Seth and Setheus and venerated under the name of Aberamentho, a title they also used as a name for Jesus, whom they acknowledged had been an incarnation of the Sethian Christ.

Their fabricated image of Aberamentho possessed an ass's head that is often ascribed to the Egyptian Set, and its human body fashioned after the Son of Adam was covered with only a scant loin cloth.[4]

The Sethians maintained that their alchemical practices to achieve both the Divine Mind and Power of Seth had both been passed down from the First Instructor directly through Adam to his son Seth, as well as been transmitted to Seth directly from the Goddess Sophia when the Son of Adam spent 40 days and 40 nights in her heavenly realm. Although it is not entirely clear if Sophia's teachings were written down, the gnostic text *The Revelation of Adam* is explicit that Adam's instructions to Seth were compiled into a sacred book or tablet that was eventually divided into numerous books and passed down among gnostics for many succeeding generations. The gnostic text is explicit regarding the sequence of events that occured after Adam's gift to Seth:

"Adam imparted revelations to his son Seth, and showed him his original greatness before the Transgression and his going out of Paradise....it was given to him to inscribe this wisdom in a book and teach it...and thanks to him, for the first time in this world, there was seen a book written in the name of the Most High. Seth bequeathed to his descendants the book thus written, and that book was handed down even to Noah...(and) Noah took with him into the ark the books of these teachings...these books of the hidden mysteries were (eventually) placed in the mountain of Victories to the east of our country of Shyr, in a grotto, the Cave of Treasures of the Life of the Silence."[5]

Some of the wisdom in the ancient Books of Seth was compiled into the "Seven Books of Seth" that some early historians ascribed to the Sethians. It was also incorporated both into the three Tablets of Seth mentioned in the *Apocalypse of Zostrian,* as well as the esoteric teachings Dositheus, one of the gnostic students of John the Baptist, who received them in a series of visions. The gnostic revelations of Dositheus were compiled into *A Revelation by Dositheus*, or *The Three Stelae of Seth.*

One of the important contributions made by the Sethains to the fledgling gnosticism of the west was their cosmological theory of emanationism and their delineation on a map that charted the various levels of the universe, or "Aeons," that a gnostic would pass through when ascending into the Pleroma. By memorizing their detailed schematic, all gnostics could momentarily escape the empire of the Dark Lord at any time of their lives, and permanently at death. When devising their map of the Aeons the Sethians astral traveled to the levels of the cosmos and learned the name of their gatekeepers and the passwords required to enter. They also discovered that some form of baptism was required at each level to achieve the high frequency required in the succeeding level. To assist the gnostics in their ascents, a gnostic gospel entitled *Zostrianos* was composed that described all the various baptisms required at each Aeon. Another important text, entitled *The Holy Book of the Great Invisible Spirit*, maintained, however, that all the required baptisms could be undergone by a gnostic on Earth before making his or her ascent to the Pleroma, and delineated specific instructions for their observance.

Cain and the Cainites

Close cousins and gnostic neighbors of the Sethians were the Cainites. Both gnostic sects venerated the same Divine Power of Seth, the only difference being that the Cainites called the power Cain and the Sethians referred to it as Setheus or Set. The synonymy between the Hebrew Cain and the Egyptian Set, both of whom murdered his own brother and fully embodied the power of destruction, is revealed in certain gnostic texts, such as *Gospel of the Egyptians,* which makes the observation that "the sacred dwelling places of the Men of Seth were Sodom and Gomorrah."[6] These Biblical towns, according to the testimony of Ireaneaus, were alternately known by the gnostics as the land of the "Men of Cain."

In more recent times the link between Cain and Seth has been further expanded upon by Madam Blavatsky and other esoteric authors, who point out that the Biblical lists of Cain and Seth and their descendents are nearly identical. Most occult historians agree, however, that the gnostic Seth was more consistently used as a name for the Divine Mind, while Set or Cain was used as a title for the Divine Power. Therefore, it follows that the perfect ancient title for the Primal Serpent of the gnostics would have been Seth-Cain.

Among the Sethians and Cainites, Cain was known for his association with fire, death, and destruction, as well as alchemy. The name Cain denotes "smith," and in ancient times smiths were respected workers in fire, as well as shamans, magicians, and alchemists. The epithet Cain also denotes "possessor" of fire, and according to one Kabbalistic legend Cain inherited his fiery, Divine Power directly from his father, Samael, the Serpent on the Tree, who had copulated with Eve when Adam was away. After inheriting all the attributes of his serpentine father, Cain became an incarnation of the Primal Serpent. Cain's formidable power was renown among the Cainites, whom the Church Father Irenaeus stated were proud to proclaim that "Cain was from the superior realm of absolute power."[7] Cain's inheritance from the Primal Serpent is also intrinsic to his name Cain, which is a form of the universal sound syllable for serpent, Can.

For those gnostic Cainites who were sincere seekers of wisdom, the most valuable aspect of Cain's power was, of course, its alchemical and transformative effect that opened a seeker to gnosis. Cain, whose Hebrew rendering is Quayin, meaning "spear," was, like his counterpart Karttikeya, intimately linked to the symbol of the spear, which denoted his inner, alchemical influence. For both deities the spear represented the spine (the shaft) and Third Eye of Wisdom (the head or blade) that they as the serpent fire would rise up to awaken. Fiery Cain was also intimately associated with another god of fire and weaponry, the Roman fire god Vulcan. According to the *The Source of Measures,* one of the early renderings in Cain's name in the Bible was V'elcain or V'ulcain, an epithet that ostensibly reflects the name Vulcan.

Author Laurence Gardner points out that Cain's Divine Power supported the throne of the earliest monarchs, the Fisher Kings and Queens, and it was passed down through long lineages of rulers (seee my book *Guardians of the Holy Grail* for their lineages). Cain's special letter Q (as in Quayin) gave rise to nouns associated with the world's highest administrators, such as "Queen" and "King." Gardner contends that Cain's mark of infamy - which he believes was a cross within a circle - was actually a noble symbol denoting rulership and synonymous with Malkuth, the Sephira at the base of the Kabbalic Tree of Life that denotes "Kingdom." A version of Cain's symbol was adopted by the lineage of rulers known as *The Order of the Dragon* and *The Imperial and Royal Court of the Dragon*, which was an organization that the Holy Roman Emperor Sigismund von Luxemburg revived in the Fourteenth Century. Its membership, which is said to have included Vlad III of Wallachia, better known as Count Dracula, wore as their emblem of membership a revised symbol of Cain with the circle perched over the cross. In this form it also becomes the symbol of Venus, who as Goddess Ishtar was patroness over all monarchs of Sumeria and Babylonia.

In Alexandria, Cain had his own gnostic sect, the Cainites, who daily applauded their ancestor for having been the first to transgress one of the cardinal laws of Ildabaoth as Jehovah. Because of the transgression of slaying his own brother, the Cainites championed Cain as the archetypal revolutionary and model for those on the Left Hand Path, and they sought to mirror him in their daily activities. The more evolved Cainites, however, focused principally in invoking Cain's destructive power in their alchemical experiments. They held Cain's definitive symbol, which was either a red or black cross, to be representative of the alchemical power of transformation he embodied.

According to Irenaeus, the Cainites honored not only Cain but all the legendary figures who had become infamous for transgressing the laws of Jehovah, including Esau, Korah, Judas, and the Sodomites. They revered Judas as a great liberator and touted the *Gospel of Judas* as the greatest of all scriptures. Eventually, the unruly behavior of some Cainites is said to have reached such immense heights of debauchery and anarchy that it led to the downfall of the entire sect. But, amazingly, not even the infamous Cainites would later hold the title as the most deplorable or despicable of all the gnostics.

The Barborites

The aberrant behavior of the Cainites was both matched and exceeded by the gnostic sect known as the Barbelo Gnostics or "Barborites," a name that denoted "filthies" or "muddies" in reference to their unwashed and abhorrent appearance. Ephianius maintained that the Barbelo Gnostics even indulged in the repulsive ritual of cannibalism, a practice that has also been associated with the Left Hand Path practitioners of both India and Greece. One of their more "disgusting" practices related to their method of birth control. According to the Church historian Epiphanius, the Barborites, who considered it the worst sin to bring souls into this evil world through childbirth and induced abortions whenever possible, would often capture their ejaculations and "pray while gazing towards Heaven" before imbibing their holy sacrament. Little did Ephiphanius know that they, in fact, regarded the consumption of seminal fluid to be a form of spiritual communion. Like other alchemists and yogis worldwide, the Barborites recognized that the seminal fluids are infinitely precious to the body and support inner alchemy. Not only do these inner fluids feed all the inner organs and support longevity, the inner alchemical fire is stoked by feeding off them. So the more seminal fluid a gnostic retains, the stronger will their Kundalini power be, and the quicker they will achieve gnosis and immortality.

The Carpocratians

Intimately related to the unruly Barborites and Cainites were the enigmatic Carpocrations. The Carpocratians believed that a soul must continue to reincarnate in this oppressive world lifetime after lifetime until it has gone through every possible experience Earth has to offer. Thus, their eccentric behavior was born out of the need to meet this criteria, even if it meant attracting the extreme censure and repulsion of the Right Hand Path. As one Church Father observed:

"...(they) are so abandoned in their recklessness that they claim to have in their power and to practice anything whatsoever that is ungodly and impious. They say that conduct is good and evil only in the opinion of men."[8]

While remaining true to their gnostic heritage and ideology, the Carpocratians denied the divinity of Jesus and claimed that his past incarnations and his experiences in the Pleroma had prepared him for his ascension to gnosis in only one lifetime. He was held as a model gnostic seeker by the Carpocratians, but they were also adamant that they too could achieve the same gnostic transcendence and immortality that he had. Irenaeus commented that one of the prized possessions of the Carpocratians was a portrait of Jesus supposedly painted by Pontius Pilate. They honored this portrait alongside the images of their other, equally great heroes and gnostics: the great Greek philosophers Plato and Pythagoras.

The Ophites and Naaseni

The Sethians and Cainites were additionally linked to another gnostic sect in Alexandria known as the Ophites and Naaseni. The Fourth Century historian Philaster maintained that these three sects were specially united by having descended directly from the First Instructor and Serpent on the Tree, and he therefore grouped them together as the "Head of the Heresies." Of the three sects the Ophites (from Ophidian, "snake") and Nasseni (from Hebrew Naas or Nachash, "snake") were most closely affiliated with the Primal Serpent and became well known as the pre-eminent worshippers of live snakes in Alexandria. They also merited the title of those gnostics most opposed to the dictates of the Right Hand Path since they claimed that the Serpent on the Tree had specifically instructed them to directly defy the oppressive son of Sophia.

The Naaseni are believed to be some of the original gnostics in the west, existing well before the birth of Christ. Originally they were known by their peers as the "Serpents" who had "knowledge of the deepest things."[9] They may have been a branch of the illustrious Nasurai, the enlightened gnostics of the Mandeans from Lemuria who founded the Nasorean or Nazarene sect of the Essenes when the most spiritual branch of Judaism and the Mandaeans merged together. During the time of his ministry, both the Mandaean Nasurai Jesus and his Apostles were collectively known by their peers as Nasoreans (or Nazarenes), and this gnostic title remained among the Apostles long after the Ascension when they were governed by Jesus's brother, James. One historical incident that irrefutably links the Nasoreans with the Nasseni has James the Just sending some very secretive "Serpent" teachings to the Nasseni via his chosen envoy, Mariam. This Nasorean Mariam is believed to be none other than Mary Magadalene, who was apparently in association with the Apostles and their Nasorean sect long after the departure of Jesus.

According to Epiphanius, the Nasseni departed from the Mandaeans and the Nasoreans by incoporating live snakes into their rites.The most important of snake was venerated as the First Instructor and commonly kept in a special chest known as the Cista Mystica, which was only opened during the most sacred of rituals. At mealtimes the favored snake, which the Ophites addressed as their Savior, was coaxed out of its box and let loose to consecrate the gnostics' food by slithering over and around it. Afterwards, the Ophites would take turns kissing the sacred snake upon the mouth and then sinking to their knees in humble worship of the reptile. The nocturnal rites of the Ophites were timed with the ascension of the celestial serpent, the constellation of Draco the Dragon, which was acknowledged by them to be the eternal heavenly manifestation of the First Instructor. Under the influence of the Middle Eastern gnostics the constellation of Draco went through numerous phases of evolution. At one time in its history it was given a tree made of adjoining stars to encoil itself around like the Serpent on the Tree; at another time the seven stars of the Little Dipper were concieved of as seven serpent heads; and at one period the Big and Little Dipper were attached to it as its two wings.

The Ophites and Nasseni employed various Greek and Hebrew names for their Serpent Savior, including Nachash, Kneph, Chnouphis, and the Agathodeamon. For protection they carried coins, talismans and gems with images of their serpent deity carved deeply into them. The gems and talismans were often bright red in color, thus reflecting the fiery nature of the serpent engraved upon them, and covered with Greek mantras and symbols.

For their academic contemplation the Nasseni studied *The Gospel According to Thomas* and were known to have been great fans of a *Gospel According to the Egyptians*. They were also inverterate devotees of the Goddess and adopted many of Her rites that had been observed in the Elusinian Mysteries and other Left Hand Path schools of alchemical initiation. Sometimes they worshipped the Primal Serpent as the Goddess' Son Hermes, especially in his form as the Agathodaemon.

The Archontici

The final sect associated with the Sethian-Cainite group of gnostics was the Archoniti, a group spread throughout Alexandria and Asia Minor whose members learned methods to neutralize and transcend the power of the Archons, the planetary spirits, which worked as prison guards for Ildabaoth to prevent humans from developing gnosis. The members of this sect were astrologers and astronomers who had studied the *Symphonia,* which were treatises associated with planetary transits, as well as the words of the prophets Martiades and Marsanes, who had risen into the celestial heavens while in their etheric bodies and ferreted out the secrets of the planets and stars by astrally exploring them for three days.

In order to neutralize the power of the Archons, the Archontici carried gems and talismans and utilized the power of ancient mantras and invocations. They also called upon the superior power of their Savior Serpent for assistance, and often had its image engraved upon their protecting gems.

The Sons and Daughters of Thoth-Hermes

The Sons and Daughters of Seth who settled in Atlantis and Egypt knew and embodied the Primal Serpent as Thoth-Hermes. They are known in history as the lineage of Thoth-Hermes Masters. Ancient historians have identified many of these Thoth-Hermes adepts. The Roman orator Cicero, for example, alluded to

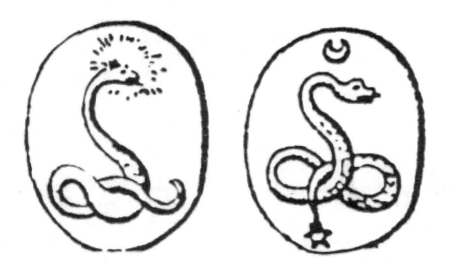

Ophite Coins with Serpent images

A Gnostic Orgy

five Thoth-Hermes Masters, and in *The Secret Doctrine* Madame Blavatsky alludes to numerous owners of this honorable epithet. She states:

"Hermes, or rather Thoth, was a generic name. Abul Teda shows in *Historia Anti-Islamitica* five Hermes, and the names of Hermes, Nebo, Thot were given respectively in various countries to great Initiates... They were all "Serpents of Wisdom," as connected with the Sun astronomically, and with [gnostic] Wisdom spiritually."

Other historians have also alluded to the fact that there were an abundance of scribes and adepts in Egypt who signed their works Thoth-Hermes. Together, these channels of the Divine Mind of Thoth authored 36,000 texts or scrolls that covered all the mundane and spiritual sciences.

One of the first recorded Thoth-Hermes in Egypt arrived in the country from Atlantis before the Great Deluge. He is remembered in the writings of the Carthaginian historian Sanconiathan, who referred to him as the leader of the "Serpent Tribe" and one of the "Seven Sons of Sydyk" (or Melchizedek), thereby identifying him as a member of the lineage of adepts descended directly from the Primal Serpent itself. Sanconiathan's Thoth-Hermes and his entourage are apparently also referenced in the hieroglyphic texts that cover one of the walls at the temple of Edfu, where they are called the Seven Sages that arrived in Egypt from the "Homeland of the Primeval Ones" and then constructed temples and pyramids across the land. Most esoteric historians have associated the Homeland of the Primeval Ones with Atlantis and maintained that the incipient Thoth-Hermes traveled to Egypt from the Atlantic Motherland just before the Great Deluge in order to build the Great Pyramid to serve both as a beacon for future generations as well as a water-tight storehouse for important Atlantean records and power objects. According to the great gnostic sage of Neoplatoism, Iamblichus, the records of Thoth-Hermes were also inscribed by the ancient serpent master on two columns and then placed in an impenetrable cave near Thebes. One of these columns was made of stone, to resist destruction by fire, and the other was formed out of brass, to resist destruction by water. A reference to this pre-flood Thoth-Hermes was also recorded in the holy books of the Hebrews, where he is referred to as Enoch, the patriarch who is similarly said to have inscribed ancient secrets on columns of stone and brass before secreting them in southern Egypt preceding the Great Deluge. The link between the two figures is undeniable within the texts of the Moslems, where they are both referred to as "Idris."

When the flood waters of the Great Deluge abated to reveal the bare ground again in Egypt, a second Thoth-Hermes is reputed to have arrived in the land to reclaim the records and power objects placed there by his predecessor. This later missionary, who is believed to have also come from Atlantis, recovered the columns hidden in Thebes and then transcribed their engravings into papyrus scrolls for the benefit of the Egyptian priesthood. This later Thoth-Hermes is also famous for having brought to Egypt the *Tabula Smaragdina*, or "Emerald Tablet," which was destined to become the foundation of all alchemical wisdom in not only Egypt but the entire western world. It is the mummified body of this second Thoth-Hermes that both Abraham's wife Sarah, as well as Alexander the Great, are averred to have discovered entombed in a cave near the Palestinian city of Hebron with the famous Emerald Tablet between his hands. The sacred city of Hebron was the "City of the Kaberoi," the twin snakes and sons of Melchizedek who had founded the Atlantean school of alchemy attended by Thoth-Hermes.

The secret wisdom recovered by the second Thoth-Hermes was eventually written both in coded hieroglyphs upon the walls of the Egyptian temples and tombs, as well as on hidden papyrus scrolls. One of these scrolls became known in history as the *Book of Thoth* which was studied by the priests and priestesses of Egypt and later incorporated into the Tarot. It is believed that the most important scrolls of Thoth-Hermes were kept in secret underground vaults at Heliopolis and only accessible to high priests and officials trained to facilitate initiations in the King's Chamber of the Great Pyramid. During these final initiations the priests would become mouthpieces for the Divine Mind of Thoth in order to intone Thoth's sacred mantras and summon his Divine Power to alchemically transform the body of the candidate.

After the traditional three days and nights sealed within the sarcophagus of the King's Chamber, a new initiate would arise as an awakened gnostic and be welcomed into the ancient lineage of Thoth-Hermes Masters by a circle of his or her new gnostic peers. He or she was now alternately known as a Djedhi, an enlightened "Serpent" master in the tradition of Djehuty, which was the Egyptian "serpent" title accorded Thoth-Hermes. A Djedhi was recognized as one who had united with Thoth-Hermes by raising the Dj, the inner serpent, up the Djed column or inner Tree of Life, and awakened all the inner centers of gnosis and power. Such a priest or priestess now wielded both the Divine Mind and Divine Power of Thoth-Hermes and could direct their powers into teaching, officiating ceremonies and initiations, and some would achieve renown as magicians. With magical accouterments that included a wand, a crystal ball, and several books of incantations, a Djedhi could move the Divine Power of Hermes through his or her staff while intoning the magical words of Thoth. According to the *Westcar Papyrus*, one Djedhi acquired notoriety for being able to reattach severed heads to their animal bodies. Another Djedhi possessed the Divine Power to magically animate a wax crocodile to devour his wife's lover.

The Hermeticists

Some of the magical formulary of the early Egyptian Djedhi was passed down to the later Alexandrian Gnostics who incorporated it into a series of Hermetic volumes known as the *Corpus Hermeticum*. The *Corpus Hermeticum* was later taken into Europe along with the precepts of the Emerald Tablet and became the foundation of many alchemical and magical textbooks. During the Middle Ages the laboratory alchemists of Europe would daily dedicate themselves to mastering the 13 Precepts of the Emerald Tablet by first invoking the Divine Mind and Power of Thoth-Hermes, the Lord of Alchemy, to guide them from within and bring success to their experiments. They would begin their alchemy by creating Mercury (the Latin name of Thoth-Hermes) in his Primal Dragon form as the Prima Materia, the "Primal Material," which they then separated into the twin snakes of the Primal Serpent, called Philosophical Sulpher (fire) and Philosophical Mercury (water). These separated "snakes" were then purified and subsequently rejoined as the Primal Serpent, which then vibrated at a much higher frequency than its original form of the Prima Materia. The end product of this alchemy was a fiery red-colored Philosophers Stone or Red Lion Elixir that carried a similar transformative property as the inner serpent fire. When powdered and sprinkled on a base metal it could transform it into gold, and when it was imbibed as an elixir it could both heal and endow one with great longevity.

The Hermetic alchemists of Europe were also accomplished astrologers and timed their experiments to coincide with supportive planetary influences. They closely watched the planet closest to the Sun, Mercury, which they identified as a celestial form of the Thoth-Hermes. It represented Thoth-Hermes as the Primal Serpent after it had initially emerged from Spirit (the Sun) at the beginning of time. Ultimately, Mercury would become synonymous with Thoth and more specifically associated with the Divine Mind of the Primal Serpent rather than the Divine Force. As such, in astrological interpretations it was given rulership over the logical or intellectual mind, and the Zodiacal sign of the intellect, Gemini. Gemini, the twin snakes or boys, represented the divided polarity of the Primal Dragon. In its earliest rendition the glyph of Gemini consisted of twin pillars encoiled by twin serpents and appeared very similar to the Caduceus of Mercury.

The Sons and Daughters of Enki

The earliest Sons and Daughters of Seth who arrived in Sumeria were led there by human embodiments of the Primal Serpent Enki. Known by the Babylon historian Berossus as the lineage of Oannes, a Greek name for Enki, these early gnostic adepts arrived four times in Mesopotamia at 30,000 year intervals with an entourage of gnostic adepts called the "dragon-faced" Annedoti. Their mission

Hermes Tresmegistus
The Lord and Patron of Alchemy

Thoth-Hermes and his Emerald Tablet

was to promulgate both the mundane and sacred sciences to humanity that was developing in the ancient Middle East. Eventually, these waves of gnostics established Eridu, the first city of Sumeria, as their base and made Enki the city's patron. Thereafter, Eridu served as the principal headquarters for all those Sumerian aspirants who sought to embody both the Divine Mind and Divine Power of Enki for their magic and alchemical practices.

The priests of Eridu would eventually became known as the Ashipu. The Ashipu were formidible magicians who channeled Enki's wisdom and power into their ceremonial rites. In order to completely merge their identities with Enki, during their rites they would cover themselves in ceremonial fish suits that resembled their deity, and then through their "fish" hands they channeled his Divine Power into their magical wands. After inscribing protective circles around themselves with their wands, they chanted:

"In my hand I hold the magic circle of Enki, in my hand the cedar wood, the sacred weapon of Enki, in my hand I hold the palm tree of the great rite."

Their ensuing magical incantation described Enki's Primal Dragon form and was calculated to provide both protection and abundance to the people of Eridu:

"The head is the head of a serpent...
His horns are twisted in three curls
The body is a sun fish full of stars
The base of his feet are claws..."[10]

Recognizing their deity as supreme in the spiritual pantheon, the Ashipu would also use the power of the summoned Enki to tame and control the other gods and spirits when they became unruly. The most efficacious incantations to invoke Enki, as well as the minor deities, were eventually compiled into the magical books of the Ashipu, and these were later transcribed into the Hebrew language by Jewish magicians who collected them during their Babylonian exile. These incantations would eventually find their way into Europe by Jewish immigrants and become part of the many grimoires used by the continent's magicians during the Middle Ages. These grimoires included the famous *Greater Key of Solomon* and the *Lesser Key of Solomon,* both of which were said to have been written by King Solomon, a master magician who used a supernatural ring with the pentagram signet of Enki to control the inimical spirits and force them to build his temple.

Some of Enki's alchemical rites studied by the Ashipu were part of the Sippar texts that Enki had earlier presented to Ziusandra, the Sumerian Noah, before the the Great Deluge so he could preserve the gnostic-alchemical path into the new cycle of time. Many of these alchemical rites were baptismal purifications

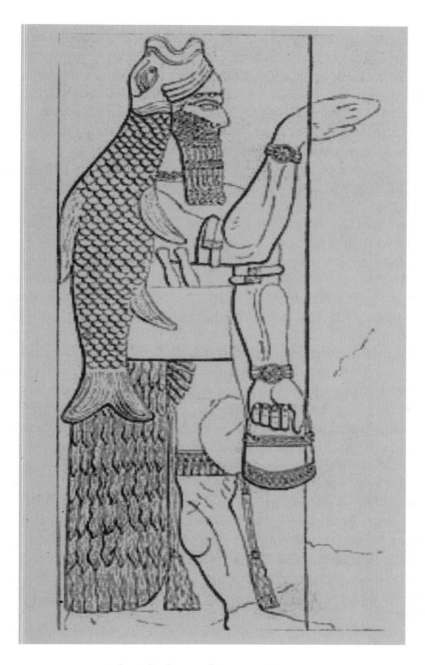

The Culture-bearer Oannes

designed to be observed adjacent to or within the Tigris and Euphrates Rivers, both of which had celestial counterparts in higher dimensions. Enki lived within these terrestrial arteries as the subtle, transformative life force, or "Water of Life," that moved through the physical water. By activating and enhancing Enki's subtle current through the recital of his sacred names, the Ashipu priests were bathed by his transformative power and ultimately acquired Enki's Divine Wisdom. Those Ashipu seeking to move quickly on their path to gnosis baptized themselves daily in the sacred rives and continually called out the names of their Savior.

The Mandaeans, who are the modern descendants of the Ashipu, continue to baptize each other in the Tigris and Euphates just like their ancestors once did. In the tradition of the Ashipu, once a week the Mandaeans participate in a special "full baptism" that is presided over by a priest who places his hand upon the head of the worshipper in order to transfer more of Enki's Divine Power into them. This ritual is completed when the priest inscribes a cross on the forehead of the worshipper with sacred oil. The cross, which is an ancient alchemical symbol of Enki, awakens Enki at his seat within the Third Eye of Wisdom.

The Mandaeans also studied the alchemical rites of Enki during their long sojourne in Egypt, where they lived many years before traveling to Palestine and merging with the Essenes. At that time the rites of Enki flourished in the cities of Mendes and Panopolis, the City of Pan, where they had been transplanted by missionaries from Atlantis and their descendants. Some of Enki's rites had arrived in Panopolis via the Atlantean Danaans, who as magicians and adept seafarers had succeeded in transplanting the rites of Enki and their primal Goddess Dana, Danu or Diana all around the globe. The Danaans of Panopolis founded a lineage of priest kings that included King Belus and his son, Danaus, who later established a kingdom in another headquarters of the goat-god Pan, Arcadia in Greece.

In Mendes, Enki's goat rites merged with those of Osiris, whose venerated form of a ram was eventually assimilated into the image of the Goat of Mendes. The goat god rites were principally fertility rites in Mendes, and the city became famous for the promiscuous sexual festivals that frequently occurred there. These rites later attracted the censure of Christian missionaries and a campaign for their complete eradication eventually proved successful. But the fertility rites of Mendes were only an outer veneer of the city's more hidden esoteric activities. As any alchemist of the time period knew, wherever the energy of the fiery billy goat was venerated through creative, sexual rites, his destructive/transformative power was also called upon. Thus, Mendes and Panopolis became Meccas for magicians, sorcerers and alchemists who sought to tap into the goat's occult power.

The image of the Goat of Mendes was eventually taken into the Middle East by the Islamic Sufis, who recognized it to be a symbol of the alchemical force they sought to manifest in their alchemical experiments. Their venerated alchemical image of the Goat of Mendes, known by the Sufis as "Baphomet," was later passed to the Knights Templar and made public by the Eighteenth Century occultist Eliphas Levi. The caduceus of Thoth-Hermes served as the phallus of Baphomet, and its other bisexual features were symbolic of the polarity that united to create what the black goat symbolized: the alchemical force. The androgyny of Baphomet manifested as its female breasts combined with a male phallus, and it united the polarity of Heaven and Earth with its hands that pointed both up and down. The destructive, fiery nature of Baphomet was reflected by its goat head and its dark, black color. Recently, the name "Baphomet" has given up clues about how the Sufis and Templars understood this unique androgyny. The name has been translated as both "Head of Wisdom," as well as "Baptism of Wisdom." Moreover, author Hugh Schonfeld has discovered that the name is written in the coded language of the *Atbash Cipher,* which was once used by the Knights Templar. Translated via the *Atbash Cipher* the name Baphomet becomes "Sophia." Thus, Baphomet was known by the Sufis and Templars to be the embodiment of the Divine Mind and Power of the gnostic Goddess Sophia.

The Goat of Mendes was still residing in Egypt many centuries after the heyday of the Sufis when the great British occultist Aliester Crowley visited Cairo in 1904 with his wife, Rose. While resting within their hotel room Rose spontaneously began channeling the wisdom of Baphomet. Calling itself Aiwass, it communicated through Rose what was to become the *Liber Al vel Legis*, "The Book of the Law," which was 21 page poem with one foundational mandate: "Do as thy wilt shall be the whole of the Law." This, of course, is the eternal anti-law of the gnostics of the Left Hand Path. When Crowley subsequently identified Aiwass to be his own guardian angel and higher self he decided it was fitting to refer to himself by the epithet of Baphomet.

During their sessions together, Aiwass instructed Crowley to prepare humanity for the Age of Horus, a coming Golden Age which would be the culmination of the preceding male and female ages of Osiris and Isis. Aiwass transmitted to Crowley a series of Left Hand practices involving alchemy and gnosis that the Brit was to use in preparing humanity for its next evolutionary leap. Crowley's mission also became heavily influenced by Sirian extraterrestrials who had anciently established a foothold in Egypt, and under their guidance he formed the Argenteum Astrum, the "Silver Star," an occult fraternity named after Sirius. The Argenteum Astrum, or A.A., was a full-on Left Hand Path sect centered on both the practices of alchemy and the wisdom contained within The Book of the Law.

One of the ancient gnostic practices taught by Crowley within the A.A. was astral travel, a practice he was to become particularly obsessed with. Crowley adopted the ancinet gnostic guidebook of moving through the dimensions that had been rewritten in the Seventeenth Century by John Dee and Edward Kelly and

Eliphas Levi's Baphomet

renamed Enochian Magic. Through it he was able to reach the highest levels of the Pleroma. Whenever the astral rites failed to give the desired result Crowley would supplement them with the occult power gained through sexual magic. This, however, proved his spiritual undoing, and in the eyes of the conservative Victorian public he acquired the reputation of a licentious guru preying upon on his naïve followers. Crowley never developed the discipline that accrues through following the Right Hand Path, and he thus became prey to the addictive tendencies that often accompany the Left Hand Path.

Crowley also taught his students of the A.A. how to create a magician's studio where they could channel the Divine Power of Baphomet while opening to gnosis. Their rites and invocations were based upon the Kabbalistic rites of the Jewish magicians, many of which had their origin with the Ashipu priests of Enki. Crowley was known to even assume the regalia of the ancient Ashipu priests while performing some of his magic.

Sons and Daughters of Bacchus

In Greece and its satellite countries of Greek-speaking inhabitants, the Sons and Daughters of Seth established commun ities and mystery schools where the goal was to achieve oneness with Dionysus or "Bacchus" who was an embodiment of the Divine Mind and Power of the Primal Serpent. In the tradition of their gnostic peers the world over, these gnostic Bacchae of Greece became renown for living the lives of recluses and eccentrics, or as radicals who were constantly rebelling against the laws of the Right Hand Path.

The origins of the Dionysian cult are very remote and seemingly swallowed up in the mists of antiquity, but inscriptions on archeological artifacts and the testimonies of ancient historians, such as Diodorus, seemingly trace its beginnings to Egypt, Crete and Aisa Minor. The wild, orgiastic rites of Dionysus were a staple of Thrace, which is now part of Bulgaria, as well as on Crete where Dionysus was venerated as Zagreus, the "Hunter." The earliest Dionysian revelers would meet in remote regions during full moon nights and ingest sacraments of very strong wine and/or hallucinogenic mushrooms in order to loose themselves in communion with the Divine Son. While under the influence of their sacraments those who venerated Dionysus as Zagreaus would embody their deity's hunting instincts and try to capture and devour the wild animals roaming the surrounding countryside. The most zealous revelers would tear apart animals with their teeth and lustily consume bloody, raw flesh as their legendary Savior, Zagreaus, once did.

Dionysus was also the Lord of Nature and Green Man, so his enebriated devotees sought to unite with him through communing with the surrounding forests and vegetation. Once they united with the spiritual essence within all the physical forms of nature, they then found themselves in ecstatic communion with their beloved Dionysus. Eventually, however, as their gnostic training progressed, they would recognize that the same Dionysian spirit that pervades nature also exists within their own hearts, and that they could commune with Dionysus at any time by simply going within. In this way communion with Green Man Dionysus served as a gateway to inner gnosis and self-knowledge.

When the Dionysian rites were eventually taken to Asia Minor and Rome they spawned groups of Dionysian revelers where every form of licentious behavior became the norm. Orgies of both a heterosexual and homosexual nature became commonplace, as did the exorbitant consumption of consciousness-expanding wine and herbs which were ingested to the point of stupefying inebriation. Sadly, the Left Hand Path rites of Dionysus succeeded in going completely out of control. This was a red flag to the authorities of the Right Hand Path, and soon the destructive and socially unacceptable nature of the Dionysian orgies would precipitate their abolition when the Roman Senate was pressured into outlawing their gatherings throughout the empire in 186 BCE. But this did not curtail the aberrant behavior of most Bacchae, who were dedicated gnostic rebels. Their goal was to live life to the fullest by continually allowing their actions to be inspired solely by Dionysus. By their very nature their abnormal actions could never be understood by the masses because their inspiration came from the heart, not the mind.

The Dionysian rites also managed to survive because they eventually acquired structure and discipline through the reforming influence of the great prophet Orpheus. Orpheus's promise to the Dionysian revelers was to permanently establish them in a gnostic communion with their deity, not just during their nocturnal orgies. Some Right Hand Path structure and academia thus took their place alongside the Left Hand Path practices of the Bacchae.

Like Thoth-Hermes, Orpheus was not one person but a lineage of gnostic masters who had succeeded in incarnating the Divine Mind. Collectively, all those masters called Orpheus were culture bearers of multiple mundane and sacred sciences, including medicine, writing and language, and especially the rites of the gnostic mystery traditions. Orpheus and Thoth-Hermes were names for the Divine Mind in the Greek and Egyptian spiritual traditions respectively, and for this reason they became recognized by the initiates of those traditions as one teacher and one consciousness. Since there was continual intercourse between Greece and Egypt for many centuries, especially during the time of the Ptolomies, the gnostic sects of Orpheus and Thoth-Hermes became mirror images of each other as the same rites and ideologies freely passed wisdom back and forth between them. One result of their intercourse was that the early historians claimed that the Greek mysteries ascribed to Orpheus had originally been taught in Egypt by the Thoth-Hermes Masters. Diodrous alluded to this truth when he claimed that Orpheus had studied the esoteric rites of Osiris and Thoth-Hermes in Egypt and

Bacchantes, Roman Priestesses of Dionysus

A Greek Priestess of Bacchus
with her initiating Thrysus Staff

then transported them to Greece, where they became the rites of Dionysus. The transference of secrets between these two deities and their cults is also revealed in the Greek legend that maintains that the famous lyre ascribed to Orpheus originally belonged to Hermes.

Perhaps the most important result of the exchange of the Egyptian and Greek mysteries was the synthesis of the rites of Osiris and Dionysus formulated by the Orphic Masters. During these fabricated initiation ceremonies each Orphic candidate would emulate the dying god Dionysus, the Greek counterpart of the Egyptian archetypal initiate, Osiris, as he was torn into pieces and later reborn and ressurected. Legend had it that Osiris had been slayed and carved up by his brother Seth, and it was said that Dionysus had met the same fate through his relatives, the Titans. Both had been magically resurrected. In ceremony, the Dionysian initiate was resurrected by the Thrysus, which was a Greek version of the the caduceus of Thoth-Hermes that had revived Osiris. The "Thrysus," which was typically a fennel stalk encoiled in serpentine ivy and surmounted with a pine cone, representing the Third Eye and its underlying pine-al gland, would assist the inner arousal of the serpent power and its ascension up the inner Tree of Life. This activation was enhanced by a live snake, the living symbol of Dionysian as Sabazios, that was simultaneously let loose in a candidates shirt to gyrate and sympathetically activate the inner serpent. In order to accentuate the inherent electro-magnetic properties of the Thrysus, it was often given a metal tip and made into a Dionysian spear similar to that carried by his eastern counterpart, Karttikeya. When it was not being used in ceremony, the Thrysus served as both the staff and weapon of a priest or priestess of Bacchus.

Following their initiations, the Orphic initiates were required to adopt a collection of disciplined alchemical practices and observe them daily. Their purpose was to complete the initiate's alchemical transformation and immerse them permanently in a gnostic union with Dionysus, who dwelled within them as their own inner spirit. The Orphics contended that the flesh of the human body came from the unruly Titans, and the heart and indwelling Spirit was from the divine Son, Dionysus. In order to subdue the unruly passionate nature of the Titans, sensual abstinence and ascetisim was highly encouraged by the Orphic Masters.

The austere and disciplined alchemical practices of the Orphics, which became known as the "Arts of Orpheus," would ultimately replace most of the orgiastic festivals of the Dionysian revelers. In Greece, these rites were called Teletae, "Perfections," and those seekers who achieved human perfection through their observance became known as Teloumenoi and Tetelesmenoi, meaning "Brought to Perfection." Itinerant Orphic priests called Orpheotelestae officiated over the Teletae in Greece; and on the Aegean islands the same rites were administered by priests known as Dactyloi, Kouretes, and Korybantes, who were repesentatives of the most ancient priests of the Goddess, the Kaberoi Twins. When the Dactyloi priests of Crete gave initiation into the mystreries of Dionysus in their cave-temples high upon the sacred mountains of the island they would use special Orphic mantras and bull-roaring instruments along with "Thunderstones" placed along the candidate's back. These were huge meteorites whose stimulating electro-magnetic field would catalyze movement in an initiate's etheric body and root chakra, home of the serpent fire. When Pythagoras underwent the Thunderstone initiaiton on Crete with the Dactyloi priests, the activation of his inner serpent catalyzed an intense alchemical reaction and for 24 hours he resembled a dead corpse.

The Sons and Daughters of Shiva

The Sons and Daughters of Seth in India established colonies and mystery traditions wherein they became the wielders of the Divine Mind and Power of the Primal Serpent, which became known to them as both the Goddess, Shakti, as well as her Son, Skanda-Murugan or Karttikeya. Their ultimate goal, however, was complete transcendence and identification with the Infinite sea of pure witness consciousness that transcended both Mother and Son, known as Shiva.

The incipient path leading to a perpetual union with transcendental Shiva was the Left Hand Path first promulgated on Lemuria by gnostic adepts in the alchemical tradition of Karttikeya or Sanat Kumara. The alchemy they practiced and taught their students involved using the Divine Power and Divine Wisdom of Shakti or Karttikeya to alchemically purify and transform their dense human bodies and raise them to a frequency compatible with Shiva consciousness. Thus, through the vehicle of Shakti - which was Shiva's own power and wisdom - Shiva's transcendental nature was achieved.

A guru in the Karttikeya tradition, the late Subramuniya Swami of Kauai, received a series of visions from Murugan in the 1970s that revealed many of the alchemical practices taught by Sanat Kumara and observed on Lemuria by those on the path to Shiva. In his *Lemurian Scrolls*, Subramuniya Swami also reveals the ashram environments where these practices occured: energy conductive structures erected upon vortexual fields of energy that once covered the landscape of Mu. The enlightened Subramuniya Swami was no doubt also aware that union with Shiva was also achieved through meditation on Skanda-Karttikeya, the Green Man and Lord of Nature, just as the Greek revelers had achieved gnosis through communing with Skanda's counterpart, Dionysus. Meditation on Skanda's vegetative form could similarly transport the Lemurian worshipper into union with Shiva, which was the Green Man's spiritual essence (and their own). For the fortunate few, Skanda-Karttikeya would bless his devotees with his radiant peacock form to meditate upon. They would be ushered into Skanda's special fourth dimensional realm where virtually everything, including the trees and mountains, assumed the form of peacocks and peacock plumes. In time, the meditator would identify with the peacock feathers as their own, and then they would be one with the radiant Son Karttikeya. This was one of the special experiences available to those early humans living in the Garden of Eden.

Shiva also sometimes manifested to the gnostic seekers of Lemuria and India in a special symbolic form for them to meditate upon. In his form of the "Lord of the Yogis" Shiva would appear as an ascetic yogi with long matted locks sits, legs crossed, and with his vision directed inwards towards his own inner Self. When meditated upon the symbolic meaning of the image would soon emerge: the true essence of Shiva is the inner, Infinite Spirit within everyone's heart. The color of the Lord of Yogis was also instructive; as either blue, the color of pure spirit, or covered with grey ashes, the image revealed that Shiva is dead to our world and dwells solely in the transcendental realms beyond it. The other symbolic components of the image revealed how the universe emerges from the pure consciousness of Shiva at the beginning of time. The tiger skin that the Lord of Yogis wore as a loin cloth and sat upon represented the solar or male creative Spirit that emerged from him. The snakes that coiled upon Shiva's neck and arms, as well as the three powers of the life force he wields as represented by his three-pronged trident: creation, preservation, and destruction, denote the life force that emerges from Shiva and eventually condenses into the forms of the physical universe.

On Lemuria, and later in India, yogis would seek to achieve union with Shiva by emulating and indentifying with his image as Lord of the Yogis. They grew matted locks, painted their bodies in sacred ash, and covered themselves solely with a loin cloth just like Shiva. Some would hike the length and breadth of India with a trident, while others would sit with cross legs in absolute stillness while immersed in the transcendental consciousness of Shiva.

The Shiva yogis of India and Mu followed the Left Hand Path, which by its Sanscrit name is also known as the Vamacara Path. These Vamacara gnostics typically lived outside the mainstream of society. Their homes were caves, ashrams, cremation grounds, thick jungles or any remote place in nature their inspiration directed them to. Like the Lord of Yogis, they covered themselves in ash and considered themselves dead to the world of social consciousness. Their reclusive lifestyles and habitations also mimicked Lord Shiva, who according to scripture is said to sit alone in deep meditation on top of sacred Mount Kailas, in cremation grounds, or other places removed from society. Shiva typically only enters society long enough to destroy a Vedic sacrifice or transgress the social customs of the Right Hand Path while displaying repugnant and obscene behavior. Shiva's rebellious nature as the enemy of God's law, as well as his image as the wild looking and the trident-wielding deity of fire, destruction and the underworld, eventually became a model for the Right Hand Path's greatest enemy. When Shiva's form accompanied the Kali-worshipping Gypsies into Europe it served as a contributing model for the fabrication of the Christian Devil.

Another reason that the gnostic seekers of Shiva removed themselves from society is because their Left Hand Path practices were not understood by the masses of humanity and would quickly attract both censure and persecution. Such practices included ignoring the scriptural injunctions by consuming meat and wine, indulging in an abundance of casual sexual liasons, living in cremation grounds and consuming food and drink out of skulls while utilizing skeletal bones as eating implements. Even digging up corpses to consume and/or use them in their rituals has been a commonplace occurance among the Vamacara yogis in the past. When not understood, these activities are naturally viewed as nauseating and repulsive, but for the Vamacara initiate their observance provides a key to spiritual growth. They are consciously performed by a Vamacara yogi to help him or her move beyond the dualistic considerations that society places upon all humans at a young age. Such encoding, or "brain washing," serves to dictate a person's positive or negative responses to their environment throughout life, but through the cultivation of an even mind and balanced temperament while involved in what society normally considers repulsive, a yogi can become re-programmed and acquire equal vision. He or she can then begin to realize the essence of the Hindu scriptures, which collectively entreat the yogi to see and experience all things as equal, including praise and blame. Once a perpetual even mind and tranquil nature is achieved, the next step is transcendence and union with the witness consciousness of Shiva.

The greatest Vamacara yogis who have completed the Left Hand Path and live eternally united with transcendental Shiva are known as the Avadhoots. Any personal motives, worldly desires, needs and ambitions have disappeared from within these adepts, and they live completely by the inner inspiration that comes directly from Shiva, their inner Self. Unless they feel the inner command from Shiva, they may spend the entire day sitting immovable in a chair or even lying down upon a hard floor while immersed in ecstatic communion with Shiva.

Being completely detached and disconnected from society, the Avadhoots can often be found living naked and free from all restrictions in dense jungles or on remote mountains. When they do move around they often appear mad or insane, and there is no rational explanation for many of their actions. A blessing from one of them might arrive as a hard blow to the face, or as a rock or coconut beaten against the worshipper's skull. However, the devotees of Avadhoots take such "abuse" in stride because they know that the blessing from a great adept never goes to waste and will eventually bare positive fruit. They also acknowledge that Avadhoots can not act maliciously since they only remain in a human form to raise the consciousness of humanity.

Shiva, Lord of the Yogis

Yogi emulating Shiva

Shiva Lingum
Shiva and Shakti as phallus and yoni unite to produce Skanda-Murugan, the serpent

Dattatreya, Avadhoot of the Treta Yuga

Entrance to Baba Kinaram Ashram
Headquarters of the Vamacara Aghoris
Varanasi, India
Photo by Mark Amaru Pinkham

One of the greatest of Avadhoots, and an important reformer of the Avadhoot tradition, was Dattatreya. Dattatreya first walked the Earth during the Treta Yuga, which is an age that coincides with the latter days of Lemuria. Some believe he still roams around the region of Junagarh in Gujarat, where legend has it he met the Avadhoot Baba Kinaram in the Sixteenth Century and designated him the modern revivalist of the ancient Avadhoot tradition. The ashram that Baba Kinaram subsequently founded in the center of the holy city of Varanasi has since become the world headquarters of the Avadhoot tradition. A sacred fire ignited by Baba Kinaram has burned continually within the ashram for nearly five hundred years. The current head of the Avadhoot lineage at the Baba Kinaram Ashram is Avadhoot Siddhath Gautama Ramji, who was materialized out of thin air as a baby by his predecessor Avadhoot Rajeshwar Ramji.

Since the time of Dattatreya the preeminent scripture that describes the state of the Advadhoot has been his masterpiece, the *Avadhuta Gita*. Through this text the great Vamacara master attempted to articulate the exalted awareness he perpetually dwelt within as an Avadhoot. He states:

"There is no doubt that I am that God who is the Self (Shiva) of all, pure, indivisible, like the sky, naturally stainless."

"All is verily the absolute Self (Shiva). Distinction and nondistinction do not exist. How can I say, "It exists; it does not exist"? I am filled with wonder."

"Union and separation exist in regard neither to you nor to me. There is no you, no me, nor is there this universe. All is verily the Self (Shiva) alone."

Today, the Left Hand Path rites that lead to the exalted state of an Avadhoot are typically not enrolled in until a yogi has acquired the discipline that comes through following the Right Hand Path. The union of the two paths was found necessary when undisciplined yogis acquired addictions to some of the sensual Left Hand rites, or they sought to acquire some of the supernatural powers to harm others that can be earned from observing the more gruesome Vamacara practices. It was for this reason that the Kuala Path, which unites both the Right and Left Hand Path practices, came into existence. During the first four stages of this eight-stage path a yogi observes the Vedacara practices of the Right Hand Path, which include worship, study, and adherence to the Vedic laws and injunctions. Then during the last four stages of the Left Hand Path the yogi undergoes the intensive alchemy and aberrant rites that will culminate in equal vision and gnostic union with Shiva. During these latter stages of the Kaula Path the yogi often chooses one of the many alchemical yogas that unite the male and female principles within the human body and arouse the fire serpent. There are literally hundreds of these yoga paths to choose from, each of which is designed for a different temperament. Those who take to the path of Hatha Yoga, for example, are more athletic and disciplined in their lifestyle. Those who gravitate to the path of Bhakti Yoga are more devotional in nature and resonate with the path of love and service. Those yogis who are involved in continual work often find themselves most suited to the path of Karma Yoga, within which they learn to dedicate the fruits of their labors to a higher power. And lastly, those yogis with a contemplative temperament inevitably find a home following the path of Jnana Yoga, the path of knowledge (see Chapters 11-13).

Some Vamacara yogis take to the path of Siddha or Maha Yoga, which involves being initiated by an enlightened guru who has achieved union with Shiva and wields the Divine Power and Divine Wisdom of the Goddess Shakti. Initiaiton from such a teacher is known as Shaktipat, meaning "falling power," during which a particle of their Kundalini power "falls" into a disciple via an adept's thought, word, look or touch and then awakens their dormant serpent power. One benefit of having a guru is that he or she can control the movement of the serpent fire as it moves through the body and ascends the Tree of Life. Sometimes the heat of the inner fire or the visions that it produces seem overwhelming to a yogi. According to the yogic scriptures, the guidance and support of a guru becomes especially necessary when the inner serpent rises to the Third Eye of Ajna Chakra of the yogi. At that point the blessings of a guru are indispensible for guiding the serpent to its final destination, union with Shiva in Sahasrar Chakra at the top of the head.

After the various paths of yoga of the Vamacara Path were taught on Lemuria for thousands of years they were finally taken into the heartland of India. One Lemurian guru, the great sage Agastyar, took the alchemical teachings into south India and set up a school of yoga in the Pothagai Hills, where rumor has it he still resides while awaiting those seekers worthy of his blessing. Agastyar's closest disciples left south India and took the ancient teachings of Mu to different parts of the country where they established many schools of yoga that continue to exist today. Collectively known as the Mahesvara (Shiva) Siddhas (perfected ones), they include Goraknath, the founder of Hatha Yoga; Babaji, the founder of Kriya Yoga; Patanjali, the author of the Yoga Sutras; and Bogarnath, founder of Siddha alchemy or "Rasayana," which involves the use of herbal and mineral formulas for longevity and immortality.

The Sons and Daughters of Sanat Kumara:
The Great White Brotherhood

One branch of the Left Hand Path founded by the Sons and Daughters of Seth during the Lemurian era is the Great White Brotherhood (GWB). This planetary organization is called "white" in reference to the purity of its members, not the color of their skin. The network is also considered "white" because it is inclusive of all people and all races, just as the color white is the synthesis of all the seven colors of the spectrum. The initiates of the Great White Brotherhood have served as an exceptional vehicle for equality and the spread of the Left Hand Path around the globe.

During Lemurain times the GWB was administered by Sanat Kumara and his six twin brothers, the Seven Kumaras or Seven Archangels, each of which represented one of the seven aspects, rays, or divisions of the Creation that became manifest by the crystallized Primal Serpent, and they oversaw their respective division on Earth. Since that early epoch numerous gnostic adepts and Ascended Masters have evolved on Earth to a level where they could assume some of the important administrative positions previously held by the orignal Seven Kumaras. It is said, for example, that at the Ascended Masters Morya and Kuthumi recently assumed the roles of Lords of their First and Second Rays respectively. Below is the standard chart of the individual rays and their lords, past and present:

Ray	Color	Lords
1. Will and Power	Blue	Sanat Kumara, Master Morya
2. Love and Wisdom	Yellow Gold	Sananda Kumara, Kuthumi
3. Activity	Red, Orange	Sanaka Kumara, Paul the Venetian
4. Harmony/balance	White	Sanatana Kumara, Serapis Bey
5. Science/Healing	Green	Ribhu Kumara, Hilarion
6. Devotion/Mysticism	Purple	Sananda Kumara, Lady Nada
7. Alchemy/Transmutatin	Violet	Sanat Kumara, Saint Germain

According to legend, Sanat Kumara came to Earth from the Pleiades via the planet Venus some 18 million years ago with an entourage of 104 gnostic adepts who became the first initiates of the Great White Brotherhood. References to the arrival of Sanat Kumara on our planet have come principally from H.P. Blavatsky's Theosophical Society and its satellite members and organizations, including the clairvoyant Alice Bailey and her Lucis Trust. Bailey wrote massive tombs on esoteric history and the GWB compiled from information transmitted to her principally from the Ascended Master Djwhal Khul. Regarding the functions Sanat Kumara assumes as head of the GWB, Bailey writes:

"At the head of affairs, controlling each unit and directing all evolution, stands the KING, the Lord of the World...He Who is called in the Bible "The Ancient of Days," and in the Hindu scriptures the First Kumara, He, Sanat Kumara it is, Who from his throne at Shambhala in the Gobi desert, presides over the Lodge of Masters, and holds in his hands the reigns of government...he has chosen to watch over the evolution of men and devas until all have been occultly "saved." He it is Who decides upon the "advancements" in the different departments (of the GWB), and Who settles who should fill the posts."[11]

Bailey's Shambhala, the original headquarters of the GWB, originally sat upon the "White Island" where it was surrounded by an inland sea. Eventually the sea drained and was replaced by the parched Gobi Desert of modern China. However, as Bailey asserts, court still convenes at Shambhala with representatives of the GWB just as he did nearly 18 million years ago. Today, Shambhala consists of "matter of the higher ethers of the physical plane, and only when man has developed etheric vision will the mystery (of its location) beyond the Himalayas be revealed."[12]

According to Bailey, instructions from Sanat Kumara at Shambhala are dispatched to various Ascended Masters and members of the Great White Brotherhood during their gatherings and telepathically. Some recipients of the instructions will know their origin, while less advanced members of the GWB will simply experience them as an inner inspirations or commands. These commands, and the power and wisdom to execute them, come directly from Sanat Kumara. Bailey asserts that the high frequency power of Sanat Kumara expands beyond the borders and into the world especially during times when major alchemical changes are needed on our planet in preparation for new cycles of time. Thus, many individuals should be feeling the power of Sanat Kumara moving through them now or in the very new future as we proceed into the prophesied Golden Age.

The Sons and Daughters of Vishnu- the Avatars

Intimately related to the Great White Brotherhood are the Avatars of Vishnu. The "Avatars" are those who incarnate fully enlightened during times of upheaval on Earth solely for the upliftment and protection of humanity. To accomplish their missions they live in continual union with Shiva while wielding principally Shiva's power of preservation, one of the three powers symbolized by Shiva's trident that is associated with the demi-god Vishnu. Thus it is said that the Avatars are embodiments of Vishnu. Over many millennia these representatives of Vishnu have repeatedly taken physical incarnation during times of planetary crisis, which normally coincide with the beginning or end of a major cycle of time.

There are various lists of avatars in the Puranas or legends of India. The accepted list mentions 11 avatars, with the last, Kalki, due to arrive at the end of the Kali Yuga, the age we are passing through now. Before him, the Avatar Krishna took birth during the previous Dwarpa Yuga and his death signaled the beginning of the Kali Yuga. Other avatars on the list include the Matsya or "Fish" Avatar that assisted humanity during the time of the Great Deluge; as well as Avatar Parasurama, who saved the world from the oppressive rule of the Kshatriya kings. The Avatar Lord Rama defeated the Rakshashas, the demons, who threatened humanity during the Treta Yuga; and the Avatar Lord Buddha made the path to enlightenment available to everyone. In other Avatar lists Sanat Kumara and his brother Kumaras are sometimes listed as the very first avatars since they were the first saviors of humanity and the incipient teachers of the gnostic-alchemical path.

In recent times the list of avatars has grown to include those souls who have come into incarnation already enlightened during the present Kali Yuga and live solely for the upliftment of humanity. Jesus Christ is on this extended list, as is Sri Ramakrishna of Calcutta, India and the contemporary Avatar Mata Amritanandamayi or "Ammachi" of Kerala, India.

The Sons and Daughters of Quetzlcoatl

In Middle America, the Sons and Daughters of Seth first appeared as Atlantean missionaries known as the Quetzlcoatls, or "Plumed Serpents," who founded a lineage of gnostics that embodied the Divine Wisdom and Power of the Plumed Serpent. According to the testimonies of the Native Elders of Mexico gathered by the Spanish chronicler Sahagan and the first US consul in Mexico, Edward Thompson, the Quetzlcoatl lineage initially arrived in Mesoamerica from the east with a very advanced culture that possessed pyramid technology, writing, a system of numbers, a calendar system, and held special veneration for the Morning Star, Venus. Arriving on boats covered in snakeskin, these missionary Quetzlcoatls are said to have worn the symbol of their patron, the primal serpent, over their third eyes and also covered their own bodies in snakeskin. After arriving along the coast of Veracruz and sailing down the Panuco River, these Quetzlcoatls founded the first civilization of Middle America, Tamoanchan, which Thompson was told means "The Place where the People of the Serpent Landed." With Tamoanchan as their base, many Quetzlcoatl missionaries traveled throughout Middle America to found other civilzations, including that of the Olmecs, the Toltecs, and the Maya. Many of the Quetzlcoatls became the priest kings and high priests within these civilizations.

The Middle American records also allude to individual Quetzlcoatls who arrived in boats sometime after the Tamoanchans and similarly served the Mesoamerican culture as monarchs and teachers. One of these Quetzlcoatls is

Images of Quetzlcoatl, the Serpent Culture Bearer

remembered as having arrived in a long gown covered with alchemical, red crosses. With a large entourage of builders in his wake, this Quetzlcoatl assisted in the building of many pyramids in Mexico and then served as a Toltec priest king. At the completion of his sojourne among the Toltecs, Quetzlcoatl made a raft covered in snake skin, and after promising his people that he would one day return he sailed back from whence he had come.

In the Mayan language Quetzlcoatl translates as Kukulcan, a term that similarly denotes "Plumed Serpent" and awarded to those adepts who had united with the Primal Serpent. One Mayan Kulkucan is famous for having served as king of the great Maya city-state of Chichen Itza and for inculcating his subjects with great spiritual teachings. Both the Kukulcan and Quetzlcatl kings revealed themselves as embodiments of the Divine Mind and Power of the Primal Serpent through their title of "The Twins" (they united the Maya twins Hunapu and Xbalenque, or the Toltec twins Quetzlcoatl and Tzcatilopoca) and by wearing the radiant plumes of the quetzl bird within their ceremonial crowns and ponderous jaguar gloves over their hands. Both the jaguar and serpent were assocaited with shamanic power in Middle America and used interchangeably, although the serpent generally represented the life force power that moves under the ground and the jaguar was its symbollic embodiment as it moved above the ground. To further emphasize and identify the source of their power, the Kukulcan monarchs would seat themselves upon jaguar thrones during special ceremonies. In order to keep their kingdoms strong and prosperous, these shamanic rulers would occasionally observe a ritual to release their own power into their kingdoms. This rite required them to ceremoniously cut themselves with obsidian blades in the most sensitive and excruciating parts of the body, including their genitals and tongues, which were also areas in the body associated with personal power.

The later Aztecs inherited the Quetzlcoatl tradition of the Toltecs and founded the Calcemac or "College of Quetztlcoatl" so their young warriors could learn the wisdom of the Quetzcoalt. Some of those who graduated from this school went on to become enlightened gnostic teachers of the Plumed Serpent, or perhaps a chief priest of the Aztecs. Two Quetzlcoatls were specially elected to preside over the religious life of the Aztecs. The high priest Quetzlcoatl Totec Tlamacazqui oversaw the rites of the highest Aztec deity, the Sun god Huitzilopochtli, and the second high priest Quetzlcoatl Tlaloc Tlamacazqui administered the rites of the rain god Tlaloc. According to the Spanish historian Sahagun, those gnostics elected to serve as the Quetzlcoatl high priests were the wisest and most powerful of all the ordained Aztec priests. They were the true embodiments of the Plumed Serpent and honored as such.

The Daughters (and Sons) of Sophia

Besides the Sons of Seth, there was another movement of gnostics that spread the Left Hand Path and its teachings around the globe following the Garden of Eden epoch. These gnostics, known as the Daughters and Sons of Sophia, established gnostic and alchemical sects around the world that espoused communion with the Goddess by fully embodying her divine power and wisdom. The Daughters and Sons of Sophia can be traced back to the heyday of the primeval Goddess civilization on Lemuria, where they emerged following Sophia's compassionate descent into the Garden of Eden. The Goddess tradition became defined and structured under the influence of the "Sons of God" on Mu, who taught their wives, the Daughters of Men, the various components of the Left Hand Path including divination, healing, astrology, herbology and alchemy. In the aftermath of Lemuria the Daughters of Sophia manifested on Atlantis as the Amazons and Danaans and then they could be found in settlements throughout Asia and Europe as the votaries of the Great Goddess of the Neolithic Age. Since then their manifestations have included the devotees of Goddess Shakti in India and the contemporary Dianic Wiccans of modern times.

The Alchemical Rites of the Amazons

On Atlantis, the rites of Sophia were embraced by the male and female venerators of Dana or Danu, the Goddess of profound wisdom and power, as well as by the purely female Amazons, who came to know Dana as the Maiden Diana, as well as Artemis, Neith, and Athene. Possessing excellent sailing skills, the lovers of Dana eventually left Atlantis as traders and spread the mysteries of their deity around the globe. They subsequently settled in Greece and Egypt, where they became known as the Danaans. In India, they were known as the magical Danavas; in Britain they were powerful wizards known as the Tuatha de Danaan; and in Palestine they were the Tribe of Dan, whose symbol was the transformative serpent. Meanwhile, the intrepid Amazons, who were also itinerant merchants, became the merchant warrior women of Hesperius or the Hesperides (two inter-related names of Atlantis), and adopted a fiercely independent and highly skilled warrior-huntresses deity as their patroness. Many Amazons sailed from Atlantis to Lake Tritronis (part of the Triton Sea) in Libya, where they founded a colony and continued to venerate their patroness under the names of Neith and Athene, while other Amazons continued sailing east to Asia Minor and the islands of the Medi-terranean and the Aegean where they set up numerous temples and shrines to their beloved huntress deity under the name of Artemis.

On Atlantis, the Amazons acquired the reputations of great alchemists and gnostics. They were worshippers of all three aspects of the Triple Goddess, Maiden, Mother and Crone, which personified the three powers of the Primal Serpent. Later, in their settlements on Libya's Lake Triconis, the Amazons continued their veneration of the Triple Goddess as Anatha, whose androgynous manifestations included the Primal Serpent and the double-headed battle axe. Serpent Goddess Anatha, who was also worshipped by the Amazons as the Great Mother, had her Divine Wisdom and Divine Power individually venerated by her "Twin Serpents" or two daughters, the Maiden Neith-Athene and the Crone Medusa. It is said that Medusa was initially a very beautiful Maiden, but during a vicious battle with Athene she was transformed into a grotesque, serpentine deity. After her transfor-mation, serpent-haired Medusa fully embraced her new role as the dreaded Crone. As for Athene, she remained the embodiment of the Divine Mind, and later, when the patriarchal Greeks assimilated her, she was recognized as the Divine Mind of Zeus who had been born directly out of the head of the highest god.

When the Amazons settled in the Mediterranean and Aegean Seas they gravitated to many of the same power spots that other migrating Atlantean alche-mists before them had previously colonized. Such energetic zones enhanced the transformative power of the Crone. The Amazons established temples on certain volcanic islands that possessed intensely active electro-magnetic fields, including Lemnos, Rhodes, and Samothrace, the Holy Island of the Kaberoi Brotherhood, where they built their most sacred alchemical cave-temple dedicated to the Crone as Hecate. Hecate, whose name denotes "mistress of fire," was sometimes re-ferred to as the mother of the Kaberoi "Twin Flames" and addressed as Kaberia, the "Mother Flame." The greatest of Hecate's initiations occurred in Samothrace's Zerynthian cave-temple, where the redeeming fire of the Savior Hecate trans-ported the Amazons beyond illusion and into the soul's true home of gnosis.

Many of the Amazons who migrated into Asia Minor settled in the city of Colchis on the shores of the Black Sea and its vortexual power. It was there that they are reputed to have often summoned the Divine Power of Medusa during their alchemical rites. During secret moonlit ceremonies it is said that Amazon

Atlantis, Lake Triconis and the Triton Sea

Hecate, Goddess of Alchemy and Gnosis

Medusa, Embodiment of the Divine Power

Athene, Embodiment of the Divine Mind

The Alchemical Image of Artemis-Diana

priestesses would strive to identify with and fully embody the power of Medusa by donning fiery red or black masks featuring Kali-like blood-dripping fangs and serpentine hair. To further invite the destructive power of Medusa into their rites, the Amazons are reputed to have let loose live snakes to bite them. The snake venom "induced a hallucinatory state in which oracular visions were revealed."[1]

When not in volcanic regions, and/or to enhance the alchemical power of a volcanic island, the Amazons incorporated tools made of meteorites and igneous rock into their initiations. Meteorites and igneous volcanic stone, both of which possessed radiant electro-magnetic fields, were venerated as embodiments of the Dark Goddess with the power to activate the inner fire serpent. The Amazons are known to have used their alchemical black stones on the volcanic island of Crete, where priests called Dactyloi initiated with huge meteorites called "Thunderstones."

Among the Amazons and other Goddess worshipping sects of Asia Minor, meteorites were forms of the Great Mother, especially in her form as Venus or Aphrodite, with whom the meteorites shared a common origin. Both the Goddess Venus and meteorites were born from Heaven, fell to Earth as fire, and then cooled on land or in water. The legend of the birth of Venus maintained that she had fallen from the sky as the flaming genitals of the Heaven God, Uranus, and then splashed into Mediterranean Sea where she subsequently arose in a cloud of steam as the alluring Aphrodite. The closest dry land to her fall was Cyprus, the island she proceeded to make her home and the headquarters of her cult.

Meteorites, which were natural "androgynous" alchemical tools capable of sympathetically uniting the inner polarity within an initiate and awakening the fire serpent, became so sacred to the populace of the Middle East as manifestations of the destructive/transformative power of the Goddess that when these fiery masses of molten metal landed anywhere along the Asia Minor coast - either on land or in the Mediterannean Sea - they were immediately gathered up and either set within temples dedicated to the Goddess or taken by Her priests and priestesses to be used in the Goddess's initiation rites. One of the collosal meteorites that fell near the Asia Minor coast was discovered by the Amazons and then carved into a statue of their beloved Artemis. This life-size black image was placed within their main Temple of Diana-Artemis in Ephesus, thereby filling the Amazons' principal Asia Minor headquarters with the power of the Dark Goddess and making it an alchemical crucible for transformation. Future statues of the Goddess interred within the temple were made of black wood and did not vibrate with the same electro-magnetic intensity as a meteorite, but by virtue of their ebony color and the intense devotion daily directed towards them by the Amazons and other Goddess worshippers, they eventually emanated some measure of the destructive alchemical power of the Goddess. These later wooden images of Artemis were some of the first examples of Black Madonnas in the Middle East.

The Gnostic Cult of Diana

The ancient Amazon tradition of Artemis-Diana was eventually transported by missionaries of the Left Hand Path to Rome, and from there they spread into the rest of Europe. In time, this Dianic tradition assimilated various streams of Goddess worship from the South and East to form the amalgamated rites of witchcraft that became immensely popular during the Middle Ages. Goddess Hecate was absorbed into these alchemical rites, as were some of the remaining orgiastic practices of Dionysus. Gypsies from the East arrived to share their Tantric rites of Kali and Shiva, whose fiery, trident-carrying form contributed to the Christian's version of the Devil. The Sufis also entered Europe with their special alchemical wisdom after traveling from the Middle East to eastern Europe or Spain. The Sufis shared their ancient rites of Enki, the Sabbatical Goat, as well as the Halka circle of 13 participants that would eventually evolve into the witches' coven of 13 members. The dance of the "Cone of Power" that subsequently emerged from the coven gatherings was also a gift of the Sufis and based upon the spiraling dance of the Sufi Dervishes.

With its thirteen swaying and spiralling paticipants, the Cone of Power was used by the Dianics to intensify the amount and frequency of the life force so that it could effectively be used for healing, magic and alchemical transformation. Since thirteen was also a number of the Goddess Diana, the Lady of the Moon, whose annual full moons numbered thirteen, the Cone of Power could also assist in the manifestation of her presence.

Before or after creating the Cone of Power, gathering witches of a coven might intensify their communion with Diana through the consumption of mushrooms, wine and a host of vision-inducing herbs including datura, mandrake, henbane, etc. Experiences of "flying" could then be induced during which a witch could leave her body, gnostic style, and travel to distant realms in the astral dimensions. The witches' sacraments also had the potential to activate the inner alchemical force of the Dark Goddess to further enhance gnostic vision.

One of the vestigial rites of the early Goddess nature religion adopted by the European covens was the "Great Rite," during which males and females would sexually mate to produce an abundance of creative life force. The Great Rite was often observed during the beginning of the growing season to generate fertilizing power for the crops, but it was also performed during the dark winter months of the Dark Goddess to trigger the alchemical awakening of the inner serpent power. Once activated, the inner power of the Dark Goddess could also be used for healing, magic and transformation. Many of the alchemical sexual rites of the witches had their origin in the Tantric rites of the East that had been brought west by both the Gypsies and bands of Mascara Revelers from Persia and India.

Some sexual rites of the Goddess also evolved out of the Neolithic agrarian tradition of the Goddess that annually gave birth to a Son, who later in the year evolved into her lover. This legend of the Goddess was passed down through Sumeria and Babylonia to Rome, where rites in Italy's Alban Hills annually reenacted the mating of Diana and her Son and lover, Janus. Janus was the Roman name for the ancient Son of the Goddess known as Jnana, Ioannes, and John, a name or title denoting "Lord of Wisdom." Each year two Roman slaves would meet in deadly combat to decide who would take Goddess Diana as his wife and rule as Janus, the King of Nemi, for the coming year.

The Goddess is All and Does All

Typically, the sacred Goddess rites of the Amazons, Dianics and other Goddess worshippers of the past and present have been designed to enduce a gnostic communion with the all-pervasive Goddess. Through their communion with the Goddess Her devotees learned first-hand about the true nature of the Mother of the Universe. They discovered that the Goddess is omnipresent and that She created the universe and rules over it. She does All and She is All.

The awareness of the Goddess's all-encompassing presence was first cultivated during the primeval Goddess civilization on Lemuria, and it was then experienced on Atlantis, duirng the Neolithic Age and into the proto-historic period of Europe and Asia Minor. The Goddess's omnipotent rulership as Queen of Heaven and Earth acknowledged by Her Neolithic devotees is reflected in many of the artifacts recently discovered within excavations in Yugoslavia, Bulgaria, Anatolia, Crete and Romania. Within these sites images of the Goddess possesses both snake and avian or bird features. As the Snake Goddess, the Mother Goddess was venerated as Earth's ruler, and as the Bird Goddess she was given homage as queen of the sky and the heavenly regions.

The Bird Goddess/ Queen of Heaven and Snake Goddess from Crete

The Goddess is the Doer

"All actions take place in time by the interweaving of the gunas and Prakriti [the Goddess], and the deluded man thinks that he is the doer of the actions."
The Bhagavad Gita

According to the ancient cosmology of the Daughters and Sons of Sophia, in the process of becoming the entire cosmos the Goddess as the Primal Serpent first emanated as energy from the Infinite Spirit. She then proceeded to create the universe out of Herself, and when the cosmos was finally complete, the Goddess proceeded to nuture and animate all life forms, which became Her "children." She then became not only Queen of the Universe, but the primal animator and the doer of all actions.

When the Goddess created the human body, Her various frequencies of energy congealed to become our mental, emotional and physical bodies. She then became both the animator and nourisher of these vehicles of experience. Because of Her our cells continually replicate, blood perpetually pumps in and out of our hearts, and neurons spontaneously fire in our brains. All the functions of our body are overseen and performed by the Goddess in Her form of dynamic energy, or life force, much of which enters us through the air we breathe and the food and water we consume. Upon entering the bloodstream, the Goddess as life force moves to all parts of the body and both nourishes each inner organ and activates their respective functions. To fuel all our bodily processes, claim the Hindu scriptures, the Goddess as life force, or prana, divides herself into ten sub-pranas, including prana, apana, samana, etc. which perform all the bodily functions including breathing, digestion, and elimination. States the *Sandilya Upanishad*:

"The functions of Prana are inspiration, expiration, and cough. Those of Apana are the excretion of the feces and the urine. Those of Vyana are giving and taking. Those of Udana are keeping the body straight, etc. Those of Samana are nourishing the body. Those of Naga are vomiting, etc.; of Kurma, the movement of the eyelids; of Krkara, the causing of hunger, etc.; of Devadatta, idleness, etc.; and Dhananjaya, phlegm."

The balance of the male and female principles, or water and fire, within the body is also controlled by the Goddess. As the life force She cycles every ninety minutes through the two main energy meridians of the body that control the water/fire balance. These vessels are known by the Hindus as the Ida and Pingala Nadis, and by the Chinese as the Ren and Du Meridians. The balance of the five elements that comprise the physical matrix of the body are also controlled by the

Goddess when she moves through the lower five chakras, each of which is associated with one of the five elements.

One of the most important seats of the Goddess is at the base of the spine, where She resides as the Source Chi and Mundane Kundalini. As the primal life force, the Goddess enters the two principal energy meridians and afterwards moves to all 72,000 subtle energy vessels that connect to every cell and organ. The ability to speak and articulate sounds, say the yogis, also comes from the Goddess at her lower seat. The Goddess as sound begins to vibrate at the base of the spine or "Para" level, before moving to the solar plexus or "Pashyanti" region, followed by its ascent to the "Madyuma" level at the heart and then emerging as fully developed "Vaikari" speech in the throat. According to the Tantric gnostics of India, all letters and sounds originate at the base of the spine from the Goddess as Kali, whose necklace of 50 skulls represent the 50 letters of the Sanscrit alphabet.

The Goddess also controls all human activity both internally and externally via the power of the planets and stars that are broadcast to Earth. Each planet and Zodiacal sign rules over and controls a portion of the human body. The ancient gnostics maintained that the Goddess' sevenfold nature manifests as Her Seven Rays, or Sons, who took their seats within the seven astrological planets and from there they continue to control all life as the Archons. The early gnostics dedicated themselves to understanding the planetary spirits and how to either neutralize their negative influence or amplify their positive effects through gems and metals.

The Goddess is our Inner Wisdom and Guide

The Goddess also manifests as everyone's inner wisdom and guidance. Understanding, wisdom, and the inner words, feelings and phrases that spontaneously emerge when a seeker looks within for answers to his or her questions are all manifestations of the Goddess.

In the Wisdom Texts of the *Holy Bible* Sophia explicitly identifies herself as the inner aspects of self. She proclaims:

"I am wisdom, I bestow shrewdness and show the way to knowledge and discretion." (Proverbs 8.1.12)

"From me come advice and ability; understanding and power are mine."
(Proverbs 8.1.14)

"Through me kings hold sway and governors enact laws."
(Proverbs 8.1.15)

"...[W]hoever listens to me will live without a care, undisturbed by fear of misfortune." (Proverbs 1.33)

Many of the Biblical prophets and monarchs embraced Sophia, and She became their guiding light of gnosis. The grateful King Solomon waxed poetic regarding the support her received from the Goddess in ruling his kingdom. With high praise and great love, Solomon exclaimed:

"She knows and understands all things; she will guide me prudently in whatever I do, and guard me with her glory." (Wisd 8.9.11)

"...I called for help and there came to me the spirit of wisdom. I valued her more than health and beauty; I preferred her to the light of day, for her radiance is unsleeping..." (Wisd 7.7-8)

"She is an inexhaustible treasure for mortals, and those who profit by it become God's friends...." (Wisd 7.14)

"...I was taught by wisdom, by her whose skill made all things." (Wisd 7.22)

As to the method of finding Sophia, the Biblical prophets are explicit that She can be discovered within by all sincere seekers of wisdom:
"She [Sophia] is quick to make herself known to all who desire knowledge of her; he who rises early in search of her will not grow weary in the quest, for he will find her seated at his door." (Wisd 6.13-14)

"...[S]he herself searches far and wide for those who are worthy of her, and on their daily path she appears to them with kindly intent, meeting them half way in all their purposes." (Wisd. 6.16)

"Wisdom working through a holy prophet, gave them success in all they did." (Wisd 11.5)

The Goddess takes us to Gnosis

Lastly, the Goddess is the Savior of Humanity that takes all of us to gnosis. When a person is ready, the Goddess initiates their next step of evolution by awakening a higher frequency of herself at the base of the spine, the Spiritual Kundalini, which then drives the process of alchemical transformation to its completion. As the Goddess in her serpent fire form moves from the base of the spine through the network of 72,000 channels or nadis its high frequency alchemically purifies and raises all the body tissues and organs to a higher frequency, and everything that remains at a lower frequency is either brought to the surface and released or burned in the fire of alchemy. This includes the physical, emotional and mental toxins that are creating blockages in a person's physical, etheric, emotional and mental bodies. Ultimately, the serpentine Goddess will rise up the central channel, the Sushumna Nadi and inner Tree of Life, to evolve the chakras to their highest level of functioning while releasing their inherent gnostic wisdom and power.

When the ascending serpent Goddess reaches the skull and activates the dormant two-thirds of the brain, she reacquires the wings she had lost when she initially descended the Tree of Life. At this stage a person truly becomes a Serpent of Wisdom and wields both the Divine Mind and Power of the Primal Serpent. The two inner wings reclaimed by the Serpent Goddess are the two hemispheres of the brain, which are represented on the caduceus as two wings. Through their activation the Primal Serpent becomes reconstituted and reintegrated. The hemispheres are the two petals of the Ajna Chakra or Third Eye that when fully awakened endows a person with both gnosis and immortality. The highest gnosis, however, occurs when the highest part of the brain corresponding to the Sahasrara Chakra becomes fully activated. This occurs simultaneously with the full blossoming of the heart chakra and the revelatory awareness that proclaims, "I am the Infinite" or "I am Shiva and Goddess Shakti is my Divine Mind and Power."

Kali and her necklace of 50 skulls, symbol of the 50 Sanscrit letters
Kali emerges out of the Infinite Spirit, the "sleeping" Shiva,
at the beginning of time. As the destructive aspect of the
Triple Goddess, she takes us to gnosis.

The Eternal Union of God and Goddess

According to the cosmologists of Sophia's Left Hand Path, although the Goddess emerged from the Infinite Spirit at the beginning of time and then created the cosmos, She remained united with Him. She was an embodiment of the Divine Wisdom and Power of the Infinite Spirit, and through Her the Infinite succeeded in manifesting the universe. An instructive Jewish name for the Goddess that reveals Her function as the body and character of the Infinite Spirit is Shekhinah, meaning "Royal Residence."

An understanding of the eternally interlocking relationship between the Infinite and the Serpent Goddess is an essential part of Left Hand Path cosmology and theology. Left Hand Path images that represent the origin of the universe have consistently depicted the Infinite Spirit as a male figure with "female" snakes and serpents emanating and/or dangling from it. This has been a ubiquitous theme in India, where the Goddess Shakti is pictured as snakes dangling from the body of Infinite Shiva, and similar motifs can be found in Mesopotamia and Egypt. At this stage of universal creation the Infinite God becomes the Goddess. She becomes the finite form of the Infinite. Other Left Hand Path icons that reflect a later stage of the creation cycle are comprised solely of snakes, the symbol of energy that crystallizes to become the physical cosmos. These include the famous Serpent on the Tree motif. The Infinite Spirit is absent or invisible in these icons, although it is known by gnostics of the Left Hand Path that the Infinite is alway present as the spiritual essence of all matter. They acknowledge that the Infinite Spirit is the essence of the Goddess, and they are always locked in an eternal embrace.

The eternal interplay and interdependence of God and Goddess, the Infinite and its serpentine emanation, have been commented upon for ages by members of the Left Hand Path. Jnaneshwar Maharaj and Sri Ramakrishna, two famous teachers of the gnostic culture in India, wrote poetically on this union.

"Because of God, the Goddess exists,
And, without Her, He is not.
They exist only because of each other."

Amritanubhav of Jananeshwar

"…When I think of the Supreme Being as inactive, neither creating, not preserving, not destroying, I call Him Brahman or Purusha, the impersonal God. When I think of Him as active, creating, preserving, destroying, I call Him Shakti, or Maya, or Prakriti, the personal God. However, the distinction between them does not mean a difference. The personal and the impersonal are the same being- in the same way as milk and its whiteness, or the diamond and its luster, or the snake and its undulations. It is impossible to conceive of one without the other. The Divine Mother and Brahman are one."[2] *Sri Ramakrishna*

98

In the "Wisdom Texts" of the *Holy Bible* a similar sentiment is conveyed by Jewish gnostics regarding Sophia and Yahweh. It states the following:

"All wisdom is from the Lord; she dwells with him for ever."

"Wisdom (Sophia) is from the Lord; She is with Him eternally…and it is He who created Her…and infused Her into all His works." Ecclesiastes 1,1-9)

"By Sophia the LORD laid the earth's foundations and by understanding he set the heavens in place." (Prov. 3, 13-26)

Sophia, the Wisdom of the Infinite Spirit

The Johannite Gnostics

In the aftermath of the Garden of Eden one migration of the "Sons of Seth" traveled west from Sri Lanka and across Asia, eventually establishing their gnostic path in the Middle East. These were the Mandaeans, a group of gnostics who left Sri Lanka approximately 250,000 years ago (by one count) when it was part of the continent of Lemuria and successively became part of the Sumerian, Persian, Egyptian and Jewish civilizations. Finally merging with the Jewish Essenes, the Mandeans founded the gnostic sect of Nasoreans and the lineage of the Johannites, the "Followers of John." The name John, which had evolved from Jnana Pandita, a name for the Sri Lankan Serpent on the Tree, became the honorary title of the grand masters of this lineage and denoted "He of Gnostic Power and Wisdom." The Johannite lineage, which passed along a line of Nasorean Mandaeans who were denominated John I, II, III and so on, eventually included John the Baptist, Jesus, John the Apostle and a long line of grand masters that survived until the time of the First Crusade when the Knights Templar assimilated the Johannite sect into their fledgling Order.

The Gnostic Mandaeans

The Mandaeans were first "discovered" in the Nineteenth Century by Portuguese missionaries along the banks of the Tigris and Euphrates Rivers in southern Iraq. When the missionaries discovered that John the Baptist had been a great prophet of Mandaeans they designated them the "Christians of St. John the Baptist." This was a very inaccurate moniker for the Mandaeans because they were not Christians, nor had their sect originated with St. John. Another hundred years would pass before their true history would be revealed to Lady Ethel Stefana Drower. This was in the early 1920s, when the British lady was accepted into the Mandaean community as a foreign delegate and allowed to study their very ancient history and sacred baptismal rites.

Lady Drower's hands-on research revealed that the most enlightened of the Mandaeans, including John the Baptist, were known as Nasurai, a term related to "Nass" and the Hebrew "Nachash," meaning "Serpent." The Nasurai were distinguished by their peers as being wielders of the Divine Wisdom and Power of the Jnana Pandita, the Serpent on the Tree, whom the Mandeans had evolved into Manda d'Hiya, meaning "Embodiment of Gnosis," "Embodiment of Life," or "Gnosis of Life." As Manda d'Hiya, the ancient Jnana Pandita still retained his earlier Sri Lankan associations, and he continued to be venerated as a warrior, a savior, a divine son, a forever-young boy, as well as the embodiment of "Life," which included both Divine Wisdom and Power. In acknowledgement of this last association, whenever the Mandaeans observed their daily baptismal cermonies or cleansed their water or food they always invoked the purifying Divine Power of Manda d'Hiya. At sunrise of each day he was summoned by the Mandaeans with the following prayer:

"In the name of Life Almighty; Life to be praised with pure heart; Life exists. Living Ones exists; Manda d Hiya, Knowledge of Life exists"[1]

The Mandaean Nasurai

The "serpent" powers that the Nasurai acquired through their worship of Manda d'Hiya are mentioned in the holy books of the Mandaeans and include the ability to heal, walk through fire and even raise the dead. One of their common names in the Mandaean texts is Bnia d bnia d Ardban, meaning "skilled in religious matters and white magic." In *The Story of Qiqel and the Death of Yahya* the Nasurai are remembered as having miraculously survived the invasion of a nieghboring tribe and its blood-thirsty chieftain. When they would not surrender their renowned wisdom and power to the coveting chieftain, a huge fire was built and the Nasurai thrown upon it. Neither the chief nor his men could believe what happened next:

"...[W]hen the Nasurai were pushed into the fire they didn't burn; instead, they walked on top of the fire! A white light descended from the sky and enclosed each Nasurai in an envelope of divine, protective radiance. When the frustrated chief loudly lamented "Can you not prevail against them?" One Nasurai unhesitatingly answered "Never! For (we) do not use magic, but knowledge. [Our] power, it is of God."[2]

To achieve their enlightened state and miraculous powers the Nasurai adhered to certain alchemical practices, the principal one being water baptism. They understood, however, that the alchemical substance that purifies and transforms a Nasurai is not the physical water but the etheric power or "Water of Life" that flows through it. The subtle Water of Life is the primal chi or prana that the

A Mandaean Priest performing a Baptism

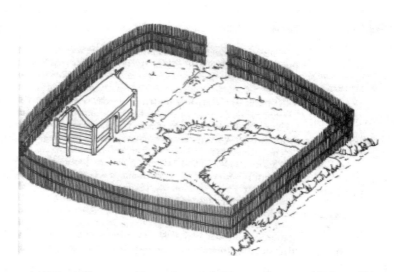

A Mandaean Baptismal Temple or "Mandi"

universe was created out of, as well as the subtle essence that eternally sustains it. It is also the material and "flesh" that the Primal Serpent was composed of. For this reason, the Mandean cosmology states that the Water of Life (the Primal Serpent) was the first emanation of the Supreme Being, Malka d' Nhura, and from the Water of Life emerged the physical universe. One Mandean scriptural passage delineates this cosmic sequence:

"…[F]irst [comes] Water [the Water of Life]; from Water, Radiance; from Radiance, Light; and from Light, uthri, the spirits, whose function it is to govern natural phenomena."[3]

The term Water of Life is very ancient and originated in Sumeria, where it was a name for the subtle power of the Primal Serpent Enki that moved within physical water. Sumeria was an ancient homeland of the Mandaeans, and later in their history it became the region they returned to following persecutions from the Jews in Palestine. Today, the Mandaeans in Iraq continue the water rites of Enki in baptismal pools situated next to "Mandi," which are replicas of the ancient Sumerian temples used by their ancestors. Just as their forebears once did, the Mandaeans summon the alchemical power of Enki to purify and transform them on all levels, although they currently refer to it as the essence of Manda d'Hiya.

The Lord of Wisdom is Enki, Manda d'Hiya, & Jnana Pandita

Manda d'Hiya is easy to comprehend when it is understood that he is synonymous with both the Jnana Pandita and Enki. All three are personifications of the Divine Mind and Divine Power. Each is an indigenous manifestation of the archetypal Lord of Wisdom and exist in a body composed of the Water of Life. It is possible that the Jnana Pandita transformed into Enki when the Mandaeans became the Sumerians, and that Enki later evolved into Manda d'Hiya.

The undeniable links between Enki and the Jnana Pandita have been commented upon and are fully presented in Chapter 1. For example, their Greek names, Oannes and Ioannes, are nearly identical and essentially carry the same meaning. In his magnum opus, *Anacalypsis*, Godfrey Higgins reveals why he believes that *both* Oannes and Ioannes evolved from the name Jnana. In reference to a work by his friend, the philologist, Georgius, he states:

"Georgius maintains that the Tibetan word, which he renders GNIOS in Latin…is the same as the Gnosij of Greece, and Agnitio in Latin. If the Gn be written as the Hebrew letter was corrupted in Tibet, it will be O, the next letter will be Y, I or Yod, and both read from right to left, OI the Deity of Wisdom. In the same way, the Jnana for Wisdom in the Sanscrit is OANA. Here we have the Oanes."[4]

In another passage of the same text Higgins also explains that John or Ioannes and its counterpart, Oannes, are united by being equivalent but alternate names assigned to those adepts who have taken birth at the beginning of each great age and venerated as incarnations of the Lord of Wisdom and the returning Messiah. He states:

"I suspect the Johns, or Oanneses, are like the Merus, the Buddhas, the Manwantaras, the Soleimans, etc. They are renewed incarnations, and the name was given after death, and sometimes during life, to any person whom the priests thought proper to designate as the guardian genius of the age."

The Johannite Messiah

One of Higgins' messiahs, who was also the "guardian genius" of his age, was the great Nasurai and Mandean prophet, John the Baptist. In a later passage of *Anacalypsis*, Higgins specifically identifies the Baptist as the manfestation of Oannes who served as the Avatar or Messiah of the Age of Pisces. He remarks:

"...And John the Baptist, or Savior of Men by means of water, was the Oannes or Avatar of Pisces, as Buddha was of Taurus, and Cristna [Krishna] of Aries...."[5]

Higgins' pronouncement of the return of Oannes as John the Bpatist at the beginning of the Piscean Age was consistent with the prophecies once made by the soothsayers of ancient Sumeria and Babylonia. The historians and diviners of Mesopotamia predicted that the ancient culture-bearer Oannes would arrive at the beginning of each new age to teach the indigenous people the sacred and mundane arts while spending half of each day immersed in water. Their prophosies of Oannes were assimilated by the Essenes during the time of their Babylonian captivity. So later, when the Sumerian-Mandeans merged with the Essenes, the entire Essene population knew what signs to look for in the coming avatar. Thus, John the Baptist, the great teacher who spent half his life immersed in water, was recognized as an incarnation of the returning Lord of Wisdom who had been known as Oannes and the Jnana Pandita. Moreover, his spirit, that of the Prophet Elijah, became synonymous with the returning spirit of Oannes. Elijah was henceforth the Tishbite, a name derived from the Hebrew Ha Tishbi, meaning "he who returns." Today, current belief has it that Elijah is synonymous with the Moslem deity al-Khadir, who in turn is synonymous with Oannes and similarly lives within water as the subtle Water of Life. Since al-Khadir is also synonymous with the Jnana Pandita, all four deities, Elijah, al-Khadir, the Jnana Pandita and Oannes, are collectively recognized as being synonymous.

The prophosied embodiment of the returning Primal Serpent Oannes for the Age of Pisces, John the Baptist, also lived up to his calling by being an embodiment of the Serpent's Divine Wisdom and Power, which was referred to in the Hebrew and Jewish tradition as the Holy Spirit or Holy Ghost. His possession of the primal power is confirmed in *The Gospel of Luke*, where it is stated that John was "filled with the Holy Ghost, even from his mother's womb." This gospel also states that the angel Gabriel insisted that the Baptist be named John (or the Hebrew John, "Yohanan"), because this name specially denoted "Holy Spirit." The name of John, along with its variants, such as Jonah, meaning "Dove" (the symbol of the Holy Spirit), have since become traditional names and forms associated with the Holy Spirit.

The True or CO-Messiah?

During the last fifty years, and especially since the translation of the *Dead Sea Scrolls* and certain Mandaean texts featuring John, there has been increasing speculation regarding the ancient status of John the Baptist. Was he CO-Messiah with Jesus, or could he have been *the* awaited one of prophecy? The Mandaeans maintain that both John and Jesus were members of their sect and powerful Nasurai, but of the two they regard John as the only true Mandaean prophet and therefore of a higher status than Jesus. Certain Mandaean texts even speak negatively of Jesus, calling him a "liar" and "traitor" because he and his apostles broke many of the Mandaean laws, including the rite of baptism, which is absolutely never administered in standing water. Jesus encouraged his apostles to disregard many Jewish and Mandaean scriptural injunctions, including regulations regarding the Sabbath, and the mandate to marry and produce children. Even John himself considered Jesus a deviant and had resolved not to baptize him when a message arrived from his Mandaean colleague, Abathur, stating:

"Yahya [John], baptize the deceiver in the Jordan. Lead him down into the Jordan and baptize him, lead him up again to the shore, and there set him."

John heeded the instructions and baptized Jesus, but according to the Mandaean *Book of John*, the baptism only occured after an acrimonious debate between Jesus and John over whether the "deceiver" merited the Mandaean initiation rite. While Jesus presented a case in favor of his baptism, John produced a litany of reasons why the "deceiver" was not worthy of it, stating:

"Thou hast lied to the Jews and deceived the priests. Thou hast cut off their seed from the men and from the women bearing and being pregnant [i.e., promoted celibacy]. The Sabbath, which Moses made binding, thou hast relaxed in Jerusalem. Thou has lied to them with horns and spread abroad disgrace with the shofar."

John then continued his diatribe by further proclaiming:

"A stammerer becomes not a scholar, a bind man writes no letter. A desolate house mounts not to the height, and a widow becomes not a virgin. Foul water becomes not tasty, and a stone does not with oil soften."[6]

John's severe judgement against Jesus illustrates what the other Mandaean Nasurai must have also known, that Jesus was not the returning Lord of Wisdom for the new era. And apparently John's doubt never wavered. According to the *New Testament,* John continued to be uncertain about Jesus' identity down to the time he was imprisoned by King Herod, when he sent a message to the "deceiver" inquiring if he was indeed the prophesied Messiah or should John "look for another." As Hugh Schonfeld rightly points out in *The Jesus Party*, if John had indeed regarded Jesus to be the Messiah why was it that many of the Baptist's other disciples had never even heard of Jesus? Their ignorance was strikingly apparent to St. Paul when he visited John the Baptist's gnostic circle in the Asia Minor city of Ephesus and discovered them oblivious of even the existence of Jesus. Author A.N. Wilson makes the logical conclusion that had it not been for the work of St. Paul championing Jesus, John the Baptist might today be regarded the Messiah. He states:

"Had Paul been a weaker personality…or had he never written his epistles, it easily could have been the case that the "Baptism of John" would have been the religion which captured the imagination of the ancient world, rather than the Baptism of Christ…."[7]

Even among John's own circle of disciples that were aware of the existence of Jesus, the Baptist was recognized as the true Savior and Messiah. Their belief is illustrated in the apocryphal text, called the *Recognitions*, which is part of the Pseudo-Clementine Texts. It features a debate between the disciples of John and Jesus, during which one of John's students plainly asserts:

"He [John] is the Christ, and not Jesus, just as Jesus himself spoke concerning him, namely that he is greater than any prophet who had ever been. If he is thus greater than Moses, it is clear that he is also greater than Jesus for Jesus arose just as did Moses. Therefore, it is right that John, who is greater than these, is the Christ."

The Infancy Gospel of James is another apocryphal text which elevates John into the role of the Messiah. This text maintains that when King Herod decreed the murder of the firstborn sons of the Jews in order to slay the future King of the Jews, his intention was to kill John, not Jesus. John's parents were alerted of Herod's carnage before it began and they arranged for Elizabeth and John to quickly depart into the surrounding hill country. When Herod's men subsequently arrived to question Zacharias, John's father refused to tell the whereabouts of his son and he was promptly slain for his insubordination. Then, states the text:

"...[T]he agents went away and reported all this to Herod, who became angry and said, "Is his son [John] going to rule over Israel?""

Another reliable source regarding the spiritual status of John the Baptist is the principal First Century historian of the Jews, Titus Flavius Josephus. In his *Antiquities of the Jews*, Josephus had very little to say about Jesus while thoroughly championing John as the great savior of the Jewish people. Apparently Jesus was not nearly as well known as John by the Jews, and he certainly was not held in as high regard by them as the Baptist. However, the authors of *The Templar Revelation* might be right in asserting that the true smoking gun in the debate of John's status may be the fact that even Jesus' own disciples did not even initially recognize their teacher as the Messiah. They state:

"He was their leader and their teacher, but there is never any suggestion that they originally followed him because they believed he was the long-awaited Jewish Messiah. Jesus' identity as the Messiah seems to have gradually dawned on the disciples as his ministry progressed."[8]

However, even if history proves Jesus to be the Messiah, there is reason to beleive that John was his CO-Messiah. The historical documents known collectively as *The Dead Sea Scrolls* state clearly that the Jewish Essenes expected not one but two messiahs. One messiah was to be the King Messiah born into the Tribe of David, and the other was to be a Priest Messiah born into the Tribe of Levi. The Priest Messiah appears to have incarnated among the Mandean-Essenes as John the Baptist, which means that the King Messiah manifested among them as Jesus. If John was indeed the awaited Priest Messiah, the intensely religious Essenes would have held that he was closer to Yahweh and therefore the superior of the two. Dead Sea Scrolls author Geza Vermes comments:

"...[T]he Priest-Messiah comes first in the order of precedence; he is also called the Messiah of Aaron, the 'Priest,' the 'Interpreter of the Law.' The King-Messiah was to defer to him and to the priestly authority in general in all legal matters.... The 'Messiah of Aaron' was to be the final Teacher, "he who shall teach righteousness at the end of days."[9]

The Life of Avatar John the Baptist

According to the Mandaeans' scripture *The Book of John*, John the Baptist's special training as a child was designed to prepare him for his destiny as their greatest prophet. Almost as soon as John came forth from the womb of his mother, Elizabeth, an angelic messenger named Annosh-Uthra appeared and

Enki-Oannes was incarnate as John the Baptist
Enki-Oannes personifies the Water of Life

Al-Khadir, the Moslem's Elijah, was incarnate as John the Baptist
Al-Khadir lives in the water as its Water of Life

The Messiah John the Baptist as Bacchus, by Leonardo DaVinci
*John incarnated the spirit of the Lord of Wisdom known variously as
Bacchus, Enki, al-Khadir and the Jnana Pandita*

Leonardo DaVinci's heretical "Virgin on the Rocks"
*A young John the Baptist touches his element, water,
while blessing his disciple, the infant Jesus*

quickly whisked the newborn child away for training. John was taken to another world, the Frat-Ziwa, which the Mandaeans maintain is the heavenly double of the territory in and around the Euphrates River. Here John was baptized in the heavenly Waters of Life on the thirty-first day of his life, and then over the following twenty-one years he was regularly baptized and taught his "ABCs," which included the wisdom contained within the Mandaeans' *Sidra d Nishmatha*, the "Book of Souls." His training complete, John was taken back to Palestine to begin his ministry in the River Jordan.

According to an additional account of John's early training, at some point the Baptist was also groomed for his future mission upon the sacred Mount Parwan, the "White Mountain." Mount Parwan may have been in the vicinity of or even synonymous with the Mandaeans' most sacred mountain, Tura d'Madai, the "Mountain of the Madai," which was home to a colony of enlightened Nasurai and located somewhere in Turkey, or possibly in the mysterious Albourz Mountains of Iran. There has also been some speculation that Mount Parwan is a name for Palestine's holy Mount Carmel, which is revered for having been home to the Prophet Elijah and many of the Essene and Mandaean prophets. In *The Book of John* the Baptist is portrayed as visiting Mount Carmel on several occasions, thus revealing its importance to John and his mission.

When John suddenly reappeared among the Mandeans after so many years away, his family and peers were taken aback by his towering spiritual attainment. The leaders of the Jews, who were not accustomed to being in the presence of a Nasurai of John's caliber, were instantly put on the defensive. Those who were full of pride in their intellectual dogma sought to oppose and even banish him from Jerusalem. The following scene documenting John's arrival comes from Slavic edition of Josephus' *Antiquities of the Jews*:

"Now at that time [John] went about among the Jews in strange garments; for he had put pelts on his body everywhere where it was not covered with his own hair; indeed to look at he was like a wild man....

"He came to the Jews and summoned them to freedom, saying: 'God hath sent me that I May show you the way of the [high] Law, wherein ye may free yourselves from many holders of power. And there will be no mortal ruling over you, only the Highest who hath sent me.'

"And [John] did nothing else to them save that he plunged them into the stream of the Jordan and dismissed them, instructing them that they should cease from evil works....

"And when he had been brought to Archelaus and the doctors of the Law had assembled, they asked him who he was and where he has been until then. And then to this he made answer and spake: 'I am pure; the Spirit of God hath led me on, and [I live on] cane and roots and tree-food.' However, when they threatened to put him to torture if he would not cease from those words and deeds, he nevertheless said: 'It is [rather] meet for you to cease from your heinous works and cleave unto the Lord your God.'

"And there rose up in anger Simon, an Essene by extraction, a scribe, and he spake: 'We read every day the divine books. However, thou, now only come from the forest like a wild animal, thou darest in sooth to teach us and to mislead the people with thy reprobate words.' And he rushed forward to do him bodily violence. However, he [John], rebuking them, spake: 'I will not disclose to you the mystery which dwelleth in you, for ye have not desired it. Thereby an untold calamity is come upon you, and because of yourselves.

"And when he had thus spoken, he went forth to the other side of the Jordan; and while no one durst rebuke him, that one did what (he had done) before."

John had nothing more to say to his boastful accusers. As a gnostic guide and teacher, John's role was to unite seekers with their inner wisdom, however the Jews who confronted him were obviously too attached to their own egos and the laws of the Right Hand Path to unite with the Spirit dwelling inside their hearts. So rather than debate further with his accusers, John began to baptize and work miracles with his prodigious Holy Spirit power. According to the Mandaean text known as the *Haran Gawaitha:*

"...[John] opened the eyes of the blind, cured the sick, and made the lame to walk."

John's healing prowess angered the Jewish priests, whose goal was to control the Baptist, and they pressed for his immediate exile. However, states the *Haran Gawaitha*, they fell far short of their goal:

"The [Jewish] priests were angry and came to Yahya [John] and ordered him to leave Urshalam [Jerusalem] immediately. Yahya refused to go and defied them saying, 'Bring swords and cut me, bring fire and burn me, or water and drown me!' And the priests replied, 'Yahya, we know that swords will not cut thee, nor fire burn thee, nor water drown thee.' Then, when his detractors had left, Yahya began to read in his *Ginza Rabba* [another Mandean scripture], the birds of the air spoke, praising God, and the fishes opened their mouths and glorified the Life."

The Jewish hatred against him did not prevent John from commencing with his baptisms in the River Jordan. John soon gathered around him a train of followers to whom he daily admonished "prepare for the great and dreadful day of the Lord," which was a call to the faithful to purify themselves in the transformative Water of Life. John's most famous recorded baptism was of Jesus, whose dramatic activation of the inner alchemical forces is described as being "the Spirit of God descending like a dove and lightning upon him." The dove and lightning are two symbols of the Holy Spirit, and their auspicious appearance can indeed accompany its transmission into an initiate.

Because of his many hours spent in the River Jordan and the initiations he provided to the true seekers of wisdom, John eventually became known by his peers as the "Fisher of Souls." He was a Fisher who gathered the souls for purification in the Water of Life. John the Baptist refers to himself thusly:

"A Fisher am I who among the fishers is chosen, the Head of all catchers of fish…The fisher-trident which I have in my hand [is] a staff of pure water, at whose sight tremble the fishers…. A Poor Fisher am I who calls to the souls, collects them together and gives them instruction."[10]

Among John's "Fish" were those who became long term members of the Baptist's inner circle of disciples. During the gatherings of his inner circle John honored the Goddess and his Left Hand Path heritage by placing them in a Lunar Circle of thirty participants that reflected the approximately thirty days of a lunar cycle. The elect would gather during important phases of the Moon, and the thirtieth member would always be a female representing the Gnostic Goddess Sophia. Regarding John's circle, Clement of Alexandria commented in his *Recognitions*:

"[Just] As our Lord [Jesus], the Sun, had 12 apostles, so John, the Moon, had 30 disciples, or even more accurately answering to the days of a lunation, 29½, for one of them was a woman."

John's instructions to his inner circle of thirty disciples included daily baptismal ablutions in the Mandaean tradition. The importance that John placed on the baptismal rite became so ingrained within his disciples that they later passed on both the rite and its spiritual importance to their disciples and the various gnostic sects they founded. Because of John's seminal influence, eventually most gnostic sects in Asia Minor and Egypt came to accept baptism as "closely associated with the reception of gnosis" and a vehicle "to enable the gnostic to overcome death."[8]

In time, John the Baptist's teachings regarding baptism, alchemy and gnosis would be spread throughout the entire Middle East and ultimately earn the Baptist a large "international following"[9] that extended south to Alexandria and north to Ephesus. The disseminators of John's teachings were principally his disciples and their students, who were collectively Johannite Gnostics, the "Gnostics of John."

The Heretical Johannites

Following the tragic murder of John the Baptist, the leadership of his circle of 30 disciples passed to his most advanced disciples, Simon Magus and Dositheus, who competed among themselves for the role. Contention built quickly between these elite disciples when both claimed to be the Messiah or Chosen One sent from on high to succeed their master. Each campaigned rigorously among the other disciples for the right to be called "He who is upright" or "The Standing One," which would distinguish them as an embodiment of "the Supreme deity."[11]

The issue of who should succeed John was settled when Dositheus announced himself successor during a period when his opponent Simon was away on business in Alexandria. As part of his ruse, Dositheus even claimed that Simon Magus had passed away. Simon was, of course, completely incensed when he returned from Alexandria, but instead of confronting Dositheus in a quorum of fellow disciples and creating any further dissension among them, he quietly found a seat in the circle and waited for the right opportunity to prove himself as the true Standing One. According to the Clementine *Recognitions,* the opportunity quickly arrived. During a discourse given by Dositheus Simon found reasonal cause to heckle and humiliate his brother disciple over what he perceived to be a gross mis-understanding by the spurious Standing One. The ensuing pivotal scene is described by Clement of Alexandria:

"Dositheus, when he perceived that Simon was depreciating him, fearing lest his reputation among men might be obscured [for he himself was supposed to be the Standing One], moved with rage, when they met as usual at the school, seized a rod, and began to beat Simon; but suddenly the rod seemed to pass through his body, as if it had been smoke. On which Dositheus, being astonished, says to him, 'Tell me if thou art the Standing One, that I may adore thee.' And when Simon answered that he was, then Dositheus, perceiving that he himself was not the Standing One, fell down and worshipped him, and gave up his own place as chief to Simon, ordering all the rank of thirty men to obey him; himself taking the inferior place which Simon formerly occupied. Not long after this he died."

Clement's account may not be completely accurate because Dositheus is on record as having lived many years following his confrontation with Simon. After departing with a few chosen disciples, he eventually settled in Syria, where his teachings caught fire, especially at his new headquarters in the city of Damascus. The gospel Dositheus' promulgated to his Syrian following included the Mandaean ways he had meticulously learned from John the Baptist. Dositheus was apparently so adamant about following the strict Mandaean regimen that the later Samaritan chronicler Abu al-Fath of the Fourteenth Century was convinced that the sect of Dositheus must have been the forerunner of the Mandaeans, rather than the other way around. Through regular observance of baptism and other alchemical practices, it is said that Dositheus eventually acquired perfect clairvoyant ability and was able to clearly read ancient gnostic wisdom straight out of the Akashic Records. His greatest contribution to future gnostics was his gospel, *The Three Steles of Seth,* which was a transcription of akashic tablets that had originally been written by the gnostic patriarch Seth.

Simon Magus and the Simonians

After taking over the circle of thirty disciples, Simon founded his own gnostic sect known as the Simonians, wherein he was recognized by his students to be a fully enlightened gnostic and addressed by them as the "Great One." Simon codified and expanded the teachings of the Baptist, and he is especially famous for introducing sexual rites and occult magic into the evolving gnostic paradyne in the West.

Many of the sexual rites Simon taught his disciples were probably learned from and endorsed by his teacher, John the Baptist, because according to the Mandaean *Book of John,* John himself once took a sexual partner and even fathered a small family. Other sexual rites espoused by Simon and his fellow disciple, Jesus, came from their partners, Helen and Mary, who were masters in the sexual arts. The sexual mysteries engaged in by Jesus and Mary Magdalene have been kept relatively secret, but throughout the centuries authors have hinted at them, including St. Mark, who is believed to have written a "secret gospel" about them.[12] Simon Magus was much less discreet about his sexual affairs and eventually chose as his partner Helen, whom he found working in a brothel in Tyre. Simon stated that he chose Helen because he recognized her to be a direct incarnation of the Gnostic Goddess Sophia. In his later writings, Simon referred to Helen as Ennoia, "Divine Wisdom," while annointing himself an incarnation of the Infinite God from which Ennoia had emerged at the beginning of time. Thus, according to Simon, it was fated that he and Helen should unite. In his *Panarion* the gnostic historian, Epiphanius, summarized Simon's unique understanding and teachings regarding Helen:

"In the beginning God had his first thought, his Ennoia, which was female, and that thought was to create the angels. The First Thought then descended into the lower regions and created the angels. However, the angels rebelled against her out of jealousy and created the world as her prison, imprisoning her in a female body. Thereafter, she was reincarnated many times, each time being shamed. Her many reincarnations included Helen of Troy; among others, and she finally was reincarnated as Helen, a slave and prostitute in the Phoenician city of Tyre. God then descended in the form of Simon Magus, to rescue his Ennoia, and to confer salvation upon men through knowledge of himself."

The Magician and Johannite Grand Master Simon Magus

Simon Magus in flight

After satisfactorily identifying her as the primal Goddess, Simon made Helen the honorary Sophia of his own inner circle of 30 disciples. During their sexual rites together Simon also honored Helen as the incarnation of Sophia and himself as the Infinite Spirit, thus elevating what would have been simply a mundane tryst into a divine union of God and Goddess. Simon taught his disciples sexual rites from this higher, spiritual perspective, and was thus able to assist them in transcending their personality limitations so they could soar into a cosmic union of two spiritual essences. There is no doubt that this sacred approach and understanding was observed by Jesus and Mary Magdalene who, like Helen, was similarly regarded by her partner as an incarnation of Sophia.

Ultimately, many of the sexual rites observed by the Simonians and later gnostics were attributed to Mary Magdalene and Helen. Historian Clement of Alexandria confirmed this truth when he maintained that some of the gnostic sects of Alexandria had inherited their sexual observances directly from Mary Magdalene, Martha and Salome.[13] Apparently Mary and Helen had both come from Left Hand Path traditions that encouraged alchemical sexual practices, as well as orgies, as these rites became commonplace among Simon's disciples and the later gnostics. In regards to the activities of Simon's promiscuous students, gnostic historian Jean Doresse comments:

"In imitation of their master, Simon's disciples seem to have repeated, in their wilder moments, that one aught to give oneself up to carnal intercourse without limit: 'All earth is earth, it matters little where one sows provided that one does sow.' It was in this, they proclaimed, that 'perfect love' consisted."[14]

But there was also a subtle discipline involved with Simon's sexual exploits and teachings that made them more Tantric. Simon's disciples learned the importance of preserving their sexual fluids both during and after their sexual liaisons in order to transform them into spiritual power. Through methods of seminal rentention and imbibing their sexual fluids, Simon's students generated an abundance of inner power that eventually engendered both supernatural abilities and expansive gnostic wisdom. Simon himself was never shy about exhibiting the abilities he had attained, and it became known that he could spontaneously become invisible or fling himself off a mountain top without being injured. He could also walk through fire without being burned, and he could bring to life any inanimate object.[15] The Clementine *Recognitions* quote Simon as having once announced:

"I shall change myself into a sheep or a goat. I shall make a beard to grow upon little boys. I shall ascend by flight into the air, I shall exhibit abundance of gold. I shall make and unmake Kings. I shall be worshipped as God, I shall have divine honors publicly assigned to me, so that an image of me shall be set up, and I shall be adored as God."

116

Although he often projected the appearance of a magician and madman, there was also a very serious and academic side to Simon. The writings of Simon Magus are some of the first examples of gnostic cosmology and theology introduced in the West. His most important contribution was his groundbreaking work, *Great Revelation,* within which Simon presented the foundational gnostic myth that was to become the bedrock of many gnostic sects to follow. States Doresse:

"...[He] postulated the existence of one supreme god, alien and superior to the wicked universe. The Wisdom, the Mother of All, had come down through the heavens from the higher universe into this base world created by the god of Genesis, the wicked god."[16]

Simon's reward for the work he contributed to the path of gnosticism would eventually merit him the title of the "Father of Gnosis," but in the estimation of the heresy hunters, including Irenaeus, Hippolytus and Eusebius, he also merited the derogatory epithet of "Father of all Heretics." It is because of the disparaging comments made by the early Church Fathers against him that Simon has been maligned as a demonic figure since the First Century.

Simon's successor was, like himself, a Samaritan. This was Menander, a gnostic teacher who chose Antioch, Syria to be the headquarters for his ministry. In his writings Ireanus stated that, like his teacher Simon, Menander similarly proclaimed himself a Messiah and "the man sent down as Redeemer by the Invisible [Spirit] for the salvation of men." Menander claimed to have achieved oneness with the Infinite Spirit and acquired the divine power of the Goddess, some of which he used while earning a reputation as a supernaturally endowed magician. However, Menander was also a formidable baptizer in the tradition of John the Baptist and the Mandaeans, and he transmitted the sacred alchemical fire during the ancient water rite. Referring to Menander's initiatory baptisms, Irenaeus proclaimed: "Through their baptism by him [Menander], his disciples receive the gift of resurrection, and therefore can no longer die; and do not age, but remain immortal."

Menander's two successors, Saturnius and Basilides, were both natives of Antioch and became his students at an early age. Saturnius was the more austere of the two and acquired a reputation for being a harsh task master to his own students. Besides enforcing the daily observance of the Mandaean baptismal rites, Saturnius also instructed his disciples to fast and spend long, solitary hours in gnostic meditation in the barren and scorching Syrian deserts. Basilides, by contrast, tended to be more academic and cerebral. After taking the gnostic teachings of Simon Magus south into Alexandria it is said that he studied with Glaucias, a student of St. Peter, and then incorporated Christian mysticism into his gnostic teachings. Basilides' gift to developing gnosticism included his twenty-four volume

Exegetics, within which he gave a deeper, gnostic interpretation to the Synoptic Gospels in order to further broker a philosophical fusion between Johannite Gnosticism and Christianity. Basilides also commited himself to the further development of the gnostic cosmology of emanationism that had been taught by Simon and within the Neo-Platonic schools of Alexandria. His advanced theories were eventually funneled into his gnostic sect, the Basilideans, and adopted by many other progressive Alexandrian sects as well. One of Basilides great contributions to gnosticism was the famous image and esoteric understanding of Abraxas, the serpentine deity adopted by the Basilideans, Ophites and other gnostic sects.

Basilides was part of a common stream of gnostic wisdom that flowed in Alexandria among all the "Adepts of the Mother," including the Ophites. In one way or another each gnostic sect was affiliated with the gnostic tradition that had emanated from John the Baptist and the Mandaeans. The Ophites' link to the Nasurai John the Baptist and the later Nasoreans has been mentioned. They received at least some of their serpentine gnostic wisdom from the surviving Nasoreans via James the Just and Mary Magdalene. The Sethians were also indebted to the Johannite tradition and acquired much of their wisdom from the texts of John the Divine, including *The Gospel of John* and *The Secret Book of John*, the latter of which contained teachings Jesus gave to John following his supposed Ascension.

Like the Basilideans, both the Sethians and Ophites made important inroads into the creation of an amalgamated Gnostic Christianity, but the true artist behind this synthesis was the Alexandrian philosopher Valentinus, a student of Basilides and the founder of the sect of Valentians. Valentinus' academic training had been a mixture of Gnosticism and the Christain mysteries of St. Paul, which had been imparted to him from his teacher Theudas, a direct disciple of the Apostle. After synthesizing the two traditions, Valentinus began to teach many abstract Christian ideas from a gnostic perspective, especially those found in the Synoptic Gospels. One of his greatest works was a treatise on the Christian Trinity, which he published as the *Tripartite Tractate*, and another was a critque on Christ's divinity. In regards to the Gnostic-Christian synthesis Valetinius labored to create, G.R.S. Mead remarks:

"...[He embraced] everything, even the most dogmatic formulation of the traditions of the Master [Jesus]. The great popular movement and its incomprehensibilities were recognized by Valentinus as an integral part of the mighty outpouring; he labored to weave all together, external and internal, into one piece, devoted his life to the task, and doubtless only at his death perceived that for that age he was attempting the impossible. None but the very few could ever appreciate the ideal of the man, much less understand it."[17]

Abraxas
A model of Creation
**The Cock's Head represents the Solar Sun or Infinite Spirit that descends
as energy before dividing to become the dual serpents,
which are the two legs of Abraxas.**

Valentinus eventually took his Christian Gnostic teachings to Rome in 136 A.D. where he became both a respected gnostic teacher and a high official of the Catholic Church. When Valentinus became a candidate for pope (or "bishop") in the wake of Pope Hyginus' passing, all of Christendom was suddenly on the cusp of becoming gnostic. Instead, the brilliant Valentinus was passed over for someone less qualified for the position. The painful event was recorded by Tertullian in his *Adversus Valentinianos*:

"Valentinus had expected to become a bishop [Pope], because he was an able man both in genius and eloquence. Being indignant, however, that another obtained the dignity by reason of a claim which confessorship had given him, he broke with the church of the true faith. Just like those [restless] spirits which, when roused by ambition, are usually inflamed with the desire of revenge, he applied himself with all his might to exterminate the truth; and finding the clue of a certain old opinion, he marked out a path for himself with the subtlety of a serpent."

Valentinus' brush off by the Catholic hierarchy left him bitter and resentful. He left Rome soon afterwards and resettled in Cyprus where, according to Tertullian, he became a heretic of the Church and fully embraced both gnostic theology and a heretical gnostic lifestyle. His resentment towards Chrisitanity remained, however, until he gained a measure of vengence by insulting the entire Christian world through his famous expose on the three types of seekers. Of the three types, the first category of "spiritual" seekers were principally the gnostics; only they had the potential to receive true wisdom and gnosis. The second category, which included the ordinary Christians, could possibly attain a much lesser degree of enlightenment, and the third category, that of the Jews and pagans of a "material nature," would probably acquire virtually no true wisdom whatsoever.

Johannite Christianity

Although Valentinus failed in his ultimate goal of creating a Gnostic Christian religion, a synthesis of sorts emerged among many of the gnostic sects which accepted Jesus as a gnostic adept and their Savior. They composed and studied scriptures containing what they beleived was the true life and gnostic teachings of Jesus. When orthodox Christianity sought to destroy these texts, the Alexandrian gnostics inscribed them on papyrus scrolls and buried them deep within the Egyptian desert. There they remained for nearly two thousand years, until 1945, when the most important cache of these texts was discovered in the area of Nag Hammadi in middle Egypt. They have since been translated and shown to contain dialogues between Jesus and his disciples, as well as previously unknown facts regarding the interrelationships that existed between Jesus, Mary Magdalene, John the Divine and the other Apostles. Both Mary and John are, for the first time, revealed in these texts to be the true gnostic successors of Jesus in the Johannite lineage.

The Nag Hammadi Texts

Following the recovery of the Nag Hammadi scrolls, other gnostic manuscripts and papyrus scrolls that had been previously purchased on the black market in Cairo resurfaced and gained renewed importance within the academic community, especially among the Johannite researchers. Included among these gnostic texts was the *Bruce Codex,* which had been purchased in Thebes in 1769 by the Englishman Lord James Bruce, and the *Codex Askewianus*, which was also bought in Egypt in the Eighteenth Century and later gifted to the British Museum.

Today, all the recovered texts comprise an extensive Christian Gnostic library. Of these texts, two stand out as being the best preserved and most informative: the *Pistis Sophia*, which was one of the texts of the *Codex Askewianus*, and *The Secret Book of John,* which was among of the Nag Hammadi scrolls. Both these texts purport to be teachings given by Jesus to his closest disciples many years after his Ascension. Each is a comprehensive gnostic text covering the intricacies of Gnostic Christian cosmology, including Sophia's fall and humankind's path to gnostic redemption through Christ. While using cryptic gnostic terms such as the First Mystery, the 12 Aeons, Barbelo, and the Pleroma, Jesus describes the evolution of the universe and the creation of humanity in a traditional gnostic nomenclature that was only familiar to gnostic initiates. *The Secret Book of John* has exceptional value for the modern gnostic student since its wisdom was only given to John, who along with Mary Magdalene was one of Jesus' two most evolved gnostic students and an important figure in the Johannite lineage. The *Pistis Sophia* is similarly invaluable since it explicitly identifies John and Mary as being the Apostles closest to Jesus and the ones who would rule alongside of him for eternity in Paradise. In *Pistis Sophia*, Jesus explicitly describes this afterlife scenario:

"Where I shall be, there will be also my twelve ministers. But Mary Magdalene and John, the Virgin, will tower over all my disciples and over all men who shall receive the mysteries of the Ineffable. And they will be on my right and on my left. And I am they, and they are I."[18]

Mary's exalted status as Jesus' future successor is also disclosed in a passage of the *Pistis Sophia* wherein Jesus refers to her as the "one who is the inheritor of the Light," meaning it was she who inherited the true gnostic wisdom or "Light" from the Master. In the Nag Hammadi texts Mary is repeatedly revealed to be the closest disciple to Jesus and the one who received secret teachings from the Christ that the others did not. In *The Gospel of Philip*, we read that the Apostles' inquired about the lack of attention they received from Jesus:

"…[Christ] loved her more than all the disciples, and used to kiss her often on her mouth. The rest of the disciples…said to him 'Why do you love her more than all of us?"

The Apostles' jealousy toward Mary reached a boiling point in *The Gospel of Mary*, which recounts a gathering of Jesus' disciples following the Ascension. At the beginning of this scene, Mary attempts to console the disciples by sharing some secret teachings with them that had been transmitted solely to her from the Master. Then, states the text:

"Mary stood up, greeted them all, and said to the brothers, 'Do not weep or grieve or be in doubt, for [Christ's] grace will be with you all and will protect you. Rather, let us praise his greatness, for he has prepared us and made us truly human.'

"When Mary said this, she turned their hearts to the good, and they began to discuss the words of the [savior].

"Peter said to Mary, 'Sister we know the savior loved you more than any other woman. Tell us the words of the savior that you remember, which you know but we do not, because we have not heard them.'"

With love for her brother Apostles, Mary then recounted a special teaching from the Master, prompting Andrew and Peter to respond with great indignation...

"Andrew answered and said to the brothers, 'Say what you think about what she said, but I do not believe the savior said this. These teachings certainly are strange ideas.'

"Peter voiced similar concerns. He asked the others about the savior: 'Did he really speak with a woman in private, without our knowledge? Should we all turn and listen to her? Did he prefer her to us?'

"Then Mary wept and said to Peter, 'My brother Peter, what do you think? Do you think that I made this up by myself or that I am lying about the savior?'

In Mary's defense, Levi harshly berates Peter: 'Peter, you always are angry. Now I see you arguing against this woman like an adversary. If the savior made her worthy, who are you to reject her? Surely the savior knows her well. That is why he has loved her more than us."[19]

The events of this contentious gathering were prophetic and destined to become a mirror to the future. The seeds of a future split among Jesus' Apostles were evident at that time, and eventually two divergent churches began to take shape. Mary and John the Apostle would found the Gnostic Christian or Joahnnite Church and Peter would found what would become the Catholic Church. Mary's church would be based upon the Left Hand Path that exalted the female principle, while Peter's patriarchal church would be founded upon the God tradition of the Right Hand Path that denigrated the female principle. The name Peter, and the Latin Pater, or "Father," is instructive as it reveals Peter to be the emissary of patriarchy and the Right Hand Path, while the name Mary, with its prefix of Ma, or "Mother," reveals Mary to be the embodiment of matriarchy and the Left Hand Path.

According to authors Lynn Picknett and Clive Prince, Peter's distain towards Mary is graphically portrayed in Da Vinci's *The Last Supper*. They claim that Mary rather than John is seated on the right of Jesus at the table, and Peter looms threateningly in back of Mary while making a murderous gesture with his hand across her neck. Picknett and Prince's conclusion regarding the identity of the person to the right of Jesus is corroborated by another of Da Vinci's painting, *Mary Magdalene,* wherein Mary's features are nearly identical to her proposed appearance in *The Last Supper.* Their conclusion is additionally confirmed by the *Pistis Sophia*, wherein Jesus states that Mary's rightful place is on his right side.

In recent years Mary's special place among the Apostles has even been admitted to even by the Christian orthodoxy, who hold her in high esteem for having been the first blessed disciple to see Jesus following his Resurrection. The familiar scene is recorded in the Gospel of St. John:

"[Mary] turned herself back, and saw Jesus standing, and knew not that it was Jesus. Jesus saith unto her, 'Woman, why weepest thou? Whom seekest thou?' She, supposing him to be the gardener, saith unto him, 'Sir, if thou have borne him hence, tell me where thou hast laid him, and I will take him away.' Jesus saith unto her, 'Mary.' She turned herself, and saith unto him 'Rabboni; which is to say, Master" Jesus saith unto her, 'Touch me not; for I am not yet ascended to my Father: but go to my brethren, and say unto them, I ascend unto my Father, and your Father; and to my God, and your God." (John 20:14-17)

The Synoptic Gospels also acknowledge Mary's elevated position among the Apostles by portraying her as one of only two disciples stationed at the foot of the cross during the Crucifixion. Along with the second disciple at the Crucifixion, John, Mary was given the ultimate honor by Jesus of guiding and protecting the Master's beloved Mother Mary after he was gone. With the blessings and spiritual power of Jesus guiding them, the three would subsequently travel together to Ephesus, which was one of the principal seats of gnosis in Asia Minor. Although on legend has it that Mary eventually sailed to France and ended her days there, the historian, Gregory of Tours, and Modestus, a patriarch of Jerusalem, states otherwise. According to Modestus:

"After the death of Our Lord, the mother of God and Mary Magdalene joined John, the well-beloved disciple, at Ephesus. It is there that the myrrhophone ended her apostolic career through her martyrdom, not wishing to the very end to be separated from John the Apostle and the Virgin."

The Johannite Lineage after Jesus

When John and Mary arrived in Ephesus they firmly rooted the Johannite Church and lineage in the city that had become a bastion of gnosis and the Left Hand Path. Both of the Beloved Disciples had been trained by John the Baptist and Jesus for their mission, and they carried it off so perfectly that one of the world's Johannite leaders still has his seat in Ephesus.

Mary Magdalene

According to the alternate history of Mary in *Legenda Aurea,* the "Golden Legend," by the Mideaval historian Jacobus de Voragine, the Magdalene may have traveled from Asia Minor to France and spent her remaining years spreading the Johannite gospel of Jesus in the West. She arrived weather-worn and ragged in an oar-less and mast-less vessel that also held many of her fellow disicples, including Mary Salome, Mary Jacobe, her brother Lazarus, and Maximinus. Together they landed on the French coast at the city of Oppidum-Râ, now called Saintes-Maries-de-la-Mer, and from there Mary Magdalene proceeded to convert much of southern France to the Johannite Christian teachings.

There are many stories of the miracles Mary performed during her years in France, including blessing couples with children and bringing the dead back to life. One of the famous women Mary blessed with a son was the Princess of Marseille, who unfortunately drowned when she fell off a ship bound for Rome soon after giving birth to her progeny. Her grieving husband resolved to complete the journey without the Princess, and left both her and his son together on a sheltered rock. Upon his return a full two years later, the Prince miraculously found his son still alive from having continually suckled the beast of his dead mother, which the grace of the Magdalene had made ever-plentiful. The joy of the reunion with his son was so overwhelming that the returning father immediately sunk to his knees and between sobs of joy thanked Mary. Hearing his prayer, the compassionate Magdalene bestowed yet another blessing on the couple, and she brought the princess back to life. As an interesting postscript to this unusual story, when the prince recounted to his wife his two-years of adventures he discovered that she was oblivious to the fact that she had even been dead. On the contrary, she remembered having been on a two-year pilgrimage with Mary in Jerusalem!

Another legend of Mary's sojourne in France claims that for forty years she lived the life of a hermit in a desolate cave high on a cliff face in Sainte Baume. While deep in meditative trance she is said to have sometimes levitated for many hours, and if she ever needed any material sustenance she simply manifested it out of thin air. Supposedly there was a time she subsisted solely on pure life force. When she transitioned, Mary's body was entombed by St. Maximin in a chapel in southern France and was later transported to the small town of Vézelay to become the treasure of the Abbey Church of Saint Marie-Madeleine. The Magdalene continues to produce miracles in the lives of those who pray to her; and because of the immense spiritual power that still surrounds her relics, people from all parts of the world regularly receive profound healing at Vézelay.

John the Apostle: John III

Following Jesus, whose title had been John II, John the Apostle took over as head of the Johannite lineage with the title of John III. John's status as grand-master of the Johannites has been passed down through history in secret Johannite documents, including one written in the Fifth Century that eventually came into the possession of the Knights Templar. After studying this document, in 1154 the Templars rewrote this ancient history to read as follows:

"Jesus conferred evangelical initiation on his apostles and disciples. He transmitted his spirit to them, divided them into several orders after the practice of John, the beloved disciple, the apostle of fraternal love, whom he instituted Sovereign Pontiff and Patriarch...."[20]

When he was annointed John III, the Evangelist received a special gnostic dispensation of wisdom and power from Jesus, and through it he achieved renown as a visionary teacher and miracle worker. John's *The Book of Revelation* is one of the greatest masterpieces of gnostic visionary insight ever produced, and his spiritual power was reputed to be second only to the Master's. When John left Ephesus on his premier mission to Rome, his power was tested on numerous occasions by the Emperor Domitian, who sought to martyr the Johannite Christian emissary by putting him through a series of tortures that no normal human could possibly survive. Domitian forced John to drink some deadly poison, but not only did the apostle not succumb to the liquid but he even resurrected from the dead another condemned prisoner who had imbibed the same fatal poison. The indomitable Domitian then had John thrown into a cauldron of boiling-hot oil, but again the Johannite master easily survived. Finally, having reached his wits end, the frustrated Roman Emperor sent John away to the Island of Patmos to work himself to death in the emperor's mines. It was here that John received his gnostic visions recorded in *The Book of Revelation*, which along with *The Gospel of John* were to become required reading within most of the Johannite and gnostic sects that were founded in the centuries to follow.

When Domitian passed away John was set free and journeyed back to Ephesus, where he performed some of his greatest miracles. One legend states that after a fire suddenly consumed the city's famed Temple of Diana and killed 200 of its worshippers, John brought the entire congregation back to life. Soon afterwards, when John denounced idol worship to an assembly in front of the

Mary Magdalene
Johannite Grand Master & Incarnation of Sophia

John the Evangelist, Johannite Grand Master
by El Greco

127

Temple of Diana, a frenzied crowd of worshippers tried to stone him to death. However instead of reaching John, the rocks boomeranged and fatally wounded those who had tossed them.

When John was laid to rest in Ephesus his tomb became one of the most important pilgrimage places in the Christian world, and remours of the Apostle's incredible miracles from the grave reached far and wide. John's dynamic serpent power perpetually emanated from his tomb, and miraculous healings took place either via the Holy Spirit or from the tomb's particles of dust that were saturated with it. One popular legend asserted that John had never truly died, and that he simply slept soundly in his tomb. This intriguing notion was later corroborated by St. Augustine, who maintained that the earth under John's tomb would rise and fall in rhythm to the sleeping Apostle's breathing patterns.

John's tomb received the ultimate honor in the Sixth Century when the huge Basilica of St. John, a citadel that was 380 feet in length and rose up 90 feet in height, was built over it by the Emperor Justinian. The church was later captured and destroyed by Seljuk Turks, and a mosque arose in its place.

The Johannite Knights Templar

Before his death, John continued the process of installing the long line of grandmasters named John. They would become "the Grand Pontiffs of the sect [who] took the title of Christ, and laid claim to an unbroken chain of succession in their office..."[21]

Following John as John IV was his close disciple, Brother Zebedee, and after him the dynastic title of John V fell to Brother Simon. He was followed in the lineage by Brother Titus, the titular John VI, and then the lineage continued in succession, with one John following another as grandmaster until the time of the First Crusade. At that time Theoclete, John LXX, passed the lineage to a French knight known as Hugues de Payens, "[who] was invested with the Apostolic Patriarchal Power and placed in the legitimate order of the succession of St. John the apostle or evangelist."[22]

This important investiture occurred soon after the First Crusade, in 1118 CE, when nine French knights banded together to form the Poor Knights of Christ of the Temple of Solomon, or the Knights Templar, with Hugues de Payens as their first Grand Master. Hugues had joined Theoclete's Church of John in Jerusalem in the same year and he was annointed John LXXI. From 1118 CE onwards the Knights Templar were the official guardians and representatives of the ancient Johannite lineage.

The acquisition of the Johannite Church to the Knights Templar and Hugues de Payens was later alluded to in *The History of Magic* by the Nineteenth Century occultist Eliphas Levi:

"The inmost thought of Hugues de Payens, in establishing his Order, was not precisely to serve the ambition of the [Christian] patriarchs of Constantinople. At that period there was a sect of Christian Johannites in the East who claimed to be alone initiated into the inner mysteries of the Savior's religion; they claimed also to know the true history of Jesus Christ…let it suffice to say that the Johannites went so far as to make St. John the Evangelist responsible for this spurious tradition and that they attributed to the apostle in question the foundation of their secret church. The grand pontiffs of this sect assumed the title of Christ and claimed an uninterrupted transmission of powers from the days of St. John. The person who boasted these imaginary privileges at the epoch of the foundation of the Temple was name Theoclete. He was acquainted with Hugues de Payens, whom he initiated into the mysteries and the hopes of his superstitious church; he seduced him by his ideas of sovereign priesthood and supreme royalty; in fine he designated him his successor."

In *Isis Unveiled* Madam Blavatsky similarly corroborates the Templars' Johannite inheritance, but she also affiliates the Knights with the Johannite Grand Master John the Baptist. She states:

"The true version of the history of Jesus, and the early Christianity was supposedly imparted to Hugues de Payens, by the Grand-Pontiff of the Order of the Temple [of the Nazarene or Johannite sect], one named Theoclete, after which it was learned by some Knights in Palestine, from the higher and more intellectual members of the St. John sect, who were initiated into its mysteries. Freedom of intellectual thought and the restoration of one universal religion was their secret object. Sworn to the vow of obedience, poverty, and chastity, they were at first the true Knights of John the Baptist, crying in the wilderness and living on wild honey and locusts. Such is the tradition and the true Kabbalistic version."

Finally, in the mid Nineteenth Century no less authority than Pope Pius IX made this public statement regarding the Templars and the beginning of the Johannite "heresy"in his *Allocution of Pio Nono against the Free Masons*:

"The Johannites ascribed to Saint John the foundation of their Secret Church, and the Grand Pontiffs of the Sect assumed the title of Christos, Anointed or Consecrated, and claimed to have succeeded one another from Saint John by an uninterrupted succession of pontifical powers. He who, at the period of the foundation of the Order of the Temple, claimed these imaginary prerogatives was named Theoclete; he knew Hugues de Payens, he initiated him into the Mysteries and hopes of his pretended church; he seduced him by the notions of Sovereign Priesthood and Supreme royalty, and finally designated him as his successor.

"Then the Order of the Knights of the Temple was at its very origin devoted to the cause of opposition to the Tiara of Rome and the crown of Kings, and the Apostolate of Kabbalistic Gnosticism was vested in its chiefs. For Saint John was the Father of the Gnostics....

"The Templars, like all other Secret Orders and Associations, had two doctrines, one concealed and reserved for the Masters, which was Johannism; the other public, which was the Roman Catholic. Thus they deceived the adversaries whom they sought to supplant."

Pope Pius' announcement made it clear that the Church had been aware of the existence of the Johannites for many centuries. The Church was no doubt aware of the Johannite-Templar succession since Vatican spies continually swarmed the Middle East, which is apparently one reason that the early Templar Johannites kept their affiliation hidden even from those Knights in the lower ranks of the Order. Only those at the highest level of the Templar hierarchy were allowed entrance into the Johannite tradition while the other knights remained primarily Catholic in faith. As Eliphas Levi explains:

"The tendencies and tenets of the [Templar] Order were enveloped in profound mystery, and it externally professed the most perfect orthodoxy. The Chiefs alone knew the aim of the Order; the subalterns followed them without distrust."[23]

In order to keep their veil of secrecy drawn, the Templar elite organized their order into a concentric arrangement consisting of outer and inner circles of initiates. The Johannite hierarchy comprised the three inner circles, while the rest of the knights occupied the seven outer circles. According to Jean Robin, another French occultist of high repute, only those advanced Templars of the three inner circles were aware of the Orders' gnostic practices. He states:

"The Order of the Temple was indeed constituted of seven 'exterior' circles dedicated to the minor mysteries, and of three 'interior' circles corresponding to the initiation into the great mysteries."[24]

The Templars' documents regarding their Johannite affiliations were also kept hidden and secret. Their current hidden locations are believed to include Rosslyn Chapel and the Langueduc region in southern France. Some Johannite documents were passed down the long lineage of Johannite Grand Masters who were able to keep the Order functioning as a clandestine organization following the mass arrest of the Knights in 1307. Then, in 1705, the Templars reappeared among the masses when Philip II, the Duke of Orleans, was elected Templar Grand Master during a special gathering of Templar Knights in Versailles, France. Grand Master Philip, who was in line of succession to the throne of France and therefore relatively immune to censure, asserted that the Templars had never ceased to exist and he was part of a lineage of grand masters that stretched back to the martyred Jacques De Molay. Grand Master Philip eventually passed both his mantle and many of the ancient Templars Johannite documents to his successor, the Duke of Cosse-Brissac. These documents included the *Statutes and Election Charter* of the Templars; as well as the *Larmenius Charter*, which gave lineal authority to the Templar Grand Masters.

The Duke of Cosse-Brissac was executed soon after his installment as Grand Master during a French Revolution massacre, but the secret Templar documents he received were preserved by his doctor, Ledru de Chevillon de Saintot, who in 1804 united with a brother Freemason of the Chevaliers de la Croiz, Bernard-Raymond Fabré-Palaprat, to continue the revival of the Knights Templar. Then, in a famous public ceremony in 1808 honoring the martyred Jacques de Molay, the two Freemasons donned the uniforms of the early Templars and officially proclaimed the revival of the Knights Templar in France.

Perhaps to keep the ancient secrets intact, Fabré-Palaprat did not invest his new Templar sect with the Johannite teaching until 1828. The result was a newly revived Johannite Church which he called the *Église Johannites des Chretiens Primitif*, meaning the "Johannite Church of Primitive Christians."

To give lineal authority to his Johannite Church, Fabré-Palaprat produced one of the old Templar documents that was supposedly written in 1154 and designated the Templars to be the true guardians and lineal successors of the Johannite Church. Another related Johannite document he had access to was the *Levitikon*, which was an introduction to a version of *The Gospel of St. John* known as the *Evangelicon*. The *Levitikon,* which included a history of the Johannites that was hand written hundreds of years before the First Crusade by a Fifth Century Greek monk from Athens named Necephorus, identified John the Apostle as Jesus' chosen successor. The document specifically recounted Jesus' sojourn in ancient Egypt where he acquired both gnostic wisdom and power within the Priesthood of Osiris, and then his return to Palestine where he transmitted all he had received in Egypt to his favored gnostic disciple, John the Apostle. Regarding Jesus' momentous initiation into this very ancient gnostic-alchemical tradition that extended back to Atlantis and the Thoth-Hermes Masters, Kenneth MacKenzie remarks:

"[Jesus] was initiated into the occult sciences, and the priests of Osiris, regarding him as the long-promised Horus, *expected by the Adepts*, finally consecrated him Sovereign Pontiff of the universal religion." [25]

Additional Johannite documents possessed by Fabré-Palaprat may have included the *Heavenly Jerusalem* and/or documents of a similar genre. Currently on display at the library in the University of Ghent in Belgium, the *Heavenly Jerusalem* is a drawing done by Lambert de St. Omer, a cleric of Flanders, who copied it from a document the Templars brought into Europe nine years after their founding. Those who have made a close study of the copy, including Christopher Knight, author of *The Hiram Key,* consider the document a perfect example of the Johannite heretical wisdom subscribed to by the Templars. Jesus is suspiciously absent in the drawing, and John the Baptist is apparently represented as the founder of the Heavenly Jerusalem, thus implying that he is the true Messiah. The original document that the *Heavenly Jerusalem* was copied from, as well as other Johannite documents, were eventually taken to Scotland and are now believed to reside in the crypt under Rosslyn Chapel.

Fabré-Palaprat eventually passed the revived Johannite Templar tradition to Sir William Sidney Smith, a retured British admiral, who immediately expunged its Johannite teachings and returned Templarism to what he beleived was its orginal form. The Knights Templar Order then became a full-on military and charitable organization, and it has remained so until today.

The Johannite Revival

The gnostic wisdom of Fabré-Palaprat's Johannite Church did not simply pass away under Sydney Smith, however, but became assimilated into a Universal Gnostic Church that united the wisdom of a host of gnostic sects that simultaneously arose in Nineteenth Century France and were directly or indirectly linked to the ancient Johannite tradition. These sects included the *Church of Carmel* founded by Eugene Michel Vintras, a mystic who proclaimed himself to be a reincarnation of the Prophet Elijah, the spirit that had previously incarnated as the Johannite Grand Master, John the Baptist. Vintras identified himself by a symbol of John the Baptist, the Holy Spirit Dove, that he wore over his forehead, and he claimed as authority for his gnostic sect the Archangel Michael, Joseph and the Virgin Mary, who had collectively appeared to him in a vision and anointed Vintras as the founder of the Age of the Paraclete, the new age of gnosis. Vintras' ensuing *Church of Carmel* eventually spread throughout much of Europe, ultimately founding branches in Spain, Belgium, England and in the City of John the Baptist, Florence, Italy.

Vintras' successor, the Abbé Joseph-Antoine Boullan, followed the example of his teacher and annointed himself an incarnation of John the Baptist. For many years previous to this appointment Boullan had been a dedicated devotee of the Left Hand Path and the Goddess, whose symbol of the pentagram he had tattooed next to one of his eyes. After receiving Vintras' mantle as head of the *Church of Carmel*, Boullan incorporated within it numerous sexual rites of the early gnostics he had been practicing. These rites had been part of the gnostic sect he had founded, the *Society for the Reparation of Souls*, and supposedly they once had been observed by the Simonians and other early gnostics.

The revival of Johannite gnosis and the Era of the Paraclete continued to gain momentum with Jules Doinel, a librarian who was visited one night by Jesus Christ and two Bogomil Bishops and anointed first Patriarch of a revived Gnostic

Church. Dionel named his church the *L'Eglise Gnostique*, "The Gnostic Church," and in order to gain instruction on its organization, Doinel held a series of nocturnal séances. Guidance for his church eventually came through the arrival of the spirits of 40 Cathar bishops known as the "Very High Synod of Bishops of the Paraclete." He also received for his church the blessings of the Gnostic Goddess Sophia, who spoke to Doinel through the voice of a woman in his gnostic congregation:

"I address myself to you because you are my friend, my servant, and the prelate of my Albigensian Church. I am exiled from the Pleroma, and it is I whom Valentinius named Sophia-Achamôth. It is I whom Simon Magus called Helene-Ennoia; for I am the Eternal Androgyne. Jesus is the Word of God; I am the Thought of God. One day I shall remount to my Father, but I require aid in this; it requires the supplication of my Brother Jesus to intercede for me. Only the Infinite is able to redeem the Infinite, and only God is able to redeem God. Listen well: The One has brought forth One, then One. And the Three are but One: the Father, the Word, and the Thought. Establish my Gnostic Church. The Demiurge will be powerless against it. Receive the Paraclete."

When Doinel founded *L'Eglise Gnostique* in 1890 he assumed the dynastic name of Valentin II, thereby affiliating himself and his church with the gnostic adept Valentinius. The catechism of his church incorporated the ancient gnostic teachings of both Simon Magus and Valentinius, and its leadership was equally divided among both men and women whom he designated "Bishops" and "Sophias." Eight specially selected Bishops and Sophias were given the highest rank of Tau, which is an alternate name for the Egyptian Ankh, thus further cementing their alignment with the ancient gnostics of Alexandria.

One of Doinel's dissenting Bishops, Jean Bricaud, eventually split off from *L'Eglise Gnostique* to create a church that would unite all the new gnostic sects in France under one roof. After becoming a high initiate in most of these sects, including Vintras' *Church of Carmel*, and Fabre-Palaprat's *Église Johannites des Chretiens Primitif,* Bricaud brought them all the sects together as the *Universal Gnostic Church.* As titular head of his new amalgamated gnostic church, Bricaud anointed himself Tau Johannes, thus ostensibly designating himself to be a Johannite dignitary and a latter-day successor of the two Johns, John the Baptist and John the Apostle.

Bricaud's *Universal Gnostic Church* has since undergone many transformations. Some sects initially split off from it, while others joined its ranks as it gradually moved around the globe. Finally, in 2002, the Universal Gnostic Church was remolded in North America as the *Apostolic Johannite Church*. The new head or "Primate" of the church was another John, Primate James Foster, the honorable Tau Johannes III. Today, the *Apostolic Johannite Church* remembers the grand masters of the Templars as their Johannite predecessors and mentions many of them in their liturgy. However, since its revival by Fabré-Palaprat in the Ninthteenth Century, many elements of patriarchal Christianity have crept into the Johannite Church and it is currently far from being a pure gnostic organization.

The Lineage of Johannite Grand Masters

1. John the Baptist
2. Jesus Christ
3. John the Apostle - Mary Magdalene
4. Brother Zebedee
5. Brother Simon
6. Brother Titus
7. Brother Joseph
8. Brother Theodecte
9. Brother Jonas
10. Brother Zacharias
11. Brother Joseph of Caesarea
12. Brother Marc
13. Brother Jerome
14. Brother Cyril
15. Brother David
16. Brother Adrian Anthony
17. Brother Agathon
18. Brother Mathias
19. Brother Athanasius
20. Brother John Titus
21. Brother Felix
22. Brother Thomas
23. Brother Agrippa
24. Brother Matthew of Alexandria
25. Brother Chrysostome
26. Brother Issac
27. Brother Diodore
28. Brother Julian
29. Brother Prosper
30. Brother Justin
31. Brother Auguste
32. Brother Aurelian
33. Brother Faustin
34. Brother Paul of Judea

35. Brother Eusebius
36. Brother Irenaeus
37. Brother Epicrate
38. Brother Maxime
39. Brother Anthony the Roman
40. Brother Christopher
41. Brother Gregory
42. Brother Leonce
43. Brother Eugenien
44. Brother Samuel of Antioch
45. Brother Theobald the Byzantine
46. Brother Raphaël
47. Brother Machaël
48. Brother Priscillian
49. Brother Valere
50. Brother Cornelius
51. Brother Claude
52. Brother Sylvester
53. Brother Stephen Simon
54. Brother Andrew Philip
55. Brother Cleophas of Egypt
56. Brother Ovid
57. Brother Porphyry
58. Brother Jacob of Samaria
59. Brother Anatome
60. Brother Irenaeus Cephas
61. Brother Damase
62. Brother Simeon Claude
63. Brother Romain
64. Brother John Leon
65. Brother Zacharias
66. Brother Alexander Dactyle
67 Brother Lazare Idumean
68. Brother Cyprian
69. Brother Eustate
70 Brother Theoclete
71. Hugues de Payens

Hughes de Payen, Johannite Grand Master

The Knights Templars unite with the Johannites
The Agnus Dei Symbol of John the Baptist is united with the Knights Templar Flag of St. George

The Agnus Dei, symbol of John the Baptist
became the Seal of the Knights Templar, The "Knights of St. John the Baptist"

Philip II, Duke of Orleans
Johannite Templar Grand Master

Bernard-Raymond Fabré-Palaprat
Modern Reviver of the Johannite Templars

The Heavenly Jerusalem

The Gnostic Knight Templars

After assimilating the ancient teachings of the Johannite Church, the Order of the Poor Knights of Christ of the Temple of Solomon, or Knights Templar for short, amalgamated their Johannite gnostic wisdom to the alchemical rites they acquired from the latter-day Essenes, the Jewish Kabbalists, and from various sects of Islamic Sufis. These diverse streams of knowledge were taken into Europe by the Templars, where they were synthesized as the Holy Grail Mysteries. In *The Hidden Church of the Holy Grail: Its Legends and Symbolism* A.E. Waite denominates this Templar tradition as the "Holy Grail Church," and maintains that it began a movement that provided Europe with an Underground Stream of gnostic and alchemical wisdom for centuries to come.

The Origin of the Gnostic Knight Templars

The Knights Templar initially arrived in the Holy Land on a mission to reclaim some treasure that they believed was rightfully theirs. According to the modern Templar historians, Tim Wallace-Murphy and Christopher Knight, the knights who banded together as the Knights Templar were part of a wave of European royalty descended from Jewish Elders that had fled the Holy Land around 70 CE. Before leaving their homeland, these Elders had hidden their temple treasures and priceless Essene and Kabbalistic scrolls in strategic regions of the Holy Land so that the Roman invader Titus could not plunder them as the spoils of war. The Jewish Elders then immigrated to Europe and many of them married into the continent's noble families. Of these Elders, twenty-four would become the patriarchs of a group of European families known by the sobriquet of the "Rex Dues" or "Star" families. For hundreds of years the secret locations of the Jewish treasure filtered down through the families of the Elders until the First Crusade, when knighted members of the Rex Deus joined the procession of holy warriors traveling east with the dual goal of defeating the Moslems and recovering their family treasure. The original nine Knights Templar were either born into or related to the Rex Dues families, as was Godfrey de Boullion, the French general who led them during the First Crusade. His cousin, King Baldwin II of Jerusalem, assisted the Templars in retrieving the treasure by donating the al-Aqsa Mosque for their use. Traces of the Templars' ensuing excavations were later discovered in the 1800s by a detachment from the Royal Engineers of Great Britain and are now in the possession of the Knight Templar archivist of Scotland, Robert Brydon.

Apparently the Jewish Elders had stashed much of their treasure under Solomon's Stables, because it was there that the Templars spent most of their time excavating. After nine years of digging, the original nine Knights had accumulated enough treasure and documents to fill four large trunks. When their patron, King Baldwin II, suddenly took ill and died, the Knights took their four cases into Europe, stopping briefly at St. Omer in Flanders to have the Johannite illustration, the *Heavenly Jerusalem* mentioned in the previous chapter, copied and then replaced by cleric Lambert de St. Omer. They then proceeded to the French city of Troyes.

After a special ceremony with Pope Honorius III at the Council of Troyes in 1128 that made their organization official in the eyes of the Church, two of the Knights, Hughes de Payen and Andre de Montbard, carried their four cases of treasures to Kilwinning, Scotland, the location of the "Mother" Grand Lodge of Freemasonry. The trunks resided there for many years before eventually being moved to Sinclair Castle in Roslin, near Edinburgh. The Sinclairs were one of the Rex Dues or Star families whose destiny had, according to one legend, become forever entwined with the Knights Templar when their ancestress Catherine de Saint Clair married Hugues de Payen a decade or so before he took the vows of a monk in 1128. It is because of the Sinclair-Templar bond that much of the Knights' treasure, including the prodigious wealth that landed in Scotland after the Templar escape from France in 1307, ended up in the coffers of the Sinclair Clan.

Rosslyn Chapel, Bastion of the Johannites

The Sinclair Earls of Roslin kept the four cases of Templar treasure safe in their castle until a fire unexpectedly broke out and they were forced to remove them from the collapsing edifice. The calamitous event apparently had a silver lining, however, because legend has it that soon after the fire construction on nearby Rosslyn Chapel began in earnest. Thus, the safekeeping of the four boxes may have been the original purpose for the construction of Rosslyn Chapel.

Recent confirmation for the survival of the four cases in Rosslyn has come through ground scans in the chapel taken over the past twenty years which reveal a vault in the crypt containing four large boxes. This vault is located directly under the keystone and within the most energetically protected part of the chapel. If

The Council of Troyes

Roslin Castle

Rosslyn Chapel

Andrew Sinclair is Knighted at Rosslyn Chapel by Grand Prior Ian Sinclair

143

Rosslyn Chapel was built as a copy of Solomon's Templar or Herod's later temple, as many believe, then this region of the chapel would correspond to the inner sanctum or Holy of Holies. Researcher Christopher Knight contends that Rosslyn Chapel is a model of Herod's Temple, which is why it contains a so-called "unfinished" outer wall. Knight contends that this wall was added intentionally to give the Chapel the appearance of the ruins of Herod's Temple as it looked when the Templars excavated under it. If this is true, then Rosslyn Chapel was built to duplicate Herod's Temple so that the Knights' treasure could be symbolically returned to a version of its original hiding place in the Holy Land.

The internment of the four cases, along with their indwelling treasures and Johannite documents, made the small Gothic church of Rosslyn Chapel an important bastion of the Templars' Johannite legacy. One of the conspicuous symbols inside the chapel that noticeably affiliates Rosslyn with the Johannite tradition is the Agnus Dei, the symbol of John the Baptist, which dominates a upper wall near the north entrance of the chapel. An image of the head of John the Baptist may also be on display in Rosslyn. This is the carving of a bearded head attached to the west wall of the Chapel that is commonly referred to as the head of the apprentice mason even though apprentices did not sport beards. Rather, it possesses the long-haired and bearded features commonly associated with the Baptist along with a gash over the right eye, which was a feature that was commonly incorporated into John's iconography at the time Rosslyn Chapel was built. The legend associated with John's pronounced gash started at Amiens Cathedral when its priests received the supposed head of John from the crusading knight, Wallon de Sarton, in the Thirteenth Century. At that time the skull possessed a gash over the right eye, so the priests wove a myth which asserted that Salome's mother, Herodias, had slashed the skull when it was brought to her on a platter. Their fabricated story became widely accepted, and for the next few centuries John's gashed head was consistently featured in his iconography all over Europe. In *Répertoires des saints; noms, patronage, attributs,* French author Louis Réau mentions two surviving examples of this period. He cites a Fourteenth Century relief in Lyon cathedral and a Sixteenth Century fresco at Saint-Denis d'Anjou, both of which feature the gash on John's forehead.

Other symbols that indirectly affiliate Rosslyn with the Baptist are the more than 100 Green Men faces that peer out from behind a tangled web of leafy vines artistically molded under and between the chapel's widows. John was linked to the Green Man via Elijah, who in the Middle East was synonymous with al-Khadir, the Green Man of the Sufis. The Freemasons, who also regard Rosslyn Chapel to be one of their bastions, similarly equate John with the Green Man. Within the Craft the two Masonic patrons, John the Baptist and John the Apostle, are associated with the two heads of Green Man Janus, the Romans' Lord of the Year. The

Masonic year was divided between the two Johns, with John the Baptist's six month reign beginning at the Summer Solstice (actually June 24) and John the Apostle's period commencing at the Winter Solstice (actually December 27). The solstice associations of the two Johns affiliates them with the Apprentice and Master Pillars of Rosslyn, which are symbolically associated with the Summer and Winter Solstices, respectively. Author Keith Laidler contends that there is a head buried under the Apprentice Pillar and suggests that it is Jesus.' This may be true, however since the pillar is so closely linked to John the Baptist and the Baptist's head is recreated on the west wall, there is a much better chance that it belongs to the Templars' patron and Savior.

Baphomet: The Head of John the Baptist

There are, of course, many legends regarding the wherabouts of John's head, which to the Templars was anciently known as "Baphomet" and considered their most prized sacred object. One legend has it that John's mummified was taken into Europe by crusader knights after being discovered during the Fourth Crusade in Constantinople's magnificent Boukoleon Palace, where it was stored in a small chapel along with the Holy Shroud, the Veil of Veronica and a piece of the True Cross. Once it reached the heart of Europe, the head was placed in the hands of the Templars' Johannite hierarchy and used principally for initiations into their ancient gnostic tradition. At their French trial the Templars claimed that the head emanated the same prodigious Holy Spirit power as it had when attached to the body of John. The Knights stated that it "made the trees to flourish and the earth to germinate." Supposedly during the time leading up to the Fourth Crusade the head had healed an emperor of the Eastern Roman Empire and then continued to keep him strong and healthy by being daily passed over his body. So later, when a candidate for Johannite initiation was brought before the head he would have found himself immersed in a tremendous power that activated his inner alchemical process and gnostic development. It is also said that the Knights of lower rank profited from John's power by wearing a cord that had been wrapped around Baphomet and given to them during their premier initiation into the Order. They were told to continuously wear the cord around their waist while they were members of the Order, even if they did not understand its origin or importance.

Besides the head of John, the Knights Templar were also in the possession of many other Holy Grails, including the Crown of Thorns, the Holy Shroud, the Holy Chalice and the pieces of the True Cross. What made an object a Holy Grail was its etheric, alchemical power, which it typically received from a great master full of the Holy Spirit, such as John the Baptist or his disciple Jesus, who had infused power into the Articles of the Passion when they came into contact

The Agnus Dei in Rosslyn Chapel

The Gashed Head of John the Baptist

The Green Men of Rosslyn Chapel
Photos by Mark Amaru Pinkham

with his body and fluids. When a Knight drank from or touched a Holy Grail, its power would enter him and initiate the process of alchemical unfoldment. The Templars were the authority on the power of the Holy Grails, and according to Knight Wolfram von Eschenbach, the author of *Parzival*, they were also their eternal guardians and keepers.

The term Baphomet, meaning "Baptism of Wisdom," was an appropriate name for the head of John, whose Holy Spirit power would baptize and purify a Templar Knight while awakening the inner centers of gnosis. Baphomet was also a name applied to other Holy Grail objects since it simply denoted the fiery power of the Holy Spirit; i.e., Baphomet *was* the alchemical power. The famous monstous image of Baphomet that was popularized by Eliphas Levi and placed upon the inner and outer walls of Gothic Cathedrals by Templar-trained masons was a symbollic image of the alchemical power in the form of an androgynous, black goat. Baphomet was androgynous because the alchemical power results from the reunion of the polarity, and it projects an ominous dark and destructive nature because the serpent power it represents destroys everything that prevents a person from knowing their divine nature. According to author Hugh Schonfeld, when translated via the Atbash Cipher used by the Templars, the name Baphomet becomes Sophia, thus making Baphomet and Sophia synonymous. Strickly speaking, Baphomet is a name of the Serpent Son and Sophia is the name of his Mother, the Serpent Goddess. But, as mentioned, they are simply two names for pure energy, which is by nature neutral and non-gender specific.

The Johannite "Chakra" Pilgrimage

When the Knights Templar left the Holy Land and returned to Europe many of them called upon the sacred building skills they had acquired from the Sufis in order to create a new form of alchemical architecture on the continent. This was to become the "Gothic" style, which was specially designed to generate the alchemical force and initiate all those within a structure on the path to gnosis. In regards to the Templars' seminal influence on the new Gothic design, Picknett and Prince remark:

"The Knights Templar were the prime movers behind the building of the great Gothic cathedrals, especially that of Chartres. As the predominant, and often the only 'developers' in large European centers of culture, they were behind the formation of the builders' guilds, including that of the stonemasons, who became lay members of the Templar Order and who reaped all their benefits, such as exemption from paying tax."[1]

Seven of Europe's Gothic cathedrals were especially important to the Templars. These were constructed over the seven chakras or principal vortexual power points on the continent which greatly empowered them. The location of the

European chakras had been known about since the time of the Celtic Druids, who had built primitive nature temples over them and dedicated each to one of the seven known planets. Druid priests and priestesses then served as oracles for each temple's associated planet. The Templars, or Templar-trained masons replaced the Druid temples with their own Gothic churches and cathedrals.

Since Tim Wallace-Murphy and Marilyn Hopkin traveled up the spine of Europe and successively visited each of these seven chakra cathedrals - a journey they recorded in *Rosslyn: Guardians Of The Secrets Of The Holy Grail* - many other contemporary pilgrims have taken the pilgrimage route, including the author. Besides being palpably charged with energy, each cathedral contains both gnostic and alchemical symbols inside and out, including the recurring Johannite image of John the Baptist holding his baptismal scallop shell. According to the great European alchemist Fulcannelli who visited most of these cathedrals in the early 1900's and recorded his assessments of them in his magnum opus *Le Mystere des Cathedrales,* the majority of the cathedrals had indeed been designed by Templars or Templar-trained masons and intended to be used as special initiation chambers. Apparently most of the cathedrals, including the small Gothic church of Rosslyn Chapel that is situated over Europe's seventh chakra, once possessed one or more Black Madonnas, symbol of the transformative power of the Goddess, gracing their main altars. Many also possessed a labyrinth, which is a geometrical form of the Goddess, painted upon their tiled floors. The labyrinth was known to possess both alchemical and gnostic properties. The back and forth movement of a person walking through a labyrinth naturally balances and unites the left and right hemispheres, and the inner male and female principles. One of the cathedrals particularly noted for both its alchemical symbols and its labyrinth is Amiens, the cathedral built over Europe's sixth chakra that was dedicated to John the Baptist. The alchemical properties of the labyrinth of Amiens were enhanced by giving it the form of an octagon.

Although the precise rites performed at the seven "chakra" cathedrals have been lost or hidden, it is not inconceivable that they would have involved activities designed to awaken the corresponding chakra within a pilgrim. At the very least, when a pilgrim entered each shrine he or she would have used the scallop shell acquired in Santiago at the start of the pilgrimage route to baptize him or herself with holy water. If performed with the appropriate attitude and prayer invocations, this rite would have been both purifying and activating.

Theoretically, the rite performed by the Templars at Europe's first chakra of Santiago de Compostella wouild have been designed to promote the awakening of the alchemical force that resides within the Root Chakra. Not surprisingly, the base chakra of Santiago became renown for its alchemical powers and nicknamed the "Alchemist's Pilgrimage" and the "Pilgrimage of Initiation." Its patron saints were two powerful Johannite initiators, James the Greater and James the Lesser or Just, both of whom had a special relationship with John the Baptist. James the Greater had been a direct disciple of John the Baptist, and James the Just, the brother of Jesus, had represented John as the Priestly Messiah after the Baptist met his fateful demise at the hands of King Herod.

The second chakra of Europe, and the second stop of the Johannite Pilgrimage route, is L'eglise de Notre-Dame la Dalbade in Toulouse, France. The second chakra is specially associated with the symbol of the peacock, an important motif that reflects one of the latter stages of alchemy, and this church displays an array of peacock-like murals and stained glass windows. Past Templar influence in the church appears to be indicated by rows of columns with attached cross pattées.

The third chakra on the Johannite pilgrimage, the Cathedral of Orleans, is famous for its life-size image of John the Baptist holding his famous scallop shell. The symbol associated with the third chakra is a knight, so there is reason to believe that this was an initiation stop-over for some Johannite Templars.

The fourth chakra at Chartres Cathedral was once the greatest of the Druid oracles and the headquarters of Europe's Arch Druid. It has always been the eternal home of the Goddess, and a Madonna was once venerated here by the Celts well before the birth of Christ. Chartres is the heart chakra point, and therefore the home of the nurturing, loving aspect of the Goddess, as well as an important place where the polarity unites in Europe. Through walking the labyrinth at Chartres, and communing with its two Madonnas, the Lady of the Pillar and the subterranean Lady of the Underground, a pilgrim's inner polarity could unite and produce both an awakened heart and an active Third Eye. The Eye of Wisdom would also be additionally stimulated by the cobalt color of the stained glass windows that flood the cathedral with dark blue light.

The Cathedral of Notre Dame in Paris, which Fullcanelli refers to as the "Philosopher's Church," marks Europe's fifth chakra. It was here, according to the master alchemist, that the local alchemists built their headquarters, complete with alchemical symbols, such as salamanders, which are symbollic of alchemical fire. He states:

"The alchemists of the Fourteenth Century used to meet [at Notre Dame] once a week on the day of Saturn, either at the main porch, at the Portal of St. Marcel or else at the little Porte-Rouge, all decorated with salamanders."[2]

Today, still greeting those of an alchemical predilection at the main entrance of Notre Dame is the symbol of a Goddess figure, probably Sophia, who identifies the nine stages of alchemy as a ladder with nine steps. About this image Fullcanelli remarks:

"Supported between her knees and leaning against her chest is the ladder with nine rungs-scala philosophorum-hieroglyph of the patience which the faithful must possess in the course of the nine successive operations of the hermetic labour."[3]

Another important meeting place for French alchemists was just north of Paris at Amiens, whose cathedral sits over Europe's sixth chakra. According to Fullcanelli, the alchemical symbols that embellish the entrances of Amiens Cathedral are in many ways identical to those at Notre Dame, and they similarly depict all the stages involved in the alchemical process. Amiens Cathedral sits over Europe's Third Eye, the chakra specially associated with gnostic wisdom, which is perhaps why it is dedicated to John the Baptist, the Lord of Gnosis. Amiens is full of John's symbols and relics, including what is believed to be his head and the bone of a finger. John's alchemical power of destruction and transformation is represented by the inverted pentagram that looks down from a very large stained glass window near the ceiling of the cathedral. The labyrinth of Amiens, which is in the shape of an octagon, possesses tremendous potential for alchemical activation. The center of the labyrinth was originally covered with solid gold representing the alchemical purity and gnostic wisdom waiting at the end of its pathway. States Fulcanelli:

"In the center of the labyrinth at Amiens a large flagstone used to be visible, encrusted with a bar of gold and a semi-circle of the same metal, showing the sun rising above the horizon."[4]

The supposed skull of John the Baptist at Amiens that was brought to the cathedral from the Middle East in the Thirteenth Century by crusading knight Wallon de Sarton sits within a reliquary in Amiens Cathedral. The skull is set into a gold plate that is on display in a glass case on the left side of the cathedral. The skull is most likely not the true mummified head of John the Baptist since it lacks the alchemical power that the Knights Templar attributed to Baphomet. Moreover, since its arrival at Amiens corresponded to the height of the Cult of Relics in Europe, it may forever remain impossible to be completely sure of the identitiy of the head since all churches and cathedrals of the period attempted to distinguish themselves, and thereby attract greater financial endowments, by acquiring the body part of one or more saints, even if it meant falsifying the real owner of the relic. Besides Amiens, there were at least four other churches and cathedrals that claimed to possess John's head, including St. Mark's Cathedral in Venice, St. Chapelle in Paris, St. Chaumont in Lyonnais, and the Abbey of Tyron in France. Even a mosque in Lebanon has laid claim to being its possessor. However, even if the real head of John the Baptist is not enshrined in Amiens, the skull that currently resides there was probably highly regarded by the Templar Knights or it would not have become the centerpiece of one of their most important alchemical cathedrals.

The Cathedral of Santiago de Compostella
Photo by Mark Amaru Pinkham

John the Baptist with Scallop Shell, Orleans Cathedral
Photo by Mark Amaru Pinkham

Chartres Cathedral, Alchemical Crucible
Its design unites the polarity and incorporates the Golden Proportion
Photo by Mark Amaru Pinkham

The Madonna of the Pillar, Chartres Cathedral
Photo by Mark Amaru Pinkham

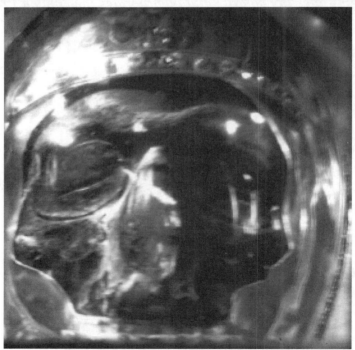

The Head of John the Baptist at Amiens Cathedral
Photos by Mark Amaru Pinkham

The Chartres Alchemical Labyrinth

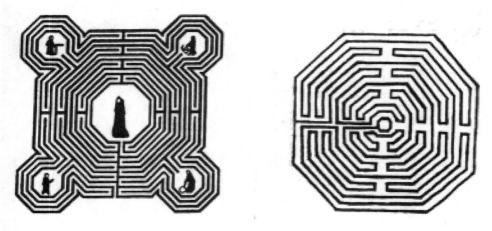

Octagonal Labyrinths of Reims and Amiens Cathedrals

Sophia holding the Book of Alchemy
The Ladder of 9 Steps or Stages of Alchemy, Notre Dame Cathedral

The Philosophical Mercury, Notre Dame Cathedral
Photos by Mark Amaru Pinkham

The Philosophical Sulpher, Notre Dame Cathedral
Photo by Mark Amaru Pinkham

The Union of Mercury & Sulpher, Notre Dame Cathedral
Photo by Mark Amaru Pinkham

The final chakra and power point of the Johannite pilgrimage is occupied by Rosslyn Chapel, whose esoteric affiliation is a golden crown and the human crown chakra, which can conceivably be awakened here. Rosslyn, which is known to have originally served as a mystery temple before it became a church, was the crowning glory of the Johannite's pilgrimage up the spine of Europe. All initiations culminated here. Rosslyn Chapel's design, which incorporated both the six and eight pointed stars of alchemy, made it highly charged for a pilgrim's final initiation.

The Knights Templar, Emissaries of the Left Hand Path

The Templar Knights' intimate association with the Left Hand Path was cemented in the Middle East, but it was also long in the making well before the Knights even set foot in the Holy Land during the First Crusade. Most of the original nine knights hailed from either the Langueduc region of southern France, which was famous for its heretical, Goddess-driven gnostic and alchemical sects, or from northern Champagne with its capital of Troyes, a bastion of Kabbalistic wisdom and alchemical research. Most of the nine knights were also students of or related by blood to St. Bernard, who was himself a lover of the Goddess in Her form of Mary Magdalene and preached the Second Crusade from her European headquarters in Vezelay. Because of the tutelage they received from St. Bernard, it was natural for the Templars to swear an oath of obedience to Mary Magdalene, whom they referred to as "Our Lady,"when they took their formal vows of monkhood in 1128. Of course, by then the Templars were Johannites and recognized Mary as their official patroness.

The Templars and the Sufis

The Templars' education regarding the Goddess and Her gnostic-alchemical tradition was expanded upon and accelerated in the Holy Land under the Sufis who in the eyes of the Moslem hierarchy were themselves mystical renegades and heretics "attempting to ignore the Law and substitute personal experience for what religion really meant."[1] As adherents of the Left Hand Path, the Sufis had exchanged the laws of the Right Hand Path for direct experience of the Divine.

When the Templars met the Sufis these desert roaming "People of the Wool" had been Goddess venerators for hundreds and thousands of years, well before the advent of Islam. For many years they were the official caretakers of the Goddess shrine at Mecca, right up until it was usurped by the patriarchal followers of Allah. When Sufism was integrated into Islam, it retained its Goddess-loving predilections, which is why the original Islam flag designed by the Sufis contained the Goddess' symbols of the crescent moon and the eight-pointed star. Only much later did the eight-pointed star evolve into the modern five-pointed star we commonly associate with Islam.

158

The Templars learned from their Sufi mentors that the eight-pointed star had been one of the most ancient and definitive symbols of the Goddess, beginning as far back as Inanna of Sumeria and her Babylonian evolution, Ishtar. Inanna-Ishtar was the Goddess of the planet Venus, the "Queen of Heaven," which shined nightly in the heavens as the eight-rayed star. Venus was associated with the number eight because of her sacred eight year cycle with the Earth, but also because she was the heavenly manifestation of the Goddess and the union of the polarity, which appeared as the Morning and Evening Stars. The two circles united as the Arabic eight is a symbol of polarity union of the male and female principles, as well as a glyph of Heaven united with Earth. When the polarity unites it engenders immortality, or infinity, which is another interpretation of the Arabic eight.

To reveal their affiliation to the Goddess and Her Left Hand Path gnostic-alchemical tradition the Templars adopted the red-colored, eight-pointed Cross Pattee as their distinctive symbol. The eight-pointed cross denotes the Goddess as the union of the male and female principles, and its red color refers to Her nature as the alchemical fire created by polarity union.

The Assassins and al-Banna

One Sufi sect that profoundly influenced the Templars was the Assassins, another knighted order with whom the Knights made numerous treaties and pacts, including one wherein the two orders agreed to jointly fight against a Moslem chieftian, the Atabeg of Mosul. The Assassins were formed just prior to the First Crusade as a renegade knighted order of alchemists of the Left Hand Path, and they preceded the Templars in adopting the alchemical colors of white and red for their uniforms. It is believed that Templars' choice of uniform was influenced by the Assassins; as was their adoption of their foundational three degrees. In fact, the Templars reflected the Assassins in so many ways that the researcher and historian Godfrey Higgins was prompted to remark in his *Anacalypsis*:

"As the society of the Assassins and Templars were [I have no doubt] of the same philosophy and religion…. I believe the Templars were Assassins."

The alchemical influence of the Assassins on the Templars also inspired the design of the Knights' alchemical black and white flag, the Beausant, and their mastership of the game of chess. Another Sufi sect was especially instrumental in the transmission of sacred, alchemical building design to the Knights. This was the al-Banna, which Idries Shah refers to as the "Sufi Freemasons." The al-Banna were responsible for the construction of many Islamic mosques and temples in the Middle East within which they incorporated sacred, geometrical dimensions and shapes, including the circle and octagon, to make their enclosures alchemical crucibles. Their mastership of the art of alchemical construction was daily on display

159

The Beausant: Templar Alchemical Flag

The Assassin Leader and Alchemist, Hasan-i-Sabah

A Templar and Assassin play "alchemical" chess

The Templar Alchemical Cross Pattee Symbol

The Sinclair Engrailed Cross
At the center of the Engrailed Cross is the Templar Cross Pattee
The scallops along the shafts of the cross are indicative of the wavy
Water of Life that is produced through the union of the polarity.

161

for the Templars to study in the form of the circular dome and octagonal body of the Dome of the Rock, which provided the Knights a continual visual aid for their study since it was situated just a few hundred feet from their headquarters in the al-Aqsa Mosque. As mentioned, the number eight is an alchemical number associated with the union of the polarity of the male-female principles, especially as Heaven and Earth; and this truth was incorporated into the Dome by Sufis who painted the upper half of each of the structure's eight panels the color of the sky (and the heavens) and their lower portions the color of the Earth. Thus, the Dome of the Rock revealed itself to be a Heaven-Earth mediator and the generator of powerful alchemical energy. As a Heaven-Earth mediator the Dome was also meant to be a launching pad for travel into the heavenly dimensions. It was specifically built to enhance the power of the indwelling Stone of Foundation, which was the platform from which Mohammed ascended into Heaven and where many priests and imams ascended their consciousness into a holy communion with the Infinite. The Templars used their Sufi-inspired knowledge of the circle and octagon when they rebuilt the Church of the Holy Sepulchure, and they later drew upon this wisdom when they designed their alchemically enhanced preceptories and churches in Europe in the shape of octagons, circles and domes.

The al-Banna had been founded by Dhul'Nun al-Misri, an Egyptian alchemist who is credited with transmitting sacred geometry, alchemy and gnostic wisdom into the synthetic mysteries of the Middle Eastern Sufis. The title, Dhul'Nun, meaning "Of the Fish" or "Of the Snake," reveals that the alchemist was regarded to be an embodiment of serpent wisdom. Through decoding the ancient Egyptian knowledge inscribed on the temples of Abydos and Memphis, Dhul'Nun came to understand the ancient alchemical rites of Osiris and the Master Craftsman Ptah, who together had been revered as the synthesized deity Ptah-Sokar-Osiris. Dhul'Nun's indepth study enabled him to contribute to the foundational alchemical myth of Masonry, that of the Master Craftsman, Hiram, Hermes or CHiram, who is slain and resurrected like Osiris. It also qualified him to build alchemical temples where death and rebirth initiations could occur. The myth of the resurrected Master Craftsman Hiram would become the principal teaching tool in European Freemasonry for the initiates of the three Blue Degrees of Entered Apprentice, Fellowcraft, and Master Mason. It has been suggested that the Blue Degrees were named after the original Master Craftsman of Egypt, Ptah, the blue-man.

The Order of the Garter

Dhul'Nun's work was also influential on the Templars by helping to introduce them to the mysteries of al-Khadir, the Green Man. When the Knights learned from the Sufis that al-Khadir was synonymous with their own St. George or Green George, they amalgamated the mysteries of the two deities and observed each

April 23rd as their joint holiday. When they took the synthesized warrior St. George-al-Khadir back into Europe, he became the patron of many esoteric knighted orders, including the Order of St. George that was founded by the British King Edward III. This knighted order, which soon after its founding became known as the Order of the Garter, was given Windsor Castle and its Chapel of St. George for its official headquarters. The badge and seal of the Garter Order was a version of al-Khadir's alchemical form that was venerated by the Sufis; and the colors of al-Khadir, gold and blue, were chosen for the initiation chamber and knighting room of the royal Order of the Garter in Windsor Castle.

The Templars and the Essenes

Another important influence on the Knights Templar came from the Essenes, who transformed the Knights into experts of their secret Kabbala. Through their Essene teachers the Templars came to learn of two ancient Nasorean Messiahs, with John the Baptist having been the first and the greatest of the two. They also learned the art of Kabbalistic Magic.

According to one tradition, the Knights Templar encountered some latter-day Essenes in the Holy Land who were vestiges of those that had flourished during the time of Jesus. These "Seven Syrian Christians" sought refuge with the Templars after fleeing some inimical Moslems, and the Knights let them live among them as long as they needed to. In recompense, "the Syrians [Essenes] communicated their sublime knowledge to the [Templar chiefs], who remained as the depository until the suppression of the Order."[5]

Alchemical Legends of the Holy Grail

As mentioned, with the wisdom learned from the Essenes, and the Sufi sects of the al-Banna, Assassins, Druses, and the Yezidis, the Knights Templar were able to synthesize a Holy Grail Mystery Tradition with the Johannite Church as its foundation. The secret alchemical wisdom of their mystery school was eventually incorporated into the series of Holy Grail legends that were written by knights or Templar-influenced scholars in the Thirteenth and Fourteenth Centuries. According to Templar scholar A. E. Waite, it was through these Holy Grail legends that the Hidden Church of the Holy Grail was able to hide and transmit many of its esoteric secrets.[6]

The most extensive of all the written Holy Grail legends, and the one that explicitly reveals the foreign influences on the Templars' mystery school, is *Parzival* written by Knight Wolfram von Eschenbach around 1200 CE. Wolfram states in his text that his rendition of the Holy Grail legend was acquired from his teacher, Kyot, who had himself discovered it in one of the Sufi libraries of Toledo, Spain.

Kyot's research uncovered that the Holy Grail tradition had originated in the Middle East with an astrologer known as Flegetanis, which is a Persian name meaning "Familiar with the stars." Since Kyot found many other Persian names sprinkled throughout the legend of the Holy Grail, including Parzival or Parsifal, the protagonist of the story whose name is Persian for "Persian faith," it appears that the Holy Grail tradition must have either originated in Persia, or that Persian Sufis inserted Persian names into the legend of the Grail after migrating to the Middle East. Some modern researchers, such as the authors of *From Scythia to Camelot*, have speculated that if the legend had indeed originated in Persia, it was no doubt an evolution of the Persian Holy Grail legends, known as the *Nart Sagas*, that recount the legends of the fabled Kayanid Dynasty and its renown King Key Koshrow, the Persian counterpart of King Arthur. Key Koshrow is reputed to have ruled over a Camelot-like court with a circle of knights, called Narts, who drank from a Grail chalice called the Nartmongue.

Parzival traces the journey of the archetypal initiate, Parzival, as he goes in search of the Holy Grail to achieve immortality. In this version of the Holy Grail legend the Grail is not a cup, but the Lapis Exillis, the "Stone of Heaven," which appears to be synonymous with the Philosophers Stone of the alchemists. The text's reference to this particular manifestation of the Holy Grail clearly reveals the important influence of Sufi alchemy on the Knights Templar. Another foreign influence revealed in *Parzival* is the Fisher King, whom von Eschenbach portrays with a crown of peacock feathers. This version of the Fisher King is no doubt related to Tawsi Melek, the "Peacock King," who was the principal deity of the Yezidis, a Sufi-inspired sect that existed in Syria, Iraq, and other parts of the Middle East during the time of the Templars.

Hindu Yoga is also evident in *Parzival* as the gruesome Kundry, whose name according to the Rosicrucian adept, Manley Palmer Hall, is an evolution of Kundalini. These epithets are obviously united through their common prefix, Kun, which in the Sanscrit language denotes "burning,"a reference to the heat produced by the transformative alchemical force as it destroys all tendencies and blockages within a person which keep him or her from knowing their divine nature.

The Templar Alchemical Initiation

Sufis influences were also pronounced in the Templars' initiation rites, especially those related to Kundalini. The secret yogic wisdom of Kundalini most likely reached the Sufis when the Molsem empire extended into India, or perhaps before that time period when Hindu and Buddhist missionaries visited the Middle East during the first few centuries of the Piscean Age. The Templars' Sufi-inspired initiation rites included having an incoming Knight kissed below the navel, at the base of the spine, and upon the mouth by a receiving Knight. The two lower regions have for ages been recognized in the East as dwelling places of the Kundalini, and both are often touched or kissed by gurus today to awaken the indwelling Serpent Power. Typically, an initiating guru transmits a spark of his own Kundalini into the initiate, so the process is described as "one candle lighting another." Eastern gurus and Sufi Masters also transmit their alchemical power through their breaths, which they do by blowing or kissing parts of the body, including the face and mouth.

A Thirteenth Century manuscript, entitled *The Secret Rule*, provides proof that the Templars' infamous initiation kisses were not sexually motivated but designed to awaken the inner force. One of the many "Articles" contained within the manual states:

"Article 11.-Ritual of Reception of the Brothers-Elect: Oath to guard the secret of the Order, the least indiscretion being punishable by death. The Receiver shall kiss the Neophyte successively on the mouth, to transmit to him the breath; on the sacral plexus [base of the spine], which commands the creative force; then on the umbilicus, and finally on the virile member, image of the masculine principle."[7]

According to author Nesta Webster, other so-called heretical acts involved in the intiation of a new Knight Templar were similarly "alchemical" in that they were designed to trigger an inner reaction that would ultimately lead them to gnosis. Certain of these acts were specifically calculated to induce terror within the candidate, and thereby ultimately expand him beyond the limitations imposed upon him by his deeply ingrained beleifs. She states:

"...we have today the certainty that the Knights endured a great number of religious and moral trials before reaching the different degrees of initiation: thus, for example, the recipient might receive the injunction under pain of death to trample on the crucifix or to worship an idol, but if he yielded to the teror which they sought to inspire him he was declared unworthy of being admitted to the higher grades of the Order."[8]

The Fall of the Johannite Templars

The final fall of the Johannite Knights Templar occurred not when the Knights were arrested in 1307, but later when they were invited to the court of Pope Clement V in southern France. Fearing that the Inquisition's torture chambers had given it an unfair advantage for extracting confessions, Clement handpicked 70 Knights to visit him at his headquarters in Poitiers, where he assured them that whatever was said in his presence would not be used as evidence against their Order. However, even with the Pope's assurances, the inner circle of Templar Knights simply reiterated the same confessions of heresy that they had given to the

Inquisition while under torture. French author, Jean Robin, later commented that those 70 Templar Knights were the "nucleus" of the Templars, meaning that they were the Johannite Templars who had been most involved in the heretical practices.[9]

Of all their confessions, the curiosity and anger of the Pope was, however, most inflamed not by the Templar kisses but by the Knights' references to the mummified head of Baphomet. The Vatican hierarchy had good reason to believe that Baphomet was the head of John the Baptist; and it that were indeed true, then the alternate Johannite gnostic lineage from Jesus was very much alive and needed to be eradicated. The confessions extracted by the Inquisition regarding Baphomet revealed that the head had been in the special care of Hughes de Peraud, a Templar officer who served as second in command to Grand Master Jacques de Molay. One of the few Knights that saw the head, Knight Stephen de Troyes, confessed that Baphomet was a human head that was only put on display once a year for all the Knights to see. He claimed that the head was "very pale and discolored, with a grizzled beard like a Templar's," but that it had been given a regal appearance by having its neck covered with gold, silver and precious stones.

The current suggested locations for John's head include Rosslyn Chapel and the Languedoc region of southern France, where legends also have it that the Templars deposited the body of Mary Magdalene after transferring it from a location in the Middle East. The Languedoc has always been the headquarters of the Goddess tradition, as well as a bastion of Johannite ideology and worship. It is well known that at their height at least one-third of all the Templars' hundreds of preceptories were situated in the Languedoc. Their preceptory of Bezu was strategically constructed at one of the five corners of a huge landscape pentagram, the symbol of the Goddess, through which the continental Rose Line traverses. The Rose Line, which is another suggested location for John's head and the lost Templar treasure, runs straight north through the Languedoc and then cuts a swath through both Paris and Amiens. The rose was a symbol of alchemy and gnosis, and the Rose Line marks a dynamic energy meridian where these Left Hand Path practices can effectively be practiced, as well as where precious relics could be buried. A second Rose Line in Scotland is another candidate for the buried Templar treasure. It runs through the volcanic peaks surrounding Edinburgh and straight into Rosslyn Chapel. Perhaps John's head and the body of Mary Magdalene will resurface soon along one of these Rose Lines and serve as a stepping stone to lead us into the current revival of gnosis and alchemy across the planet.

Knight Templar Grand Master Jacques de Molay

Templar Octagonal Church in Eunate, Spain

Templar Circular Church in London

Templar Circular Preceptory in Gisors, France

Templar Alchemical Symbol
Union of Male-Female, Sun-Moon Polarity
with skull of John the Baptist

The Sub-Rosa Gnostics

According to a secret Masonic history, many years previous to their arrest in 1307 the Knights Templar had entered Europe as the "Knights of the Rosy Cross." At that time they initiated a movement of alchemical sects on the continent that adopted the symbol of a rose, or a rose attached to a cross, as their definitive symbol, thereby revealing their special affiliation to alchemy, the Goddess, and the Left Hand Path. When the French Templars were later dissolved in 1314 many of the "rose' sects they helped to form inherited the gnostic and alchemical wisdom of the Knights and officially became the new guardians of their very ancient lineage and tradition. With their help, the Johannite gnostic tradition was able to survive in Europe as the network of Sub-Rosa alchemical sects for many centuries to follow.

The Templars' title of "Knights of the Rosy Cross" was how Freemason Baron de Westerode referred to them in the 1780s during conclaves of Secret Society members that gathered together to discuss their common histories, goals and identities. Westerode, who claimed for his authority some secret archives preserved in his lodge in Sweden, also stated that the Templars and many of the other Secret Societies of Europe shared a common symbol, the rose or rose cross, as well as a common heritage that reached back to the Alexandrian Ormesius, or Ormus, founder of the Society of ORMUS whose members, the Sages of Light, were given a red cross to wear as their disinguishing symbol. Ormus was one of the gnostics of the First Century who worked within the milieu of the period to create a synthesis between the path of gnosis and fledgling Christianity. Ormus' amalgamated Society of ORMUS was, in the estimation of Westerode, the official launching pad for an ensuing Sub-Rosa movement in the West. Unfortunately, no other information about Ormus has surfaced since the time of Westerode, leaving many historians doubting his very existence. However, since "orm" in Swedish denotes snake or serpent, it is possible that Westerode's assertion cloaked a deeper meaning: that the ancient gnostic-alchemical tradition had been reshaped by one or more gnostic "Serpent" adepts of Alexandria.

Of course, as any "rose" historian will tell you, the path of the rose and its association with alchemy and gnosis is much older than Alexandria. In fact, since the dawn of history the red rose has been the symbol of both the Goddess and her alchemical power. The red rose has symbolized both the fiery, magnetic passion that results through the union of a man and woman, as well as the transformative fire that results through alchemically uniting the male and female principles, while the blossoming of the rose has represented the final blossoming and goal of alchemy, which is gnosis. Referring to the flower's alchemical associations, the great French alchemist, Fulcanelli, once proclaimed: "The rose alone represents the action of the fire and its duration,"[1] while the British esoteric historian, A.E. Waite, similarly maintained that the symbol of a rose attached to a cross was used "to indicate the work of Sacred and Divine Alchemy…."[2] Wigston, another historian of the rose tradition of alchemy, added that the symbol of the rose and its cross have been used to signify "the secret of immortality."[3] This last association has, apparently, overstepped the secret boundaries of alchemy and seeped into mass consciousness. Roses as symbols of immortality and everlasting life have adorned the caskets of the populace for many centuries.

In recorded history, the association of the rose to alchemy and passionate love can be traced back to the Middle East and the Goddess of Love in her evolution from Inanna, Ishtar, Astarte, Aphrodite and later to Venus. Among the ancients, Venus and her red rose represented the fiery power of love and attraction, whose influence through sacred sex or the inner union of the polarity can result in the production of alchemical fire and gnosis. According to Waite, the association between Goddess Venus and alchemy even included the planet she ruled, which the ancients portrayed as a star shining "before the Portal of Regenerated Life."[4] The Knights Templar, who were both alchemists and great lovers of the Goddess Venus, identified Venus as their patroness Mary Magdalene, and thereby accorded her the distinctive symbol of the rose. As an enchantress and an adept in the sexual arts and alchemy, Mary fully personified the Goddess of Love.

But besides being a traditional symbol of the Goddess, throughout the centuries the rose has also been associated with the Son of the Goddess. As noted by Waite in *The Brotherhood of the Rosy Cross*, "…the Rose belonged as much to Iaachus (Dionysus) as it did to Aphrodite." This is because the Goddess and her Son were synonymous; as mentioned, both were embraced by the Left Hand Path as the First Instructor, the Serpent on the Tree, and as embodiments of the powers of creation and/or destruction that manifest in nature as both fertility and alchemy. As a symbol of the Son of the Goddess, however, the rose might possess certain distinguishing features, such as a green center, thereby representing the Green Man residing in the bosom (the rose petals) of his mother.

Six-Headed Karttikeya emerges within a rose-colored lotus

Horus emerges from a lotus

During previous eras of history the red rose has been the special symbol of the Divine Son, Dionysus, the torch-bearing initiator of the Greek mystery rites whose early Thracian festivals included the Rose Festival, or Rosalia. The rose and/or rose cross was also a symbol of the Middle Eastern Green Man, al-Khadir, as well as his counterparts, Tammuz and Adonis, the Sons and lovers of the Goddess Venus. A close relative of the rose, the rose-colored lotus of India and Egypt, was closely associated with both Karttikeya and Horus, both of whom were born from the Goddess in Her form of a lotus.

Following the First Crusade, al-Khadir, who had been venerated by the Sufis' as their personification of the fire of alchemy, became an important figure among the Templars when the Knights identified him as the Middle Eastern counterpart of their patron, St. George or Green George. While acting on this cross-identification with the Sufis, the Templars amalgamated many of the characteristics of al-Khadir to St. George, and declared al-Khadir's holiday of April 23 to be a grand rose festival that would celebrate both deities.

According to Baron de Westerode, it was the year 1188 CE when as Knights of the Rosy Cross, the Templars rode into Europe to begin their mission of spreading the rites and wisdom of their amlagamated "rose" deity and the gnostic-alchemical path of the rose cross. Through their disseminating work, the Rosy Cross initiation rite that had been used by the Templars themselves in the Holy Land became incorporated into many or most of the fledgling Secret Societies of Europe. A few of the numerous Secret Societies that eventually adopted the Templars' Rose Croix rite included the Brethren of the Golden Rose-Croix, the Royal Order of Scotland, the Rite of Memphis and Mizraim, the Scottish Rite of Freemasonry and the Martinists.

As new initiatic societies arose in Europe under the influence of the Knights of the Rosy Cross it became common for them to choose as their patron saint the Templars' "rose" warrior that was the union of St. George and al-Khadir. In Britain, the synthesized warrior became the patron of the Order of St. George that was founded in 1348 by King Edward III. Renamed the Order of the Garter soon afterwards, this most prestigious of British knighted orders mirrored certain aspects of al-Khadir's Sufi Order, which it had been modeled after. Its membership of 26 (the King, the Prince of Wales, and 24 knights), was twice the 13 members utilized in the Sufi mystical circles of the Middle Eastern Order of St. Khadir. The knighting room of the Order of the Garter in Windsor Castle was decorated with gold and blue, the mystical colors of al-Khadir, and these colors were also incorporated into the flowing ceremonial robes of the order and its medallion of St. George. The other medallions of the Garter incorporated either al-Khadir's rose or his symbol of a red cross set within an eight-pointed star, which had been an ancient alchemical emblem of both al-Khadir and his mother, the Goddess. Even

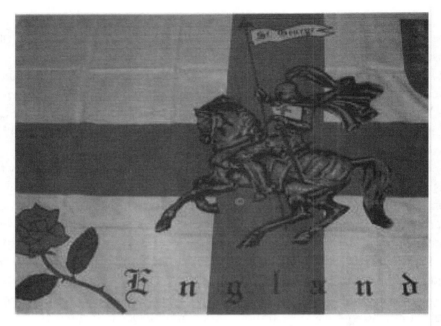

St. George and his alchemical symbols:
The Red Cross and the Red Rose

The Rose Collar of the Order of the Garter

The Alchemical Symbol of the Order of the Garter

The Knighting Room of the Order of the Garter
Windsor Castle, England

the headquarters of the Order of the Garter, the circular Windsor Castle, revealed the influence of al-Khadir. According to Idries Shah in *The Sufis,* one of the branches of the Order of St. Khadir was known as *el-mudawwira*, "the round building."

It is interesting to note that when researching her book *The Rosicrucian Enlightenment,* historian Francis Yates turned up so much evidence associating the rose cross with St. George that she was forced to conclude that the symbol's origin in Europe must have coincided with St. George and the founding of the Order of the Garter, thus indirectly linking it with the Sufis' al-Khadir and the entrance of the Knights of the Rosy Cross onto the continent. She states:

"What then of the origins of 'Rose Cross'? ... I have suggested a chivalrous origin, that it referred to the red cross of St. George of the Order of the Garter ...."[5]

An eastern clone of the Order of the Garter would surface soon after the founding of the elite British Order. Known as The Imperial and Royal Court of the Dragon, this Order was founded in 1408 by the Emperor Sigismund von Luxembourg and placed under the patronage of St. George. It was composed of 26 members, and its insignia was St. George-al-Khadir's symbol of a rose attached to a rosy cross. The medal of the Order pinned to the lapel of each member was a dragon-shaped, circular ouroborous with a fiery rosy cross attached to it. The fiery red cross revealed the fiery, alchemical nature of St. George.

The Royal Dragon Court claimed a tradition extending back to the ancient dragon courts of both the Middle East and Egypt, as well as to the Holy Grail lineage of Grail Kings of Anjou. The Court was founded on the gnostic-alchemical tradition and practiced various alchemical rites. It appears that the supposed blood sucking of one of its most notorious members, Count Vlad Basarrab, the infamous Count Dracula, may have been based on an alchemical "Starfire" ritual that can make a person immortal. The rite of "Starfire," which was descended from the earliest Dragon Kings, involves the consumption of pineal gland secretions with alchemical properties that flow out of a woman with her menstral blood.[6]

The Sufi "Path of the Rose"

In 1614 the rose cross and its undeniable link to the Sufis was publicly confirmed with the publication of a document in Germany called the *Fama Fraternitatis,* which alerted the world to the existence of the fraternity of Rose Cross initiates. This document told the story how the Rose Cross initiates were descended from the Sufis in the form of the allegorical life of Christian Rosencrutz, the supposed founder of the organization. CRC, as he is referred to in the text, was said to have been born in Germany in 1378 but left his home at an early age

The Rose Cross Insignia of
The Imperial and Royal Court of the Dragon

The Royal Court's Flaming, Alchemical Cross of St. George

in search of knowledge. He visited two prominent Sufi cities, Damascus and Fez, where he received initiations and an abundance of esoteric and alchemical wisdom from the Sufi adepts residing there. Returning to his homeland via Islamic Spain, where he received additional instruction from the Sufis, CRC compiled the knowledge he had gained into a series of books. He then gathered three dedicated and worthy students to his mission and founded "The Fraternity of the Rose Cross," later known as the Rosicrucian Order. The membership of the organization quickly expanded to eight brothers who promptly left for various parts of the globe to spread their Rose Cross wisdom. Before departing, however, they agreed that their descendants would return to their headquarters, the "House of the Holy Spirit," after 120 years.

When the Rose Cross initiates eventually returned they discovered, not unexpectedly, that CRC had long since passed away. While searching for clues regarding the location of the burial tomb of the deceased Master, the brothers were led to a chamber wherein CRC had apparently hermetically sealed himself. Breaking open the seal, the initiates immediately found themselves bathed in the glow of a supernatural light that illuminated the entire tomb. CRC was situated in the center of the tomb and his well-preserved body appeared as though it had been interred only the day before. He looked quite young, even though the brothers determined that he had lived to the ripe old age of 106 years. Studying the tomb that CRC had created for himself, they found its dimensions incorporated the Golden Mean Proportion, and it immediately became obvious to them that it had been designed to perpetually generate the preserving life force, like the tombs and pyramids of Egypt.

CRC may or may not have been a real person, however, his life story has served as an allegory to reveal the Sufi roots of the Rosicrucians. Any survey of the early Rose Cross alchemists of Europe has consistently born out the truth that many had studied with the Sufi Orders. Some had been mentored by the Sufis of the Order of al-Khadir, just as the Templars had, while others had trained within Sufi sects associated with the al-Khadir tradition. One popular Sufi sect of this genre was the Dervish Order of Qadiriyyah which was founded by the "rose" alchemist Abdul al-Khadir al-Jillani, nicknamed "The Rose of Baghdad." This distinguished Sufi is renown for having been a recluse in the Iraqi deserts for 25 years before achieving full gnosis, after which he exclaimed "Whoever understands his own self, understands God." He became an adept of the "rose" alchemical path of al-Khadir, and transmitted the power of al-Khadir when giving Baraka, or "blessing," through his hands and feet. In his *Qala'd Al-Jawahir*, "Necklaces of Gems," Abdul al-Khadir disclosed the mystical state of gnostic awareness he experienced daily. He states:

"There is a time when I do not eat until God is pleased to say: 'Abdul Khadir, get up and eat for My sake, or wear these robes to please Me.' It is men like him who would do even their daily chores only when God wants them to; of course, not for their own sake but for the sake of God, for whatever they do, they do it to please Him."

Since the Dervish Order of Qadiriyyah was one of the largest Sufi sects in the Middle East, Abdul al-Khadir's famous students came to include Europeans from many walks of life, including the great psychic and astrologer Nostradamus, who adopted some of the rose alchemical practices to help him see into the future.

Although its roots extend back to the Garden of Eden, historically the al-Khadir tradition of "rose" adepts can be traced back to Sayed Khidr Rumi Khapradari, the "Cupbearer" of Turkestan, who was an incarnation of Khadir and filled like a vessel with his alchemical power. Later, within the same lineage emerged the Sufi Suhrawardi, a famous teacher of the "Path of the Rose." Legend has it that Suhrawardi began his rose path to gnosis after a life-changing vision, when the Greek philosopher Aristotle instructed him to put aside everything and, "Know Thyself." Suhrawardi subsequently became both a great alchemist and a gnostic visionary of the Illuminist Sufi tradition that espoused the mystic teachings of the Inner Light of Gnosis. He was to become a great influence on many later Sufi Masters, including Muhyiddin Ibn 'Arabi, whose teachings were summarized by Mahmud Shabistari in his esoteric treatise, *The Secret Rose Garden*. In this fascinating expose the "Rose Garden" is defined as the inner sanctuary of contemplation and gnostic revelation. One passage of the text metaphorically summarizes the ecstasy of gnosis that is felt by an adept as "walking" among the roses of the inner Rose Garden. It states: "I shall pluck roses from the garden, but I am drunk with the scent of the rose bush."

Over time, when a Sufi on the rose path has attained the highest gnostic truth he or she becomes a Khizr (Turkish name of Khadir), a "completed Sufi,"[7] who embodies the wisdom and power of al-Khadir. Such Sufis have been known to publicly proclaim "Ana al-Haq!", meaning "Truth is Me" or "I am God." Besides the famous Sufis Suhrawardi and al-Hallaj, other Sufis who have ascended to this exalted gnostic awareness include Bayazid Bistani, Mansur Manstana, Abu Yzid and the ecstatic, Rabia, who was renown for walking through the streets of her village while announcing her plans to burn down Heaven and drown the fires of Hell so that all persons could live exclusively in each ecstatic moment on Earth.

According to the Sufi Idries Shaw, the Sufis of the rose tradition eventually produced their own "rose" vernacular to pass secret messages back and forth among themselves. They developed many "rose" words that incorporated the root, WRD, including WaRD, the term for a rose, and WiRD, the name of the Sufi Dervish dance designed to awaken the inner rose. Thus, "WiRD" or "WiRDed

Way" became synonymous with the rose path to gnosis. Shaw explains that even the German name of "Rosicrucian" originally came from an Arabic "rose" word that combined WRD with SLB, another root that denotes both "cross" and to "extract the marrow." The name Rosicrucian is, therefore, an Arabic alchemical term meaning to "extract the marrow from the rose cross." With pride, the great Sufi alchemists were known to proclaim: "We have the marrow of the Cross, while the Christians only have the crucifix."[8]

The European Sub-Rosa Sects

The Knights of the Rosy Cross and other "rose" alchemists who studied with the Sufis before returning to Europe as missionaries succeeded in creating a panoply of Rose Cross organizations across the continent. Many of the orders they helped found incorporated "rose" in their official name, while others adopted the degree of Rose Cross or Knight of the Rose Cross as one of their higher levels of advancement. The image of a crusading Knight of the Rosy Cross also spread into other mystical and artistic milieu in Europe. It became part of the legend of King Arthur and his Knights, who were often portrayed sitting around a Round Table with a huge rose at its center, and a skeletal Knight of the Rosy Cross flying his rose banner was adopted as a symbol of the 13th card of the Major Arcana of the Tarot, revealing that "death" referred to by the card was an alchemical death.

The Royal Order of Scotland

One of the first "rose" organizations founded by the Knights of the Rosy Cross was the Royal Order of Scotland. Legend has it that when many Templars escaped to Scotland in 1307 they were protected by the excommunicated monarch King Robert the Bruce, who founded the Royal Order for them to disappear into after the Knights had shown impeccable courage and loyalty to the Scottish throne by assisting him in the defeat of the English at the Battle of Bannockburn. The Royal Order he created consisted of two degrees, one of which was, not surprisingly, Knight of the Rose Cross.

Once in Scotland, the fleeing knights were met by an earlier wave of Rosy Knights who had settled upon land given them by King Robert and the earlier Scottish King, David I. According to Baron de Westerode, these Knights had arrived in Scotland in 1188CE as a delegation consisting of three Knights of the Rosy Cross. In their new home they founded the "Order of Masons of the East."

King Robert's Royal Order of Scotland was a Freemasonic organization headquartered at Kilwinning, the "Mother Grand Lodge" of all Freemasonry. This order of Speculative Freemasonry gave the Templars a prime vehicle to transmit, and thereby preserve, a good measure of their Johannite and alchemical wisdom. The Royal Order revealed its affiliation to the Knights of the Rosy Cross by choosing

Knight of the Rosy Cross on the Tarot Death Card
The Death is an Alchemical Death

King Arthur's Round Table with its Central Rose
Arthur's Grail legend is based upon Knights of the Rosy Cross

181

as its emblem a cross covered by five small roses. Its official charter also revealed that the Royal Order was not only linked to the Templar Order, but a continuation of it. It stated that the earliest roots of the Royal Order were Mt. Moriah, which is a name of the "Temple Mount" where the Knights had their first headquarters in Jerusalem.

According to Waite, one of the immediate goals of the Royal Order was to realign Freemasonry with its Templar origins and "to correct the errors and reform the abuses that had crept in amongst the Three Degrees of St. John's Masonry."[9]The Blue or St. John's Degrees apparently had arrived in Scotland in 1188 with the Knights of the Rosy Cross and, over time, had become distorted through their wrongful observance in the Lodge of Kilwinning.

Robert the Bruce made himself, as well as all future Scottish monarchs, the Grand Master of the Royal Order, and instituted two degrees: Knight of the Royal Order of Heredom of Kilwinning, and Knight of the Rose Cross. The "Heredom" of Kilwinning was a metaphorical "Mountain of Initiation"[10] that had to be climbed by the rose alchemist before gnosis could be achieved. This concept may have been an adaptation of the metaphor once promulgated by the Assassin Grand Master, Hasan-i-Sabah, who made the ascent of consciousness to the highest levels of gnosis a metaphorical climb up mythical Mount Kaf. Hasan fully developed this concept in his *Sargozast-I Sayyid-na*, wherein he referred to the steps of alchemy that lead to gnosis as stairs leading to the summit of Kaf.

Legend has it that Robert the Bruce also appointed one of the Rex Deus families of Scotland, the Sinclairs, to serve as the hereditary Grand Masters of the Crafts and Guilds of the country. This important position included overseeing both the Royal Order and all the other Freemasonry lodges. Later, when the Grand Lodge of Scotland was founded in 1736, William Sinclair was elected as its first Grand Master, thus perpetuating the Sinclair lordship. The destiny of the Sinclairs ultimately became entwined with that of both the Templars and Freemasons, a truth revealed in Rosslyn Chapel where motifs of both organizations are displayed.

When the Royal Order was taken to France with its Grand Master, the exiled King James II, it began its evolution into what would become the modern Scottish Rite of Freemasonry. One of the patriarchs of the future Scottish Rite was Michael Ramsay, a Knight of the Order of St. Lazarus, who resided in Paris but had been born near Kilwinning and was very well educated in the rites and history of the Royal Order. From his days in Kilwinning Knight Ramsay knew the important link between the Templars and Freemasons and inculcated this truth to a forum of Freemasons during his famous Paris oration in 1736. During his pivotal speech Ramsay publicly stated that the true originators of the Craft were the Crusading Knights, i.e., the Templars. Ramsay also stated that according to the records at his disposal, the Lodge of Kilwinning had been founded in 1286, thereby re-

*The Two Johns: Johannite Grand Masters
who became the Patron Saints of Freemasonry*

vealing that Freemasonry had been in existence in Scotland even before the founding of Robert the Bruce's Royal Order. Apparently not only the Blue Degrees or St. John's degrees were introduced at Kilwinning, but the patron saints of the Johannite Templars, John the Apostle and John the Baptist, were also chosen there to be the patrons of all Freemasonry.

Legend has it that the two degrees of the Royal Order evolved into the 25 degrees of the Rite of Heredom at Kilwinning, and then this "Rite of Perfection" was taken to Paris by Prince Charles Edward Stuart, the "Pretender" to the throne of Scotland. Charles assumed the postion of Grand Master of this Rite and initiated into it new aspirants from all over France. Later, in 1762, at Charleston, South Carolina, the 25 degrees of the Rite of Heredom evolved into the 33 degrees of the Scottish Rite of Freemasonry.

The Scottish Rite currently contains the Knight of the Rose Croix as its Eighteenth Degree, and another Templar-related level, that of the Knight of the East and West, comprises its Seventeenth Degree. Both levels are a direct evolution of the Knights of the Rosy Cross tradition and are full of Johannite, gnostic, and alchemical symbolism. During initiation into the Knight of East and West, which is essentially an initiation into the Johannite Templar tradition, the initiating "Venerable Master" assumes the role of John the Baptist and all the attending Freemasons are recognized as the "disciples of John the Baptist." The new Knight of East and West receives a new regalia with both alchemical and Johannite symbols, including an alchemical collar with polar opposite white and black strands of fabric. He also acquires an alchemical medal with the image of a lamb seated on John the Divine's *Book of Revelations* that is composed of the polar opposite silver and gold metals. The medal itself is seven sided, corresponding to the "Seven Seals" within Revelations which, for the alchemist, are also the seven chakras or gnostic centers and the seven alchemical stages that culminate in gnosis.

When the Masons enters the Eighteenth Degree of the Knight of the Rose Croix he becomes fully inducted into the mysteries of the Knights of the Rosy Cross. He also becomes known as Perfect Prince of Heredom and Knight of the Eagle and Pelican, and receives a Masonic apron embroidered with the alchemical symbols of a skull and crossbones, roses and a serpent encoiled around a globe. The medal of the Eighteenth Degree incorporates the rose, the cross, the compass and both the pelican and the eagle, one on each side. According to the 33rd degree Freemason, Manly Palmer Hall, the image of the pelican feeding its chicks engraved on the medal is an alchemical motif. He states:

"As the Rose Croix degree is based upon Rosicrucian and Hermetic symbolism, it follows that the pelican presents one of the vessels in which the experiments of alchemy are performed and its blood that mysterious tincture by which base metals are transmuted into spiritual gold."[11]

***Emblem of the Royal Order of Scotland
with its five roses***

***The Medal of Knight of the Rose Croix
18th Degree of the Scottish Rite of Freemasonsy***

The Strict Observance

One of the aspirants initiated by Charles Edward Stewart into the Rite of Perfection was the German born Baron Karl Gottlieb von Hund. In attendance of those elite Knights gathered for his induction was Prince Charles Edward Stuart and the mysterious "Knight of the Red Feather," whose epithet may reveal an affiliation to the Rose Cross tradition. According to the recent research of authors Baigent and Leigh, the identity of the Knight of the Red Feather was Alexander Seton, a member of one of Scotland's Rex Deus families.

Following his initiation, Baron von Hund was instructed to found a satellite organization of the Scottish Templars in Germany. His ensuing organization became known both as the Strict Observance, as well as "The Brethren of John the Baptist." Although the Baron was the visible leader of the German order he claimed his instructions came from an unseen Templar hierarchy headquartered in Scotland. These were known as the Baron's "Unknown Superiors," and supposedly included Prince Charles Edward Stuart as well as a lineage of Scottish Knights Templar descended from the French Templar Pierre D'Aumont, the Prior of Auvergne, who fled France in 1307. Von Hund claimed that Pierre D'Aumont had succeeded Jacques de Molay as Templar Grand Master and then brought the knighted Order directly to Scotland following its invasion by the Inquisition.

Although the Strict Observance grew slowly, it soon went through a major growth spurt that made it the most popular Templar sect in both Germany and throughout most of Europe. At its apogee the Strict Observance assimilated into its fold some of the most important luminaries of the Templar hierarchy in Europe, including St. Germain and Cagliostro, who were also lifetime members of the alchemical rose tradition. Then, just as quickly, the appeal of the Strict Observance diminished and it flamed out. States historian Robert Freke Gould in *Gould's History of Freemasonry*:

"For twenty years from its birth [the Strict Observance] either lay dormant, or made only infinitesimal progress; during the next twenty years it pervaded all continental Europe to the almost entire exclusion of every other system; within the next ten it had practically ceased to exist...."

The Rosicrucians

"The Successors of the Ancient Adepts Rose-Croix, abandoning the austere and hierarchal Science of their Ancestors in Initiation, became a Mystic Sect, united with many of the Templars, the dogmas of the two intermingling, and beleived themselves to be the sole depositaries of the secrets of the *Gospel of St. John*, seeing in its allegorical series of rites proper to complete the initiation."

Albert Pike in *Morals and Dogma*

This passage by Grand Master Freemason Albert Pike discloses an ancient union between the Knights Templar and Rosicrucians and the founding of a united Johannite sect. Their union occured numerous times over the course of hundreds of years, one of which was July 27, 1586, when in Luneberg, Germany, a special conference was held known as the Cruce Signatorum Conventus, the "Sign of the Cross Convention." It was here that the Knights of the Rosy Cross officially united with the "Brotherhood of the Rosy Cross," or Rosicrucians, to produce the Militia Crucifera Evangelica, the "Evangelical Army of the Cross," whose stated goal was to protect the symbol of the rose cross from being used in the future as a symbol of war or any other destructive movement or purpose, even thought its hidden agenda was to spread and practice the gnostic-alchemcial rites symbolized by the rose cross. The architect behind this union, and the organizer of the conference, was Simon Studion, a high ranking Rosicrucian. Little more is known about the Militia Crucifera Evangelica other than what Studion later recorded in succinct passages inserted into his magnum opus, *Naometria*.

The Militia Crucifera Evangelica was revived in 1990 by Gary Stewart, a former Imperator of the Rosicrucian sect of AMORC, the Ancient Mystical Order Rosae Crucis, who named his new organization the Order of the Knights of the Militia Crucifera Evangelica. Since then, both knight chivalry and the Templars' predilection to spread the gnostic-alchemcial path and raise the consciousness of humanity have been showcased and championed by the KMCE. The altruistic mission statement of the organization is as follows:

"The KMCE is directed to peacefully promote religious freedom, freedom of thought, and freedom of inquiry. The purpose of the KMCE is to establish an exoteric body of Light to direct and guide humanity towards evolution and personal development."

Gary Stewart and the other historians of KMCE currently maintain that the Militia Crucifera Evangelica was an important stepping stone that culminated in a Seventeenth Century movement marked by a massive outpouring of previously secret alchemical and gnostic wisdom. The beginning of this outpouring coincided with a public manifesto in 1614 announcing the existence of the Rosicrucians. Under the explicit title of the *Fama Fraternitatis Rosae Crucis*, meaning the "Existence of the Brotherhood of the Rosy Cross," this manifesto claimed that the Rosicrucians were not a new organization but had been in existence for many centuries. Their sudden appearance on the world stage at that time was part of their continual cycle of outer and inner activity, and it was again time to take the rose teachings of alchemy into the world. In their follow-up manifesto issued in 1615, the *Confessio Fraternitatis*, meaning the "Confession of the Brotherhood," the members of the Rose Cross tradition made it irrefutably clear that they were ready to protect their gnostic-alchemical practices and teachings at all costs from those who would seek to destroy or denigrate them. They even instructed the faithful to "denounce" the Pope who, since the publication of the *Fama*, had become one of their prime detractors. Thus, it appeared that the members of the Rose Cross tradition were ready to become an army of spiritual warriors and a major force for positive change in the world.

In the wake of the Confessio arrived an alchemical treatise called the *Nuptia Chymica* or "Chymical Marriage." Authored by the Rosicrucian leader Johan Valentin Andreas, this treatise ostensibly gave additional information regarding the Brotherhood of the Rosy Cross, along with some of their previously secret mysteries of alchemy. Written in cryptic and allegorical imagery, which was typical of the alchemical writing of the period, this treatise revealed the stages of alchemical transformation in the form of a wedding allegory that occurred between a king and queen (symbolic of the male/female polarity) over the course of seven days (representing seven alchemical stages). At the outset of the treatise its narrator and protagonist, the archetypal alchemist, Christian Rosencrutz, is fully immersed in the activities at the wedding, which allegorically reveal the seven stages of alchemy. The culminating moment of the alchemical wedding arrived on the Seventh Day when all the guests simultaneously completed their alchemical activities and were collectively annointed "Knights of the Golden Stone." CRC recounted his own induction into this exclusive order:

"Hereupon I prepared myself for the way, put on my white linen coat, girded my loins, with a blood-red ribbon bound cross-ways over my shoulder: In my hat I stuck four roses."

Through the description of his new regalia as a Knight of the Golden Stone Rosencrutz ostensibly identified himself and his new order with the Knights of the Rosy Cross. A knight covered in white linen crossed with a blood red ribbon and surmounted with a hat covered in roses was one of many descriptions of a Knight of the Rosy Cross and his regalia in the Seventeenth Century.

After the fanfare accompanying the *Nuptia Chymica* had subsided, a noticeable pale and silence fell over much of Europe as the next eagarly waited treatise failed to materialize. This, or course, fueled speculation that the organization was a hoax or that it had returned to another long period of secrecy. We may never know what clandestine operations were launched during this time by the Order of the Rose Cross, but many alchemists of the age confessed later that, after reading the manifestos, they had gone in search of the fraternity. Most were dissapointed in their quest, including the great alchemist, Robert Fludd, who confessed to having been repeatedly frustrated while trying to draw the Rosy Cross brothers out of the shadows. However, even if he had achieved contact with the order there is no guarantee that he would have ever publicly confessed to the liason. As Rosicrucian Manly Palmer Hall informs us, a true Rosicrucian was always silent regarding his connections to the mysterious Rose Cross order. You were chosen by the secret votaries of the Rose Cross, not the other way around. And if you were one of the fortunate few, sooner or later an initiate would mysteriously show up at your door. As Hall states in *The Secret Teachings of All Ages:*

"Efforts to join the Order were apparently futile, for the Rosicrucians always chose their disciples. Having agreed on one who they believed would do honor to their illustrious fraternity, they communicated with him in one of many mysterious ways.

"Alchemists were sometimes visited in their laboratories by mysterious strangers, who delivered learned discourses concerning the secret processes of the Hermetic arts...."

One reason secrecy was paramount among the Rosicrucians is because many of their practices had been labeled heretical and/or illegal by officials of the Right Hand Path. The Pope and many of Europe's Catholic royalty had made it illegal to produce alchemical gold, and charges of heresy would be swiftly brought against anyone subscribing to an alchemical philosophy linked to the Sufis, the Jews or any other "heathen" tradition. The Vatican was well aware that certain alchemists had studied in Moslem countries beginning with the premier alchemist, the Spaniard Ramon Lully, who had spent much of his life studying with the Sufis in the North African countries of Tunisia and Morocco. The renegade Swiss physician, Paracelsus, was also under scrutiny by the Catholic authorities for having spent much time traveling among the Sufis in the Middle East, as well as for creating alchemical elixirs back in Europe that he claimed were efficacious for healing, longevity and transformation. Paracelsus also contributed to the growing alchemical vernacular of the continent by identifying the alchemical force by its Sufi name, the "Azoth." Another Rosicrucian alchemist and eternal archenemy of the Church, Alessandro Cagliostro, also learned the art of transmutation among the Sufis of North Africa and the Middle East. In his autobiography he specifically mentions the Sufis of Medina, Mecca, and Fez as the teachers who most profoundly influenced him and the adept alchemist he became.

The Jewish alchemical influence on the Rose Cross alchemists came through the Kabbalistic alchemists of the Middle East who migrated to Spain and the Languedoc region of southern France to disseminate their wisdom. Later, with the rise of a Protestant Europe, Jewish Kabbalistic adepts found themselves suddenly free to settle in many of the progressive regions on the continent associated with alchemical research, including Prague and the city of Troyes in northern France. The Frenchman Nicholas Flamel is well known for having acquired his alchemical wisdom from a manual written by "Abraham the Jew, Prince, Priest, Levite, Astrologer, and Philiosopher." Flamel ventured to Spain where he found a Jewish

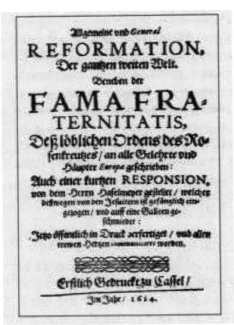

The Fama Fraternitatis

Johann Valentin Andrea
Rosicrucian Grand Master

190

The Alchemical Marriage of the King and Queen from Andrea's Chemical Wedding

The Alchemist Paracelsus and his Azoth

alchemist to help him decode the book. When his Jewish mentor fell ill and died soon afterwards, Flamel returned home and succeeded in creating both the Philosophers Stone and the Elixir of Immortality.

Another important influence on the European alchemists was the Hermetic tradition of Thoth-Hermes that had originated in Egypt. After hundreds of years of being hidden and preserved in Greece following the decline of Alexandria, the manuscripts comprising the *Corpus Hermeticum* were taken to Italy and translated into Latin by Marsilio Ficino (1433-1499). The most important of these texts was, of course, the Thirteen Precepts of the Emerald Tablet, which, with its numerous commentaries, became the definitive manual for all European alchemists seeking to create the Philosophers Stone and the Elixir of Immorality.

A less pivotal Egyptian influence on the Rose Cross tradition apparently predates Alexandria and the *Corpus Hermeticum* by at least one thousand years. According to Harvey Spencer Lewis, founder of the American Rosicrucian sect known as *The Ancient Mysticathe Order Rosae Crucis,* or AMORC, much of the Egyptian wisdom in his Roscrucian Order can be traced back to the Pharaoh Thothmoses III of the Eighteenth Dynasty who founded the first historical Rose Cross sect in a temple in Karnak. His incipient sect, known as the Illuminati, reached its pinnacle under his great grandson, the Pharaoh Akhenaton, who is said to have moved his government administration to Tel El Amarna and built a temple-monastery in the alchemical shape of a huge cross. After Akhenaton, the rose tradition apparently became somewhat circumspect and hidden in Egypt until its revival in Alexandria.

Rosicrucian Sects Worldwide

AMORC is one of many Rosicrucian sects that appeared on the horizon during the Nineteenth and Twentieth Centuries. These sects followed of the heels of the pioneering work of the *Order of the Golden and Rosy Cross* that was founded in Germany by Rosicrucian alchemists claiming to be direct lineal descendants of the authors of the Seventeenth Century manifestos. The founders of the *Order of the Golden and Rosy Cross* adopted the three primary degrees of Freemasonry as their novice levels, and the higher degrees were comprised of the alchemical practices of the Left Hand Path. "Rose" legend had it that some of the early initiates of the Order of the Rosy Cross had founded Freemasonry as a preparatory organization for the higher, alchemical degrees of the Rose Cross, so the *Order of the Golden and Rosy Cross* was simply following that tradition. When ready, however, the Order's members were introduced to the practices of pure alchemy contained within their source-books that included *The Perfect and True Preparation of the Philosophers Stone according to the Secret of the Brotherhoods of the Golden and Rosy Cross* by the Rosicrucian Sincerus Renatus.

The *Order of the Golden and Rosy Cross* would ultimately become the most popular Rosicrucian society to ever exist in Europe, and it would eventually establish many franchises in Germany, Austria, Hungary and Poland. The organization also established a standardized model that was adopted by many future Rosicrucian fraternities. Its levels and curriculum were replicated in the 1800s by the *Societas Rosicruciana in Scotia*, as well as other spin-off sects that arose in England, America and around the globe. The most famous and influential of these, the *Societas Rosicruciana in Anglia*, was founded in 1865 by the Freemason, Robert Wentworth, and gained prominence under its Supreme Magus, William Wynn Westcott, the coroner of the British Crown. Westcott, and his Rosicrucian brothers, Samuel Liddell "MacGregor" Mathers and William Robert Woodman, united as co-founders of the *Hermetic Order of the Golden Dawn*, which was modeled after the *Societas Rosicruciana in Anglia*, albeit with guidance and esoteric information provided from the secret German adept, Fraulein Anna Sprengel, and some of Baron von Lund's Unseen Superiors.

Through a series of levels or degrees, the alchemical rites of the Golden Dawn were designed to transport an initiate into the transcendental realms of gnostic consciousness. Mathers synthesized these rites from clues he discovered while translating numerous old esoteric books in the British Museum, including *The Book of the Sacred Magic of Abramelin the Mage, The Kabbalah Unveiled, The Key of Solomon, The King*, and *The Lesser Key of Solomon*.

The most renown member to emerge within the Golden Dawn was Aleister Crowley, a towering genius whose brilliant intellect was exceeded only by his prodigious vices. Crowley was alternately a leading member of the *Ordo Templi Orientis* (OTO), the "Oriental Templars," whose founders, Carl Kellner, Heinrich Klein, Franz Hartmann, and Theodor Reuss, professed to have inherited the sexual tantric secrets of the original Templars. Crowley took these ancient sexual rites to new extremes and claimed to have achieved exalted gnostic states of consciousness through his experimentation with them. He supposedly traveled astrally through many of the Thirty Aeons that had once ben mentioned by the Alexandrian gnostics and later revised and updated in the Seventeenth Century by John Dee as Enochian Magic. Crowley became notorious for taking the title, Baphomet, the "Beast of Revelation," and for authoring the *Book of the Law* whose salient passage reflects ancient gnostic sentiment: "Do as thou wilt shall be the whole of the Law."

The Rosicrucian movement in America began in earnest in 1868 under the pioneering lead of Pascal Beverly Randolph, who claimed that he had been initiated into the *The Societas Rosicruciana in Anglia* while traveling in Great Britain. The Rosicrucian sect that was founded by Randolph was principally based around sexual rites and magic that he had learned from tantric masters but not sanctioned by the SRIA. Following the demise of his organization Dr. George

The Rosicrucians' Alchemical Rose
Bees collect the sweet nectar, the Gnosis

The Rosicrucians' Alchemical Rose Cross

The Rosicrucians' "Hidden College" of Alchemy

Winslow Plummer made further inroads in America with his *The Societas Rosicruciana in America*, but he soon lost interest in the sect and it languished for just a short time afterwards.

The heyday of American Rosicrucian sects was soon to follow during the early years of the Twentieth Century. In 1908, Max Heindel founded *The Rosicrucian Fellowship* after claiming to have been initiated on a mountaintop in Germany by Rosicrucian adepts who were in direct line to the authors of the *Fama* and *Confessio*, but it soon became obvious to his peers that many of his Rosicrucian teachings came predominantly out of his own head. Heindel's organization, which still exists in California, was succeeded in 1920 by the *Fraternitas Rosæ Crucis* founded by Reuben Swinburne Clymer, an irascible maverick who claimed descent from Pascal Beverly Randolph's group. Clymer stubbornly maintained for many years that his was the only true authorized Rosicrucian organization in America, even after Harvey Spencer Lewis made similar claims for AMORC. Clymer lashed out at AMORC, but his ruthless attack backfired when Harvey Spencer Lewis was able to produce evidence that his group was not only the first and oldest American Rosicrucian sect, but that it had a direct link to Rosicrucians who had settled Pennsylvania in 1693. Lewis' own initiation into the Rosicrucians had supposedly been administered through the auspices of the *Antiquus Arcanus Ordo Rosae Rubae Aureae Crucis*, which he claimed to have visited in Toulouse, France, in 1909. Lewis eventually embellished AMORC with rites acquired from the OTO, thus linking AMORC with the original Knights Templar.

The Priory of Sion

Another branch of Rose Cross alchemists in Europe was the Priory of Sion, an esoteric sect that made its existence known in the 1950s with claims of being historically linked to the Knights Templar. The Priory of Sion, whose name can be translated as "The Priory of John," thus linking it to the Johannites, came suddenly and prominently into mass consciousness with the publication of *Holy Blood, Holy Grail*, an international bestseller of the 1980s that referred to the organization as the guardian of a supposed bloodline created through the union of Jesus and Mary Magdalene. The authors of the book were able to establish contact with Pierre Plantard, the Grand Master of the Priory of Sion, and through him learn the secret history of this mysterious organization.

Holy Blood, Holy Grail contains a history of the Priory of Sion that is identical to that of other Rosicrucian sects, thereby revealing it to be a branch of the Rose Cross and corroborating the testimonies of many authors who had alluded to an early union between the Templars and Rosicrucians. The book traces the Priory's history back to the Alexandrian gnostic adept, Ormus, the founder of the "Order of the Rose Cross" mentioned by Baron de Westerode, before moving forward in time to its affiliation with the Knights of the Rosy Cross. The book states that the Knights Templar began as a branch of the Priory of Sion, so apparently for many years they manifested together as the united Knights of the Rosy Cross. These two orders coexisted under the same Grand Masters until 1188, when a split occurred that history records as the "Splitting of the Elm." This is the year Baron de Westerode maintained that the Knights of the Rosy Cross rode into Europe to transmit their alchemical wisdom into fledgling Freemasonry. Following the split, the Priory of Sion functioned principally under its alternate name, L'Ordre de la Rose-Croix Veritas, "The True Order of the Rose Cross," and established itself in the heartland of Europe with the express purpose of protecting the Bloodline. As latter-day Johannites, the Priory continued the tradition of designating its Grand Masters John I, II, III. Supposedly John XIII of this line was the great artist, Leonardo da Vinci, whose paintings of John the Baptist revealed the classic Johannite wisdom that John was superior and ascendant to Jesus. The rest of the Prioy's Grand Masters are identical to those of the Rosicrucians so there can be no doubt the organization has been a branch of, or synonymous with, the fraternity of the Rose Cross.

The Count of Saint Germain

There were many administrators of the panoply of Sub-Rosa sects, but one will always stand head and shoulders above the rest as the universal Grand Magistrate of them all. This was Count de Saint Germain, an initiate of all Secret Societies and the honorary head of their united Sub-Rosa alliance. St. Germain typically wore a Cross Pattée around his neck to reveal his link to the latter-day Johannite Templars, which manifested in Europe as the Brethren of John the Baptist and the "Knights of St. John the Evangelist from the east of Europe." He continually served as the official representative of the Johannite Templars and was often found "going from Lodge to Lodge to establish communication between them."[12]

St. Germain's knowledge of alchemy and gnosis is legendary. He is reputed to have mastered most languages and traveled throughout China, India and the Middle East on numerous occasions while gathering gostic and alchemical secrets that he used back in Europe to make both the Philosophers Stone and the Elixir of Immortality. He is even reputed to have been able "to fuse diamonds so that there was no trace of the operation."[13] His synthesized potions apparently kept him alive and young looking for many centuries, and European witnesses, including Voltaire, are on record as having seen St. Germain on occasions many years apart and testifying that he had not aged a day in the interim. Saint Germain would occasionally give his age away in social gatherings by referring to conversations he had had with Cleopatra or the Queen of Sheba. At other times, Saint

*St. Germain (far right) poses with Kuthumi, Master Morya
and Madam Blavatsky one hundred years
after his supposed "death"*

Germain, who was a great gnostic and acted in accordance with his inner inspiration, would appear "mad" to the un-initiated. For this reason he sometimes found himself escorted to the local jailhouse for unexplainable and unruly conduct.

St. Germain claimed to have Rosicrucian roots and been the natural or adopted son of the Rosicrucian and Kabbalistic adept, Comes Cabalicus.[14] His entire life was linked to Europe's Sub-Rosa confederacy, which he rose to the summit of as its distinguished leader. Some of the later initiations he administered for those entering the Knights of the Rosy Cross occurred, suitably, in a large castle in Holstien, Germany. Here, in 1785, he inducted into the Knights of the Rosy Cross none other than the person who would become his second-in-command, Count Alessandro Cagliostro, and his wife, Lorenza.

When it appeared that reform was needed within Freemasonry, Saint Germain rose to the occasion and became one of the principle driving forces behind the creation of Paris' Lodge of Amis Reunis, which served as a dynamic vehicle for change. The goal of this progressive lodge was to synthesize all the divergent Freemasonry sects into one planetary Masonic tradition. To support this effort, St. Germain was known to have regularly given lectures to the members of the Amis Reunis regarding the unification of all religions and the gnostic-alchemical path that underlies them. His meetings are documented to have attracted a large audience in lodges located upon the Paris' Rue Platriere and Rue de la Sourdiere.[15]

Saint Germain is reputed to have passed away sometime in the late 1780s, although it is believed by many occultists that he eventually achieved immortality and has been residing somewhere in the East down to the present time.

The Masonic Congress of the Lodge of Philalethes

The Lodge of Amis Reunis, the "Reunion of Friends," was officially founded in 1771 as a synthesis of the teachings and rites of all Masonic lodges. Its founder, Savalette de Langes, was a high initiate of Freemasonry and "versed in all the mysteries, in all the lodges, and all the plots."[16] As Keeper of the Royal Treasury and Officer of the Grand Orient, Savalette was recognized as one of the leading experts of all the Secret Societies of the period and a friend of St. Germain. His work of synthesis bore fruit when in 1773 he devised the Rite of Philalethes "out of Swedenborgian, Martinist and Rosicrucian mysteries…"[17] This was calculated to be the Masonic rite that would unite all Freemasonry.

Savalette's Lodge of Amis Reunis eventually sponsored a Masonic Congress in Paris in 1785 to officially discuss the links that united all the Masonic and Sub-Rosa sects and reunite them into one grand order. Besides working to create one universal Masonic lodge, this pivotal congress answered many unspoken occult questions regarding the chain of Secret Societies that had sequentially begotten each other since the time of the Alexandrian Gnostics and the Knights Templar.

The findings of the conference were later summarized by Gérald Encausse, or "Papus," a high ranking member of the Martinist sect of Freemasons that co-sponsored the conference. Papus stated that the long chain of transmission had moved from "The Gnostic sects, the Arabs [Sufis], Alchemists, Templars, Rosicrucians, and lastly the Freemasons...."[18]

The list of attendees at the Paris Congress read like a who's who of Secret Society royalty. At the top of the list were the elite nobles, Saint Germain and Cagliostro, who came together as official representatives of the Johannite Knights Templar. The French initiates included the famous hypnotist Mesmer, as well as St. Martin, Grand Master of the Martinists, and the Swedish delegation included historian Baron de Westerode. The German attendees included Duke Ferdinand of Brunswick, Ludwig Prince of Hesse, as well as the conference's Secretary General, Baron de Gleichen, an intimate friend of both St. Germain and Cagliostro. De Gleichen set the tone for the conference when he disclosed some Rosicrucian history that maintained that the members of the Rosy Cross were the true founders of the Freemasons, and that the ancient Rose Cross Grand Masters were denominated John I, II, III and so on, thereby revealing that the Craft had emerged from a branch of the Johannite Templars. De Gleichen's disclosure was not new. The Johannite affiliation to Freemasonry had previously been established by many esoteric sources, including the *Cologne Record,* which in 1535 published an article that stated that after 1440 the Johannites, or the "Brotherhood of St. John," had naturally evolved into the Freemasons.[19] Johannism had also become visible in almost every aspect of Freemasonry, including its patron saints, the Johannite Grand Masters, John the Apostle and John the Baptist. The "staffs" of the two Johns lined almost every lodge floor, and their holidays, June 24 and December 27, were the most sacred days in the Freemasons' annual calendar. Possibly the most important day in the history of Freemasonry is John the Baptist's day in 1717. It was on June 24, 1717, that Freemasonry became a public institution through the unvieling of the world's first Grand Lodge of Freemasonry in London.

Ultimately, the Masonic Congress of the Lodge of Philalethes would become pivotal in another way. It paved the way for the French Revolution and the possibility of creating a one-world spirituality based upon gnosis and alchemy. To accomplish this global mission, the Lodge of Amis Reunis submitted a plan to bring together a unique group of revolutionaries. They would include:

"...[T]he subversives from all other lodges: Philalethes, Rose-Croix, members of the Loge des Neuf Soeurs [The Lodge of the Nine Sisters] and of the Loge de la Candeur and of the most secret committees of the Grand Orient, as well as deputies from the Illumines [the Illuminati] in the provinces."[20]

The greatest of revolutionaries, the Illuminati, were represented at the Congress by two of their Bavarian initiates, Johann Joachim Christoph "Amelius" Bode and Baron de Busche, who sought to rally the assembled congregation to their conspiracy of destroying all the royal houses of Europe, beginning with the French monarchy. Their grandiose plan, although radical, was certainly not new. It was simply the end product of a conspiratorial movement that had been in motion since the time of the Sufis.

A Knight of the Rosy Cross
by Ron Richardson

The Gnostic Conspiracy

The Rose Cross Confederacy

The plot hatched at the Paris Congress for a one-world spirituality had many analogues in the past. There had been previous attempts at the creation of a one-world spirituality by the Sufis, the Knights Templar, and most recently, in the Sixteenth Century, by Sub-Rosa sects who hatched a plot to create a Rose Cross Confederacy across Europe wherein the gnostic-alchemical path could be promulgated and practiced without fear of censure and/or torture by the Catholic Church. The Sub-Rosa plot pivoted around the strategic marriage of Princess Elizabeth, daughter of James I of Great Britain, to Frederick V, Elector Palatine of the Rhine, who together would rule as monarchs over a united Rose Cross Confederacy.

The success of the Sub-Rosa plot was predicted because it came on the heels of Martin Luther's Reformation and the panoply of Protestant nations that resulted from it. One leader of the Protestant movement who arose to disempower the Vatican was Queen Elizabeth I, the Tudor "Rose Queen" and champion of serpent wisdom who sought Protestant alliances for England against the juggernaut of Catholic nations that maintained their supremacy on the continent was God-given. One spy in Elizabeth's employ who was instructed to to keep tabs on the multitude of intrigues among the Catholic countries was none other than the famous alchemist and court astrologer John Dee, the original 007, who would later be instrumental in the public unveiling of the Rosicrucians in Bavaria in 1614. When Elizabeth's successor, James I, followed her to the throne of Great Britain he inherited the queen's court of astrologers and alchemists, as well as her ambitious campaign to liberate Europe. He also inherited the Queen's newly restored Order of the Garter, whose revival coincided with a great influx of renewed interest throughout Europe for the Knights Templar and their Holy Grail Mysteries.

Queen Elizabeth I, the Tudor Rose Queen

Elizabeth wears the Serpent of Wisdom on her arm

When the Sub-Rosa plot was put into motion with the strategic wedding, Frederick V began his ascendency as leader of the Rose Cross Confederacy by becoming formally inducted into the Order of the Garter, thereby aligning him with all the Sub-Rosa sects and their "rose" deity, St. George. Frederick's future thus became inextricably linked to the ambitions of both the early Templars and the British monarchy when in a special ceremony:

"A jewel-studded George-the pendant of St. George and the Dragon which depends from the great collar of the Order-was presented by the King to his future son-in-law, and his fiancé also presented him with a George, probably a Lesser George of the smaller version of the pendant worn on occasions when the full regalia of the Order were not worn…"[1]

To cement his affiliation with St. George and the Order of the Garter, during a public display of fireworks that night Frederick V played the role of St. George while donning the special regalia of the ancient Knight of the Rose. The festivities reached a cresendo with the ensuing marriage nuptials of Frederick and Elizabeth in London, and then the royal couple set off in their flamboyant royal robes to a new life together in Heidelberg, the famous city of progressive thinkers that was to become the capital of their Rose Cross Confederacy.

When Princess Elizabeth and Frederick V finally arrived in Heidelberg they were feted with a hero's welcome and a city swarming with with fresh roses and alchemical symbols. Frederick had called ahead to make sure his Castle of Heidelberg had been completely renovated for his new bride. His architect, Salomon de Caus, a student of Vitruvius, followed the monarch's specifications and transformed the castle into a monument to the gnostic-alchemical tradition, which the new royals now represented. His greatest achievement was the design of the new castle grounds, wherein he set "musical grottos, singing fountains, and pneumatically controlled speaking statues" that were set in "geometrical garden designs of great complexity."[2] De Caus earned hearty praise from the new royal couple for his achievement of creating an outdoor paradise that was both a museum of ancient culture and an alchemical laboratory for the expansion of consciousness. The garden was so magnificent that, in some circles, it was touted as the Eighth Wonder of the World.

After they had settled into their new palace, Frederick and Elizabeth set about dedicating their first years on the throne to overseeing a tremendous outpouring of alchemical texts and previously secret information throughout the Palatine. Among the revealed texts were the works of the great Rosicrucian alchemist, Robert Fludd, whose *Ultrusque Cosmi Historia* was "profusely illustrated" and freely circulated among the masses. The dramatic increase in esoteric knowledge was so profound that the grateful faculty at the University of Heidelburg built ornate arches on their campus in honor of their beloved new Queen.

Frederick V wears the Rose Collar of the Order of the Garter

The Marriage of Frederick V and Elizabeth

Heidelburg Palace with its Alchemical Grounds

Robert Fludd's Ultrusque Cosmi Historia

King Rudolph II and an Alchemist in Prague

Unfortunately for Fredrick, the end of the young monarch's short reign was in sight almost from the day he ascended the throne. The final chapter of his rule occurred when Bohemia, the bastion of alchemy and gnosis in the eastern part of Europe, petitioned to join the new Rose Cross Confederacy and adopt Frederick as their new King. The Bohemians were desparate, having recently lost much of their religious freedom during the reign of the Catholic Holy Roman Emperor Ferdinand, the successor of the Emperor Rudolph II. Rudolph, by contrast, had fully supported the gnostic-alchemcial tradition of the Bohemians and even made the city of Prague a European headquarters for alchemical study and experimentation. With the overthrow of the oppressive King Ferdinand, the Bohemians sought a return to a better era.

The Bohemian's plot to become affiliated with the Rose Cross Confederacy did not sit well with the Hapsburg monarchs of the Holy Roman Empire, who counted Bohemia as one of their gems. They were determined to hold onto the territory at all costs and made a plan to quickly and decisively defeat any attempts Frederick made in securing it for himself. Therefore, after allowing Frederick and Elizabeth to spend one winter in Prague within the comforts of the exotic alchemical mystery school that King Rudolph had used as his castle, they attacked. With the rank and file of the Holy Roman army bearing down on them, the royal couple left the country in such a hurry that Frederick's badge of membership in the Order of the Garter was completely lost in the confusion. The symbolic disappearance of the badge represented an end to the plot to create a united Rose Cross Confederacy, at least until the rise of the Illuminati.

Sufi Beginnings of the Illuminati Conspiracy

The year 1776 arrived with a flourish. This was the pivotal year that saw the founding of the first Sub-Rosa nation in the New World, the United States of America, and the official beginning of the gnostic Order of the Illuminati in Germany. Founded by Adam Weishaupt, the Professor of Cannon Law at the University of Ingolstat in Germany, the Illuminati was calculated to be the final vehicle in the movement to precipitate a one-world spirituality. Although this movement had, in recent history, begun with the Knights Templar, its roots were much more ancient and could be traced at least as far back as the Sufis.

The visionary Sufi Master who first proposed a crusade to create a one-world spirituality was Abdullah ibn Maymun during the Ninth Century. Maymun was born in southern Persia and brought up in an eclectic environment of intellectuals, which included both Persian Gnostic and Ishmaili Shiite teachers. Endowed with both mystical insight and a very ambitious temperament, from a young age Maymun proved his ability to understand the highest and most abstruse gnostic teachings of the Ismailis. So when the first opportunity arose to ascend the Ishmaili hierarchy Maymun easily found support among his peers. His subsequent activities and reforms as an Ishmaili chief would prove pivotal not only to the Ishmaili but to the later Knights Templar and the Illuminati.

Maymun was one of the first Sufi synthesizers to amalgamate the numerous ancient religious and alchemical traditions gobbled up by the conquering Moslems into a new mystery school tradition. His mystery sect of the Batinis, which was founded in 909 CE with seven levels of advancement, became a model that would be adopted by many future Sufi mystery sects. Maymun's exceptional ability to synthesize both people and spiritual traditions together set him apart from his peers and ultimately gained him fame. One Islamic historian remarked:

"To link together into one body the vanquished and the conquerors; to unite in the form of a vast secret society with many degrees of initiation free thinkers-who regarded religion only as a curb for the people...to induce conquerors to overturn the empires they had founded...such was Abdullah ibn Maymun's general-an extraordinary conception which he worked out with marvelous tact, incomparable skill and a profound knowledge of the human heart...."[3]

Maymun's predilection to champion the gnostics was also recognized and commented by historians. One stated: "It was...not among the Shiites that he sought his true supporters, but among the Ghebers (the Persian Gnostics), the Manichaeans, the pagans of Harran (Mandaeans), and the students of Greek philosophy...."[4] Thus, it was recognized that Maymun was more interested in creating a gnostic-alchemical sect than one based upon Islamic ideology.

Maymun's mission quickly gathered many converts, but it also quickly imploded when his followers began to resort to violence to achieve their goal of a one-world gnostic spirituality. When his teachings became embraced by the warring Karmathites, thousands of innocent persons who refused to convert to Maymun's doctrines were slain. The final debacle occurred when 30,000 Moslems were massacred for standing in the way of the Karmathites' campiagn to conquer Mecca. When the Karmathites were themselves soundly defeated soon afterwards it had become crystal clear that another approach was needed if the world was to be won over to a higher cause.

The basic principals of Maymun's mystery tradition and his global movement were both were adopted in 1004 CE by the Dar-ul-Himat, the "House of Wisdom" mystery school of Cairo, which became the premier training ground for Ishmaili Sufis. The House of Wisdom adopted Maymun's seven levels of mystical advancement, to which two more were added to make nine degrees. These nine degrees mirrored other gnostic mystery traditions, such as the Kuala tradition of India, by embracing Right Hand Path practices and theology in their early degrees, and then progressing through the Left Hand Path practices in their later degrees to achieve transcendance and gnosis. The complete elimination of all Right

Hand Path religious doctrine and observances occurred in the ninth degree, which is summed up by Nesta Webster in *Secret Societies & Subversive Movements*:

"…Finally, in the ninth (degree), the adept was shown that all religious teaching was allegorical and that religious precepts need only be observed in so far as it is necessary to maintain order, but the man who understands the truth may disregard all such doctrines."

The Illumined Ones

Those Sufis who founded their own mystery schools after graduating from the House of Wisdom adopted many of Maymun's degrees, but to their detriment they also adopted the predilection for violence that often accompanied them. One such Sufi pioneer was Hasan-i-Sabah, founder of the Order of Assassins. Another was Bayezid Ansari, founder of the Roshaniya, the "Illuminated Ones," who spread throughout the mountains of Afghanistan during the Sixteenth Century. Bayezid Ansari and his family claimed to be direct descendants of Mohammed's Ansar, or "Helpers," who as early Sufis had "been granted initiation into the mysteries of the Ishmaelite religion…which dated from Abraham's rebuilding of the Temple of Mecca, the mystical Haram."[5]

In creating the Roshaniya, Bayezid shortened the nine degrees of the House of Wisdom to eight while also adopting the far-reaching planetary goals of Maymun. His vision was to produce an army of enlightened gnostics willing to sacrifice themselves in service to a "supreme power" that both ruled over the world and dwelled within all people. As the initiate progressed through the eight alchemical degrees of the Illumined Ones, he or she would gradually become empowered by the Divine Power and Wisdom of the Supreme and learn to recognize the Divine Presence both within themselves and throughout the world. Apparently their advancement to the fourth degree, that of the "Enlightened One," was extremely pivotal for achieving spiritual freedom and gnosis. It was then that the initiate was finally allowed to discard all Right Hand Path religious mandates and adopt the iconoclast and free-spirited attitude of an enlightened gnostic. States author Arkon Daraul:

"The Enlightened One of the fourth degree was he who could attain, during the rituals, complete identification with this overall power, and was guided by it in all he did. This meant that, apart from the guidance of the chief, he was free to suit his own pleasure in life. No theological or social bonds limited him."[6]

Bayezid, who became known by his grateful and devoted followers as the Sage of Illumination, eventually built an impregnable castle in the mountains of Afghanistan from where he sent his warriors into many parts of Asia. One of his greatest achievements was founding a city in Hashtnagar, now in Pakistan, which he intended to use as the world headquarters of Illuminism. However, the beginning of the end was already in sight, and Bayezid's mission soon devolved through the mis-use of the sword and the mismanagement of his descendants.

The Illuminati

The mysteries and modus operandi of the Illumined Ones survived their demise and were adopted forty years later by the European Illuminati, a gnostic order that embraced both the Roshaniya's eight levels of advancement, as well as its campaign to manifest a one-world spirituality through planetary revolution. The list of the eight respective levels of the two orders were nearly mirror images of each other:

Roshaniya	Illuminati
Seeker	Apprentice
Disciple	Fellow-craft
Devotee	Master
Enlightened One	Illuminatus Major
Master	Illuminatus Dirigens
Commander	Prince
Priest	Priest
King, Chief	King

Where the two lists diverge is in their first three degrees. This is because Masonic degrees were incorporated into the Illuminati by Baron Adolph Knigge, a high ranking member of the Strict Observance, whom Wieshuapt hired to revise his Illuminati degrees.

According to historical speculation, Weishaupt was initiated and trained by a direct initiate from the Ismailis' House of Wisdom five years previous to his founding the Illuminati. At that time Weishaupt is said to have been visited by a gnostic adept who had spent years in Egypt studying the mystical traditions of the Dar-ul-Himat. This charismatic and persuasive adept is said to have possessed both an exceptionally strong personality and a high level of gnostic awareness.

One identification that has been suggested for this mysterious adept is that of a Danish merchant named Kolmer, who after sojourning in Egypt for many years, arrived in Europe seeking converts for both the Ishamaili and gnostic Manichaeaism teachings he had become a proponent of. His predilection for the Persian Gnostic path aligned him directly to the early Sufis, many of whom had originated in Persia, including the Sufi Maymun.

Before meeting Weishaupt, Kolmer is said to have stopped off in Malta to enroll the Knights of Malta in his scheme for a one-world empire. He was, apparently, less than successful and the Knights sent him packing, but not before he had

Illuminatus Adam Weishuapt, "Spartacus"

Illuminatus Baron Adolph Knigge, "Philo"

a pivotal meeting with the alchemist and gnostic, Alessandro Cagliostro, who was residing in Malta at the time. Cagliostro never mentioned Kolmer by name in his diaries, but he repeatedly alluded to one of his teachers named Althotas, which is believed to be a cryptic name for Kolmer. Althotas, who was credited by Cagliostro for introducing him to many elements of the gnostic-alchemical path, has been referred by esoteric historians as a "universal genius, almost divine...[whose] system [of alchemy] was derived from those of Egypt, Syria and Persia."[7] A hint to this adept's mastery in the art of alchemy is his name, Althothas, which incorporates the title Thoth, thus possibly designating him to an adept in the Egyptian alchemical tradition of Thoth-Hermes.

After Weishaupt's visit with the mysterious adept from Egypt, he spent the following five years gathering together the components of an organization that in 1776 would become officially known in Bavaria as the Illuminati. In its synthesized form the Illuminati was a gnostic-alchemical mystery school with strong Sufi, Persian, Egyptian, Greek, Manichaean and Freemasonic influences. Of these, it was perhaps the Persian influence that was most salient and foundational. Weishaupt adopted both the Persian calendar, as well as the floppy hat of the Persian savior, Mithras, which became the Illuminati's most recognizable symbol. Apparently the higher levels of the Illuminati also came directly out of Persian mysticism, as Weishaupt himself comments:

"The allegory in which the Mysteries and Higher Grades must be clothed is Fire Worship and the whole philosophy of Zoroaster, or of the old Parsees who nowadays only remain in India, therefore in the further degrees the Order is called 'Fire Worship,' the 'Fire Order,' or the 'Persian Order'-that is, something magnificent beyond expectations."[8]

From the start, the members of the early Illuminati gained a measure of credibility by referring to themselves as modern Templars; and like the Secret Societies before them, they also made it clear that their agenda included vengeance for their knighted ancestors. When Alessandro Cagliostro was officially inducted into the Illuminati order he was delighted to find his initiators referring to themselves as Templars. Later recalling the event in his diary, he wrote:

"I met with two men, whom I can not reveal...but they were chiefs of the Illuminati...in the middle [of the room] was a table, upon which I saw a metal chest, that contained a quantity of writing, among which...was a manuscript upon which was written, "*We the Grand Masters of the Templars*," followed by oaths and expressions that were [meant to] horrify, but which I could not recall, and it contained obligations to destroy despotic sovereigns...."

Caglisotro was informed by his initiators that the prime targets of the Illuminati would be the Templars' archenemies, the Catholic Church and the French monarchy. Later, in order to trigger the French Revolution, Caglisotro was instructed to compell the citizens of Paris to destroy the Bastille, after which throughout the city could be heard cries of, "The Templars have their vengeance!"

The Illuminati began as a small fraternity of five men who initially held closed-door meetings while sitting at the five points of a pentagram, the ancient symbol of the Goddess, perhaps in honor of the Left Hand Path roots of their tradition. As was common within other occult orders, each of the first five members chose an initiated name. Weishaupt took the name, Spartacus, because, like the Roman warrior, he was dedicated to freeing the slaves (the oppressed masses) from the oppression of all monarchies and religious powers. Ultimately, his desire to shake off the yoke of limitation would include not only governments and organized religion, but also the institution of marriage, and even family. Thus, what has so often been commonly referred to by many as the beginning of a New World Order was, in truth, the seeds of a New World Disorder. Weishaupt's vision for a future world was a full-on communism, with all possessions, even children, held in common. It never manifested the way he hoped, but his coummunistic ideals did precipitate a series of short lived communes in France.

At its beginning, the Illuminati was not a Masonic order, and Weishaupt himself did not enter a lodge until 1777, when he received induction into the Lodge Théodore de Bon Conseil in Munich. However, once inside Masonry Weishaupt immediately saw its potential value to be a vehicle for the realization of his Illuminati dreams. To orchestrate an official union between the Illuminati and Freemasonry, Weishaupt set about organizing the Congress of Wilhelmsbad at the Castle of William IX of Hesse-Kassel, to occur on July 16, 1782. That special event, which was momentous in both size and aspirations, was attended by elite representatives of Masonic lodges from all over the world, including Cagliostro, St. Germain, and the Masonic historians Baron de Gleichen and Baron de Westerode.

Wilhelmsbad was to become historically relevant as the venue where the the initial Illuminati plan to overthrow of the world's governments and monarchies was first unveiled. It was also there that a decision was reached to allow the previously excluded Jews to be granted admittance into Freemasonry. The Illuminati creed maintained that all people were equal, so the Masonic union with the Illuminati at Wilhelmsbad stipulated that the previously outcast Jews be allowed admittance into the predominantly Christian organization. However, there was another, tacit reason for the change in Masonic policy towards the Jews. Money was needed to help fund the series of revolutions the Illuminati had planned for the future, and the Jews were the principal bankers of Europe, a role they had assumed since the time of the fall of the Knights Templar. Jews could lend money and support themselves with the accrued interest, while usury was considered a major sin within the Christian community. When the time came for a vote on their admittance at Wilhelmsbad, the Jews were so anxious to win the day that they

The Gnostic Serpent Seal of the Alchemist Cagliostro

The Mithriac Cap
Symbol of the Illuminati-led French Revolution

215

*Castle of William IX of Hesse-Kassel
Site of the Wilhelmsbad Congress*

The Emblem of the united Illuminati-Freemason Order

completely filled the hall with other Jewish supporters.[9] It was not long afterwards that the Illuminati membership included an abundance of Jewish banking families, including the Rothschilds, the Oppenheimers, the Wertheimers, the Schusters, Speyers, and Sterns.[10] New lodges of predominantly Jews were formed in Frankfurt, the Rothchild's financial capital in Europe, and soon all of Illuminized Freemasonry would make the city its world headquarters.

The induction of Jews into the Illuminati at the Congress of Wilhelmsbad did, however, put a cramp in the future agenda of the organization, and its long term goals began to move in a different direction. The Illuminati succeeded in gaining the funds to finance its revolutions, but in the process the Order's hierarchy gave up much of its decision-making power to the Jewish bankers. Ultimately, the goal of creating a one-world gnostic civilization was replaced by the establishment of a one-world economy designed to support the interests of the Jewish bankers. The New World Order of contemporary conspirators had truly begun.

The first order of buisness for the Illuminati-initiated Jews, who were the world's premier disenfranchised race, was to manifest their prophesied Zion, a world ruled by the chosen people of Yahweh. Plans were set in motion for the Zionist Jews to finally have their land of milk and honey that had been promised to them for so long, and it would be the entire world!

The opportunity for manifesting their Zion arrived with the Russian Revolution, which was financed by the Jewish bankers. One of their own, the German Jew, Karl Marx, had catalyzed the event with the publication of his *Communist Manifesto*, within which he preached the merits of communism. The Bolshevik leader of the Revolution, Lenin, whose ancestors had been Jewish on both sides of his family, then contributed his plan for a centralized government that would be controlled by a Jewish oligarchy. After Lenin and his Illuminati cohorts raised their victory flags at the end of the Russian Revolution, their new communist government quickly emerged with Jews occupying at least 75% of its highest positions. Zion had been won, but not for long. Following the sudden death of Lenin, the Jewish hopeful, Trotsky, was soundly defeated by Stalin, a Christian, and the dictator murdered all those Jews who stood in the way of his new policies.

The Jewish campaign to rule the world as their Zion was all the justification Hitler and the Nazis needed to commit genocide against the entire Jewish race. A document entitled *The Protocols of the Meetings of the Learned Elders of Zion,* which was apparently written before the Russian Revolution and outlined the entire Jewish plan to rule the world, found its way into the hands of Hitler. The Fuhrer, who already blamed the Jews for all the woes that had beset Germany, was expectedly enraged. Although parts of the document may have been a hoax, its underlying plan for Jewish domination proved accurate.

Following their failed attempt at world domination through communism, the Jewish bankers took another tact and slowly built up an empire of financial institutions to oversee a capitalistic infrastructure that would govern the world. Zion could still be won. As one Jewish banker and Illuminati patron, Amshel Rothschild, is known to have famously remarked, "Give me the control of a country's finances, and I care not who governs the country!"

Amschel Rothschild wears the Maltese Cross

Mayer Carl Rothschild wears Secret Society badges

THE PROTOCOLS
OF THE MEETINGS OF THE
LEARNED ELDERS OF ZION
TRANSLATED BY VICTOR E. MARSDEN

1923 Edition published by Britons Publishing Society

Star Missionaries of a
World Gnostic Civilization

Although the modern movement for a one-world gnostic civilization began with the Sufis, its true origin was in the fabled Garden of Eden. During that era star missionaries arrived on the Pacific continent of Lemuria to plant the seeds of a one-world civilization that they clairvoyantly predicted would fully blossom at a much later epoch. Their akashic visions revealed that humanity would first need to experience a divisive patriarchal era during which the ego and intellect could be fully developed. Only after enduring a dark age of conflict and divisiveness would humankind be ready to forge a world gnostic civilization that would be a balance of intellect and intuition, matriarchy and patriarchy. Therefore, with their eyes on the future, the star missionaries resolved to assist humanity through its dark period and then help guide it into the era of world unification that would follow.

The original star missionaries were the Sons of God, or the "Nephilim," a term meaning "those who were cast down upon the Earth." These missionary "Sons," who were, essentially, androgynys, are referred to in almost every creation myth worldwide as the two or more forever-young twin boys who suddenly appear from the heavens to teach Earth's human population language, writing, medicine, agriculture, alchemy and various other mundane and sacred sciences that are essential components of a civilization. They are remembered not only as culture bearers, but also as heroes and saviors who were dedicated to eradicating ignorance and uniting all humans in fraternal love.

As to the original homes of Earth's first extraterrestrial culture-bearers, the legends passed down through the Knighted Orders, including the Knight Templars, Freemasonry and the other Secret Societies, point to a region of the heavens that is home to the archetypal warrior-protector and first gnostic teacher of humanity, Karttikeya/St. Michael. This is the region occupied by Sirius, Orion and the Pleiades, and recognized astronomically as the starry home of the celestial warrior, Orion, who with his attending dog, Canis Major (which incorporates the star Sirius), is forever in pursuit of the Seven Doves, the Pleiades. It is within this region of our galaxy that Orion, the "male" Divine Mind, seeks to tame and mold his prey, the "female" Divine Power of the Pleiades, with a club, arrows or a spear, in order to encode "her" with a blueprint that will determine the physical forms that will eventually crystallize out of the asterism. The great hunter Orion is the cosmic maniestation of Karttikeya and St. Michael (Orion), who eternally seek to subdue and tame their dragon or unruly peacock in the form of the Pleiades. A cosmic motif with the same purport can be found at the center of the Milky Way, wherein another fountainhead of creative power is inhabited by the centaur Sagittarius shooting his arrows into Ophiucus, the great serpent that embodies the life force that is preparing to crystallize.

The brightest star in the cosmic warrior region of our celestial sphere, and the one most often referred to by the Secret Societies as a guiding influence, is Sirius. According to Alice Bailey, a channel of the Great White Brotherhood, this is because the founders of Masonry were missionaries from Sirius, the "Great White Lodge" in the cosmos, who came to Earth many millennia ago. In her book *The Rays and the Initiations*, Bailey announces:

"Masonry, as originally instituted far back in the very night of time and long antedating the Jewish dispensation, was organized under direct Sirian influence and modeled as far as possible on certain Sirian institutions...."

Bailey also asserts that since the time of their first visitations the influence of Sirius and the Sirians has never abated, and in subtle ways they continue to guide the Secret Societies. She states explicitly that "The entire work of the Great White Lodge (The Great White Brotherhood and the Secret Societies) is controlled from Sirius."[1]

The Sirians' eternal support of Freemasonry is currently honored in many Masonic lodges by their prominently featured five-pointed Blazing Star, which according to the late Freemason Grand Master Albert Pike is the definitive Masonic symbol of Sirius. The Sirian support began on the Motherlands of Lemuria and Atlantis where the extraterrestrials began using the Knighted Orders as their vehicles to evolve humanity to a point where it could accept a one-world government and a one-world spiritual tradition. One of the Sirians' premier gifts to humanity through Masonry and the Knighted Orders has been alchemy, which was disseminated to help humans evolve beyond the limited boundaries that separate them. Historically, an intimate link between Sirius, Masonry and alchemy was acknowledged as early as the Egyptian Masons, who referred to Sirius as Sa Ptah, the Master Mason who embodied the fire of creation and destruction. Dur-

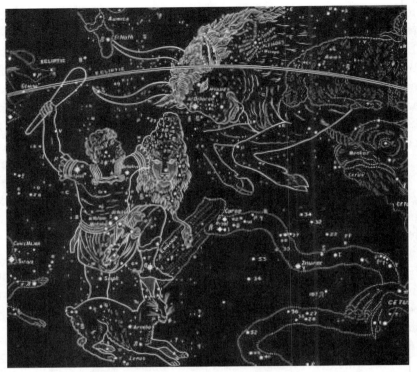

Orion, the Divine Mind, in pursuit of the Pleiades, the Divine Power

***Sirius, the Blazing Star of Freemasonry
Set into the exterior of a Masonic Lodge***

ing pre-historic times, legend has it that one special alchemical gift from the Sirians to humanity was a version of the Philosophers Stone known as the Chintamani Stone, which they brought from their celestial homeland. Supposedly this stone was first given as a gift to the Emperor Tazlavoo of Atlantis and later placed in a temple in the secret Himalayan kingdom of Shambhala. Over the years pieces of the rock have found their way out of Shambhala and into the possession of certain rulers and conquerors, including Solomon and Genghis Khan, whose exploits in some way served the Sirian agenda of precipitating a one-world civilization. Legend has it one piece of the stone was given to the founders of the League of Nations when it appeared that a one-world government was imminent. When that project failed to live up to expectations, the League was disbanded and the stone was returned to its home by the Russian explorer and artist Nicholas Roerich.

Through the Freemasons, the Sirians apparently had a hand in founding the nation of the United States, which they have always intended to use as one of their primary vehicles to precipitate the coming one-world civilization. While working in tandem with the Sirian agenda, the Masonic "Founding Fathers" were inspired to choose July 4, 1776 as the birthday of the new nation, thus placing the destiny of the United States directly in the hands of the Sirians. This special date corresponds to the annual transit of the Sun moving into a direct alignment with Sirius, thus making the astrological birth chart and destiny of the United States forever aligned with the Sirian agenda. The symbol of Sirius and the country's eternal link with the star is evident in the obverse of the Seal of the United States, where Sirius radiates its influence as the all-seeing eye that surmounts a pyramid of thirteeen levels. The Masonic five-pointed star of Sirius is also the geometrical shape that underlies the nascent design of Washington D.C..

To evolve the United States into their perfect vehicle on Earth, the Sirians have been working to evolve the citizens of the country beyond their personal and nationalistic biases, and into a nation with unity awareness. According to Alice Bailey, the energies of Sirius are "applied to the centers [chakras] of the initiate with terrific force" and can culminate "in an expansion and an apprehension of the truth as it is, and is lasting in its effect."[2] As the Sirian influence uplifts the consciousness of the citizens of the United States, many of them will ultimately transform into world teachers who will assist in ushering in a world gnostic civilization.

The Coming New World

The current Sirian agenda of unification is designed to culminate in an age when the Left Hand and Right Hand Paths will come into balance and harmony, and there will finally be an end to the enmity that has separated them for so long. This age is the prophesied era appopriately named the "Age of the Son" because it will unite the previous two ages of the God and Goddess, patriarchy and matri-

Nicholas Roerich and the Chintamani Stone from Sirius

The Chintamani Stone returns to Shambhala

archy, and bring forth a balanced "progeny." It is the union of God and Goddess that makes the coming era so special. For the first time since the Garden of Eden gave birth to humanity, there will finally be perfect harmony and equality between male and female, intellect and intuition, and the Right Hand and Left Hand Paths.

The coming age and how to prepare for it was transmitted to the British Aleister Crowley in the early Twentieth Century by a Sirian named "Lam." Lam was instrumental in founding the A:A, the organization through which Crowley taught the alchemical practices needed to prepare humanity for the new era. Crowley called it the coming Age of the Son and described it as the union and culmination of the previous two epochs, the Age of Osiris and the Age of Isis. Unfortunately, Crowley failed in his mission as a way-shower because of his free spirited abhorrence for structure and discipline, which he summarized in the A:A gospel, *The Book of the Law*, as "Do as thou wilt shall be the whole of the Law." His anti-law and anti-structure modis operandi did not make Crowley the best choice for catalyzing a synthesis between the Left Hand and Right Hand Paths.

According to the prophesies of the Dogon of Mali, a group of extraterrestrial missionaires from Sirius, called the Nommo, visited the North African tribe sometime in their colorful past and will be returning to usher in the new era of light on Earth. The Dogon have baffled anthropologists by their knowledge of the two stars that revolve around Sirius, Sirius B and Sirius C, as well as their insight regarding the rings of Saturn and the moons of Jupiter. All these celestial points require a powerful telescope to observe, something the primitive Dogon have not possessed through most of their history. The Dogon also maintain that the Nommo manifest as part humanoid, but most of their bodies are covered with fish scales and terminate in fish tails. The Nommo thus mirror Enki, making them adrogynys and serpent culture-bearers in the tradition of the Sumerian missionary of legend.

Finally, according to Hopi prophesy, it will be the appearance of Sirius in the heavens that will officially mark the beginning of the new era. They refer to Sirius as the Blue Star Kachina, whose appearance as a blazing blue light will signal the united civilization on Earth that the Sirians have worked towards creating for many ages.

Sirius, the Blazing Star on the reverse of the US Seal

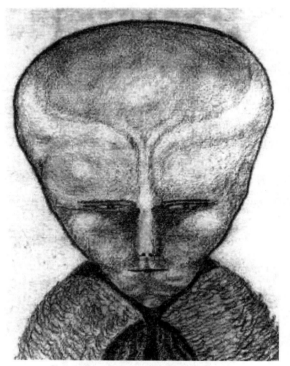

Crowley's Lam from Sirius

Nommo of the Dogon: Culture-Bearers from Sirius

A Ceremonial image of the Blue Star Kachina of the Hopis

Part II
The Coming Gnostic Civilization

The Elixir of Immortality
by Chadwick St. John

Gnostic Civilization since the Garden of Eden

Both Aleister Crowley's and Adam Weishaupt's visions of a worldwide gnostic civilization were either directly or indirectly inspired by the Sirians. The Illuminati symbol of the Eye of Wisdom surmounting a pyramid with 13 levels is considered to be a direct reference to the extraterrestrials' pivotal influence on Weishuapt's order (the Eye has been associated with the star Sirius), and the symbol also links the Illuminati with the most ancient gnostic civilizations that originated on Lemuria. Weishaupt brought his organization prominently in alignment with Lemuria when he stated the Illuminati intent of creating a one-world civilization based upon the mystery traditions and civilizations of the Greek and Persian Gnostics. The Greeks and Persians had, of course, inherited the components of their gnostic civilizations from the "Sons of Seth," the "Daughters of Sophia," and other missionary groups of the Left Hand Path that had left the Motherlands during their time of decline and final destruction. Therefore, nearly a direct link can be made between the earliest gnostic civilizations and the Illuminati.

This chapter will chronologue the world's gnostic civilizations beginning with the primeval Goddess civilization on Lemuria and then down to the modern era. Most have been interrelated to each other and contained some combination of the following components:

1. A caste system in the early stages and its abolution in the latter stages.
2. Rule by a priest-king and/or gnostic spiritual leader(s).
3. A belief in reincarnation.
4. Both Right Hand Path teachings for the masses and Left Hand Path teachings for the initiates ready to achieve gnosis.
5. Alchemical practices, herbs, and elixirs to separate from and/or evolve the physical body in order to experience complete spiritual freedom.

The very ancient "Illuminati" Symbol
A symbol of Lemuria, Babylon and other Gnostic Civilizations,
this artifact is part of Father Crespi's collection in Ecuador
Courtesy of Klaus Dona
www.unsolved-mysteries.info

6. An understanding and direct experience of the levels and astral dimensions that separate the Earth from the highest heavens, or Pleroma.

7. Baptism and the transmission of spiritual power to initiate inner alchemy.

8. Veneration of the Goddess and the universal female principle.

Lemuria, The First Gnostic Civilization

The Garden of Eden, or the Lemurian epoch that brought forth our planet's first gnostic civilization, is remembered in by those of the Left Hand Path as the fabled era when the Goddess Sophia spiraled down Her universal tree and taught fledgling humanity the secrets of gnosis. Adherents of the Right Hand Path remember it as the time of the "Fall" mentioned in *The Book of Enoch* when the Sons of God mated with the Daughters of Men and then taught their new wives the various subjects of the Left Hand Path, including herbology, divination, gemology and alchemy. These teachings became the foundation of Earth's premier gnostic culture and many later Left Hand Path sects. The practices and ideology of this incipient culture were able to survive unhampered on the Lemurian continent for thousands of years, and a multitude of ages would pass before the divisive ego and intellect of patriarchy would have sufficiently developed within the human race to restrict or abolish them. Thus, the first gnostic civilization was able to function with unrestricted freedom.

Many legends have survived among the Hawaiians and other Polynesians which allude to the free-spirited culture that once thrived upon the ancient Motherland of Lemuria. Some of these legends refer to the Pacific continent as the Land of Rua, the land of R'ai Rai, the Goddess of Sunshine and Joy, and they maintain that it was a land that supported the joy, spontaneity and the sunny openness that characterizes a young child. Such perpetual spontaneity, it was believed, filled a person with spiritual power, or "mana," which could be used to manifest all one's desires and to ultimately achieve complete gnosis. An ancient Lemurian on the path of gnosis would never have imagined stealing another's possessions or striking a neighbor out of anger, because they understood intuitively that "All are One." They lived thier lives according to the gnostic maxim that you could not hurt your brother or your sister without hurting yourself.[1] The social structure of this premier gnostic civilization on Lemuria was communal, and even children were held in common. Sexual encounters were spontaneous and uninhibited, and even relatives were allowed to mate. The concept of sin had not entered the consciousness of the early Lemurians, so there was less judgment dividing the masses and much more love for self anf others. Everyone was an embodiment of the Divine, and the world was their playground.

Some of the freedom felt by the earliest Lemurians was the product of existing within energy bodies of very high frequency. This gave them the ability to teleport to various locations around the Earth and to easily move between the various levels and dimensions of the universe.

A window into the latter days of the Lemurian gnostic civilization comes from the late Subramuniya Swami of Kauai, author of *Lemurian Scrolls,* who was shown by the spirit of Sanat Kumara, the ancient King of Lemuria, a series of clairvoyant visions of Mu. Subramuniya Swami was given visions of a Motherland covered with temples and ashrams, where its citizens could actively, and with discipline, dedicate themselves to the Left Hand Path. Subramuniya was subsequently directed to a location on Kauai that once harbored an ancient temple and instructed to build a contemporary ashram there. The Swami's Saiva Siddhanta Ashram was to become perhaps the first step in the revival of the ancient Lemurian civlization. Before his death, Subramuniya began construction on a stone temple called "Iraivan," which was designed to solidify the new consciousness and survive at least one thousand years.

The work on Iraivan has continued by Subramuniya's disciples and should be completed soon. Together, the temple and ashram will give visitors a direct experience of the gnostic civilzation that once covered Lemuria.

Thus, Subramuniya's visions revealed that the necessity for structure was eventually acknowledged on Lemuria. This, in turn, provided an opening for the gradual development and spread of the Right Hand Path upon the continent. This patriarchal development was important since it led to the essential evolution of the intellect, a process that was greatly accelerated when visiting extraterrestrial missionaries brought developing humanity language so they could articulate complete thoughts and classify the flora and fauna of Earth according to useful and shared characteristics. Such classifications promoted the new divisive consciousness among the population of Mu wherein all animate and inanimate life forms began to be seen as different from each other, and it was just a matter of time before the ego would firmly take root and all humans would begin to feel complete separation and alienation from each other. This divisiveness would signal the end of the Garden of Eden, and the free-spirited and heart-centered gnostic civilization of Lemuria would gradually come to a close.

The Right Hand Path agenda began to fully exert itself upon the gnostic civilization of Lemuria when it became necessary to separate souls according to their levels of earthplane experience. Many souls incarnating on Mu were entering the third dimension for the first time and needed special training and attention. Institutions dedicated to their orientation, protection and

*The grounds of Saiva Siddhanta Ashram
and its Iraivan Temple, under construction.
Is this the Revival of the Lemurian Gnostic Civilization?*

assimilation into Lemurian society were thus established. To accommodate souls with different levels of Earth experience, a striated society gradually came into existence, thus allowing each soul the lessons appropriate to its level of growth. Thus, the first caste system was developed, although by being fluid it differed from the stringent ones that would come later. A developing soul on Lemuria could fluidly move through all castes in only one physical incarnation and achieve gnosis. This Lemurian system was similar to the one alluded to by Plato in his *Republic*, wherein the Greek philosopher envisioned a perfect society composed of three castes with unlimited movement between them. Of course, the Lemurians lived much longer than modern humans, so they had more time to learn the lessons needed to move between castes. This special advantage would, however, be gradually lost.

Along with the Lemurian caste system, after studying a human lifetime on Earth the sages of Mu divided it into four stages or "Ashramas." When they were later taken to India, these four stages of life became known as Brahmacharya, Grihastha, Vanaprastha and Sannyasa. The first stage of Brahmacharya espoused celibacy and was focused on education, both practical and spiritual. Discipline, and the retention of seminal fluids, was recognized as essential to both growth and mental acuity. The second stage of Grihastha was focused on meeting the responsibilities of work and a family, and for contributing to the evolution of civilization. The third stage of Vanaprastha was dedicated to providing elderly advice to society while living disconnected from it; and the last stage of Sannyasa called for complete renunciation from all family and society responsibilities so the soul could fully dedicate itself to the pursuit of gnosis. When combined with the lessons of the caste system, these four stages provided the developing soul with a full spectrum of earthplane experience.

The incipient government of Mu was a form of theocracy that completely supported the gnostic development of its citizens. The first rulers were enlightened gnostics ruling as priest-kings and queens. Some of these monarchs were directly descended from extra-terrestrial missionaries who had come to Earth as culture bearers and then remained to lead fledgling humanity to gnosis. One such lineage of enlightened rulers was descended directly from the primeval King of the World, Sanat Kumara, whom legends assert was originally sent to Earth from the highest levels of the Pleroma to awaken humanity to gnosis and afterwards remained on the planet to reign as Mu's first priest-king. When the Hawaiians were first discovered by western explorers they were still ruled by kings who claimed descent from some of these extraterrestrial and "Solar deities." Their lineages were carved upon their ceremonial staffs, or Taus.[2]

The Gnostic Civilization of Shambhala

When most of the gnostic civilization of Lemuria disbanded, there was one remote corner of the ancient continent where it survived, and there it has continued down to the present time. This is the "Land of the Immortals," commonly known as Shambhala. Shambhala had initially been part of Mu when it was united with China, and after the demise of Lemuria many aspects of the gnostic civilization that once flourished on the Pacific continent were preserved there.

According to the Theosophists, Shambhala was initially the court of Lemuria's first priest-king, Sanat Kumara, who 18 million years ago assumed an semi-physical form to help guide the spiritual destiny of Earth's humanity. Supposedly Sanat Kumara arrived on Earth from the planet Venus with an entourage of 104 advanced souls ready to assist him in his work. They became the first citizens of Shambhala and members of Sanat's court, serving him as officials and servants. Legend has it that Sanat Kumara's palace was constructed upon the "White Island" situated in the center of a lake that has since dried up and been replaced by the Gobi Desert. From his palace, Sanat Kumara exerted his influence as the Lord of Will and Power around the globe in order to guide the spiritual progress of humanity. Regarding the all-encompassing planetary influence of Lord Sanat Kumara, Alice Bailey, the former Theosophist and channel for the Ascended Master Djwhal Khul, writes:

"The Lord of the World, the One Initiator.... He, Sanat Kumara it is, Who from his throne at Shambhala in the Gobi desert, presides over the Lodge of Masters, and holds in his hands the reigns of [world] government...he has chosen to watch over the evolution of men and devas until all have been occultly 'saved.'"[3]

Other maps and legends of Shambhala of both the Tibetan and Mongolian Buddhists locate the colony in other parts of central and eastern Asia. One Tibetan legend describes Shambhala as being in the center of a ring of snowcapped peaks deep within one of the towering mountain ranges of Central Asia. Numerous tunnels connect this Shambhala to an underground kingdom known as Aghartha, which was anciently founded by Lemurians seeking sanctuary from a polar shift that drowned much of their continent. These tunnels are said to be branches of a much larger Asian tunnel system that terminates at many distant caves and holy sites, including some of the Buddhist monasteries in Tibet and Mongolia, as well as the Chinese caves of Tunhuang, and the cave temples of Ellora and Ajanta on the sub-continent of India. It is believed that some of the Tibetan tunnels also connect with the Dalai Lama's Potala Palace in Lhasa, as well as the Tashilumpo Monastery in Shigatse, home of the Panchen Lama, who has a special affiliation with Shambhala. The soul of the Panchen Lama is the peacock-riding Dhayni Budda Amitibha, Tibet's version of Sanat Kumara; so instead of claiming that Sanat Kumara is monarch of the Land of Immortals, the Tibetans have traditionally maintained that it is Amitibha, the soul of the Panchen Lama, that rules the hidden kingdom.

The Tibetans maintain that the Lemurian caste system became firmly ensconced in Shambhala when the colony began to grow beyond the boundaries of Sanat's palace city of Kalapa. Shambhala extended into eight large districts in the shape of a huge eight petal lotus with Sanat's throne in Kalapa right in the very center. Thus Shambhala, the eight petal Heart Chakra of the World, had the king and soul of the world sitting in its center just as the human soul sits within the center of the eight petal lotus of the human heart chakra. The eight petals or districts of Shambhala were eventually settled by low caste farmers and artisans whose souls vibrated at a lower frequency than Sanat's inner circle of adepts living in Kalapa, although any citizen of Shambhala could be promoted to a higher caste if they achieved the requisite soul growth.

The early reign of Sanat Kumara eventually gave way to a lineage of kings who incarnated the Divine Mind and Power of the Primal Serpent Son. One of the greatest of these monarchs was King Manjushrikirti, who today is regarded as one of the renowned reformer of the culture of Shambhala. Under King Manjushrikirti the caste system of Shambhala was abolished, and all citizens of the land became members of one all-inclusive caste, which he denominated the "Diamond Caste." This was to be a milestone in the evolution of gnostic civilization of Shambhala and merited Manjushrikirti the honorary title of Kulika, meaning "Holder of the Castes." The great ruler had effectively expunged all divisions separating the populace of Shambhala and thereby reverted back to the earlier gnostic culture of Lemuria. From that time onwards all the habitants of Shambhala were eligible to study the mysteries of the Left Hand Path and spend the vast majority of their waking hours practicing the rites of the Kalachakra Tantra. The compassionate King Manjushrikirti also reformed the Kalachakra Tantra to make it more understandable for spiritual seekers of all levels of evolution.

From the time of King Manjushrikirti until today all souls seeking incarnation in Shambhala, the "Pure Land," must be pure and advanced in soul experience. A lifetime in the Land of the Immortals is a virtual guarantee that a soul will achieve complete gnosis in no more than two lifetimes. Most of the current inhabitants of Shambhala are so pure that they live their lives virtually disease free, usually until the age of one hundred, and if they

The eight- petal lotus shape of Shambhala

have not achieved gnosis by their death they will immediately reincarnate back in the Pure Land to complete their gnostic-alchemical training. Author Edwin Berbaum gives a glowing description of life in Shambhala:

"The inhabitants of the kingdom live in peace and harmony. Their crops never fail and their food is wholesome and nourishing. They all have a healthy appearance, with beautiful features, and wear turbans and graceful robes of white cloth. They speak the sacred language of Sanskrit. Each one has great wealth in the form of gold and jewels but never needs to use it. The laws of Shambhala are fair and gentle; physical punishment, whether by beating or imprisonment, does not exist."[4]

According to prophecy, the gnostic culture of Shambhala is destined to eventually cover the entire Earth, thus reviving to a degree the primeval gnostic civilization of Lemuria. Legend states that the caste abolisher, King Manjushrikirti, founded a lineage of 25 Kulika Kings, the "Holders of the Castes," which will eventually come to an end during the reign of the final monarch, King Rudra Chakrin, the "Wrathful One of the Wheel," who will ride out of Shambhala with a huge army to defeat the forces of divisiveness and evil around the globe. Thereafter, the gnostic wisdom and social structure of Shambhala can spread throughout the world and there will be complete equality and freedom for all persons on Earth.

According to one estimate, the current monarch of Shambhala is King Anirudda, the "Unstoppable One," who will reign until 2027 CE, and Rudra Chakrin will not occupy the throne of the world until 2327 CE. However, there are many other Tibetan scribes that believe that these dates, which are based upon all the Kings of Shambhala living at least 100 years, are completely distorted. Instead, they assert that many of Shambhala's monarchs lived shorter lives than believed and that the true advent of Rudra Chakrin's reign is either now or in the very near future.

The Gnostic Civilization of India

India also perpetuated many features of Lemuria's gnostic civilization following the Motherland's demise, especially its ashram culture and caste system. It was on the Indian subcontinent that Mu's caste system completely crystallized and its early fluidity disappeared. In time, it became impossible for a person to move outside of the caste he or she was born into. This final development of the caste system was predicated on the belief that the length of a human life-span had been dramatically shortened and there was much less possibility for soul evolution in one incarnation. This determination was made by the sages of the Right Hand Path, who had aquired supreme authority through the Vedic scriptures of India. Their stringent reformation of the caste system ultimately had the effect of precipitating divisiveness and prejudice between the members of the upper and lower castes; and the equality borne from the Lemurian or Goddess understanding that people are separated only by levels of soul growth, completely vanished.

The caste system continues to exist in modern India, where it is overseen by Brahman priests of the Right Hand Path. Those of the lowest caste have become ineligible for gnostic training and recognized as outcasts, or "outcastes," with little or no freedom to advance spiritually. They are often treated like animals and not even considered human. Only when a person is incarnated in the first caste, the Sudra Caste, are they acknowledged to be accepted members of society, even though they are still looked down upon by the upper castes. The best a Sudra can normally hope for during life is to acquire a family and work the vocation of a simple laborer. A member of the second or Vaishya Caste, the "Merchant Caste," is given greater lessons and positions of responsibility within society. If a Vaishya becomes wealthy he or she will often be treated as an equal by his upper caste peers. The third or Kshatriya Caste, the caste of the warriors, politicians, and rulers, gives the inarnating soul opportunities to dedicate itself to the service of others as a public official, a protecting warrior, or as a king or queen. Finally, a soul born into the Brahman Caste is deemed ready for a lifetime of worship and initiation into an alchemical path leading to gnosis.

Fortunately, vestiges of the Lemurian Goddess tradition that is anti-caste continue to exist in India, so there is possibility for even the lowest caste seeker to achieve self-knowledge. The Left Hand Path survives in the country as the Tantra tradition, wherein all people of all castes are considered equal and allowed initiation into the practices and ideology of the gnostic-alchemical path. The Tantric path is closely affiliated with Buddhism, which at one time assimilated many of its practices. As a sibling tradition to Tantra, Buddhism was founded by the Buddha to make the path to gnosis available to both sexes and all castes.

At times during their long histories, animosity has arisen between the Tantra followers of the Left Hand Path and the Vedic proponents of the Right Hand Path. Such conflicts have reflected the war that continues to perpetually rage worldwide between matriarchy and patriarchy. However, over time a reconcillation of the Left and Right Hand Paths has manifested in India as the synthesized Kuala sect, and the pre-eminent Tantric deity, Lord Shiva, has even been accepted by some votaries of the Right Hand Path as synonymous with Brahman, the Godhead. In more than one of the Upanishads, which are the Vedic scriptures written for initiates, the name Shiva is been inserted in place of Brahman as the name of the Godhead.

The Gnostic Civilization of Tibet

Eventually, the Lemurian gnostic culture also reached Tibet through missionaries from India and Shambhala, some of whom traveled back and forth to Tibet through an underground tunnel system that linked the three lands. Missionaries from India brought to Tibet the Tantric Buddhist path of Vajrayana, the "Diamond Path," and from its neighbors in Shambhala they received the Tantric Buddhist path of the Kalachakra, the "Wheel of Time." The Kalachakra Tantra has its roots in the archetypal alchemical paths of Mu that were designed to transport an aspirant to the transcendental consciousness of Shiva that is beyond time.

The form of the Kalachakra Tantra now taught in both Shambhala and Tibet has its beginning in south India when the great Buddha transformed himself into the Kalachakra deity and transmitted its wisdom to an assembly of adepts that included Sucandra, the reigning King of Shambhala. Sucandra took the Kalachakra teachings back with him to Shambhala, and after many years they were returned to India via a Hindu pilgrim who received them from the gnostic deity Manjushri while traveling the road to Shambhala. Finally, in 1026 CE, the Tantric Buddhist adept, Somanatha, transported the Kalachakra teachings into the heartland of Tibet, where they eventually became the core teachings of the Gelugpa sect, the "Yellow Hats," of Tibetan Buddhism. This elite sect of lamas was founded by Tsongkhapa, a Kalachakra adept who received additional training in the teachings by traveling to Shambhala in his astral body. The Gelugpa sect, which eventually became the largest sect of monks in Tibet, is today headed by the Dalai Lama, who occasionally gives initiations into the Kalachakra teachings to the masses.

Once Tantric Buddhism was firmly ensconced in Tibet, it became the norm to dedicate at least one male member of each family to the Left Hand Path and a caste system soon emerged in the country. The upper caste came to include the monks and lamas, or priests, as well as the nobles and government officials, and below them in the lower caste was virtually everyone else. Although the Tibetan caste system was initially fluid, eventually it became the rule that unless a person was born into the upper caste he or she was given little opportunity to improve his or her social status. In time, the chasm between the two castes widened and a certain measure of resentment flourished within the lower caste. Their dissension was a green light for the Communist Chinese to invade Tibet and "free the downtrodden." But although the Chinese banner of socialism was supposed to herald liberation of the low caste and the creation of a one-caste social system, the hoped for positive reformation of Tibetan society never materialized. Instead, Tibet's two class system remained in place with the Chinese taking over the upper caste and

The Kalachakra Mandala
In the center is the palace of
the King of the World in Shambala

The Tashilumpo Monastery in Shigatse, Tibet
Tunnels from here lead to Shambhala
Photos by Mark Amaru Pinkham

most Tibetans relegated to the lower caste. Tibetans became disenfranchised citizens in their own country

The religious government of Tibet was initially structured in the Thirteenth Century by the Buddhist leader of the Shakya sect, Phagpa, under the guidance and support of Kublai Khan of China's Yuan Dynasty. From the start the Tibetan government was a beaucracy headed by Buddhist monks and lay officials, and supported by the Chinese. Eventually, it was given over to the rulership of the Gelugpa sect and adminsitered by its leaders, the Dalai and Panchen Lamas, although the Chinese insidiously continued to control it by infiltrating the Tibetan govenment with their own officials to both oversee and spy on the Tibetan Buddhist officials.

Following the advent of Gelugpa rule in Tibet, it is said that messengers regularly traveled through a network of underground tunnels connecting Shigatse, the headquarters of the Panchen Lama, to Shambhala. In this way the Tibetan civlization could remain linked with Shambhala and a gnostic satellite of it. When Madam Blavasky contacted members of the Panchen Lama's court in the Nineteenth Century, including Kuthumi and Master Morya, she received a full report of their subterannean journeys to Shambhala and their meetings with its adepts.

At the close of their earthly existence the Tibetans observe an important set of rites that were established by a very ancient clan of shamans known in the legends of the ancient Bon tradition of Tibet as the dMu, a name that apparently links them with the gnostic adepts of the continent of Mu. Legend has it that the dMu were "masters of the rope"[5] and could effortlessly move between Heaven and Earth. They discovered the correct astral pathways through the dimensions of the Bardo that must be navigated by the newly desceased. Their journeys through these regions and the pitfalls associated with each were compiled into a scripture known as the *Bardol Thodol,* which is memorized by the Tibetan Lamas in preparation for their own personal transition and also read at the bedside of each deceased lay person to help their souls navigate through the Bardo and into the upper heavens. Many monks who studied the *Six Doctrines of Naropa,* which was a compilation of wisdom that had previously passed into India from the Tantric adepts of Mu, prepared themselves for the afterlife by learning to disengage their physical bodies and travel astrally through the multudinous regions of the Bardo. They learned what paths to take to break the cycle of reincarnations and which would lead them to one of the heavenly regions of the Pleroma.

The Gnostic Civilizations of the Worldwide Dragon Culture

Lemuria's gnostic civilization reached other parts of the globe via missionaries who founded "Dragon Civilizations" that championed spiritual union with the Divine Wisdom and Power of the Primal Dragon or Serpent on the Tree. In their new lands, these enlightened Lemurian missionaries founded lineages of priest-kings and head priests of mystery schools who were honorably addressed by their students and subjects with indigenous titles meaning "Dragon" or "Serpent." In Middle America they founded a lineage of adepts and kings known as the Quetzalcoatls, the "Plumed Serpents;" in China, they manifested as emperors and enlightened masters known as Lung Dragons; in India, they taught the path to Shiva and governed the masses as the Naga Kings; in Britain, they became renown as the Druid Adders who were both governmental leaders of the people and gnostic masters; and in Egypt, they manifested as the Djedhi serpents who served their people as both monarchs and gnostic adepts. Thus, for a brief moment of Earth's history, a gnostic-alchemical spirituality completely encircled our planet as the Worldwide Dragon Culture.

In *The Return of the Serpents of Wisdom* I cover many of the civilizations created by the missionaries of the World Wide Dragon Culture. Collectively, they shared the following features:

1. Promulgation of the Gnostic-Alchemical Path by adepts known as Dragons and Serpents.

2. Belief that the highest goal of human life is to alchemically transform and acquire the Primal Dragon's Divine Wisdom and Power.

3. Rule by a Priest-King, who was an embodiment of the Primal Dragon and used his Divine Power to fuel his kingdom.

4. Veneration of a Primal Serpent or Dragon as the Creator of the Universe, whose serpentine nature as the Serpent Spiral or Golden Proportion was reflected in all things in the cosmos.

5. Construction of megalithic temples and pyramids over Dragon Lairs (or vortexes) that served as World Trees or World Mountains upon which the Primal Serpent spiraled down from the heavens, and where initiations occured during which the inner Serpent Power was awakened.

6. Adoption of Serpent mantras that invoked the power of the Primal Serpent and awakened the inner Serpent Fire.

7. Observance of Dragon Calendars that charted and predicted the movements of the Celestial Dragons of the Pleiades, Venus, etc.

8. Belief in reincarnation, during which a soul gradually evolved to a level suited for initiation into the gnostic-alchemical path.

9. A multilevel caste system.

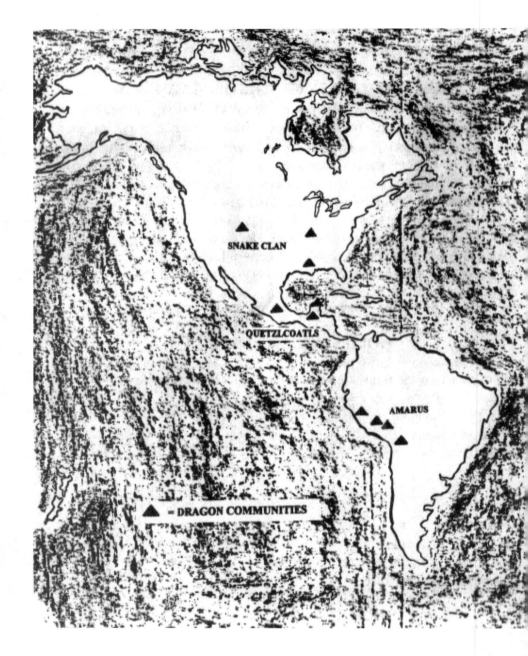

SNAKE CLAN

QUETZLCOATLS

AMARUS

▲ = DRAGON COMMUNITIES

The Worldwide

Dragon Culture

The Gnostic Civilization of China

Since it had once been part of Lemuria and always remained the country closest to the Pacific continent, China's Dragon Culture was one of the first created by the missionaries of Mu. According to Colonel James Churchward, who acquired knowledge of this early Chinese Dragon empire from secret Mu tablets he claimed to have discovered in a monastery in India, one of its earliest capital cities was Karakota in the Gobi Desert, near the Theosophists' "White Island." Karakota was visited both by Gurdjeff and later by the Russian archaeologist, Professor Kosloff, who excavated artifacts fifty feet below the surface believed to be least 20,000 years old, including the statue of an androgynous man/woman. Perhaps one remaining vestige of Churchward's early Dragon Kingdom is the world's largest pyramid located 40 miles southwest of the city of Xian in the province of Shensi. Rising 500 feet in the air and with a base width of 1200 feet, this colossal pyramid is referred to as ancient even in 5000 year old Chinese manuscripts. It was orignally painted the five colors of the five Chinese elements of metal, water, wood, fire, and earth, which collectively comprise the body of the Primal Dragon. It was, therefore, a true home of the Serpent on the Tree.

Following the sinking of much of the western portion of Lemuria, the "Islands of the Immortals", which now exist in the Gulf of Chihil, were created from the submerged mountains of Mu. Legend has it that to keep their bodies vibrating at a high frequency the residents of the Islands of the Immortals continued the Lemurian tradition of cultivating and consuming special mushrooms of immortality while daily drinking from fountains that decanted the Elixir of Immortality. When the inhabitants of the Islands of the Immortals established contact with mainland China they transmitted their knowledge of practices and elixirs to achieve immortality to an early shamanic culture of Wu Shamans that settled along the banks of the Yellow River. In time, the Yellow River colonies flourished and produced some highly evolved shamanic adepts, some of whom became the Hsia, the first historical dynasty of the Dragon Emperors of China.

The first four emperors of the Hsia Dynasty were remarkable for incarnating not only the Divine Wisdom and Power of the Primal Dragon, but also its abnormal physical features. Legend has it that these emperors possessed dragon-like heads, multi-jointed arms, two pupils in each eye (a characteristic of the all-seeing Dragon), leather-like skin, and even whiskers at birth! Some were even believed to have been fathered by dragons. The Emperor Yao's father is said to have been a great Red Dragon and Huang-ti's father was the celestial dragon, the Big Dipper, which sent a ray of golden light to Earth that penetrated and fertilized his mother's womb. Huang-ti and

The largest pyramid in the world at Xian

Androgynous 20,000 year old "Mu" image found by Dr. Kosloff

The Dragon Regalia of China's Dragon Emperors

The Dragon Symbol of China's Dragom Emperors

many of the later Dragon Emperors were born with the seven stars of the Big Dipper tattooed on their skin to signify their descent from the cosmic dragon.

The Hsia Dragon Emperors of the Wu Shamanic culture were responsible for incorporating facets of their shamanic alchemical and gnostic wisdom into Chinese religion, which was eventually distilled as Taoism, with both Right and Left Hand Path rites and practices. One of the predominant features of Taoism is its philosophy regarding the interplay of yin and yang, the universal male and female principles. Only through a balance of yin and yang can health and prosperity exist. As androgynous dragons, the Dragon Emperors of the Hsia were perfect models of polarity balance. Through the union of Heaven and Earth they embodied they were able to generate the spiritual power, or "Ling," needed to effectively govern their kingdoms and make them prosperous. The later Dragon Emperors who were not perfect embodiments of yin and yang, including the notorious Emperor Shih Huang-ti, lost both their gnostic wisdom and their Ling, and their people suffered. Devastating earthquakes, droughts, volcanoes, and epidemics resulted.

The ideology of balance that became the foundation of Taoism was first introduced by the Dragon Emperor Hung-ti, who is today considered to be the greatest of China's ancient monarchs. With his understanding and observance of the divine interplay of yin and yang, or Heaven and Earth, Huang-ti implemented laws that made his kingdom strong and prosperous and encouraged spiritual development. He himself practiced and promulgated the gnostic and alchemical wisdom passed down to him from Mu by shamans from the Yellow River, and he was eventually able to produce the Elixir of Immortality and acquire great longevity. He is responsible for codifying the practices of sexual Tantra, or "Dual Cultivation," and for assisting in the development of Chinese herbology and acupuncture, which was first used among the Taoist adepts as a tool for alchemical awakening and transformation. Legend has it that he lived until to the ripe old age of 111 and then "winged his way to Heaven" in his etheric Dragon Body.

The Eight Trigrams of Taoism, which reveal the secrets of maintaining a male/female balance and uniting Heaven and Earth, were discovered by the first historical Dragon Emperor, Fu Shi. While the ruler sat for his daily meditation next to the peaceful Yellow River, a living dragon-horse with eight legs (the eight legs symbolize the four and four, the two "worlds" of Heaven and Earth united as the Dragon) emerged from the water and stopped directly in front of the monarch so Fu Shi could study the Eight Trigrams tattooed to his back. As Fu Shi would subsequently comprehend, the Eight Trigrams represent the energies that are produced in the eight directions when the Divine Wisdom or Will of Heaven fully unites with the

Divine Power of Earth and recreates the Primal Dragon on our planet. The Trigrams reveal what energies and phenomenon the Primal Dragon will manifest in each of the eight directions and how to live in harmony with them. The Eight Trigrams, which became the foundation of the Chinese art of placement, Feng Shui, were eventually expanded to become the 64 hexagrams of the divination tool known as the I-Ching.

It is not clear if a caste system was observed during the Hsia Dynasty, but records point to its existence during the following Shang Dynasty (1766-1122 BC), which is the first well documented era of China. At the lowest rung of the Shang caste system was the slave caste, followed successively by castes populated by the commoners, the nobles and, finally, the king. It appears that initially the caste system was fluid and there was movement between its various levels, but later, when skills and property had been passed between father and son for many generations the caste structure became very rigid. The members of each caste, however, continued to be eligible to become initiates of the Left Hand Path practices of Taoism.

The Gnostic Civilization of Peru

Peru was another destination of missionaries from Lemuria's Dragon Civilization. The principal missionary was Aramu Muru or Amaru Muru, meaning the "Serpent Muru," who left the Motherland with his consort, Arama Mara, during a period of cataclysmic destruction with the records and power objects of his ravaged continent. He brought to the Andes the records of Mu, as well as the great Solar Disc that had previously hung in the premier solar temple of Lemuria and represented the Solar Spirit, or the Sun behind the Sun. According to one legend, the Solar Disc had been brought to Lemuria by Sanat Kumara and the Sons of God from Venus and was composed of metal that is not indigenous to our world. Aramu Muru initially placed both it and the sacred records of Mu in his secret monastery deep in the Andes, the Monastery of the Seven Rays, for safe keeping, but later when he felt the call from Spirit he transported them to nearby Lake Titicaca. There he was united with an entourage of builders, the Kapac Cuna, some of whom had also come from Mu, or Atlantis, while others may have been descended from extraterrestrial missionaries, such as a Venusian called Orejones, or "Big Ears," a name given her by the Spanish when they were told her enigmatic legend. According to one belief of the Andean shamans, extraterrestrials and immigrants from Mu united on the Island of the Sun to produce a fair-skinned race that produced the Incas and other peoples of the Andes. To emulate their nascent extraterrestrial ancestors from both Mu and Lake Tititcaca, the Incas were known to later lengthen their skulls through artificial deformation, and

Aramu Muru and Arama Mara arrive at Lake Titicaca

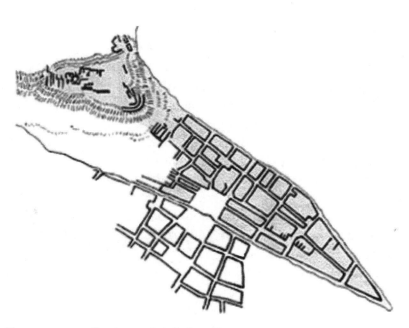

Cusco was designed in the shape of a giant puma

wear large, heavy rings to elongate their ears. One group of Incas are also known to have honored the giant size of their ancestors by wearing skirts and trousers that were five sizes too big for them.

After their pivotal liason at the lake, the Kapac Kuna assisted Aramu Muru in building many megalithic temples and pyramids, like the towering 150 foot "Akapana" pyramid that once graced the temple compound of Tiahuanco, on the shore of Titicaca. When they arrived at the Valley of Cusco they founded the Inca Empire and designed their new capital city, Cusco, meaning "navel," in the shape of a puma. According to Incan cosmology, the puma is the earthplane manifestation of the Primal Dragon after it divides itself up into the three sacred animals, the condor, puma and serpent, which serve as the patrons of three worlds: Heaven, Earth and the underworld. The puma is the Divine Power of the Primal Dragon manifest on Earth; the serpent is its power under the Earth; and the condor is its Divine Mind.

Aramu Muru ascended the throne as the first of a long line of Inca priest-kings and ruled his new subjects under the exalted title of Manco Kapac, denoting "spiritually wealthy," while his sister-wife became known as Mama Ocllo. In his capital city of Cuzco he built the Inti Wasa temple, the "House of the Sun," and placed the Solar Disc over its main altar. Manco Kapac also attached a small version of the solar disc to his ceremonial regalia, and his dynasty became known as the Intic Churincuna, the "Children of the Sun."

Manco structured a two-tiered society of rulers and commoners. The members of his own family, the Children of the Sun, made up the highest caste of nobles with himself at its apex as the ruling Inca. They and their descendants became the principal rulers of the empire.

Since Manco Kapac and his lineage of Inca priest-kings wielded the Divine Wisdom and Power of the Primal Serpent, they were required to observe strict taboos, such as only wearing an article of clothing once and then immediately burning it. For the spiritual evolution of his people Manco founded lineages of adepts and schools based upon the teachings of the Seven Rayed Gnostic Goddess of Lemuria. Through the Left Hand Path practices of his mystery tradition, an initiate could eventually command the power of Wiracocha, a name of the Creator and Primal Serpent denoting "vortexual" and "spiralling," and achieve union with the inner Solar Spirit. The gnostic revelation of Paimi Kani, meaning "I am He," would then emerge within.

The Gnostic Civilization of the Druids

The colonists of Mu also helped found the Dragon Civilization of the British Druids. The Druid Adders, or "Snakes," built a gnostic civilization with a fluid caste system composed of commoners, at its lowest rung, followed by the warriors and then the Druids, who could be either male or female. At the pinnacle of the Druid caste was the Arch-Druid, and below him were Druid Elders, who adminstered an unwritten law known as the "Tara," and sat as lawmakers and judges in Councils of Twelve. The high Druids were the final word in all matters relating to divine law and justice; they were the "Supreme Court" of a tribe and co-ruled it with a specially chosen warrior or divinely chosen king. In some cases the Druids, being the most educated of their tribe, were also the principal teachers and tutors of the young, so their close influence and guidance over the Celts began at each person's birth and continued throughout their entire life.

The Druid caste was subdivided into Bards who functioned as chanters, as well as Vates who played the roles of diviners, and the Druids who served as priests, judges and advisors to the ruling kings. The Druids relied on magical incantations and their warriors for protection, although any Druid worth his salt was not averse to swinging a sword in defense of his brethren.

Although all priestly Druids were of the same status, one sub-sect of Druids, known as the Pheryllt, appear to have been the most advanced, and possibly the most ancient. They guarded many of the antiquated secrets of alchemy and gnosis that had been passed down into the mainstream of Druidism from missionaries from the East. According to one theory, the Pheryllt were Druids of the Cymry people who arrived in the British Isles from "Defrobani," which is a Welsh translation of Taprobana, a name for Sri Lanka. It is said that the Cymry were guided from Sri Lanka to the British Isles by the Welsh culture hero, Hu Gadarn, and proof of their westward journey is the Welsh language, which is full of both Sanscrit and Hebrew root words. Once in Wales, Hu Gadarn founded what many believe to have been the incipient sect of Druids, the Pheryllt, a term meaning, "Alchemists."

The Pheryllt eventually founded a Dragon Culture along the coast of what is now Wales. In their principal headquarters of Snowdon they founded the "ambrosial city of Emrys." Emrys is also remembered as "Dinas Affaraon," the "place of the Higher Powers," i.e., the place where a Druid could achieve the apex of his or her higher spiritual powers and consciousness. Emrys was the headquarters of the "Dragons of Beli" and the dark, destructive Welsh Goddess of Death, Kerridwen, whom the Pheryllt may have brought with them to Britain from Mu. There are many similarities between her and the Sri Lankan destructive goddess, Kali.

255

An Arch- Druid "Adder"

The Seven-Tiered Spiral Castle of Glastonbury Tor
Ancient home of the Pheryllt

The alchemical initiation of the Pheryllt involved an elixir of immortality that was decanted from a chalice shaped like a crescent moon called the Cauldron of Kerridwen, or the "Cauldron of Inspiration." Within this cauldron would be mixed an elixir that included such ingredients as wheat, myrrh, silver, honey, vervain, sea foam, and sometimes mistletoe. Once it entered the bloodstream the effect of Kerridwen's Cauldron was immediate, and it would lead the new initiate into a profound inner death and rebirth. The elixir would activate the inner serpent power and lead to the subsequent awakening of gnosis, which was referred to by the Druids as Awen, meaning "inspiration." When Awen was fully active, a Druid initiate was able to access both inner inspiration and intuitive wisdom. As their Awen arose into consciousness it would take the form of poetic verse, which is the form all Druidic wisdom was transmitted and archived.

A Welsh alchemical verse within *The Book of Talieson*, known as *The Spoils of Annwn*, defines both Kerridwen and her Cauldron as intimately related to the alchemical serpent power. The allegory contained in the poem recounts the journey of King Arthur and his Knights of the Round Table as they journey through Annwn, the underworld, and discover the Cauldron of Kerridwen in the "Four Cornered Castle in the Isle of the Strong Door." This poetic metaphor is a cryptic allusion to Kerridwen's Cauldron being the British version of the Kundalini of the Hindu yogis, the serpent power which lies deep within a person (their underworld) in the four-petal Muladhara Chakra (the Four Cornered Castle) at the entrance to the Sushumna energy meridian (the Strong or Closed Door).

According to *The 21 Lessons of Merlyn*, the Pheryllt were living in Glastonbury by 2000 BCE, when the region was still under water and composed of a group of islands. Their affiliation with Glastonbury was the beginning of the sacred site becoming one of the principal headquarters of alchemy in all Britain. In the center of Glastonbury the Pheryllt built a residence for the Primal Serpent, which is known today as Glastonbury Tor, the "Spiral Castle," which is comprised of the serpentine number of seven levels or tiers. Also known as the home of the Dragoness, Kerridwen, the Tor contains polar opposite white and red springs that circulate and unite to produce the power and wisdom of the serpent which vibrates throughout the Tor. Throughout the ages alchemists have traveled to Glastonbury to capture water from the red and white springs for their experiments.

Megalithic stones found on the summit of Glastonbury Tor point to its use as a center for rituals. It has been suggested that during the most energetic days of the year, the Sabbats and Esbats of the Celts, special rites were performed by the Druids on Glastonbuty Tor, as well as within many of the most powerful stone circles of Britain, in order to channel fertilizing power through the British grid of ley lines and empower the entire land.

Because they were one of the earliest waves of Druids in Britian, it has been suggested that perhaps it was the Pheryllt who constructed the towering megalithic circles of Avebury and Stonehenge. Known esoterically as the "Temples of Kerridwen," these circles were built over very important Dragon Lairs in order to magnify and utilize their underlying energies. The building of Stonehenge by Druids through the use of magical power was alluded to by the Thirteenth Century Welsh historian, Geoffrey of Monmouth, in his *The History of the Kings of Britain.* After closely studying ancient Welsh records, Geoffrey maintained that the stones of Stonehenge were moved magically to their present location by the Druid Merlin. Magic, or the use of antigravity technology, is one of the only possible explanations for how the blocks used in the construction of many of the world's ancient megalithic structures, including those of Peru and Egypt, could have transported from their quarries and put into place.

The Gnostic Civilization of Atlantis

Atlantis was another destination of the Lemurian missionaries of the World Wide Dragon Civilization. Like its sibling Dragon Civilizations around the planet, it was also covered with pyramids and ruled over by an embodiment of the Primal Serpent. Atlantis was known as a land of immortal masters who had awakened the inner serpent power and been consumed by it. Their "Instructor" was Ladon, the Son of the Goddess and Atlantean Serpent on the Tree, whom legends maintain guarded the prized golden apples of immortality. The downfall of Atlantis occured when the power of the Primal Serpent was used to control and dominate both the Atlantean masses and other countries by a fraternity of black magicians that Edgar Cayce referred to in his readings as the "Sons of Belial."

The greatest of Atlantis' adepts were the Atlantean Kings. They were embodiments of Neptune, a manifestation of the Primal Dragon who manifested on the island continent as both Poseidon, the "Earth Shaker," as well as Volcan, the fiery volcanic deity. To represent their affiliation with Volcan-Neptune, the regalia of the kings of Atlantis consisted of a crown with a tuft of white feathers at its apex, symbolizing a volcano, and a tunic ornately covered with the dual symbols associated with the Twin Sons of Volcan-Neptune that the monarch embodied as Divine Mind and Power.

King Neptune built his palace over a strategic vortex in the center of the continent of Atlantis, and then had it surrounded with three concentric circles of land that were separated by three concentric circles of water. The

Neptune's Palace on Atlantis

The Dragon King Atlas

interspersed circles of land and water both amplified the energy of the vortex and spiralled its power outwards and into the Atlantean grid of dragon lines that nourished the Motherland. This allowed both Neptune's power and guiding will to reach every part of Atlantis, and it also promoted the transmission of fertilizing power from bulls that were annually sacrificed in his palace at the beginning of each growing season.

After Neptune's legendary reign, the rulership of Atlantis was divided among his ten sons, with the first son, Atlas, taking over the role as principal monarch. This early tradition of electing ten kings apparently continued down until the latter days of the Motherland, because the first European settlers who set foot on a surviving part of the continent, the Canary Islands, found it still being observed there.

As the embodiment of the Morning and Evening Stars, Neptune, and his continent of Atlantis, retained a close affiliation to the planet Venus. The celestial movements of Venus were closely monitored from mountain-top obsrvatories by the Motherland's great astronomers and astrologers, including King Atlas himself, and calendars were devised based upon its cycles. Venus was both the Star of Alchemy and the symbol of the resurrected initiate. When its mysteries were later taken to both Egypt and Mexico by the missionaries of Atlantis, Venus became the star of the ressurected initiate Osiris or Quetzlcoatl, and its calender was adopted by those countries.

There is reason to believe that the female principle was exalted and gender equality existed on Atlantis during its earliest epochs, especially since Greek legend tells us that its ruling deity was Goddess Venus or Hespera, and the continent was protected by Her serpentine Son, Ladon. We also know that many Goddess worshipping tribes from Atlantis settled in various parts of the globe after leaving the Motherland. After arriving in Mexico, the Goddess worshipping Atlanteans became known as the Tamoanchans, and in North Africa they became known as the Amazons and the matriarchal tribes of the Berbers and the Tauregs.

Although it was probably fluid at first, there can be no doubt that during its waning years Atlantis degenerated into a rigid caste system that was enforced by an oppressive and imperialistic patriarchy of the Right Hand Path. At that time the lowest Atlantean caste would have been populated by droves of slaves that had been transported to the Motherland from various conquered countries, as well as with an abundance of half-human, half animal creatures that resulted from the left-brained Atlantean experiments with DNA splicing that was berefit of both intuitive insight and human compassion. During the waning centuries of Atlantis, patriarchal missionaries and the Sons of Belial brought their controlling Right Hand Path agenda to Europe and laid the foundation for the militaristic nations that would later emerge to dominate most of the known world.

The Gnostic Civilization of Egypt

The gnostic civilization of Egypt was heavily influenced by missionaries of the Dragon Culture of Atlantis. References to some of the earliest epochs in Egypt and the arrival of Atlantean colonists can be found in some of the country's remaining papyrus scrolls. The Royal Payrus of Turin, for example, alludes to priest-kings ruling Egypt beginning at least 36,620 years ago. During an intermediate period lasting 13,420 years, the country was ruled by the Shemsu Hor, a title assigned to the descendants of the "Seven Sages" who are believed to have been Atlantean adepts that arrived in Egypt as part of a delegation of the Thoth-Hermes Masters.

The Atlantean colonists founded a tradition of alchemists and gnostics in Egypt known as the Djedhi, or "Serpents," who embodied the Divine Power and Wisdom of the Primal Dragon. The greatest Djedhi Serpent, the Pharaoh, was an incarnation of the Primal Dragon and the "Many-Eyed" Green Man, Osiris. His Divine Power (and inner Spirit) and Divine Wisdom were individually personified and venerated as the Twin Brothers, Seth and Horus. The Pharaohs and their Atlantean predecessors were descended from some of the early extraterrestrial missionaries of Atlantis and North Africa, which is why some Egyptian kings, including Akhenaton, were born with misshapen and elongated skulls and bodies.

Movement in Egypt's caste system is believed to have been fluid rather than static. The Greek Historian Diodorus maintained that the Egyptians had three classes: peasants, craftsmen and priests, while Plato contended that there were six: peasants, shepherds, huntsmen, craftsmen, soldiers and priests. Neither chronicler, however, mentions the scribes, which are believed have constituted their own, separate caste. Candidates for initiation into Egypt's alchemical path were taken principally from the priest caste, although members of the lower castes had the opportunity to achieve the status of a priest or priestess within one lifetime.

Egypt was ruled by a theocracy, which included the Pharaoh and his sister in the highest positions, supported by officials of the priest class. Thus, executive decisions were made with a view of supporting Egypt's gnositc spiritual culture. The country was matrilineal, so the power behind the throne of the Pharaoh came from his sister, who inherited the land of Egypt from her female ancestors. Isis, the embodiment of the universal female principle, revealed that she and her representatives on Earth were the true power behind the Pharaoh by carrying a miniture throne on her head.

Isis carries the throne of rulership on her head

The Duat and one of the creatures that dwell there

For those qualified, the final alchemical initiation into the Djedhi Order occurred in the principal dwelling of the Primal Serpent in Egypt, the Great Pyramid, which was constructed on one of the most important and powerful dragon lairs on Earth. The Great Pyramid served as a medium for the Primal Serpent to spiral down from the heavens and empower the Earth with its life-giving force. As the union of the cube (matter, Earth) and tetrahedron (fire, Heaven), the pyramid both united the polarity and returned the crystallized density of the Primal Serpent back into its original form of pure energy. The alchemically transformed power of the serpent filled the interior of the Great Pyramid, especially the King's Chamber, where the final alchemical awakening of the serpent fire was actualized within a Djedhi. It was in the King's Chamber that the polar-opposite cosmic energies radiating from Alpha Draconis and Orion streamed down shafts and then mixed together to produce an initiation chamber saturated with the serpent power.

Similar to the Tibetans, the Egyptians understood that a labyrinth awaited them in the next world when they died, and they even made a physical representation of it, complete with nefarius crocodiles, on the shore of sacred Lake Moeris. Known as the Duat, if this etheric realm was correctly negotiated the soul could achieve gnosis and immortal life, but one wrong turn and the transiting soul could find itself in a dark, hellish realm for eternity. Therefore, while alive the priests were entreated to study what was known of the next world and to take astral journeys through the Duat in preparation for their final departure. To prepare for their own personal ascents through the next world, the Egyptian nobility had their sarcophaguses and tombs covered with detailed hieroglphs and maps of the Duat.

The Gnostic Civilization of the Maya and Toltecs

Missionaries from both Atlantis and Lemuria brought their Dragon Culture to Middle America where it culminated in the Olmec, Toltec and Mayan civilizations. The records of their arrival were preserved by the Nahuatl Elders and recorded in the history of the Seventeenth Century Spanish Chronicler, Bernardo de Sahagun. Later, in the Nineteenth Century, the American consulate Edward Thompson acquired a similar historical chronology through his initiations into the Mayan Sh'Tol Brotherhood. His findings are recorded in his book, *The People of the Serpent*.

Both Sahagun and Thompson are in agreement that the first colonists were seafaring "Serpents" who arrived in Middle America from the East in ships covered in snake skins. After reaching the coast of Veracruz these Serpents sailed down the Panuco River until disembarking at the optimal spot to build a city. There they constructed the premier Dragon Civilization of Mexico,

Tamoanchan: The Garden of Eden
*Where Gnostic Civilization first
emerged in Mexico & Central America*

known as Tamoanchan, which Thompson was told translates as "Where the People of the Serpent Landed."

From Tamoanchan the Serpents spread the gnostic culture of the Plumed Serpent throughout Middle American. Under their guidance within the principle city-states of the Olmecs, Maya, and Toltecs, towering pyramidal homes of the Primal Serpent arose that were used for initiation into the mysteries of the Plumed Serpent. At La Venta, the greatest temple city of the Olmecs, the descendants of the Atlantean venerators of Volcan built a home for the Primal Serpent in the form of an artificial volcano-pyramid from rock quarried 60 miles away in the volcanic Tuxla range. In the Toltec capital of Teotihuacan, the Primal Serpent also found a home within the towering Pyramid of the Sun, which engulfed an initiate in a "redeeming fire" leading him or her to a "luminous consciousness" of gnostic wisdom.[6] At the Mayan capital of Chichen Itza, the Primal Serpent was given residence within the Temple of Quetzalcoatl and fully revealed itself during each spring and fall equinox by slithering down the steps of the edifice as as a serpent of seven triangles.

The Maya and Toltecs appear to have originally had a fluid caste system composed of nobles, priests, warriors and commoners, but at some point in history patriarchal influences arose among the Toltecs and their descendants, the Aztecs, that catalyzed its solidification. From that time onwards some city-states mandated that only the descendants of priests and nobles were eligible to receive training for the sought-after priestly positions and their accompanying initiation into the secret mysteries.

The Mayan priest caste was both striated and fluid. At the bottom were the Nacoms and Chacs who superintended the sacrifice of plants, minerals and animals. Above them were Ahua Kan Mai, the "Serpent Priests," and the Ah Kin Mai, the "Solar Priests." At the pinnacle of the priest caste was the priest-king, the Kukulcan or "Feathered Serpent," who was a living embodiment of both the Primal Serpent and the World Tree it clung to. As such, the Mayan kings kept their kingdoms prosperous by channeling an abundance of high frequency power from above into them. Many "Tree Stones" carved by the Maya portrayed their shaman kings as embodiments of the World Tree, including one that adorns the cover of the tomb holding the mummy of King Pacal Votan in Palenque. The Palanque lid also depicts the shaman king riding the World Tree as an axis mundi to other worlds.

As a shamanic culture, the Mayans produced many gnostic adepts who knew the secrets of astral traveling to the highest worlds and dimensions of the universe. Their "highway" was the Kuxam Summ, which was an inter-galactic grid "leading to the umbilical cord of the universe."[7]

The volcano-pyramids of La Venta and Teotihuacan

Mayan history closes suddenly at the end of the Classic Period (circa 800 CE) when many city-states were abandoned and their occupants simply disappeared. It has been conjectured that the ravages of war between the city-states was responsible for their abandonment, but it has also been speculated that the Maya were a very advanced civilization of gnostics that simply transcended into another dimension. A similar claim has been made for the Anasazi of the American southwest, who similarly dissappeared from the world in the Thirteenth Century without a trace.

The Gnostic Civilization of Sumeria

Another destination of both Atlantean and Lemurian missionaries of the Worldwide Dragon Culture was the Middle East. In the land of the Tigris and Eupharates Rivers they founded a constellation of Sumerian city-states beginning with Eridu, the headquarters of Enki, the Primal Dragon who was a version of Neptune-Volcan. Enki's priests were the Ashipu, the "Serpents" of Sumeria, who covered themselves in fish regalia to identify with their goat-fish deity and channel his prodigious power and wisdom.

Sumerian society centered on a fluid caste system composed of three classes: the Amelu, the Mushkinu and the slaves. The Amelu Caste was populated with the priests, as well as government officials and professional soldiers. Below them were the members of the Mushkinu Caste, the commoners, which included shopkeepers, farmers, merchants and laborers. The slaves made up the lowest caste and could be born or sold into slavery, but they could also own property and even purchase their own freedom.

The priest caste was subdivided into the Ashipu, Baru and Kalu. The Ashipu, who channeled the power and wisdom of Enki, were the highest of the three orders of priests, and it is because of their exalted sacerdotal position that their fish-head headdresses later became the mitres worn by the Cardinals of the Roman Catholic Church. The Baru served the extremely important function of divining the future for their respective city-states. Their vocation required them to become adepts at dream symbolism, cloud formations, astrology and the art of reading animal entrails. The Kalu were masters of mantra incantations, a skill that required many years of training to acquire the proper pitch and pronunciation. They were also adept musicians and would accompany their chanting with drums, cymbals and harps.

At the apex of the Sumerian and Babylonian caste system were the Dragon Kings. They were incarnations of Dammuzi, the Green Man, who was a counterpart of Enki. These monarchs received their inner serpent power to rule their kingdoms from Enki via his son Marduk, and the authority behind their reigns came from the Goddess, Inanna, whom Enki had annointed

The excavated Ziggurat of Ur

The excavated Ziggurat of Chogha Zanbil

patroness of all kings and queens. Thus, like Egypt and many other gnostic civilizations, the Goddess was the true authority behind the throne.

In Eridu, as well as many of the other Sumerian city-states, towering ziggurats were commonly erected as homes for the Primal Serpent. The ziggurat in the city-state of Nippur was known as DUR.AN.KI, meaning "Bond of Heaven and Earth," thus revealing that it was the structure by which the Primal Serpent could spiral down around as it descended from the heavens. Throughout Sumeria the ziggurats were comprised of seven tiers, each painted one of the seven "serpentine" colors of the rainbow, thus making them true embodiments of the Serpent. Known by the alternate name of ESH, meaning "heat source," they generated the serpent fire interiorly.

The Gnostic Civilization of the Yezidis

Another gnostic civilization that manifested in the Middle East was founded around 2000 BCE by missionaries directly descended from the Lemurians. These were the Yezidis, who now reside in northern Iraq and claim to be the very First People created upon our planet. Before coming to Iraq they had resided in India, and before that they were occupants of the Lemurian Garden of Eden, where according to their sacred history they had been specially produced by the Primal Serpent Son, whose name they were told was Tawsi Melek, the "Peacock Angel." Unfortunately, such an ancient and remarkable pedigree has not sheltered the Yezidis from continual attack from neighboring Moslems, who have wrongly associated their Peacock Angel with Satan and murdered up to twenty million of them over the centuries.

The Yezidis are well known for preserving one of the few remaining caste systems in the modern world. The first two and most important Yezidi castes, the Faqirs and Pirs, are said to have been created by Tawsi Melek in the Garden of Eden as part of the Lemurian caste system. The Yezidi caste system was later expanded upon by the Eleventh Century reformer Sheikh Adî ibn Mustafa, a Sufi saint. Sheikh Adî became a member of the Yezidi tribe after receiving visions of Tawsi Melek while living the life of a Sufi recluse in Baghdad. The Peacock Angel informed the Sheikh that he was to be Tawsi Melek's special emissary on Earth during the present cycle and "proclaim the religion of truth to the world." He then instructed Sheikh Adî to travel to Lalish, which had been an important axis mundi and World Tree during Lemurian times, and reclaim it for the People of Tawsi Melek, the Yezidis. When Sheikh Adî arrived in Lalish he found it occupied by a Christian sect which had erected a church upon the land. His announcement that he had been sent there to reacquire Lalish for its rightful owners did not immediately sit well with the Christians, but after some deliberation they

269

A Yezidi Community

Yezidi Priests of the Sheikh Caste

Lalish, temple-tomb of Shiekh Adî & Six Archangels

Tawsi Melek, Creater and Lord of the Universe

decided that if Sheikh Adî could show proof of the existence of Tawsi Melek they would honor his request. Calling forth the power of Tawsi Melek to move through him, Sheikh Adî tapped the hard ground with his staff and a powerful stream of clear water immediately emerged...and as a flowing artisian well it has continued to emit water in Lalish ever since. Sheikh Adî's award for his magic was the sacred area of Lalish, and he quickly mobilized the Yezidis to return to their rightful home.

Sheikh Adî continued to have visions and receive guidance from Tawsi Melek throughout his life, and in order to remain open to this high guidance he would annually observe two forty-day fasts, one in the summer and another in the winter. Some of the guidance and wisdom he received from Tawsi Melek was eventually compiled into a new Yezidi scripture, the *Kitab al-Jilwa,* the "Book of Revelation."

Ultimately, Sheikh Adî's reforms would prove pivotal to the Yezidi civilization and become the bedrock of their sect. Sheikh Adî's mission was successful, at least in part, because of the assistance he received from the other six archangels who simultaneously took physical incarnation while he was on Earth. According to Yezidi historian, Ester Spat, this was not the first time they had appeared together on our planet. She states:

"...[T]he Seven Angels appear on earth from time to time in the guise of human beings to bring religion and guidance to people. Thus the greatest protagonists of Yezidi history [Sheikh Adî, etc.] were considered earthly manifestations of the Peacock Angel, while other figures were believed to represent the other angels on earth."[8]

Sheikh Adî's reforms included strictly forbidding marriages between members of the different Yezidi castes, as well as between a Yezidi and anyone born outside the tribe. Under his guidance a lower caste, the Murids, or "Commoners," was added, and the Sheikh Caste was subdivided into the Faqirs and Qewels. The six archangels and their descendants became members of the Sheikh Caste, and the Pir Caste assimilated the descendants of the 40 close disciples of Sheikh Adî. The Faqirs, the "Poor Ones," became the highest ranking members of the Sheikh caste, and they served as the principal leaders within the various Yezidi communities they were part of. They rightfully claimed direct descent from the greatest Faqir, Sheikh Adî, from whom prodigious gnostic power and wisdom had been passed down to them. Currently, during the rites of the Faqirs at Lalish the members of the caste cover themselves in vests of black, the color of gnostic wisdom, or they walk in long white gowns covered in white vests made of the wool from a goat, the sacred animal of Tawsi Melek. During one of their annual processions, the Faqir leader adorns himself in the black fur cape and the cone-shaped hat which are said to have been once worn by the first Faqir, Sheikh Adî.

All three Yezidi castes receive continual assistance from Melek Taus in the development of both their worldly discrimination and gnosis. This is especially true of the Sheikh Caste, whose function it is to receive the inner mysteries and then disseminate them among the other Yezidis. Their model of the highest gnostic was Sheikh Adî, who was a Sufi in the mold of al-Hallaj, the gnostic adept famous for descending into trance and proclaiming, "Ana-al Haqq," meaning "Truth is me" or "I am God." While in a similar trace state, Sheikh Adî is said to have fully identified with his beloved Tawsi Melek and could be heard announcing:

"In the depth of my knowledge there is no God but me."

Today, the Faqirs and other Sheikh families are acknowledged to be endowed with both wisdom and special powers passed to them directly from Tawsi Melek and their archangel ancestors. The Faqirs and Qewels also gain considerable power by regularly reciting the prayers given them from Tawsi Melek. The power possessed by each Sheikh family is different. One family heals arthritis or fever; one cures snakebites; another cures insanity; and another provides protection against the "Evil Eye" etc.[9]

At the pinnacle of the Yezidi hierachy Sheikh Adî placed the Baba Sheikh, the "Yezidi Pope," and one rung above him he established the position of the Yezidi Prince, the "Mir," who is acknowledged to be Tawsi Melek's special envoy on Earth. The title of Mir appears to be related to Mihr, a name of Mithras, who was a Persian evolution of Karttikeya (see my book *The Truth Behind the Christ Myth: The Redemption of the Peacock Angel*), and the counterpart of Tawsi Melek. Therefore, the title Mir identifies the Yezidi Prince to be an embodiment of the Divine Wisdom and Power of Tawsi Melek.

The government of the Yezidis was initially centered around the Mir, who was the ultimate lawgiver, and the priestly support of the Baba Sheikh. They both continue to hold great influence among the Yezidis, although many of the Yezidis' most stringent laws are currently dictated to them by the neighboring Moslem Kurds. The leaders of the individual Yezidi communities continue to be the priestly Faqirs of the Sheikh Caste, who traditionally defer to the Baba Sheikh and Mir in many important disputes. Some of the most difficult conflicts are settled during the religious festivals held at Lalish, which are attended by both the Baba Sheikh and the Mir. These religious gatherings are organized and overseen by the Faqirs, who have been designated by Tawsi Melek to be the special caretakers of Lalish.

When Sheikh Adî passed away he was interred in a tomb at Lalish, and his presence can still be subtly felt by visitors there. Eventually, one by one, the bodies of the other six archangels were placed in tombs close to his own, thus making the temple that unites them exceptionally powerful.

The future of the Yezidis is bleak if the Moslem program of genocide against them is not stopped. According to the belief of many fanatical Moslems, Tawsi Melek is synonymous with Satan, but this belief is the result of a misinterpretation of the Yezidi scriptures. Moslems also believe that the Koran has instructed them to destroy all nonbelievers who will not convert to Islam, especially those who have in the past embraced the religion but later became heretics. They place the Yezidis in the latter category, even though the Yezidis are adamant that any resemblance they may have to Islam came via Sheikh Adî and their tribe has never officially been part of that religion.

It has been estimated that during the past 700 years, 20 million Yezidis have been killed by the Moslems, and the onslaught continues. Just 200 years ago the population was 2 million, and now it is estimated to be less than one million worldwide. A current "incentive" to the ongoing Moslem decimation is the belief that, if a Moslem slays a Yezidi, great awards await him in Heaven, such as 72 ripe virgins. In one of the most recent attacks in 2007, Moslem suicide bombers drove four trucks loaded with explosives into the Yezidi town of Sinjar and detonated them. The explosives decimated the town and killed more than 500 Yezidis.

The Gnostic Civilization of the Mandaeans

The Mandaeans are, like the Yezidis, a gnostic civilization in Iraq that boasts a profound Lemurian heritage. They began their history on Sri Lanka when the island was part of the land-mass of Mu and eventually migrated west where they became part of the Sumerian, Persian, Egyptian and Jewish Essene civilizations. Finally, retracing their steps, they returned to their present location in southern Iraq. In the tradition of the gnostic sects descended from the Goddess and the Left Hand Path, the Mandaeans provide equal rights and privileges for both men and women. They are a two-caste sect composed of priests at the upper tier and lay-persons below them.

The Mandaeans are governed by their priest class, which is composed of both men and women. Leading every Mandaean community is the high priest, the Ganzibra, who is a priest or priestess of "high birth" descended from priests and priestesses on both sides of his or her family. Like all priests(esses), the Ganzibra wears the rasta, the sacred ceremonial outfit of white clothing which symbolizes the "dress of light in which the pure soul is clad," and he or she covers their head with a tagha, a "crown," which represents "his kingly [or queenly] function as ruler, lawgiver, and leader."

The high priest(ess) is obligated to live an immaculate life, otherwise he or she will be disgraced and lose their high position.[10]

The centerpiece of the Mandaean religion is the rite of baptism. The Mandaean priests are adamant about the importance of regular baptism and make it clear that "the more often one is baptized the better," and that "Baptism, alms, and good deeds make the perfect Mandaean."[11] Simply by coming into contact with the Water of Life, the subtle but transforming life force moving through water, a Mandaean is purified on many levels and moves closer to the goal of gnosis. Although they do not currently refer to the Water of Life as a manifestation of Enki as their Sumerian ancestors once did, the Mandaeans do maintain that within the physical water flows the wisdom and Supreme Power, or "Great Life," of Spirit. Some rivers or streams, they claim, are more infused with this power than others, including the Karun, Tigris, Euphrates and Zab Rivers in Iraq, which is why their communities have arisen along the banks of these waterways.[12]

The private baptismal immersion of a Mandaean, known as the "Rishama," is performed each day by both men and women. A prayer is repeated while each part of the body is sequentially cleansed. At the end of the rite, the power and wisdom of ancient Enki, the Mandeans' Manda d'Hiya, is invoked with the words: "The name of the Life [the Divine Power] and the name of Manda d'Hiya [the Divine Wisdom] are pronounced upon me." The following is the Rishama rite recorded by Lady Drower during her many years living among the Mandeans in the 1920s:

"'As the Mandaean approaches the river, he says 'I bless the great yardana of Living Water.'

He then stoops and washes his hands, saying: 'In the name of the Great Life, purify my hands in righteousness and my lips in faith. Let them utter the speech of the Light and make my ablutions good [potent] by thoughts of Light.'

He washes his face three times, taking water in his hands and saying: 'I bless thy name, praised is thy name, my lord, Manda d'Hiya, I bless! Be praised that great Countenance of Splendor which of itself was manifest.'

He next takes water in his hand and signs himself from ear to ear across the forehead from right to left, saying: 'I, [name], sign myself with the sign of the Life.'

Next, three times he dips two fingers in the river and cleanses his wears, saying: 'May my ears hear the voice of the Life.'

Taking water into his palm, he snuffs it three times up into his nose, repeating each time: 'May my nostrils smell the perfume of the Life.'

He then washes the lower part of his body, saying: 'The Name of Life

Mandaean Priests

Mandaeans observing the daily Rishama Baptism rite

and the name of Manda d'Hiya are mentioned upon me.'

Next taking water into his mouth from his palm, he rinses it out three times saying: 'May my mouth be filled with a prayer of praise.'

He washes his knees three times with the words: 'May my knees bless and worship the Great Life.'

Washing the legs three times: 'May my legs follow the ways of right and faith.'

He dabbles his fingers in the river, his hands together and the palms downwards, saying: 'I have baptized myself...my baptism will gird me and lift me to the summit of perfection [the House of Life, the highest dimension].'

Lastly, he dips the right foot twice and the left foot once into the river, saying: 'May the Seven [planets] and the Twelve [Zodiac signs] not have dominion over my feet."[13]

The most powerful of baptisms are observed on Sunday under the guidance of a Mandaean priest and incorporate much more ritual than the Rishama. They include the sacraments of oil, bread, and water, and end with the sacred kiss upon the head from a priest, a rite known as as "giving Kushta." Possibly the most valuable part of the ceremony for a person's spiritual progress is a special transmission of energy given them by the priest, who after the water immersion transmits the Water of Life into a baptized Mandaean by placing his right hand upon his or her head and calling forth Manda d'Hiya.

Baptism extends into many other areas of the Mandaeans' daily life. Both before and during many of their other activities the Mandaeans also call upon the baptizing power of Manda d'Hiya. He is, for example, invoked during the preparation and washing (or baptizing) of food and then again during mealtimes to sanctify both the food and those receiving it. The support and blessings of Manda d'Hiya is paramount in the life of a Mandean who seeks to remain pure in order to open to his or her inner gnosis and spiritual power. Manda d'Hiya is invoked for his purifying power and because he is both teacher and bestower of gnostic wisdom.

Those called to the Mandaean priesthood begin to invoke Manda d'Hiya from an early age. They are normally born into the priest caste, and their education begins at home when their parents teach them all the rites and mantras. Purity is of the utmost importance, and diet is restricted to vegetables from an early age, especially among those destined to adopt the most sanctified life of a Nasurai. The rite of consecration is very rigirous and each candidate is put through an intensive battery of purificatory observances. During the first week of consecration for a priest or priestess the candidate must not sleep at night in order to prevent "nocturnal pollution." Then they are required to undergo sixty days of purity, during which they observe "triple immersion", or water baptism three times each day while living apart from their families and friends and consuming a very pure, vegetarian diet. Then there follows a litany of purificatory rituals administered by the priests.

Besides calling upon Manda d'Hiya for daily support, the gnostic Mandaeans also seek relief from the limitations of the Earth plane in other ways. They are, for example, adept astrologers who understand the energies emanating from the planets and are schooled in the remedial measures to neutralize their inhibiting, and sometimes inimical, influences. For this purpose, they often prescribe amulets and talismans for each other. One such talisman, the Skandola, may reveal an ancient Mandaean-Hindu link since Skanda is the Manda d'Hiya of the Hindus.

At the conclusion of their life, all Mandaeans rise up to Mshunia Kushta, an etheric dimension where they merge with their etheric-body double that has been waiting for them during their earthly sojourn. When Lady Drower inquired as to the location of this etheric world, she was given the description of an etheric world that apparently overlays the planet Venus. One Mandaean priest stated:

"There is a star inhabited by men, the descendants of the Hidden Adam [the etheric double of Adam], but they are semi-spiritual in nature, and not gross like ourselves. This star is called Merikh, the star of the morning."[14]

The Mandaean baptismal purifications continue on this "star" until each Mandaean is ready to shed his or her etheric forms and live exclusively in their most refined bodies of light as pure luminaries of gnosis. They are then eligible to return home to the highest Pleroma worlds of light.

The future may be bleak for the Mandaeans if their karma requires them to undergo any more decimation to their tiny population. Attacks on the Mandaeans date back to their years as Nasorean Essenes when orthodox Jews sought to exterminate them because of their aberrant spiritual practices. Not long afterwards the Mandaeans became engaged in a feud with the Moslems that has been ongoing, and most recently they suffered major setbacks from the two Gulf Wars that has reduced the Iraqi Mandeans to their present population of 15,000. Fortunately, a few thousand Mandaeans have been able to escape the Middle East and now live safely in western countries.

The Skandola

The Gnostic Civilization of the Essenes

The gnostic civilization of the Essenes was engineered by gnostic missionaries from Egypt and Sumeria, as well as by Mandaeans who endowed it with their Lemurian, Egyptian and Persian wisdom. The short-lived Essene civilization became a recognized, independent culture around 150 BCE, following the Jewish liberation from Babylonia, and then disappeared from the world stage towards the end of the Second Century CE. The Essene gnostic and alchemical wisdom lived on, however, within the gnostic sects of Alexandria, as author Robert Graves explicitly states:

"The Alexandrian Gnostics...were the spiritual heirs of the Essenes after Hadrian had suppressed the Order in 132 A.D."[15]

According to Freemasonry historian Albert Mackey, one Alexandrian gnostic sect that preserved the Essene wisdom was the Society or Ormus, or Order of the Rosy Cross, founded by the gnostic adept Ormus, which later passed the ancient knowledge down to many of the Sub-Rosa sub-sects of Europe. Beginning with Ormus and other Alexandrian gnostics, the Essene wisdom became synonymous with their most occult and secret teachings compiled in Kabbala, which was destined to become the highest authority for many of Europe's alchemists, gnostics, magicians and Secret Societies. Included in the Kabbalistic texts of the Essenes is the *Sepher Yetzirah*, the "Book of Creation," which contains traditional serpent wisdom regarding how the universe was created from vibration in the form of Primal Serpent and the Tree of Life.

The Essenes and their wisdom contained within the Kabbala, which is built around an archetypal code disseminated directly from the Divine Mind, are said to have existed since the Garden of Eden. Referring to their very ancient heritage, the authoritative Jewish historian, Josephus, declared that the Essenes had existed "from time immemorial" through "countless generations." Another Jewish historian, the famous Alexandrian mystic Philo, stated that the "[Essene] teaching was perpetuated through an immense space of ages" and brought forth "the most ancient of all the initiates."

By tracing them back to the very inception of human history, Josephus and Philo ostensibly linked the beginning of the Essenes to the fabled Garden of Eden, or Lemuria, home of the gnostics' First Instructor. Esoteric scholar Manly Palmer Hall goes one step backwards in time in maintaining that the primal Essene-Kabbalistic tradition was "...first taught by God to a school of His Angels," and then "The Angel Raziel was dispatched from heaven to instruct Adam in the mysteries of the Kabbala."[16] The Angel Raziel, whose name denotes "Keeper of Secrets" and "Angel of Mysteries," was an aspect of the Divine Mind known in the Kabbalistic tradition as St. Michael.

Michael's heavenly and earthly manifestations are manifold and include Metatron, the "Outer Yahweh," as well as the supreme monarch of the universe, King Melchizedek. It was Michael who would later give Moses a fresh dispensation of the Kabbalistic mysteries on the summit of Mt. Sinai.

Moses received two dispensations of wisdom from Michael, the first of which contained the mysteries of the Left Hand Path that were destined for the Hebrew initiates, including the Essenes, while the second comprised the Laws of the Right Hand Path that was intended for the common flock of Hebrews. It is said that Moses taught the Kabbala to 2000 hand-picked Hebrews, whom the later Essenes would refer to as their 2000 ancestors.

The wisdom of the Essenes became dualistic under the influence of the Persian Magi that arrived in the Middle East with Cyrus the Great during the Jewish captivity in Babylon. The Magi's split of the Primal Dragon into Ormuzd, the Divine Mind and Lord of Light, and Ahriman, the Divine Power and Lord of Darkness, were transformed among the Jewish theologians to become St. Michael and his archenemy, Belial. The Essenes designated themselves Michael's Army of Light on Earth and resolved to fight the forces of Belial throughout the world until the end of time. The Essene prophets predicted that Michael would eventually take a physical incarnation for his final battle with Belial, and the Essenes would then fight by his side until all the darkness and evil on Earth had been defeated.

To ready themselves for their final battle and resist the dark, coercive powers of Belial, the Essenes constantly engaged themselves in gnostic and alchemical practices. To prepare for Archangel Michael's coming each Essene would seek to fully incarnate his or her angelic spirit through intense practices of purification. In this way, when Michael finally arrived for his last battle with Belial, his army of angels would already be physically on Earth waiting for him.

Before the final battle with Belial, the Essenes welcomed a series of physical incarnations of St. Michael and the highest angels into their sect, and created special offices for them. The highest Essene office was occupied by the incarnations of the highest angel, Michael, and below him was the office of the second highest angel, Gabriel, and under him was the third highest angel, Sariel, etc. The hierachy of angelic offices within the Essene order thus mirrored the angelic hierarchy in the heavens. When Jesus was born among the Essenes, Zacharias held the office of the Michael. The office eventually passed to Zacharias' son, John the Baptist, and from him it passed to Jesus and then to James the Just. Thus, both John and Jesus were acknowledged incarnations of the Divine Wisdom and Power of Michael, a truth that is revealed by some of the sayings of Jesus in *The Gospel of Mat-*

The Essene Colony of Qumran on the Dead Sea

The cave temples of Qumran

Mount Carmel: Home to an Essene Colony

The Caves of Mount Carmel: Home to Essene Prophets

thew, which were identical to those attributed to St. Michael in the Apochryphal gospel, *The Testament of Abraham*.

At their height, the Essenes, a name which Philo Judeaus derives from hosios, meaning "holy," included around 4000 members. They were, states Philo, "Servants of God"…"an esoteric circle of illuminati," who occupied settlements in both Egypt and Palestine and commuted back and forth between the two. The Essenes in Egypt, known as the Theraputae, occupied a colony on the shores of the sacred Lake Mareotis. It was here that Jesus, Mary and Joseph are reputed to have lived after escaping Herod's carnage of the Jews' first-born sons. The two principal Essene settlements in Palestine were located at Qumran on the Dead Sea, where they lived as celibate monastics, and at Mt. Carmel, where marriage and the conception of children were allowed. In both communities all persons were treated equally, and slavery was considered an abomination. Every person was a brother or sister and a part of God's extended family, so all possessions were held in common. A vegetarian regimen was strictly followed, and prayer and meditation were observed at the beginning and end of each day. Throughout the day practical vocations, including farming and carpentry, were engaged it by all Essenes. The high regard the Freemasons currently hold for these people stems from their mastery of geometry and their building expertise, which legend has it was passed to them from Lamech, Tubal Cain and the original artisans mentioned in *Genesis*. It was because of their profound knowledge of numerology and geometry, as well as their belief in reincarnation, that the Essenes were referred to by many of the early historians as "Pythagoreans."

The Essenes were also healing adepts who had mastered diagnostic techniques and the therapeutic modalities of herbology, massage, hydrotherapy and fasting. Fasting, which was a practice some Essenes would observe for as long as 40 days, was not just for physical purification but also for alchemical transformation. To care for the sick, the Essenes built the first hospitals and welcomed into them the convalescents of all faiths and walks of life, without exception. The Essenes' compassionate temperament and generosity was renown among their Jewish neighbors. As the Jewish chronicler Josephus reports:

"The Essenes were of an exemplary morality, they forced themselves to suppress passion and anger, and they were always benevolent, peaceable and trustworthy. Their word was more powerful than an oath, which, in ordinary life, they looked upon as superfluous, and almost as perjury. They endured the most cruel of tortures, with admirable steadfastness of soul and smiling countenance, rather than violate the slightest religious precept."

Under the influence of the Mandaeans who merged with them, the Essenes integrated baptism into their daily repertoire of purifying practices. They became repositories of the true mysteries of baptism, including why it was necessary to use moving water during the rite and how to activate the inner Water of Life through mantras and invocations. History will eventually show that the Mandaeans and Essenes merged to become the sect of Nasoreans or Nazarenes. Later, when many of the Nasorean-Mandaeans fled back to the Tigris and Euphrates Rivers they continued to cover themselves in long white robes and sandals and worship the Sun, just as they had done with their Essene bothers and sisters back in the Holy Land. They also continued to maintain that their holiest mountain was Tura d'Madai, the "Mountain of the Mandaeans," which may simply be another name for the Essenes' most sacred mountain, Mount Carmel.

The requirements to become a member of an Essene community were designed to separate the casual seeker from the most dedicated aspirant. Before a person was even allowed to become a permanent member of the Essene community, he or she would be required to prove themselves by undergoing a strict probationary period of at least one year, which was then followed by a lighter probationary period of at least two years. When a candidate passed these initial trials and was accepted into a community, he or she was required to trade in all their accumulated possessions for a simple white robe, sandals, and a staff, and to swear an oath to perpetually observe the "Halakoth," the strict code of conduct and disciplines subscribed to by the Essenes.

According to *The Dead Sea Scrolls,* an Esssene community was governed by a "Guardian" at the highest level, and below him was a Council of 15. They would bestow their verdicts and judgments in accordance with the *Book of the Community Rule.* A passage from the scrolls are the statutes defining this Council. It states:

"In the Council of the Community there shall be twelve men and three Priests, perfectly versed in all of the Law, whose works shall be truth, righteousness, justice, loving-kindness and humility."[17]

As a gnostic, each Essene would prepare for an eternal residence in the Pleroma by taking periodic journeys to the upper reaches of the cosmos in their astral bodies. After becoming fully acquainted with the various dimensions and their angelic gatekeepers, he or she would draw a protective circle around him-herself and then trace the subtle Merkaba lines that would energize and extricate his-her astral body. The Essene could then rise up as high as possible into the cosmos and momentarily experience freedom from the limitations of the Earth plane.

The greatest freedom for an Essene on Earth would arrive when he or she fully integrated their guardian angel and acquired its gnostic wisdom and power. At that pivotal moment the Essene would achieve the highest gnosis and transcend the continual cycle of reincarnation. If this achievement did not occur for a member of their community during life, the Essenes would follow certain funerary injunctions to elicit its actualization in the next world.

The Gnostic Civilization of the Manichaeans

A continuation and synthesis of the Mandaean, Persian, and Essene gnostic civilizations was orchastrated by the Prophet Mani in the Third Century as the "Religion of the Prophet Mani," or Manichaeism. Mani, who was born in 217 CE to a Mandaean father and a Persian mother, became privy of his earthly mission of creating a one-world gnostic civilization when he was still a teenager. His guardian angel, who identified itself as the Paraclete, the "Comforter" promised by Jesus, appeared to Mani and instructed him to complete the work of all the great prophets who had come before him, including Zoroaster, Moses, Buddha and Jesus. They had all brought pieces of the gnostic "puzzle" to Earth, and now it was time for Mani to synthesize all these pieces into one all-encompassing universal faith designed for everyone. Mani's subsequent fabrication of the gnostic religion of Manichaeism was wildly successful, and over the course of the next one thousand years it was embraced by millions of people that lived in the chain of lands between China and Spain. At one time it counted among its elite converts St. Augustine, who later became a powerful leader in the Catholic Church.

Mani's gnostic religion encouraged the development of both the right and left hemispheres of the brain through both intellectual and intuitive training, thus supporting gnosis. The teachers of his sect were of both sexes; they were highly educated and intuitive, and most were adepts on the gnostic-alchemical path. Besides committing themselves to studying, translating and copying all the available spiritual writings of their era, the priests of Manicheaeism also observed a celibate lifestyle, a vegetarian diet, and long days and nights of meditation, fasting and prayer. They embraced a traditional gnostic ideology which maintained that all humans were divine spirits imprisoned in physical forms, and they followed Mani's guidance to extricate their souls from the shackles of dense matter. Until their release from matter was permanent they knew they were destined to continue to revolve on the wheel of reincarnation indefinitely.

In keeping with Zoroastrian dualism, Mani's ideology maintained that all matter on the physical plane was governed by an evil dark lord, while the upper, spiritual realms were ruled by a beneficent deity of light. Indulg-

Manichaen Priests

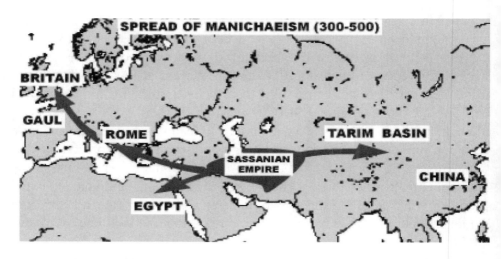

Map reference: World History Atlas, Dorling Kindersly

ing in sensual desires only served to keep a human locked in the physical world and perpetuated the dark lord's rule over them.

Manichaeism was composed of lay persons known as Auditors or "Hearers," and their teachers, priests and adepts were known as the Pure or "Elect." The Pure lived an intensely austere lifestyle that allowed only one meal per day and required at least 100 days of fasting over the course of a year, with at least one of those fasts continuing for a period of 30 days. They were required to daily chant eight very long hymnal prayers, and when not meditating or studying texts they were enjoined to enroll in service work to benefit their communities. The Elect were supported materially by the lay persons, who lived normal, worldly lives until they were ready to surrender to the life of a Pure. At the time of his or her advancement a Hearer would be absolved of all sin and have the Holy Spirit power transmitted into them by a facilitating Elect. Any future sin could be rectified with mentanoia, "repentance," except for one, observes the gnostic author Kurt Rudolph:

"Unforgivable is only the sin of the conscious resistence against the redeeming knowledge, the illumination by the light-nous, the Holy Spirit...."[18]

Apparently some of the Manichaean communities, especially those in the East, were set up like Buddhist communities, or "sanghas." States one author:

"Buddhist influences were significant in the formation of Mani's religious thought. The transmigration of souls became a Manichaean belief, and the quadripartite structure of the Manichaean community, divided between male and female monks (the "elect") and lay followers(the "hearers") who supported them, appears to be based on that of the Buddhist sangha."[19]

Mani was supported early in his ministry by the Persian King Shappur, but when the King died, his son Bharam colluded with the Persian high priest Kartir to cleanse the world of all "heretical" sects, including Manicheanism. Mani was sent to prison, and after years of torture he died an agonizing death in his cell. In the year 277 his dismembered and flayed corpse was put on public display, which at the time was the traditional fate of all condemned heretics.

Vestiges of Mani's religion continued to influence gnostic sects in Asia and Europe for more than one thousand years following his death. With minor revisions, Mani's religion was adopted in the Seventh Century by the Armenian Paulicans and again in the Tenth Century by the Bulgarian Bogomils, a sect founded by Bogomil, a gnostic adept whose honorary name meant "Dear to God." Like Mani before him, Bogomil also promulgated the existence of two opposing principles governing the universe, and championed an ascetic lifestyle as the best method for becoming extricated from the clutches of materiality. Under Bogomil's guidance, hermitages and monasteries with a strict schedule of daily prayer and meditation were founded in Bulgaria for those ready to achieve gnosis. Part of the Bogomils' heresy was his mass, which excluded the Christian crucifix. Many gnostic sects regarded the crucifix to be a symbol of torture.

The Gnostic Civilization of the Cathars

The gnostic civilization of Manichaeism experienced a revival of sorts in France in the Twelfth Century with the founding of the gnostic civilization of the Cathars by Bogomil missionaries and Manichaean gnostics who had survived in southern Europe. The Cathars departed from the earlier gnostic sects in declaring themselves Christians, albeit primitive or "Good Christians," in contrast to the "Church of Wolves," which was their derogatory moniker for the Catholic Church. In presenting themselves as the true Christians, the Cathars revived the age-old battle between the Left and Right Hand Paths and expedited their own demise.

The Cathars' claim to represent the "true Christian Church" was based on their Johannite heritage from John the Apostle and their deep and abiding love for Mary Magdalene. They reviled the Church's patriarchal control and its ostentatious ways, choosing for themselves simple and unpretentious sermons and gathering places. They dispensed with the ornate temples of the Church, choosing instead private homes and the lush, surrounding forests for their meeting places. Their temple might be a forest glen, a meadow, or a mountain clearing. Like the Bogomils, the Cathars refused to venerate the Cross, perceiving it to be a symbol of torture, and like other gnostics sects they acknowledged the equality of both sexes and eschewed any form of hierarchy. And although they may have assimilated certain structural elements of the Church, even including the offices of deacon and bishop within the sect, they recognized every officer as simply serving a special function in the community. The Cathars never considered one person better than another; all people and both sexes were completely equal and accorded exactly the same rights.

The Cathars consisted of lay believers, the Credente, and the enlightened Cathar priests and priestesses known as the Parfait. The Parfait taught that the souls of all humans began as angels, who after being lured down to Earth became trapped in material bodies by the Dark Lord, Rex Mundi, the "King of the World," to populate his evil empire. In keeping with their gnostic predecessors, the Cathars discouraged sexual union for the purpose of conceiving children. To them, bringing another soul into a world ruled by a malevolent Dark Lord was the worst kind of sin. Instead, they favored casual sex and free love that did not lead to pregnancy. Their repulsion of procreation extended into their diet, and they refused to consume any foods produced through sexual liaison, including meat and milk products. Fish was preferable, they reasoned, because fish were asexual creatures and could inseminate themselves. The Cathars also resisted consuming animals because, according to their metaphysics, angelic souls that had devolved during a past human incarnation might inhabit them.

The Parfait taught that the goal of all humans was to purify and assimilate their angelic nature. Each person's angelic soul drifted between Heaven and Earth, waiting for its owner to become purified, to become "Cathar," so it could reunite with them. The requisite purification and reunion could occur at any time in the life of a Cathar, although it normally occured during or following a special initiaition known as the Consolomentum, when they joined the ranks of the Parfait.

The Rite of the Consolomentum was designed to absolve all sins and eventually make the soul of a Cathar completely pure so it could unite with its guardian angel. This evolution occured through the reception of the Holy Spirit or alchemical force that was transmitted to them during the rite by the officiating Parfait. The rite could be administered to a Cathar on his or her death bead to insure the achievement of gnosis in the next world and ascension into the Pleroma, but normally it occurred well before death so the Cathar could fully concentrate on purifying his or her material and emotional vehicles to make them suitable for the inception of their angelic self. Through this reunion, a Cathar could potentially acquire both gnosis and special angelic abilities to heal and awaken others.

Similar to the gnostic Essenes, once initiated into the elite level of the Cathars, the new Parfaits (men) and Parfaites (women) surrendered all their material possessions except for a plain robe and sash which would be their daily clothing for the remainder of their life. Vows were taken regarding celibacy and diet, and it became forbidden to tell lies or to harm another person. Also in keeping with their Essene ancestors, when the Parfait were not teaching they engaged in practical vocations such as weaving, carpentry, healing and farming. Other Parfaits, however, found their calling deep within the forests where they dedicated themselves unremittingly to the meditative lifestyle of ascetic hermits.

The Cathars recognized Jesus Christ as a model Perfecti. He was, however, not the one and only Son of God but an angelic Christed spirit. He had been a phantom of sorts whose physical form was a mirage, and therefore he could not have suffered the crucifixion and the resurrection as the

Catholic Church taught. Some Cathars, however, maintained that Jesus had indeed possessed a physical form and needed to come to Earth to receive redemption through purification for his past sins.

The Cathars' philosophical leanings regarding Jesus, along with their other heretical revelations, including the belief that Mary Magdalene had once been married to the Christ, eventually got them in trouble with the Catholic Church. The Cathars initially attracted the attention of the Church hierarchy when they began to baptize Catholics into their heretical faith, including previously anointed Catholic priests and bishops. Eventually entire dioceses began to defect, and to add insult to injury, the new Cathar converts stopped paying their tithes to the Church.

It was not along in their history before the future of the Cathar sect began to look increasingly bleak. This was especially true when the clever Cathars, who were will educated and articulate like their Manichaean antecedents, soundly defeated leading Catholic theologians in philosophical debate. Saint Bernard may have hastened their demise when he visited the Cathars in their domiciles in the Languedoc region of Southern France and recorded his negative observations of them. Although an admirer of their faith, Bernard could not understand the Cathar's repulsion for the Catholic Church, its rites or its hierarchy. He stated:

"...[T]hey usually say of themselves that they are good Christians,...hold the faith of the Lord Jesus Christ and his gospel as the apostles taught...occupy the place of the apostles...[T]hey talk to the laity of the evil lives of the clerks and prelates of the Roman Church...they attack and vituperate, in turn, all the sacraments of the Church, especially the sacrament of the Eucharist, saying that it cannot contain the body of Christ.... Of baptism, they assert that the water is material and corruptible...and cannot sanctify the soul...they claim that confession made to the priests of the Roman Church is useless.... They assert, moreover, that the cross of Christ should not be adored or venerated.... Moreover they read from the Gospels and the Epistles in the vulgar tongue, applying and expounding them in their favor and against the condition of the Roman Church...."

In 1209, Pope Innocent III issued a bull authorizing a Crusade against the Cathar heresy. This was the beginning of the final, sad chapter in the Cathars' short history. Over the next thirty years an estimated 500,000 Cathar men, women and children would be tortured and slaughtered. Through much of this time their only protection was the gnostic sympathizers that came to their aid, especially the Knights Templar who, it was said, were "the secular arm of the Perfecti."[20]

Perhaps the lowest point for both the Cathars and their Catholic adversaries in respect to ethical and moralistic behavior was the famous debacle at Beziers. In the peaceful Languedoc city of Beziers a massive slaughter of both Cathars and Catholics occurred after Arnaud Amoury, the Cistercian abbot-commander of the Catholic forces, had been advised that members of both religions equally occupied the city and issued his famous command "Kill them all; the Lord will recognize His own." During the ensuing carnage, the Church of St Mary Magdalene was descended upon and 7,000 worshippers, including women, children, clerics and old men were summarily slaughtered.

The most powerful Vatican infantry was the second detachment of Catholic soldiers who arrived in the Languedoc under the command of Simon de Montfort. Both Montfort and his soldiers were disinherited nobility from the north seeking the free land in the Languedoc that was promised to them if they could destroy its Cathar owners. Thus began a thirty year war that would completely ravage the Cathar villages and countryside of the Languedoc, as well as all minorities living in the region, including the population of Jews.

To more efficiently deal with the Cathar heretics during the Crusade, Pope Gregory IX took advisement from St. Dominic and established the Inquisition in 1233. Inquisitors quickly sentenced Cathars by the hundreds to die in the flames. In 1234, 210 Cathars met their death by fire, and in 1239 another 183 joined them. This form of torture, of course, enraged both the Cathars and their lay supporters. As an act of vengence, Pierre-Roger de Mirepoix, a lay Cathar official of the village of Mirapoix, ordered his most powerful knights to locate two Inquisition officials and their entourages that had been dispatched to the Languedoc and slay them under the cover of darkness. Arriving with huge battle axes, the knights instantly murdered the Inquisitors and their assistants and then looted all their possessions, including their black books full of condemned Cathars. This was to be the final insult against the Church, and all the entire population of Cathars were quickly descended upon by thousands of Inquisition soldiers.

As the Church's henchmen descended upon them, four hundred Cathars fled together to the mountain top temple of Montsegur. There, during the winter of 1243-44, they found refuge while 10,000 French anxious troops waited impatiently below for their surrender. Pierre-Roger de Mirepoix, who took command of the defense of Montsegur, had at his disposal only seventy men, including the knights who had slain the Inquisitors. Other knights fighting under various commanders brought the total of troops on Montsegur to a paltry 150.

At the outset, the small, terraced settlement at the summit of Montsegur occupied by the Cathars was amply loaded with supplies, but these resources were quickly depleted during the harsh winter months. When spring arrived and the Cathars' supplies were nearly exhausted, the only expedient left was a full surrender. As the Cathars prepared to descend from their fortress to an inevitable death, 25 Credente underwent the Rite of the Consolamentum in order to fully purify themselves before their encroaching transition to the next world.

On March 15, 1244, the Inquisition messengers ascended the hill of Montsegur and presented the Cathars with their final ultimatum. They had one more day to either convert to the Catholic faith or meet their death in a raging bonfire. Later that night it is said that that several Cathars navigated through tunnels and along sheer precipices to reach the bottom of Montsegur with a mysterious treasure which they then proceeded to hide in the surrounding landscape. It has been suggested that the treasure included accumulated Cathar wealth that was earmarked for the surviving Cathar communities, as well as the original Holy Grail Chalice that Jesus and his Apostles had drunk from during the Last Supper. There is no hard evidence that this was indeed their treasure, but in recent history the German adventurer Otto Rahn was sent to the Languedoc by the Nazi Schutzstaffel specifically to recover the Grail Chalice. According to one story, the hiding place of the Chalice was discovered and it was then taken to a Grail Castle that Heinrich Himmler had specially built for it in Germany. Sometime later, when the end of the Nazi juggernaut appeared certain, the cup was supposedly taken to a German outpost in the Antarctic.

On the fateful morning of March 16, 1244, 225 Cathars marched down the southern slopes of Montesegur while chanting songs of thanksgiving. They gave thanks to the powers that be for their impending release from the shackles of the material world. Then, upon reaching the foot of Montesegur, they joyfully entered the lapping flames of a roaring bon fire and began their ascent home.

A Parfait gives a Cathar Sermon

Carcasonne: A bastion of Cathar Worship

The Cathar Temple-Fortress of Montsegur
courtesy of Wikimedia.org.

Enigmatic Cathar carvings in the French town of Mirepoix

Pope Gregory IX, Founder of the Inquisition

The Crusade against the Cathars

St. Dominic destroys Cathar texts

The Inquisition tortures a Cathar

The Cathars burn in the flames below Montsegur

The Coming
World Gnostic Civilization

The one-world gnostic civilization envisioned by Earth's cosmic mission-aries is one that contains a perfect balance of the male and female polarity. Unless this harmony is achieved and then nurtured and maintained, any civilization, be it gnostic or otherwise, cannot be sustained for any significant length of time. With-out this balance patriarchy will destroy matriarchy, or vicer-versa, and the male and female elements of society will always be in opposition to each other.

The one-world gnostic civilization envisioned by both Aliester Crowely and Adam Weishaupt was destined to fail because it was not designed with this balance. Crowley's mandate of "Do as thou wilt shall be the whole of the Law" would have culminated in a world of anarchy, and it can only be imagined what Weishuapt's new world would have evolved into. Without providing any lucid plan for a new structure, Weishaupt simply stated his reason for overthrowing the system:

"Man is not bad except as he is made so by arbitrary morality. He is bad because of Religion, the State, and bad examples pervert him...."[1]

By simply eradicating all the patriarchal structure and institutions of the world that Weishaupt felt led to corruption among men and inequality among the masses, he was, essentially, paving the way for the hippie revolution in his genera-tion. Under his guidance his Illuminati members were, as Robert Anton Wilson once put it, the "Flower Children" of their era, although their modus operandi was much more destructive than the revolting hippies of the 1960s. Both movements were equally out of balance and haunted by the desperate need for structure and organization. Taken together, they proved that the dissenters and pioneers of so-ciety of almost every century need to relearn the hard lesson that a balance of matriarchy and patriarchy, or free love and structure, must occur before a new and enduring civilization can be created. As this chapter will show, if brokered correctly, such a union can eventuate in the harmonious union of the Right and Left Hand Paths, and potentially precipitate the culmination of human evolution on Earth.

Both Weishaupt's Illuminati and the hippie revolution of the 1960's were part of a larger movement of Left Hand Path sects that began to rise up in Eighteenth Century in opposition to two thousand years of patriarchal-ruled civilization, which was itself completely imbalanced, albiet on the side of eccesive structure and oppressive laws. Thus, the ferocity of the Left Hand Path sects is easily explained, as was their fanatical and death-defying perserverance. In its darker moments, their revolution would give rise to a series of extreme Left Hand ideologies, including Nihilism, Atheism, and even Satanism, each of which was designed to resist and overthrow every feature of patriarchy, especially its religious intolerance. Weishaupt became solidly anti-religion when as a Jesuit priest he witnessed first-hand the control and improprieties of the patriarchal Catholic Church. His anti-religious attitude was additionally fueled by his study of the reprehensible and iconoclastic history of the Catholic Church and its Inquisition, which since the Thirteenth Century had become a torture machine determined to destroy the adherents of any religious ideology that differed from its its own. The most abominable example of the Church's intolerance manifested in the Thirteenth and Fourteenth Centuries with the torture and murder of the gnostic Knights Templar and the peaceful Cathars.

Weishaupt's Illuminati and the two hundred year anti-patriarchal uprising it spawned served a valuable purpose. It helped to revive the Left Hand Path and restore it to power and respectability in the world. Before it could achieve a balance with patriarchy, matriarchy needed to reassert and reempower itself. This has now been accomplished. The next step is for the human race to design a civilization where the two eternally opposing movements can co-exist together in peace and harmony. This chapter will present a vision of such a civilization. The Gnostic Civlization delineated in these pages has the potential of being the perfect balance of the male and female principles, Left and Right Hand Paths, that humanity has sought for ages.

What constitutes a Gnostic Civilization?

Before the various components of a functional gnostic civilization can be outlined its basic criteria must be defined. A gnostic civilzation is one wherein all institutions, including government, religion, business and education, are summarlily designed to support the masses in completing their human evolution and achieving gnosis. This can only occur through a balance of their male and female principles, which are the underlying forces that determine the shape and form of all facets of any civilization.

The current need for a Gnostic Civilization

At this pivotal time in history humanity has reached a crossroads in its evolution. It has gone through ages when either the male or female principle has been dominant, but never one where they have co-existed in complete harmony over a long period of time. The next stage in the evolution of the entire human race is to create such a civilization so that all people can achieve gnosis and complete their individual evolution. According to prophecy, we are currently moving into an age when the creation of such a civilization is indeed possible.

The need for a planetary gnostic civilization can not be overstated. Through a gnostic civilization we will finally be able to re-unite with our brothers and sisters around the globe that we have become separated from by national boundaries, patriarchal dogma, and the bigotry born out of ignorance. Through gnosis and the opening of the heart it engenders, humans can finally feel an inner sense of unity with each other, as well as to the flora and fauna of Earth, which they have unconsciously harmed. Such feelings of unity will be especially pronounced when each person reaches the highest gnostic awareness and realizes that his or her essence, as well as the essence of all things, is the same universal Infinite Spirit.

The Components of a Gnostic Civilization

The following components of a gnostic civilization are all designed to be a harmonious balance of the male and female principles, and the Left and Right Hand Paths they engender.

Religion in a Gnostic Civilization

It has been thought that the biggest hurdle to overcome in uniting all people and creating a balanced gnostic civilization is religion. However, all people, regardless of their predominant Right Hand or Left Hand Path ideology, can be a member of a gnostic society if they simply agree that both paths are necessary in the development of gnosis. As previously mentioned in this text, through the Right Hand Path the necessary inner male traits of structure, discipline and discrimination are cultivated, and through the Left Hand Path the important female traits of intuition and unity awareness are developed. Evolving souls typically need to progress through a Right Hand Path religion for a period of time in order to achieve the discipline and discrimination required for adhering to the practices and ideology of the Left Hand Path. Otherwise, the Left Hand Path practices can lead to addictions, anarchy, and de-evolution of the soul. In India, the classic and archetypal path to gnosis is the Kuala Path, wherein eight stages of development incorporate elements both the Left and the Right Hand Paths. The first four stages cover the practices and ideology of the Right Hand Path, and the last four exposes an aspirant to the practices and ideology of the Left Hand Path. This archetypal Hindu path is not alone in uniting the Left and Right Hand Paths, and has its analogues in other religions around the globe. Orthodox Moslems, for example, currently progress to the Left Hand Path practices of the Sufi tradition when they seek a deeper, mystical union with Allah, and Christians have been known to adopt certain Left Hand Path practices when taking to the contemplative life of a hermit or a monk.

Start with Individual Male/Female Balance

As mentioned, in a gnostic civilization all manifestation of the polarity, including the male and female genders, intellect and intuition, structure and freedom, Spirit and matter, must be balanced. The pre-requisite to balance is equality; thus, complete equality between the sexes and all races of people and levels of society is essential in a pure gnostic civilization. As we have seen in the previous chapter, the imposition of a caste system where only a few select citizens are given the opportunity to achieve gnosis does not meet the criteria of a true gnostic civilization. Such elitism promotes contempt and accentuates divisiveness among the masses.

Therefore, the first step in manifesting a gnostic civilization is to create a balance and harmony between the opposing genders. If gender balance and equality can not be achieved, then balance within any institution of a gnostic society will not be possible. To help generate this seminal male/female balance, each person in a gnostic civlization should initially strive to achieve an inner balance of the polarity. If a woman is lacking in personal strength and confidence, for example, she should consider developing her inner male; and conversely, if a man is lacking in sensitivity, social ability and compassion, he should seek balance by developing his inner female. When this inner evolution is accomplished each person will naturally become more androgynous. They will become more independant and all their relationships can become more functional. Couples can then live together because they enjoy each others company and mutual spiritual support, not because they are inherently lacking a quality or skill that the other can provide. Thus, if one member of a relationship feels guided by Spirit to move out of their relationship, he or she will not be paralyzed to leave because of a fear born of dependency and personal limitation.

When an inner and outer balance of the genders has been created, then all institutions of a gnostic civilization will reflect that balance. But until the members of a society have achieved complete gnostic awareness, a system of checks and balances must be adopted in order to preserve the male/female balance. Whenever a male policy or agenda is implemented, for example, another must be designed and adopted that supports a counter-balancing female agenda. The two party political system in the USA has, to some degree, succeeded in creating a balanced government that supports both male and female, Republican and Democratic agendas, although the party with the most representatives in Washington D.C. will typically upset this balance in order to actualize its own self-serving, male or female agenda.

Live in the Tao

The timeless archetypal spiritual philosophy that teaches how to daily create and maintain a balance of the universal male and female polarity is Taoism. The path of the Tao, meaning the "Way," is an archetypal path that balances and unites the polarity and leads to gnosis. Taoism was orignally founded on Lemuria and later codified by the Chinese Dragon Emperors and the Immortal Lao Tsu, who set down the teachings of Taoism as a series of aphorisms in 81 "chapters" of the *Tao Te Ching*. These aphorisms can serve as an excellent guide for living each moment in polarity balance, and since they were written by a fully enlightened gnostic their study can transport a person into gnostic consciousness.

Meditation on the famous Tao symbol (on the facing page) alone can help engender both an inner and outer balance of Heaven and Earth and the male and female principles. The symbol represents the body of the Primal Serpent as the Tai Chi, the "Supreme Ultimate," within which emerges the male and female polarity as two snakes or "fishes."

Achieve Balance with Sacred Movement

The study and practice of some form of sacred movement, such as the Taoist moving practice of Tai Chi Chuan, is very conducive to both establishing an inner balance of the polarity and for living a balanced existence on Earth. Sacred movement assists a person in balancing their inner yin and yang, or male and female principles, so their minds, emotions and inner organs function peacefully and optimally. When the inner polarity is balanced, there will also be a balance in the outer world. Tai Chi Chuan is traditionally observed by much of the population in China first thing each morning because the chi or life force is strongest at that time and they can then enjoy the balancing benefit of the exercise throughout the entire day. Through daily practice of sacred movement perfect health is maintained and all aspects of a person's life are brought into balance.

The long form of Tai Chi Chuan is composed of numerous stances and positions that reflect the movements of a variety of animals, which collectively are the Primal Dragon. The body of the Dragon is pure energy, and its movement includes every possible gesture, stance, and nuance of locomotion found within the animal kingdom.

The Tai Chi Tu Symbol
Commonly referred to as the Tao

Know the Divine Will through Gnostic Astrology

As the gnostics have revealed to us over many millennia, an important tool for staying in balance and discerning the Divine Will is the study of the transitting stars and planets. The Zodical signs of the planets, and the angles that they make to each other, reveal the Divine Will and what is likely to occur on Earth.

The gnostics referred to the spirits of the planets as Archons and maintained that through broadcasting their energies to Earth they determine all phenomenon on our planet. Simply by understanding each planet and what areas of life each one specifically influences, a fairly complete picture of the will of the Archons can be comprehended at any given time; and then a plan can be formulated to either neutralize the negative energies of the planets or to embrace and utilize the postive ones. The ancient rulers never made a major decision involving their empires without first consulting their astrologers.

It is also helpful to have a personal astrological map calculated for the time of each person's birth, which is a practice that has been observed in India for many ages. The astrological birth chart will reveal what areas of a person's life the Archons will act as a supporting or inhibiting influence, as well as what body parts and inner organs might be at risk. When the negative influences are identified, remedial measures involving metals, gems, and mantras that balance the potential harmful energies of the Archons can then be prescribed. Conversely, when the positive influences are identified, gems, mantras and metals can be similarly prescribed to enhance their uplifting influence.

Work in a Gnostic Civilization

In a gnostic society each person should embrace a vocation that they are best suited for. They should feel an inner balance of the polarity through such work, which in itself will assist them in remaining inwardly calm and in a meditational consciousness that is conducive to the development of gnosis. Such work will ultimately engender an intutive connection with the inner Spirit, from which the person will then receive an abundane of creative inspiration flowing directly to them. When this spiritual connection is complete, each person will experience all their work as a service to a higher power.

A person's best vocation can initially be discerned through his or her astrological positions at the time of birth, as they typically are in India, and they should be encouraged to develop the talents therein indicated. However, a person should not be confined to just one vocation throughout life. A developing soul needs room to grow, so when a person feels the inner inspiration for change he or she should have the freedom to move on to another vocation of interest.

Personal Property in a Gnostic Civilization

Weishaupt, Plato and other philosophers have decried personal property as an obstacle to a free and equal society. However, a complete communal society where all possessions are held in common is not a balance of the male/female polarity, and this is why none have endured for very long. Personal property should be allowed within a gnostic society, but it is important that each person be liberal and generous with their material resources. They should see themselves as channels or conduits for material wealth to come into this world not just for themselves by for everyone. If the members of a gnostic civilization make charity a spiritual discipline, ownership of material resources can then support their path to gnosis rather than be a hinderance to it. Charity naturally opens the heart, the seat of gnosis, and leads to unconditional love for all life.

Architecture in a Gnostic Civilization

The architecture of a gnostic civilization should utilize sacred geometry to create energy conductive structures that are a balance of the male-female, Spirit-matter polarity. A balanced structure will harmonize and unite the inner polarity within all those people residing within them while also creating a more peaceful ambiance for daily living.

When the Golden Mean Proportion, which unites the numeric values for the male and female principles, 666 and 1080, is incorporated into the dimensions of a structure it naturally engenders a male-female balance and aligns the structure with the Earth's natural energy flow. The Golden Mean Proportion is directly related to the logarithmic spiral and, when used as a base measurement, will make any structure an axis mundi that unites Heaven and Earth.

Although squares and rectangles are cost effective shapes in the building trades, they typically block energy flow and thereby impede the spriitual evolution of those living within them. Thus, certain geometrical structures that unite the polarity, including pyramids, domes (including Geodesic Domes), octagons and hexagons, should be adopted as enclosures in a gnostic society. Such structures promote the movement, accumulation, and production of an abundance of high frequency life force that naturally supports the harmony and spiritual evolution of those aspiring gnostics residing within them. Ideally, these structures should be placed over vortexes of terrestrial power in the World Grid and aligned with both the electro-magnetic and life force currents that run along the Earth. In order for them to engender optimum balance, as well as peace and prosperity for their owners, it is also helpful to orient the buildings in accordance with the principles of Feng Shui or Vaastu, which are the Chinese and Hindu sciences of right placement.

The Giza Pyramids
Ancient Power Plants

Earth Acupuncture in the World Grid

Just as the ancients once did, the World Grid of vortex points should be understood and utilized by the citizens of a gnostic civilization. Vortex points are natural whirlpools of energy where two opposing, male-female streams of energy intersect and unite to produce a standing spiral of energy. These spirals of life force can be used for healing purposes and for alchemical rites involving polarity union and the awakening of the inner serpent spiral, especially when an energy moving structure is placed around or over them. Many of the ancient indigenous people made rings of stones to mark the perimeters of vortexes, resulting in "Medicine Wheels" that became the focus of intense energy that could be used for healing and spiritual transformation. When they inserted energy conductive stone or metal conduits into the center of a vortex, Earth acupuncture was triggered that either moved life force into or out of the planetary grid, thereby minimizing the possibility of earthquakes and volcanoes. Some of the early peoples knew that with the right technology the energy that built up within vortexes could be converted into electrical energy. For this reason, the Egyptians placed pyramids over their most powerful vortexes, and then, explains author Christopher Dunn in *The Giza Power Plant,* they added some internal activating technology to transform them into dynamic energy generators that could power an entire modern city. Rather than pyramids, Edgar Cayce maintained that the Atlanteans placed crystalline "Fire Stone" into vortexes to amplify, conduct and convert their power into electrical energy. This approach was later revived by the ingenious Nikola Tesla, whose dream was to produce free energy for the entire planet by inserting a conduit into a vortex point in Colorado that would pump electrons out of the Earth and circulate it around the planet's upper atmosphere for everyone to use.

The Bagua and Feng Shui

One of the world's best tools for determining the energies that emerge from the male/female union of a vortex and how to live in harmony with them is the Taoist Bagua, meaning "Eight Directions." The Bagua is a configuration of Eight Trigrams that has been used as a tool by the Chinese for many ages in order to live in accordance with the Divine Will. The Bagua is shaped in the form of an octagon, which is one of the premier sacred geometrical forms that represent the union of Heaven and Earth, or the male and female principles. The eight trigrams of the Bagua that are situated around the eight sides of the octagon symbolize the frequencies produced at the eight directions through the union of the polarity and what activities should be performed at each direction if they are to be in alignment with the Divine Will. The Bagua can be used to determine what structures should be erected and what activities enrolled in at all the eight directions surrounding a vortex, or within the pyramid/temple built over it. Most commonly, the Bagua is used in contemporary society as an important tool of the Chinese art of placement

Eight Frequencies emerge from the male/female union

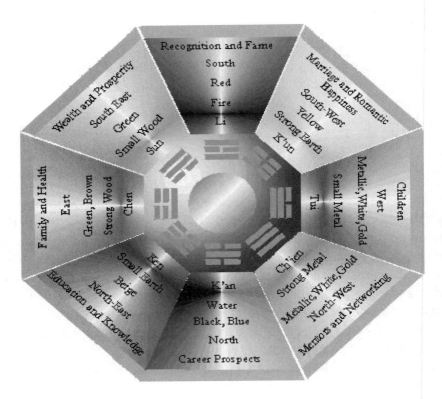

The Frequencies and Activities at the Eight Directions

known as Feng Shui to determine the placement of rooms in a home about to be built, or the activities that should be observed in previously constructed homes and buildings. When the Bagua is placed over the design of a built house, with its north direction situated directly over the structure's front entrance, the Taoist tool will inform the owner what activities should occur in each room of the structure.

Healthcare in a Gnostic Civilization

Healthcare practioners of a gnostic civilization should have a holistic approach to healing, and they should have the expertise to address all the four levels of a person. Unless all levels of a person are addressed, any dis-ease will likely eventually return. Practitioners should also have some training that will assist them in understanding the process of human alchemical unfoldment that leads to gnosis, so as not to inaccurately diagnose symptomology as simply pathological. Emotional, mental and physical toxins are likely to be brought to the surface during the process of alchemical transformation, and the health practioner needs to be able to identify them as such, and to known how to assist in their release. Visions, hearing voices, and other abnormal phenomenon can typically occur within a person as they alchemically transform, and these symptoms should not be misunderstood as mental illness or psychosis. Optimumly, the health practioner of a gnostic society will also be on the alchemical path and can then guide their patient through personal experience.

General Education in a Gnostic Civilization

Children in a gnostic civilization should be given a comprehensive education that trains them to be self-sufficient and self-reliant individuals capable of meeting most of the challenges they are likely to encounter in life. The curriculum should be a balance of male-female, left and right brain subject matter that is designed to equally develop both the inner male and female principles, intellect and intuition. Certain male or female subjects which have been principally segregated in a normal society partly because of the stigma attached to participating in them, such as homemaking and wood shop, should be fully integrated and open to all. It is also efficacious that children learn some form of martial art, as well as nutrition and a healing modality, and a modicum of business training, so they can attend to their physical needs and safety throughout life.

Religious/Spiritual Education in a Gnostic Civilization

Children should be indoctrinated into the ideologies of both the Right Hand and Left Hand Paths, and when they reach a certain age they should be given the freedom to choose the right path for them. Because of their ancestral DNA, as well as their past soul growth and experience in other incarnations, they will normally gravitate to one path or the other. If they are not sure of which path to follow, then the Right Hand Path should be recommended and then followed sequentially by the Left Hand Path, and it should be made clear that both paths are equally necessary for spiritual growth. As mentioned, in order to initially cultivate discipline within a developing child, the Hindus have, for many ages, found it most efficacious to enroll them in the Right Hand Path while they are still living with their birth families. They will have the opportunity to gavitate to the Left Hand Path once they leave the "nest."

From a young age, children should be taught that the answers to all their questions can be found within, and to begin accessing those answers they should be encouraged to "go with their hearts" when making all their decisions. To support their development of equal vision, children should also be taught that all people are inherently equal and possess the same spiritual essence. What separates all people are simply the lessons they have chosen for their soul growth.

Children should be advised that traditional belief systems can limit them. From a young age they should taught that they are special, that they are incarnations of the Infinite Spirit, not sinners, and that to "Know Thyself" as "I am Unlimited, I am Spirit" is the true goal of life. This is basic spiritualty once espoused on Lemuria and later among the Polynesians.

Children should also learn what practices they can regularly observe throughout life to maintain an inner balance and stay aligned with Spirit. These include meditation and prayer, as well as chanting, Tai Chi Chuan, Hatha Yoga, and martial arts. When youg people are enrolled in school during their formative years, these practices will help to calm and focus their minds, thereby supporting school work and all other activities they become involved in.

Government in a Gnostic Civilization
Gnostic Rulers

The rulers of a gnostic civilization should have achieved gnosis or at least aspire to its achievement, otherwise they will not be capable it leading a country of people seeking to attain that goal. They will not know what laws and policies need to be implemented to assist their citizens in achieving gnosis. If an enlightened gnostic is not elected to the highest office in a gnostic civilization, then the highest elected official should at least be a person that exhibits a good balance of the inner male-female polarity. Only then can a president or prime minister make decisions that take into consideration the needs of both males and females in the population.

Gnostic Government

The form of government adopted within a gnostic civilization should also be a balance of the male-female polarity. A middle ground should be sought that is a balance of the Left Handed matriarchal government and the Right Handed patriarchal administration. History reveals that purely Right Hand and Left Hand governments have proven themselves unsustainable. A typical Left Handed regime promotes unity and equality among its citizens, but taken to its extreme, as it often is, a Left Handed government engenders bigger and more rigid government and it can easily turn into a totalitarian communism governed by an oligarchical dictatorship. By contrast, a Right Hand government promotes a two-class society of the rich and the poor that can turn into a form of caste system. A Right Hand government emphasizes safety and abundance for its citizens aove all else, even if that requires the cultivation of an unfriendly, controlling and imperialistic attitude towards it neighboring countries. A Right Hand government supports patriarchal legislation and laws that tend to divide people, genders and races. The patriarchal government produced by the German Nationalist Party was an extreme form of Right Handed rule. It sought to conquer the world for the Fatherland while eradicating those sects and races, such as the Jews, that it deemed inferior to the fair skinned "Aryan" race.

Another reason that a predominantly Right Hand or Left Hand government can never engender a balanced gnostic society is because a Right Hand government typically supports Right Hand religions and their agendas, while Left Hand governments generally support the agendas of the alternative faiths of the Left Hand Path. Because of the support it gains through the Republican Party, the Right Hand religion of Christianity will always elect Republican officials to oversee a patriarchal government in Washington D.C., while the alternative faiths of the Left Hand Path will typically elect a Democratic and a more matriarchal government to rule the USA. Republican presidents are notorious for overstepping the boundaries that separate church and state and passing legislation that is a reflection of their Right Hand fundamentalist beliefs, including prohibitions against gay marriage and abortion. By contrast, Democratic presidents support the creation of governmental sponsored social services and impose heavy taxes on the masses to finance them. Although the Founding Fathers were on track to create a gnostic country because of their Secret Society affiliations, their Christian faith and that of their descendants has produced a predominantly patriarchal country with a patriarchal government.

The balance between the Left and Right forms of government is a mild form of Socialism, wherein the social programs of the Left Hand can coexist with the Capitalistic and patriarchal agenda of the Right Hand. But to make a socialist government support a gnostic civilization, both the Republican Party, the mouthpiece for the Right, and the Democratic Party, mouthpiece for the Left, must have equal representation in all branches of government.

Government Architecture

The city Washington D.C. was originally designed to be the perfect balance of the polarity. This was the intent of architect Pierre Charles L'Enfant, who made its geometry comply to the Golden Mean Proportion, which is a measurement based upon the union of 666 and 1080, the values of the male and female principles. He specifically laid out the buildings in the form of a series of pentacles so they would be in harmony with the Earth's energy flow. He also made the feminine dome-shaped Capital Building, which was crowned with the image of the "Lady of Freedom," the central point of Washington and had all other buildings radiate from it. This exalted "female" democracy and made the people of the USA the foundation of the country's government. When L'Enfants Golden Proportion alignments were later tampered with, and the center of the city was shifted to become the phallic-shaped Washington Monument, more power was placed in the hands of one person and made the "male", patriarchal President and Executive branch of government dominant. Another change that occured by making the Washington Monument the center of the government buildings in Washington D.C. is that the Capitol and White House no longer looked outward towards the world, but inward towards each other. This had the effect of making the US government less expansive and alturistic and more self-centered and secretive.[2]

The "feminine" shaped Capital surmounted by the Lady of Freedom

L'Enfant's geometrical design of Washington D.C.

The "male" phallic- shaped Washington Monument

Part III
The Coming
Gnostic Spirituality

When the religious dogma that controls and separates us has begun to fade away in the days to come, it will become more obvious that underlying and uniting all religions is the primal gnostic-alchemical path. Direct, gnostic experience will replace fear, and the gnostic-alchemical path can then become the spirituality that unites a one-world gnostic civilization.

All religion begins with a gnostic, who after observing intensive alchemical practices for a period of time achieves a permanent gnostic awareness. The gnostic then attempts to teach his or her profound awareness to an inner circle of disciples, who following the master's death make a religion out of his or her revelations, even though they themselves have not directly experienced the truth behind them. Consequently, the disciples' new religion is based upon conjecture and speculation. If the disciples founding the new religion are primarily men, which has generally been the case for the past 2000 years, such "fathers" will usually mandate that the converts to their new sect fully embrace their intellectual precepts and censure and/or punish those who do not. Later, after many centuries of growth, their religion will have become so full of conjecture, and spawned a theology that is so complicated, that it becomes nearly impossible to discern the pure message of the original gnostic.

Throughout the ages enlightened gnostics have not been interested in speculation, but in teaching their disciples a set of alchemical practices through which they can have direct experience of gnostic truth. Many of the alchemical practices of the early, enlightened gnostics have survived over the millennia thanks to alchemists and gnostics who have secretly preserved them in their purity. In the following section you will learn the basic theory of the gnostic-alchemical path, as well as a set of practices to experience gnosis directly. Read on and discover:

The Theory and History of Alchemy
Safe and Easy Alchemical Practices for Everyone
Living Gnosis: How to Live as a Gnostic

The Elixir of Immortality
by Chadwick St. John

The Theory and History of Alchemy

This chapter is comprehensive in scope. It covers the theory behind alchemy, as well as the various sects who have practiced it around the globe. Divided into three parts, Part I & II will cover the theory of alchemy in terms of the separation and reunion of the Primal Serpent, and Part III will present the history and practices of alchemy as they have manifested around the globe.

The Theory of Alchemy

There are two kinds of alchemy, the transmutation of a base metal into gold and the transformation of a human into a divine embodiment of Spirit. Both approaches take a subject and evolve it to its greatest possible extent through exposing it to alchemical fire. Alchemical fire, or Serpent Fire, is the final, destructive-transformative form taken by the Primal Serpent following its creation and preservation of the universe. The theory of alchemy delineated in the following pages reveals the cosmic evolution of the Primal Serpent from Creator to Preserver to Destroyer/Transformer, followed by the stages of the ensuing alchemical process it ultimately triggers.

Part I: Creation and Separation of the Primal Serpent

The Primal Serpent that emerged from the Infinite Spirit was androgynous energy. This is the Alchemist's Prima Materia, the "First Material."

When the will to create manifested within the vast sea of consciousness, which is known variously around the globe as the Infinite Spirit, Shiva, Brahman, Tai Chi, or the Ain Soph, it proceeded to congeal within itself a contracted form. This was the Prima Materia, the androgynous Primal Serpent, and the first form of Spirit. The Primal Serpent embodied the Divine Wisdom and Power of the Infinite, and through it Spirit was able create the cosmos. The initial form of the Infinite was been refered to in most pre-Christian traditions as a "snake" or "dragon" because the primal energy traveled in spirals, like a snake, and also because it contained within it the seeds of all the animal forms of nature that would condense out of it. The enigmatic dragon is the united synthesis of all animals, which is why he may be portrayed with the head of a lion, dog, snake, bird, or crocodile, etc, and the body parts of a multitude of other animals.

The Androgyny of the Primal Serpent was recognized by the Ancients.

Pure energy is neutral and "androgynous," so its personna, the Primal Serpent, has also been portrayed as androgynous. To portray the Primal Serpent's androgyny the ancients endowed it with androgynous names and forms. The Mayans portrayed it as the "androgynous" Quetzlcoatl, the "Feathered Serpent" (feathers = Spirit, snake = matter) and the Sumerians envisioned it as their androgynous goat-fish, Enki (goat = fire, male principle; fish = water, female principle). In Egypt and India, the Primal Serpent was revered as a golden cobra or asp (gold = Spirit, snake = matter), and in China it was portrayed as the "androgynous" golden, winged dragon (gold and wings = Spirit, dragon body = matter).

The Androgyny of the Primal Serpent was reflected in its blue-green color.

In China and Mexico the androgyny of the Primal Serpent was often portrayed as possessing a blue-green color, thus representing it as the androgynous union of Heaven (blue) and Earth (green).

Its Androgynous Name and Geometrical Form was the OM and Sri Yantra.

The ancients who personally experienced the Primal Serpent ascribed to it the "androgynous" name-sound of OM (O=Spirit, M=matter), which is a mantra that the Hindus refer to as the Pranava, meaning "Made of Prana." The androgynous geometrical form body of the Primal Serpent was the Sri Yantra, whose series of interlocking male and female triangles reflect its androgyny. Experiments have shown that when the sound OM emanates from a speaker that has a loose drum head set over it covered with sand, the sand will eventually assume the shape of the Sri Yantra. It has thus been proven that OM creates the androgynous Sri Yantra, the prana body of the Primal Serpent.

Images of the Androgynous Primal Serpent

When the Primal Serpent Expands and Crystallizes to become the Universe it Divides into its male-female Polarity.

The androgynous Primal Serpent must divide into its two component parts when it creates the universe in order to engender balance, stability and harmony in the cosmos. Its polarity then manifests in the cosmos as all the pairs of opposites. A short list of these multudinous pairs includes:

Spirit/matter
Heaven/Earth
Male/Female
Light/Dark
Fire/Water
Positive/Negative
Proton/Electron

The Ancients portrayed the division of the Primal Serpent as two snakes, two twin boys, or two "fishes."

The motifs used by the ancients to represent the division of the Primal Serpent include two identical snakes, boys, or "fishes." The two snakes were represented in Persian iconography as fighting amongst themselves for control of the universe, while in the Egyptian and Hindu culture they are represented as being harmoniously encoiled together. In the form of two boys, the Twins of the Primal Serpent are either diametrically opposed to each other or they compliment each other and live in harmony and friendship. These boys have been rerpesented in Greece as the Dioscouri, in India as the Ashwin Twins, and in both Egypt and Asia Minor as the Kaberio Twins. The Dioscouri twins were the Twins associated with the Zodiacal sign of the Twins, Gemini, the icon of which once consisted of twin snakes coiled around two columns. In his Primal Serpent form, Thoth-Hermes or Mercury was the father of twin serpents, which he carries on his caduceus, and why his planet, Mercury, is the ruler of Gemini. In China, the separated form of the Primal Serpent are the twin interlocked "fishes" of the Tao symbol.

The Dioscouri Twins
The "Serpent" Sons who emanted from the Solar Spirit

Hermes and his Twin Serpents

The Sumerian Twin Serpents

The Persian Twin Serpents

The Chinese Twin "Fishes"

Part II: Reunion of the Primal Serpent

The destruction of the universe begins when the snake twins, or dual components of the Primal Serpent, are reunited.

After many ages of being separated into its component parts, the Primal Serpent is reconstituted at the completion of the universal cycle of manifestation. At that time the two halves of the Primal Serpent reunite as the fiery and destructive, alchemical power.

As the Alchemical force, the Primal Serpent destroys all form and transforms the universe back into pure energy.

At the conclusion of each cycle the Primal Serpent destroys all things in the unvierse and transforms them back to their primal form of pure energy.

Since the Human Body is a Microcosm of the Universe, the human evolutionary cycle similarly comes to completion when the inner Twin Serpents reunite and a manifestation of the Primal Serpent is reconstituted.

When the inner manifestation of the Twin Serpents unite to reconstitute the fiery Primal Serpent, known variously around the globe as Kundalini, the Holy Spirit, and Serpent Fire, it completes human evolution by transforming the body to a higher frequency of energy. This human alchemy can occur at any time during the greater cosmic cycle of creation, preservation, and destruction.

As a Microcosmic Reflection of the Universe, the Human Body reflects all the stages of universal manifestation, including the Creation of the Primal Serpent, its Division into Twin Serpents, and their Reunion as the fiery Primal Serpent.

The Hindus, Chinese and many other cultures have stated that the human body is a microcosmic map of the process of the universal cycle of manifestation. Within the physical body, and more specifically in the etheric body that surrounds and underlies it, the exact sequence of events that culminated in the split of the Primal Serpent into two snakes and their evetual reunion as the First Serpent can be located and identified. Beginning at the etheric center at the apex of the head, and moving downwards and then back up the etheric body, the entire process of universal creation and destruction is revealed.

According to the esoteric diagrams of the Hindu Yogis and the testimonies of psychics worldwide, at the apex of the etheric body sits the Crown Chakra, which in the process of universal unfolding corresponds to the Infi-

321

Twin Serpents on the inner Tree of Life

nite Spirit before its finite manifestation. Below the Crown Chakra is the Ajna Chakra, or Third Eye, which corresponds to the first stage in the cycle of cosmic manifestation, when the Primal Serpent first appeared. It is approximately at this point between the eyes that the Egyptian Pharaohs and other priest-kings and adepts adorned themselves with snake images to honor the inner seat of the Primal Serpent.

The second stage in the universal cycle which corresponds to the split of the Primal Serpent is located in the body as the two serpentine energy vessels that emanate from the Third Eye and extend downwards. In China, these two inner serpents are named the Ren and Du Channels and are used in the practice of acupuncture to maintain and restore health. In India, these inner snakes are known as the Ida and Pingala Nadis and are understood to be conduits through which the male and female essences flow throughout the body. When life force enters the Pingala Nadi, which has its opening in the right nostril, the male fiery energies of the body are activated, and when the prana enters the left nostril and moves through the Ida Nadi, the female energies of coolness and sedation become ascendant. Prana alternates its movement in these two nadis in 90-minute cycles, thus, during most of the 24-hour cycle either the fiery or the watery energies predominate in the body.

Between the Ajna Chakra and base of the spine the two snakes spiral down the spine and intersect at five places, just as they do on the Caduceus of Mercury. Each of these five vertices or chakras is associated with one of the five elements the life force Serpent condenses into during the course of crystallizing and becoming the physical universe. The Vishuddha Chakra at the throat corresponds to the ether element; the Anahata Chakra at the heart is associated with the air element; the Manipura Chakra at the solar plexus corresponds with the fire element; the Svadisthana Chakra just below the navel is associated with the water chakra, and the Muladhara Chakra at the base of the spine corresponds with the earth element.

The final stage in the cosmic cycle is represented in the human body by the Twin Snakes or energy vessels that reunite at the base of the spine to produce the ressurected Primal Serpent. Alchemical transformation ensues.

Alchemy in the human body begins when the two snakes unite at the base of the spine and reconstruct the androgynous Primal Serpent. When the resurrected Primal Serpent becomes awake it moves its fiery essence out of the Muladhara Chakra and into the system of 72,000 nadis that connect the Muladhara with all parts of the body. As it circulates, this fiery, high-frequency life force of the Primal Serpent transforms the dense fabric of the body and gradually raises the frequency of dense flesh back into pure energy.

Eventually the Primal Serpent is reabsorbed back into the Infinite Spirit

In the end of the cosmic cycle the Primal Serpent as pure energy is re-absorbed into the Infinite Spirit. This final stage is mirrored in the human body as the Primal Serpent's re-absorption in the cown of the head.

Following its activation in the Root Chakra, the principal path or vessel traveled by the resurrected Primal Serpent is the middle vessel located inside the inner Tree of Life or spinal column. The fiery Primal Serpent rises up this central nadi, known as the Sushumna Nadi, while awakening or further activating the five chakras that lie along its length. As each chakra becomes fully awakened, a human gains control of its corresponding element. When the Serpent fully awakens the Muladhara, for example, a human gains control over the earth element and can easily meet his or her survival needs on Earth. When the ascending serpent eventually reaches the Ajna Chakra, the seat of the Primal Serpent, both Divine Wisdom and Power become available to the seeker. Finally, when the serpent makes its last ascension back to the Crown Chakra, seat of the Infinite, it is reabsorbed into Spirit and the seeker's consciousness is correspondingly reabsorbed into a void, or Nirvana. This is the seat of Shiva and Turiya consciousness. Here the seeker unites with the Infinite Spirit and becomes the eternal witness of creation.

All Cycles, and the Separation and Reunion of the Primal Serpent, are represented by the Signs of the Zodiac.

The Zodiac, or Circle of Signs, represents all cycles, including the macrocosmic and microcosmic (human) cycles of creation and alchemical destruction/transformation. They specifically delineate the creation, separation, and reunion of the Primal Serpent that occurs during all cycles of time.

The circular shape of the Zodiac is based upon the round Ouroboros body of the Primal Dragon. In fact, all cycles are reflected by the shape of the Ouroboros, because all time and all events begin and end with the creation and destruction of energy. Therefore, it can be said that all cycles begin with the creation of the Primal Dragon, and end with the Dragon consuming its own body.

The twleve signs of the Zodiac are divided into four parts, or quadrants, and associated with four phases of every macrocosmic and micrcosmic cycle. The first quadrant reveals the separation of the Primal Serpent into Twin Serpents ; the second quadrant reflects the period following the creation of the universe when the Twin Serpents keep the cosmos and Earth in harmony and balance; and the third quadrant reveals the phase of the universal cycle when the Twin Serpents reunite as the Primal Serpent.

The first quadrant, or first three signs of the Zodiac, is the Quadrant of Creation and Separation. The first sign of this quadrant, Aries, the Ram, represents the initial "male" will or inspiration of the Infinite Spirit to create; although like the deity of Aries, the invisible Egyptian ram-god, Ammon, at this stage of the cycle the universe remains invisible. The first manifestation of physical life force or energy in the cosmos is represented by the second sign of Taurus, the Bull, whose glyph of a sun united with a cresent moon is indicative of the male and female polarity uniting as the life force body of the Primal Serpent. Both the Taurus Bull and the cosmic Primal Serpent contained within it, i.e., the Pleiades, are interconnected. They both denote the chaotic mass of fiery life force and Divine Power that must be shaped by the arrows shot at them by the nearby hunter Orion, the embodiment of the Divine Mind. Orion, who has been venerated as the warrior Mithras sinking his dagger into the bull to shape it, pursues the Pleiades, the Seven Sisters, who collectively reside in the back of the bull as the cosmic Serpent Goddess preparing to slither down the World Tree. The Primal Serpent's descent into density occurs in the third sign of Gemini, the Twins, which denotes the separation of the Serpent's two components of Divine Mind and Power as two serpents (or boys), which separate in Gemini to provide harmony and balance within the cosmos. The intersections of the Twin Serpents as they slither down the Caduceus of Mercury, which is a symbol of Gemini, represents the sequential stages of crystallization the Primal Serpent undergoes as it lowers its frequency to become dense matter.

The second set of three Zodiacal signs, known as the Quadrant of Preservation, is led by Cancer, the Crab, which has a solid shell and represents the solid Earth that the Serpent Goddess crystallizes into. The glyph of the sign, which is a version of Chinese Tao symbol, denotes the Divine Mind and Power, or creative and destructive powers of the Goddess, that are personified and wielded by her two Twin "Fishes." These opposing forces continue to move the cycles of nature year after year. At times, as the universal male and female principles they must reunite briefly in the process of fertilization, which is denoted by the next sign of Leo, the Zodiacal sign of love affairs. And their eventual progeny together, the Earth's vegetation, is denoted by the third sign of this quadrant, Virgo, the sign of the harvest.

The third series of three Zodiacal signs, the Quadrant of Reunion and Destruction, is led by Libra, the balance. This sign denotes the phase of the universal cycle when the Twins are coming into a complete balance. The male and female principles must be completely equal and balanced before they can reunite, a process that occurs in the following alchemical sign of Scorpio. In Scorpio, the male and female polarity reunites as the destructive, alchemical fire or reconstituted Primal Serpent. There are two symbollic animals of this sign, the snake and the eagle, which occupy opposite ends of the World Tree. During the period represented by the sign of Scorpio, the snake at the bottom of the tree rises up and reunites with the eagle, thus reclaiming its lost wings. Matter has thus returned to pure energy. When this occurs within the human body, the Primal Serpent rises up the inner Tree of Life and a person reclaims his or her Divine Power and Wisdom, and their physical body ascends to a frequency closer to pure energy. The Divine Wisdom gained by this ascension is denoted by the next sign, Sagittarius, the sign of the Divine Mind and gnosis. Sagittarius is the sign of the spiritual teacher and guru, one who has elevated his or her consciousness until it is one with Shiva, the Infinite Spirit, and completed the cycle of evolution.

The fourth series of Zodiacal signs is the Quadrant of Concealment. The three signs of this quadrant are all associated with water and represent the stage in the cosmic cycle when all things in the universe have reverted to pure life force and merged back into the Cosmic Sea to await the next cycle of manifestation.

The Cosmic Ouroboros Body of the Primal Serpent

The Primal Serpent is divided into the 12 Signs of the Zodiac

Part III:
The History of Alchemical Traditions Worldwide

The following is a history and planetary survey of the various alchemists and alchemical traditions that have emerged worldwide. Although they diverge in certain aspects, they all share the alchemical process of the creation, separation, and reunion of the Primal Serpent. Within their laboratories the world's alchemists replay the three stages of the Primal Serpent in order to create the fiery, alchemical force and use it for transformation. They produce the Primal Serpent as the Prima Materia, separate it into its polarity, and then reunite it. The end product of their alchemy is the outer Philosophers Stone or Elixir of Immortality, and/or it could be an inner activation of their indwelling Fire Serpent.

Egyptian Alchemy

The term "alchemy" (al-chemy) is Arabic and denotes the "Art of Egypt."

The art of Western alchemy has its beginning in Egypt, a truth revealed by the term "alchemy," which is Arabic for the "Art of Khem," or the "Art of Egypt." Khem, Khemi or Khemit was the country's earliest name long before the Greeks renamed it Egypt. The term alchemy was coined by the Sufi alchemists when the Moslem empire expanded into Egypt.

Egyptian alchemy was first taught by the Thoth-Hermes Masters.

The alchemy of Egypt is said to have been first taught by the Thoth-Hermes Masters from Atlantis, who are reputed to have initially arrived in the land both before and after the Great Deluge. Leading up to the Flood, one Thoth-Hermes missionary engraved the wisdom of alchemy and the art of sacred design and construction on granite and brass pillars, which were then secreted in an underground vault in Thebes. These pillars and their wisdom were later recovered by a Thoth-Hermes after the Flood and then transcribed onto scrolls for the benefit of the Egyptian priests.

The Thirteen Precepts of Alchemy taught by the Thoth-Hermes Masters were engraved on the Tabula Smaragdina or Emerald Tablet.

It is said that when an ancient Thoth-Hermes Master journeyed to Egypt he brought with him the *Tabula Smaragdina* or "Emerald Tablet" upon which were engraved the 13 Precepts or stages involved in the process of alchemy. In numerology, thirteen is the number of death and rebirth. It is also a number of the fiery and destructive dragon, a truth revealed in *The Revelation of St. John the Divine* wherein the 13th Chapter is dedicated to the dragon or "Beast." The 13 Precepts of the Emerald Tablet were written in a cryptic language that describes the separation and reunion of the polarity as the Sun and Moon, and Heaven and Earth. Culminating in the "Operation of the Sun," or the completion of evolution in a Sun-driven Solar System like our own, the meaning and application of the following precepts in the alchemical process is complicated and was understood only by the most advanced practitioners of the science.

The following is one translation of the 13 Precepts:
1. Speak not fictitious things, but that which is certain and true.
2. What is below is like that which is above, and what is above is like that which is below, to accomplish the miracles of one thing.
3. As all things were produced by the one word of one Being, so all things were produced from this one thing by adaptation.
4. Its father is the sun; its mother the moon. The wind carried it in its belly; its nurse is the earth.
5. It is the father of perfection throughout the world.
6. The power is vigorous if it be changed into earth.
7. Separate the earth from the fire, the subtle from the gross, acting prudently and with judgment.
8. Ascend with the greatest sagacity from the earth to heaven, and then again, descend to the earth, and unite together the powers of things superior and things inferior. Thus will you obtain the glory of the whole world, and obscurity will fly far away from you.
9. This has more fortitude than fortitude itself, because it conquers every subtle thing and can penetrate every solid.
10. Thus the world was formed.
11. Hence proceed wonders, which are here established.
12. Therefore, I am called Hermes Trismegistus, having three parts of the philosophy of the whole world.
13. That which I had to say concerning the operation of the sun is completed.

Egyptian alchemy was influenced by "Sirian" Alchemy. Sirius was intimately associated with Ptah and Anubis, two patrons of Alchemy.

The Thoth-Hermes Masters on Atlantis were influenced by "Sirian" Alchemy that was transmitted into them by Sirian missionaries when they visited the Atlantic Motherland and bestowed upon the ruling monarch an alchemical Chintamani Stone they had brought with them from their celestial home. Later, under the influence of Sirian Alchemy, the Egyptians referred to Sirius as Sa Ptah, because the power emanated from the star was equated with Ptah, the Master Builder and alchemical force, who rebuilt the physical body into an immortal temple for the Infinite Spirit to dwell within. Sirius was also the Dog Star and equated with the Egyptian jackal god and lord of alchemy, Anubis, whose function in the alchemical process was to consume the flesh of an initiate and transmute it back into pure energy, thus elevating the frequency of the physical body and making it immortal.

The Great Pyramid served as an Alchemical Crucible of initiation.

The Thoth-Hermes Masters made the Great Pyramid into an alchemical crucible where the polar opposite energies united to produce the Primal Serpent. When an initiate moved within the force field of the Great Pyramid the same inner process or union accompanied by the awakening of the Fire Serpent would occur within them.

The shape of any pyramid, which means "fire in the middle," unites the polar opposite forms of the tetrahedron (fire) and the cube (earth). Through their interaction, the earth element, or dense matter, is transmuted by the fire element back into energy or life force. The Great Pyramid further unites the polarity in its King's Chamber, which was built with air shafts aligned with the cosmic polarity of Orion, the Divine Mind, and Alpha Draconis, the Divine Power. The male energies of Orion stream down the southern shaft and mix with the female energies of Alpha Draconis that slither down the northern shaft. They mix together in the King's Chamber to further enhance the transformative power of the Primal Serpent that is being generated throughout the pyramid. When a candidate for initiation once lied down within the sarcophagus inside the King's Chamber, his or her inner serpent fire was sympathetically activated.

The secrets of human alchemy were conveyed during the theatrical rites of Osiris, the archetypal initiate. They culminated in the raising of the Djed pillar, the spine of Osiris, and its indwelling serpent power.

The instructive alchemical myth regarding the death and rebirth of the archetypal initiate, Osiris, was dramatized specially for the Egyptian priests in the sacred cities of Sais, Philae, Busiris and Abydos. As a crowd of spiritual spectators watched with rapt attention, a priest playing the role of Osiris was murdered by his brother, Seth, symbolizing the spiritual death that occurs to an initiate through the awakening of the inner serpent power. The second act of the play was the Raising of the the Djed Pillar, which involved the raising of a pillar representing Osiris' spine and the indwelling "Dj" or serpent power within it. The final act has Osiris resurrected by his wife, Isis, and the archetypal initiate achieving the goal of spiritual immortality.

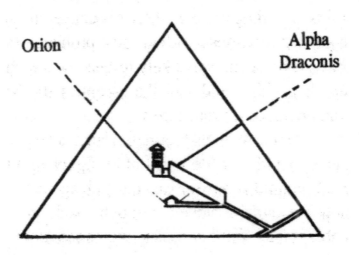

The Star Passages into the King's Chamber of the Great Pyramid

Initiation Sarcophagus in the King's Chamber of the Great Pyramid
Courtesy of www.SacredSitesJourneys.com

Thoth gives to Osiris the united Twin Serpents with one hand and the Ank, Symbol of Immortality, with the other

Raising the Djed Pillar

Egyptian Pharaoh carrying the Shewbread

Egyptian Pharaoh offering Shewbread to Anubis

Many of the stages of Osiris' death and rebirth through alchemy were also recorded as hieroglyphs covering the walls of his headquarters at Abydos. One motif has the Lord of Alchemy, Thoth-Hermes, handing Osiris the two united serpents with one hand and the ankh, or symbol of immortality, with the other. This, of course, represents that through the inner union of the twin serpents, the inner Primal Serpent is awakened and immorality is attained.

The Egyptian Alchemists also produced Shewbread or white powder gold as an Elixir of Immortality

Recent research points to the Egyptian alchemists having also produced and consumed an alchemical substance known as "Shewbread" to initiate the inner process of alchemy. According to their preserved texts, Shewbread was known in ancient Egypt and Mesopotamia by the names of "mfkzt" and "shem-an-na" respectively, both of which denoted "high-ward fire-stone," a term related to "Philosophers Stone."[1] Currently known by its modern name of White Powder Gold, Shewbread was produced especially for the pharaoh's use and for offerings to the Gods and Goddesses. Many temple hieroglyphs, like those on the opposing page, show priests or the pharaoh carrying it to the gods as an offering. The priceless Shewbread was considered one of the greatest offerings that could be made to the gods.

The first modern discovery regarding the Egyptians and their use of shewbread occured in 1904 when an expedition lead by Sir W.M. Flinders Petrie climbed Mount Serabit, the Biblical Mount Horeb, in the Sinai desert and discovered an Egyptian temple dedicated to Horus that contained literally tons of the substance. Apparently the Petrie expedition had stumbled upon a Shewbread laboratory used by Egyptian alchemists. The properties of White Powder Gold were later discovered in the 1980s by a man in Arizona named David Hudson. Hudson, a cotton farmer, was testing the content of his soil when he discovered a substance that was weightless and could completely disappear under direct sunlight. After testing the substance, lab technicians concluded that the substance was part of a family of a mono-atomic elements called ORME, an acronym for "orbitally rearranged mono-atomic elements," that include iridium and rhodium. Hudson understood the reasons for Shewbread's alchemical application in Egypt. Since it could so easily disappear, the frequency of White Powder Gold was close to that of pure energy and the inner fire serpent.

Sufi Alchemy

Sufi Alchemy was a composite science from Egypt, India, Persia, and Greece

The Sufi Alchemists received their alchemical wisdom from both East and West, but their inheritance from Egypt far surpassed what came to them from other countries which is why they named the art of alchemy after ancient Khem.

Egyptian alchemy came to the Sufis via Dhu'l Nun al-Misri

Dhu'l Nun al-Misri, whose name means "of the Fish," or "of the Snake," was born in Egypt and spent the early part of his life studying the hieroglyphs on the temples of ancient Khem and learning their alchemical secrets. After mastering alchemy and achieving gnosis, Dhu'l Nun traveled to the Middle East as a Sufi adept to teach the Art of Khem and the value of achieving gnosis.

While in Egypt, Dhu'l Nun understood that the alchemical power was personified by the ancient deity Ptah-Sokar-Osiris, the Master Builder of Egypt, whom he later helped incorporate into Masonry as the Master Builder. Dhu'l Nun also recognized Ptah-Sokar-Osiris to be synonymous with al-Khadir, who like his Egyptian counterpart was a Green Man and the embodiment of the power of alchemy. Dhu'l Nun learned that when al-Khadir was properly invoked he would arrive to initiate the process of alchemy within a Sufi by transmitting into them some of his own alchemical force, which they came to know as Baraka. Dhu'l Nun passed the wisdom of al-Khadir to the al-Banna, the organization of Sufi "Freemasons" he helped to found, and they in turn passed it to those intrepid and infinitely curious students they taught sacred geometry and Masonry to, the Knights Templar.

The basic formula used by western alchemists was standardized by the Sufi alchemist Jabir. It involves the separation of the Primal Serpent as Philosophical Mercury and Philosophical Sulphur, and their reunion.

It was the Sufi alchemist Jabir ibn Hayyan who first identified the polar opposite principles of the Primal Serpent as Philosophical Mercury and Philosophical Sulphur, which then became the standard names for the Twin Snakes or the polar opposite, or fire/water, substances that must be united before alchemy can be actuated. Philosophical Mercury and Philosophical Sulphur also became the names for the polar opposite substances of an alchemical recipe. They could be the two actual elements of Mercury or Sulphur, or more commonly, they were two substances that mimicked the "watery" properties of the metal Mercury (liquid at room temperature) and the fiery and volatile properties of Sulphur.

After Jabir, the stages of western alchemy from beginning to end inevitably always involved the separation of the Primal Serpent or Prima Materia into its two component parts, water and fire or Philosophical Mercury and Philosophical Sulphur; and then purifying these dual components before finally reuniting them back together. The resulting alchemical product, the reconstituted Primal Serpent, was known by the alchemists as the the Resurrected Mercury. Thus, Mercury was both a term for one of the alchemical ingredients, as well as the androgynous Primal Serpent that resulted from the process of alchemy. This is because of the metal's dual, or "androgynous", nature as both a solid and a metal.

Jabir, whose meritorious background included an apprenticeship to the the great Sufi, Ja'far As-Sadiq, had the good fortune of serving as court physician for the Caliph Harun al-Rashid in Baghdad, which supplied him with ample funding for his experiments and placed him at the crossroads of alchemical wisdom that was continually streaming into the Moslem Empire from conquered lands. The alchemical formulas of Jabir, who was known as Geber in Europe, were so complex and veiled in cipher that his name contributed to the term denoting incomprehensible communication: Gibberish.

Jabir would ultimately issue in a new era of exploration by pioneering the revolutionary new science of chemistry. Soon many new elements were discovered within the alchemist laboratories of both East and West.

The Sufi alchemist, al-Razi, introduced the third element of Salt.

The Sufi alchemist al-Razi introduced Salt as a third component of western alchemical formulary. Salt was the dense matter or body of a thing within which Mercury and Sulphur, its water and fire, interacted. Together, this alchemical Trinity is the Primal Dragon, CHiram, which is "One in Essence and Three in Aspect." Thereafter, all three components, Mercury, Sulphur and Salt, became recognized as the Alchemical Trinity.

The introduction of Salt added a new dimension to the philosophy and practice of alchemy. It was thus understood that when Mercury and Sulphur reunited as alchemical fire within an entity, they accomplished their transformations inside the body or "Salt" matrix of that entity. Salt was also recognized to be the "dead" matrix that resulted when Mercury and Sulfur had been removed from a substance.

The Alchemical Trinity of Mercury, Sulphur and Salt also corresponded to an entity's spirit, soul and body respectively. Thus, to fully transform a person alchemically, all three members of his or her Alchemical Trinity needed to be recognized and fully purified.

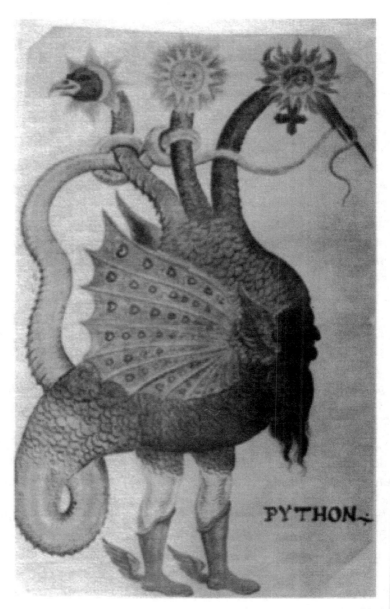

***The Trinity of Mercury (Moon), Sulpher (Sun), and Salt (Vulture)
unite as CHiram, the Primal Dragon***

The Sufis acknowledge six energy centers, the Lataif, that correspond to the Chakras of the Yogis.

The Sufi "chakras" are the Lataif-e-Sitta, meaning "six centers of spiritual cognition." These six Lataif must be awakened through alchemy and the enlivening influence of Baraka before a Sufi can achieve perfect spiritual wisdom or gnosis. They lie in areas of the body that loosely correspond to the locations of the six lower chakras. The lowest Lataif, the Latifa-i-Nafs, the Latifa of the "Self," is located under the navel; above it is the Latifa-i-Qalb, the Latifa of the "Heart," located at the physical heart; opposing it is the Latifa-i-Rooh, the Laitifa of "Spirit," on the right side of the chest; and between them is the Latifa-i-Sirr, the Latifa of the "Secret," located in the center of the chest. At the forehead is the Latifa-i-Khafi, the Latifa of the "Mysterious," and above it is the Latifa-i-Akhfa, the Laitifa of the "Deeply Hidden," in the brain near the top of the head.

European Alchemy

Many Europeans studied the art of alchemy in the Sufi universities of Constantinople, Damascus, Baghdad, Toledo, Fez and Seville, and then brought the science back to their respective homelands.

Many European alchemists, including Ramon Lully and Paracelsus, studied alchemy among the Sufis in the Middle East, North Africa, and Spain, and then later founded traditions and schools of alchemy in their native lands. The archetypal European alchemist, Christian Rosencrutz, who is said to have studied with the Sufis in Damascus and Fez, was a composite of these early, intrepid seekers of truth.

In Europe, Paracelsus introduced the branch of Alchemy known as Spagyrics.

After returning from studies with the Sufis in the Middle East, Paracelsus introduced into Europe the alchemical process of Spagyrics. Spagyrics puts plants, metals and minerals through a series of alchemical processes to create elixirs to heal the human body and prolong life. Many of the first western medicines were produced through this method. The name Spagyrics was created by Paracelsus from two Greek words meaning "separate" and "reunite," thus identifying it as a legitimate branch of traditional alchemy. Spagyrics begins with the separation of a substance's Mercury and Sulfur, which are its oils and essences. These components are then purified and reunited as tinctures and elixirs. Spagyrics also possesses the Alchemical Trinity: the oil, essence and physical body of a substance are alternately recognized as its soul, spirit and body.

European Alchemical Symbology

Reuniting the Polarity as the Sun & Moon, King & Queen

Reunitng the Polarity as the Twin Serpents

The goal of Western Alchemy was principally the production of the Philosophers Stone and the Elixir of Immortality

The final, magical product of the Western Alchemist's experiments was commonly the red Philosophers Stone, which was turned to dust and then sprinkled on a base metal to transform it into gold. The end product might also be a liquid, the Elixir of Immortality, which was taken internally to keep the body youthful and to activate the inner alchemical serpent fire.

When made correctly, the Philosophers Stone and the Elixir of Immortality were of such high frequency that they were close to pure energy. In one of his diaries the alchemist Alessandro Caglistro mentioned that his friend, St. Germain, used to keep his elixir in a capped bottle, otherwise it could interact with the air and completely disappear. In reference to the eternally undefinable nature of the Philosophers Stone, the Greek alchemist, Zosimus, described it in riddle. He stated it was a "stone which is not a stone, a precious thing which has no value, a thing of many shapes which has no shape, this unknown thing which is known to all."

The Alchemical Process took seven, nine or thirteen stages.

Western alchemists employed seven, nine or thirteen stages in their alchemical processes, all of which are numbers associated with death, completion, transformation and the Primal Serpent. When they adhered closely to the precepts of the Emerald Tablets, they usually observed thirteen stages. But regardless of the number of steps involved, the alchemical process always involved the three principal stages of separation, purification and reunion.

Today, the three stages are commonly incorporated in these seven stages:

Calcination

Dissolution

Separation

Conjunction

Fermentation

Distillation

Coagulation

Near the end of the alchemical process the transforming substance would assume the radiant colors of one manifestation of the Primal Dragon, the peacock. This is the Peacock Stage of alchemy.

Often, the closer that the alchemist got to producing the fiery red Philosophers Stone, the more their experimental matrices would take on the characteristics of the Primal Dragon as the rainbow-colored peacock.

A European Midieval Alchemist or "Puffer"

Climbing the "Alchemical Mountain"

The Peacock Stage of the Alchemical Process

341

After producing the Philosophers Stone, many Western Alchemists succeeded in transmuting base metals into gold.

Many western alchemists succeeded in transmuting base metals into gold, including the French alchemist, Nicholas Flamel, and the Spanish alchemist, Ramon Lully. It is said that while conducting his experiments in the Tower of London, Ramon Lully transmuted 50,000 pounds of mercury, tin and lead into solid gold for King Edward II. Although Lully requested that his alchemical gold be used to finance a crusade, the self-serving King Edward is reputed to have used it for other less noble purposes. Some pieces of Lully's gold were made into coins that supposedly still exist with the collection of private collectors in Europe.[2] Lully's secret alchemical wisdom eventually found its way to Scotland via his book *Of the Art of Tansmuting Metals*, which he sent to King Robert the Bruce. Thus began a Scottish alchemical tradition wherein the castles of the royals contained alchemy rooms with continually blazing furnaces. Another monarch seeking easy wealth, the Holy Roman Emperor Leopold, had a large quantity of tin transmuted to gold in his royal presence by the Austrian alchemist Wenzel Seiler. One of Seilor's transmutations is reported to still be in the imperial treasury of Vienna in the form of a piece of silver that has been partly transmuted into alchemical gold. In Bohemia, the Emperor, Ferdinand, also benefited by alchemy when the alchemist, Lubujardiere, transmuted two and one half pounds of mercury into gold for him. The occasion is commemorated by an alchemically produced coin that bears the inscription: "Divine metamorphosis caused in Prague, January 15, 1640, witnessed by his Imperial Majesty Ferdinand III." Not all transmutations benefitted the royalty, however; some were dedicated to altruistic causes. After discovering the secret for making the Philosophers Stone, the French alchemist, Nicholas Flamel, used his transmuted gold to finance the construction of 14 hospitals, 3 chapels and 7 churches in the city of Paris.

Eventually, so many alchemists succeeded in making gold that in 1310, Pope John XXII was compelled to issue a bull prohibiting alchemy and especially the practice of producing gold. It even became a crime to trade in gold that had been produced alchemically.

Many western alchemists also produced the Elixir of Immortality.

Many western alchemists, including Nicholas Flamel, are said to have also discovered the formula for the Elixir of Immortality. Some historians maintain that through the power of his elixir, Flamel lived 300 years, while others assert that he is still alive. They allude to the remarkable discovery that was made when his coffin was dug up by grave robbers a short time after his funeral; it was found to be empty! Another immortal alchemist of notoriety who was affiliated with both the European and Sufi alchemy traditions was the legendary Artephius, an elixir-consuming practitioner who is said to have lived 1025 years and may have been known as the enlightened adept Apollodorus in his younger years. The greatest of European alchemists, the Count of St. Germain, is said to have consumed a daily ration of his own brew of the Elixir of Immortality, and those who saw him at times 50 years apart swore that he had not aged a day in the interim. St. Germain, who often spoke of his intimate meetings with the Queen of Sheba and Cleopatra, is believed to have lived between 500 and 2000 years, although many believe he is still alive today. St. Germain's protégé, Alessandro Cagliostro, produced the Elixir of Immortality for both himself and a veritable army of patients and clients. While dispensing the elixir in a clinic he set up in Strasbourg, France, Cagliostro healed incurable illnesses and completely rejuvenated his aged, paralyzed and catatonic patients. He became famous for being able to restore head hair and for regenerating complete sets of new teeth. The great Swiss alchemist Paracelsus is also averred to have created an elixir, which his followers called "Tinctura Philosophorum," the "Philosophers Tincture." Through its administration, Paracelsus is known to have cured almost every fatal illness and completely rejuvenated aged bodies. In a passage attributed to him in *De Tinctura Physicorum*, "On the Tincture of the Physicians," Paracelsus comments on the efficacy of his elixir:

"This is the tincture by which some of the first physicians in Egypt, and afterwards up till our times, have lived for 150 years. The lives of many of them lasted for centuries, as history clearly teaches."

Western alchemy became famous for its elixirs known as the Four Lions

Within one school of alchemy, the Elixir of Immortality was dispensed as four elixirs of increasing degrees of intensity and effectiveness known as the "Lions." An alchemist of this school would begin with the White Lion and, when ready, would progress to the Brown and Green Lions, and eventually complete the cycle with the Red Lion, whose effect would instantly awaken the inner serpent fire. There was no turning back from the activating effects of the Red Lion, which is why the alchemist needed to be fully prepared emotionally, mentally and spiritually through imbibing the weaker Lions. Otherwise he could end up mentally unstable and even insane.

European alchemists united under the alchemical symbol of the rose.

Eventually a society of European alchemists mobilized under one roof and became Sub-Rosa, meaning that they existed under the symbol of

The Elixir of Immortality
by Chadwick St. John

the rose. The red-colored rose was the symbol of the fire of alchemy, and its opening represented the full blossoming of gnosis that results from alchemical transformation. The sweet nectar of the opened rose is what the metaphorical honey bees, i.e., the seekers of wisdom, strive to become filled with.

The most famous of all organizations that formed under the symbol of the rose or rose cross were the Rosicrucians and the Knights of the Rosy Cross, or Knights Templar. Rosicrucian denotes both "Rose Cross' as well as "Dew Cup," which is a term for the chalice that holds the Elixir of Immortality. Under the influence of the early Sub-Rosa sects the symbol of the rose, or its modified version as the rose cross, was adopted by the Royal Order of Scotland and the British Order of the Garter. Within the other orders and organizations that the Knights of the Rosy Cross helped form in Europe, most included a Knight of the Rose Cross degree.

Knights Templar Alchemy

The Knights Templar learned alchemy from Sufis and Jewish Kabbalists.

While in the Holy Land, the Knights Templar learned alchemy from the Sufis, who were acknowledged to be the best alchemists of their time. The Knights also trained under the descendants of the Essenes, the Jewish Kabbalists, whose alchemical tradition extended back to Egypt and Chaldea. The Assassins, who were founded by one of the greatest Persian Sufi alchemists, Hasan-i-Sabah, were another significant influence on the Templars' budding alchemical acumen. One Assassin chief, Rashid al-din Sinan of Syria, was a great adept of alchemy who had many recorded dealings with the Templars. Sinan was the famous "Old Man of the Mountain" who was famous for preaching the Teachings of the Resurrection, which were alchemical doctrines designed to prepare his followers for a time of mass ascension.

The Templars' Red Eight-pointed Cross Pattée was a symbol of the Goddess and alchemy.

Although it denoted a Christian affiliation to the Templars of lower rank, among the inner circle of Johannite Knights Templar the red eight-pointed cross pattée revealed their affiliation to the Goddess and Her art of alchemy. The Templars learned from the Sufis that the eight-pointed cross was the eternal symbol of both the Goddess and Her Son, St. George or al-Khadir. The fiery alchemical nature of the Goddess and Her Son was symbolized by the fire engine red-colored four and eight-pointed crosses. When Saint George became the patron saint of the British Order of the Garter, the ancient symbol of al-Khadir, a four-pointed red cross set inside an eight-pointed cross, became the order's badge of membership.

The Templars learned the alchemical power of the eight-sided octagon.

While living in the al-Aqsa Mosque on the Temple Mount, the Templars spent many days and nights studying the alchemical power of the octagonal shape of the nearby Dome of the Rock. After returning to Europe, the Knights Templar built many of their preceptories and churches in the shape of an octagon to make them alchemical crucibles that continuously generated a subtle fire for spiritual transformation. An eight-sided structure is a natural focus for the energies of Heaven and Earth to unite within.

Gothic Cathedrals designed by the Templars generated the alchemical force.

The Gothic Cathedrals of Europe were also designed and built by Templars or Templar-trained masons to generate the alchemical force. These cathedrals, many of which were literally covered inside and out with alchemical symbols, were often built on vortexes whose alchemical power they amplified and expanded. To further enhance and move the natural life force within, their dimensions incorporated the Golden Mean Proportion, which aligns a structure with the geometrical spiral pattern of the planetary life force. To make them crucibles, the Gothic Cathedrals were typically built in the shape of a cross, which Fulcanelli calls "the alchemical hieroglyph of the crucible," and to make them perpetual unifiers of the polarity they normally incorporated within their structures twin spires, or two polar-opposite spires of unequal size. Alchemical practices were encouraged inside the Gothic Cathedrals, a vestige of which survives as the numerous labyrinths which remain within the cathedrals of Chartres, Amiens, Sens, Rheims, Auxerre, St. Quentin, Poitiers and Bayeux. The alchemical properties of the labyrinth at Amiens was further enhanced by being designed in the shape of an octagon. The stained glass windows of the original Gothic Cathedrals also created a profound alchemical effect, especially the "rose windows." Fulcanelli believed that the symbol of the rose, as well as rose-colored stained-glass windows, further enhanced the power of Gothic Cathedrals.

The Johannite Templars made alchemical pilgrimages to cathedrals that were placed over Europe's Seven Chakras.

It is believed that the Templars and their masons constructed cathedrals over seven ancient power centers known of by the Druids, the seven chakras of Europe, and then made a pilgrimage to each of them while sequentially moving up the continent's spine. These cathedrals and their underlying chakras were located at Santiago de Compostella in Spain, Toulouse, Orleans, Chartres, Paris, Amiens in France, and Roslin in Scotland. It has been speculated that rituals performed within these chakra centers were designed to awaken the corresponding chakras inside a Templar pilgrim.

Some sacred structures were also built along the alchemical Rose Lines.

Some of the churches and cathedrals built by Templar-trained masons were placed along alchemically empowered terrestrial lines, known as Rose Lines, to enhance their transformative power. One of these Rose Lines was found to run north from the Langueduc through a terrestrial pentagram of churches and temples, which includes at one of its points the Templar Preceptory of Bezu. This line then continues to Paris, where it energizes the cathedrals of Notre Dame, St. Sulpice and what is now the Louvre Museum. It then moves north to another very important alchemical edifice, the Cathedral of Amiens. Another European Rose Line can be found in the British Isles that traverses the country of Scotland. This second Rose Line cuts through the dormant volcanoes upon which the city of Edinburgh is built. It then carries its dynamic alchemical force right into the center of Rosslyn Chapel, a small Gothic church that sits directly over Europe's seventh chakra.

The Templar heresy arose from the Knights' affiliation with their gnostic-alchemical path.

Allegations of Templar heresy that resulted in the Knights' downfall were built around their alchemical rituals and experiments that culminated in gnosis. After infiltrating the Templar preceptories, the spies of King Philip IV witnessed numerous alchemical rites performed by the Knights, and temples covered with alchemical symbols and images, including that of androgynous Baphomet, which to any Catholic official was an obvious image of the Devil. Baphomet united numerous male and female features, including his hands that pointed to (and united) both Heaven and Earth. Baphomet exhibited a decidedly dark nature because he was an embodiment of the alchemical force that takes one to a spiritual rebirth through death of the ego and destruction of limited concepts of the universe.

The Knights Templar had many Holy Grails, including the Holy Shroud, the Veil of Veronica, the Holy Chalice, and the Head of John the Baptist.

The Knights Templar are said to have had in their possession many Holy Grails at different times of their history, including the cup that Jesus and his Apostles drank from during the Last Supper. During the Fourth Crusade, the Holy Shroud, the Veil of Veronica, pieces of the True Cross and the Head of John the Baptist were all found in a palace chapel in Constantinople and brought back to Europe where they were placed in the Templars'

Templar Alchemical Symbol of Androgynous Man-Woman

Templar Alchemical Symbol of Androgynous Baphomet

preceptories. John's Head, which the Templars admitted during their Paris trial emitted a tremendous amount of creative and healing power, was taken around to the various preceptories in Europe by Hugh de Puraud, second in command under Jacques de Molay, and set upon special altars where initiation into the gnostic Johannite tradition occurred.

The true Holy Grail of the Templars was the power of alchemy itself.
     The Holy Grails of the Templars all had one thing in common, their alchemical power. In time, the Templars learned that the true Holy Grail was not an object but the alchemical power an object possessed, which is why there had been so many of them. This Holy Grail power was passed down to the Templar Knights as the Holy Spirit from the Johannite gnostic masters John the Baptist, Jesus, Mary Magdalene, and John the Divine.

Jewish Alchemy

Jewish, or Kabbalistic Alchemy, was revealed to Adam in the Garden of Eden. It also assimilated esoteric wisdom from Chaldea and Egypt.
     The Jewish science of alchemy, which is also known as Kabbalistic Alchemy, is said to have first been taught to Adam in the Garden of Eden along with the science of gnosis. There is no consensus as to who Adam's teacher was in the Garden, but the candidates include St. Michael, the Angel Raziel, Metatron and the Serpent on the Tree. In later years, the wisdom of the Kabbala was embellished upon by the Prophets Moses and Abraham, although their sources are also subject to conjecture. Kabbala means "received wisdom," so it is possible that much of their alchemical wisdom was received as intuitive revelation, including Moses' famous download on Mount Sinai. Another Kabbalistic prophet, Shimon bar Yochai, is said to have received one of the books of the Kabbala, the *Zohar*, while mediating in a cave for 13 years. His angelic teacher of the wisdom is believed to have been the spirit of the Prophet Elijah, and therefore John the Baptist as well.

The Kabbala text, known as the Sepher Yetzirah, the "Book of Creation," is a map describing the creation of the universe from the Primal Serpent. It describes the Creation as a sequence of 22 sounds, which are the 22 letters of the Hebrew alphabet. The first three sounds correspond to the Alchemical Trinity that together comprise the body of the Primal Dragon.
     The *Sepher Yetzirah*, the oldest of the Jewish Kabbalistic texts, outlines the entire process of creation of the universe beginning with the Primal Serpent and ending in dense matter. It recounts the universal process as a succession of 22 sounds, which were rendered into the 22 symbolic letters

of the Hebrew alphabet. The 22 sounds are divided into three groups. The first group of Three Mother Letters resound first to catalyze the creative cycle and bring the body of the Primal Serpent into manifestation as CHiram, the entity who is One in essence and Three in aspect. These three Hebrew letters are Resh, Mem and Shin, the sound frequencies of the elements of Air, Water and Fire, that collectively resound as CHiram. Precipitating out of the three Mother letters are the second group of seven double letters, which represent the seven principles and seven planets that are the seven divisions of the Primal Serpent's body. Finally, the third group of twelve simple letters that are engendered by the seven double letters represent the twelve parts of the the circular dragon body that fills the night sky as the 12 signs of the Zodiac.

The Sepher Yetzirah also includes the Tree of Life, which also reveals the Creation from the Primal Serpent to dense Earth.

The Kabbalistic Tree of Life is a version of the tree that the Primal Serpent slithered down in the course of creating the universe. Above the tree is the invisible, Infinite Spirit, known as Ain Soph Aur, Ain Soph, and Ain, meaning "The Boundless Light," "The Boundless" and the "Nothingness." Below them is the emanation of the Infinite, the Tree of Life, which is composed of 10 Sephiroth or spheres united by 22 lines. At the top of the Tree is the Sephira called Kether, meaning "Crown," which symbolizes the Primal Serpent Creator as King of the Universe. From Kether, which M.P. Hall calls the "First Androgyny,"[3] branch the Twin Serpents as the two outside columns of the Tree. These columns are known as Mercy and Severity, or Wisdom and Strength, thus identifying them as the Divine Wisdom and Divine Power, or the male/female polarity of the Primal Serpent. Of the 10 Sephiroth, the three at the top of the Tree represent the original trinity of the Primal Serpent, which is "One in Essence and Three in Aspect," and the seven Sephiroth below them symbolize the seven principles that the Primal Serpent divides into while creating the cosmos.

The Tree of Life is also a representation of the Primal Serpent in the form of the Divine Man of the Cosmos, the Adam Kadmon.

The Tree of Life also represents the cosmos as the body of the Adam Kadmon. When understanding the Tree from this perspective, the central column is the torso of the Adam Kadmon, and the dual columns of Mercy and Severity are his arms. From an esoterical standpoint, the central column is the spine and path of the Cosmic Man's Kundalini, and the dual columns are his inner snakes or polar-opposite channels that unite at his root chakra, the Sephira of Malkuth.

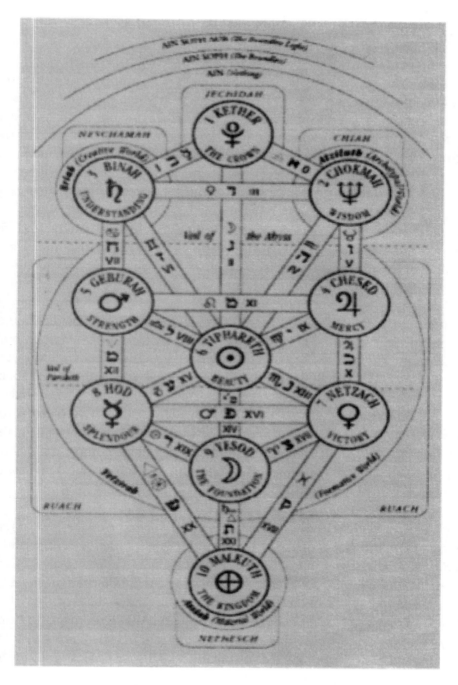

The Kabbalic Tree of Life from the Sepher Yetzirah
Courtesy of www.Thelemapedia.org

The Tree of Life is also a representation of the microcosm, the human body, and a map of human alchemical transformation.

The cosmic body of the Adam Kadmon is the macrocosmic version of the microcosmic human body, so the Tree of Life is also a representation of the human form, especially the human esoteric anatomy. This is the true meaning of humanity being "made in the image of God."

When interpreted as a representation of the human esoteric anatomy, the topmost Sephira, Kether, corresponds to the Ajna Chakra, home of the Primal Serpent in the body. The two "serpents" that stream from it and make the columns of Severity and Mercy are the Ida and Pingala Nadis (India), or Ren and Du Meridians (China), which control the balance of the male and female principles in the body. The lowest Sephira of Malkuth, where the columns or serpents unite, corresponds to the Muladhara Chakra, and the central column that rises up from it is the spinal column and Sushumna Nadi, the path of the resurrected Primal Serpent as Kundalini. The five Sephiroth along the central column include the invisible Daath. If the crossing point of the 22 paths or meridians below Daath is also considered a Sephira, then all the traditional six chakras are represented by the central channel. Another system of correspondences associates Kether with the crown chakra, both Binah and Chochmah with the Third Eye, Chesed and Geburah with the throat chakra, Tipareth with the heart chakra, Netsah and Hod with the solar-plexus chakra, Jesod with the sacral chakra, and Malkuth with the root chakra.

When the 22 Paths or meridians are added to the 10 Sephiroth, the sum is 32. Thirty-two is the number of the "Paths of Wisdom" in the Kabbalistic tradition, as well as the number of vertebrae comprising the human spine, channel of the serpent fire. Thus, the 32 Paths of Wisdom lead to the highest gnostic wisdom.

There are four levels of the Tree of Life. The four levels of the Tree correspond to the four levels of the universe and the four "bodies" of the Adam Kadmon. The macrocosmic four bodies of the Adam Kadmon are reflected microcosmicaly as the four bodies comprising the human form.

The four levels of the Tree of Life include Azilut, the World of Emanation; Beriah, the World of Creation; Yezirah, the World of Formation; and Asiyyah, the World of Action. These are the four "bodies" of the Adam Kadmon which are reflected microsmically as the four bodies of a human: the spiritual, mental (casual), emotional, and physical bodies.

The Creation Cycle represented by the descending symbology on the Kabbalic Tree of Life was incorporated in the allegory of Genesis as the Tree of the Knowledge of Good and Evil. The destructive alchemical cycle that returns matter to energy and then to Spirit was woven into Genesis as the Tree of Life situated at the east of the Garden where God placed a Cherubim with a flaming sword.

The creation cycle of the universe represented in the Kabbalistic Tree of Life is represented in *Genesis* as the Tree of the Knowledge of Good and Evil that the serpent slithered down to tempt Adam and Eve. By contrast, the destruction of the universe, as well as the process of human alchemical transformation, is symbolized in *Genesis* as the Tree of Life situated near the east entrance that God set a Cherub wielding a flaming sword to protect. The Cherub and his flaming sword is symbolic of the serpent fire that guards the entrance to the Sushumna, the path to immortal life. When awakened, the Cherub uses his flaming sword to alchemically burn through all obstacles that keep a person from knowing his or her divine nature. The Hebrew Cherub has its origin with the Sumerian Primal Serpent, Enki. Cherub is derived from Kerabu, the Akkadian name of Enki.

The Cherubs over the Ark of the Covenant were the Twin Sons of the Primal Serpent. They reunited the Primal Serpent as the fire of alchemy.

The Twin Cherubs over the Ark of the Covenant were an evolution of Enki's Twin Serpent Sons or "Kerabu" that the Primal Serpent divided itself into in the course of creating the universe. By reuniting the twin Cherubs over the Ark of the Covenant, the Hebrews resurrected the Primal Dragon, which was the power and wisdom of Yahweh.

The Ark of the Covenant was kept in Holy of Holies, the room of maximum alchemical force within Solomon's Temple.

Solomon's Temple was built according to sacred geometrical principles in order to generate the maximum Divine Power of Yahweh, which manifested as the Primal Dragon. The temple was designed to unite the Twin Serpents, which were represented at the doorway to the temple as the columns of Jachin and Boaz, although their united power was most concentrated within the Holy of Holies, the residence of the Ark of the Covenant, where as Cherubs they united by touching their wings. The dynamic fire of the united Twins was additionally enhanced by the alchemical acacia wood covered over in gold used in the matrix of the Ark, as well as the vortex energy that emanated through the floor from the underlying Stone of Foundation that the Holy of Holies was built upon. Because the power and the

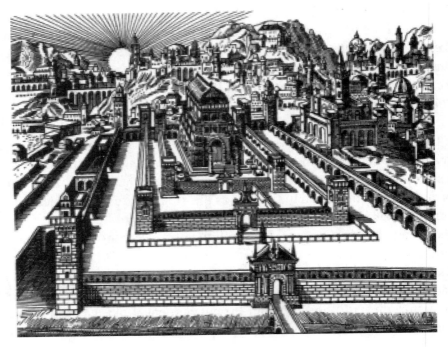

Solomon's Temple
Drawn by a Seventeenth Century Kabbalist
The four inner squares symbolize the four "Worlds" or levels of the
universe and the four bodies of the Cosmic Man, the Adam Kadmon

The Ark of the Covenant and the Twin Cherubs

presence of Yahweh was so incredibly strong within the Holy of Holies, Solomon and the Jewish high priests could use the room to directly commune with the highest deity and conduct their most important rituals.

King Solomon was an accomplished alchemist and magician.

Legend has it that much of the gold used in the building of Solomon's Temple was alchemically created by King Solomon. Clues indicating that Solomon was indeed an alchemist include his name, Sol-o-mon, or Sun and Moon, which is the premier alchemical formula, as well as the symbol he wore on his "magic" ring, the six-pointed star or Seal of Solomon, which is the definitive symbol of alchemy. The Jewish historian, Josephus, wrote that Solomon was a man of many amazing and magical abilities, a truth echoed by the European grimoires, or books on magic and sorcery, that bear his name. These include the *Clavicula Solomonis,* the "Key of Solomon the King," a text Solomon was averred to have written for his son, Rehoboam. Since Solomon consistently used his magical abilities and the serpent power they generated, it could truly be said that, "CHiram (or Hiram) assisted King Solomon to build his temple."[4]

Eastern Alchemy

Eastern Alchemy includes the alchemy of China and India, two countries that were once joined to Lemuria or Mu and received much of their alchemical wisdom from missionaries of the ancient Pacific Motherland.

Indian or Siddha Alchemy

Indian alchemy first came from Lemuria with Agastyar, a student and missionary of Skanda-Murugan, the Serpent on the Tree. Sage Agastyar established the art of Siddha Alchemy on the subcontinent of India.

Agastyar was an alchemical adept of the Pandyan Kingdom, which was a land mass that united India to Sri Lanka when the two countries were connected to Mu. When the Pandyan Kingdom sunk beneath the waves of the Indian Ocean, Agastyar traveled north to promulgate the mysteries of Siddha Alchemy, the alchemy of the "Perfected Ones," that had been passed among the adepts of Mu. He gathered a circle of students, many of whom became known as the 18 Mahesvara Siddhas, and then he assigned to each of them a branch of Siddha Alchemy to practice and teach others. Legend has it that Agastyar achieved both complete gnosis and immortality from his guru Murugan and can still be found roaming the forests of the Pothagai Hills in South India, where he occasionally appears to seekers with pure hearts.

The teachers of Siddha Alchemy in India perpetuated the Vamacara tradition of Lemuria.

The teachers of Siddha Alchemy in India were descendants of the Vamacara Masters of Mu. As members of the Shaivite tradition they emulated their Lord Shiva in both dress and temperament.

The various practices of Siddha Alchemy include yoga, pranayama (controlled breathing), meditation, and the consumption of elixirs.

There are many practices of Siddha Alchemy, most of which can be grouped under the disciplines of yoga. Yoga, meaning "to yoke" or "bring together," refers to the inner alchemy yoga sets in motion by uniting the polarity and awakening the inner fire serpent, the Kundalini. The various forms of yoga are part of the Shaivite Tantric tradition that was first promulgated in Lemuria by the primal teacher, Sanat Kumara.

Agastyar's student Bogarnath founded the branch of Siddha Alchemy known as Rasayana, which involves making and consuming elixirs to strengthen the "Rasa," the essence of the body that includes virya (seminal fluids) and ojas (bone marrow). Rasa supports all the inner organs and the immune system.

The Siddha Bogarnath inherited the Rasayana tradition from his guru Agastyar and expanded upon it to include the many herbs, metals and minerals of India which can be made into elixirs for both health and longevity. Bogarnath's formulary was adopted by yogis for alchemical transformation, as well as by healing professionals who evolved it into Siddha Medicine.

Bogarnath achieved the highest gnosis through his elixirs and his steady meditation on Skanda-Murugan, whom he came to accept as an embodiment of the primal alchemical force itself. His understanding of Skanda-Murugan compelled Bogarnath to carve a representation of his guru as the alchemical six-pointed star on a slab of purified, alchemical gold that he produced. Bogarnath's creation today resides at Murugan's shrine in Kataragama, Sri Lanka, and is only put on display once a year.

In his later years, Bogarnath made Palani in south India the headquarters for his Rasayana experiments. When he had completely mastered Rasayana, Bogarnath produced a statue of Murugan there composed of many metals, minerals and herbs that contains amazing healing and alchemical powers. This effigy of Skanda-Murugan, which remains his principal effigy at Palani, is daily washed with milk and spices which are collected and bottled as an elixir that is reputed to be able to cure any disease. Some pilgrims maintain that Bogarnath became immortal and still lives at Palani.

Palani Temple perches high on top of a sacred hill
Hills are the favorite abodes of Murugan

Siddha Bogarnath, founder of Rasayana Alchemy

Rasayana includes the production of Alchemically purified Mercury.

Some practitioners of Rasayana put great value on alchemically purified Mercury, and maintain that by itself it is an Elixir of Immortality. Alchemical Mercury is acknowledged to be a physical manifestation of the
Primal Dragon or Skanda-Murugan, and will sympathetically activate the
"inner Skanda" or fire serpent.

When alchemically purified, Mercury can be ingested through the
mouth or taken in to the body through one of its other cavities. Once inside
the body, purified Mercury, which is also known among the Siddhas as the
"Sperm of Shiva," will naturally increase the seminal fluids and even promote their transmutation into Kundalini. Just wearing purified Mercury outside the body as an amulet can have great benefit in increasing and transmuting the inner fluids. It can also assist the yogi in astral travel through detach-
ing his astral body from the physical sheath. It is, therefore, truly an embodiment of the Thoth-Hermes or Mercury, whose classical function as
psychopompos was to escort the soul to another world.

When making Alchemical Mercury, the base metal must be taken
through eight stages of purification before it is safe to ingest as an elixir. The
Rasayana scriptures state that if Mercury is taken through another 10 stages
(18 in all) it will possess the properties of the Philosophers Stone and can
then change a base metal into gold.

The Mahesvara Siddha Patanjali, author of the Yoga Sutras, wrote that the process of yoga alchemy unfolds in eight sequential stages.

Yoga alchemy proceeds through eight stages. Eight is the esoteric
number for uniting Heaven and Earth, Spirit and matter, and a human to the
Infinite Spirit. These eight stages of yoga alchemy were delineated by the
Maheshvara Siddha Patanjali, an incarnation of the Primal Serpent:

1,2. Yamas and Niyamas: the preliminary practices involved in spiritual
purification that include strict observance of a set of religious command-
ments, study of a scripture, and regular worship of a deity.

3. Asanas: Alchemical purification of the physical body through asanas, or
body stretches, and developing the ability to remain in one posture for a
period of time.

4. Pranayama: Alchemical purification of the etheric body through controlled breathing practices.

5. Pratyahara: Alchemical purification of emotional desires through the cultivation of disciplined behavior.

6. Dharana: Alchemical purification of the mind through practices involving focused concentration.

7. Dhyana: Alchemical purification of the mind through extreme concentration wherein the mind completely subsides for long periods of time.

8. Samadhi: Alchemical purification of the mind and spirit wherein the mind ceases its activity for indefinite periods of time. The mind and ego are interconnected; when one stops, so does the other. When the mind completely stops completely, the ego also disappears, and one can truly live in a state of gnostic spontaneity.

The Mahesvara Siddha, Goraknath, founded the School of Hatha Yoga

The Mahesvara Siddha, Goraknath, founded the branch of Siddha Alchemy known as Hatha Yoga. The term "Hatha" refers to the union of the inner polarity, the Sun (Ha) and Moon (Tha), that this practice catalyzes. Hatha Yoga gives special emphasis to asanas and pranayama that purify and promote the inner union, although it also incorporates concentration and meditation. Some of the asanas are called bandhas, or "locks," that both lock the body in one position and keep the in-breath and its accompanying life force locked within the lower abdomen for an extended interval of time. When energy or life force is stagnant in the abdomen for a period of time it often becomes hot and turns into fire, which would then travel to the base of the spine and awaken the Kundalini. Another feature of Hatha Yoga are mudras, body positions that both stabilize levels of gnostic consciosness and prolong life. One mudra that stabilizes the wisdom associated with an active Third Eye is known as Chin Mudra and simply involves uniting the thumb with the index finger on both hands. To prolong life yogis often perform Vajroli Mudra, which requires the yogi to suck up an elixir through his penis and thereby directly feed his seminal fluids. Another mudra, known as Kechari Mudra, involves cutting the frenulum that attaches the tongue to the bottom of the mouth and then moving the freed tongue behind the mouth and up into the head cavity. When Khechari Mudra is performed correctly the upright tongue will become a conduit and receptacle for a special elixir that the body naturally produces inside the head but normally slides down to the stomach and gets digested. When captured by the tongue, this ambrosial elixir moves down the body via a different channel and has the potential of alchemically transforming the body and making a person immortal. This was a practice specially observed by the Nath Siddhas, which was a special lineage of Perfected Masters that Goraknath and his students were members of. The Naths were especially identifiable through emulating Shiva in their dress and demeanor, and especially for their practice elongating their ears by wearing long, dangling earrings. This latter practice earned them their alternate title of Kanphatas, the "Split Earred Ones."

Siddha Goraknath, founder of the Alchemy of Hatha Yoga

Siddha Patanjali, Incarnation of the Primal Serpent

Goraknath and the Nath Alchemists also united the polarity via Celibacy.

Most of the Nath Alchemists that Goraknath trained were strict celibates. Celibacy is another efficacious practice for uniting the inner polarity. Through the practice of celibacy, the male and female hormones that exist in both genders gradually increase and eventually build up a powerful magnetic charge that unites them. Their union produces a fiery spark that then travels to the base of the spine to awaken the Kundalini energies. The observance of celibacy is even more important once the Kundalini is awakened because the serpent fire feeds off the seminal fluids. If the seminal fluids are weak, the Kundalini will begin to consume the Ojas, the bone marrow, which governs the immune system. Many health problems can then arise for the yogi.

Sexual Tantra was also practiced in Siddha Alchemy to unite the polarity.

Another practice of Siddha Alchemy to unite the polarity has simply been to unite the two polar opposite genders in intercourse. With discipline, and while observing the physical thrusts and muscular locks recommended in art of Sexual Tantra, a male and female can exchange fluids so that both become vessels for an androgynous, alchemical elixir. The heat created by the sexual passion and muscular thrusts will serve to transform this elixir into a fire that rises up the spine to catalyze exalted states of consciousness.

Agastyar's student, Babaji, founded Kriya Yoga

The Siddha Babaji, who is world renown for having attained an age exceeding two thousand years, received special instructions to found his school of Kriya Yoga from his teachers, Agastyar and Bogarnath. He also received guidance from Skanda-Murugan, whose divine vision he received after performing austerities under a banyan tree in Kataragama for six months. Murugan blessed Babaji with a high level of gnostic awareness and then sent him off to the Himalayas to complete his sadhana (spiritual practice) while developing the school of Kriya Yoga. Legend has it that Babaji eventually achieved immorality and still resides in the Himalayas in the region of Badrinath. The enlightened Kriya Yoga lineage of masters that descended from him include Shri Yukteshwar and his successor, Paramahamsa Yogananda, author of the bestselling *Autobiography of a Yogi*.

Kriya Yoga incorporates an assortment of alchemical practices that are versions of pranayama or breath control. These practices purify the etheric body, which is the body composed of energy vessels and chakras, and they can also awaken the Kundalini power that resides within the Muladhara Chakra in the etheric body. Once the serpent fire is activated then gnosis and immorality are not far away.

Badrinath, Himalyan home of 2000 year old Siddha Babaji

Badrinath Temple, Holy Shrine of Shavites

Many Siddha Adepts could awaken the alchemical force in a seeker through a thought, word, look or touch. This process is known as Shaktipat.

Once the alchemical power of Kundalini has completely purified the human body and chakras in the head, a yogi or yogini attains Shiva consciousness and the ability to emanate and control energy or Shakti just the Infinite Spirit did at the beginning of time. The yogi can then manifest material objects out of thin air, and they can transmit a particle of their own Kundalini or Shakti into a disciple and awaken their inner serpent fire. This transmission is known as Shaktipat, which literally translated means "Falling Shakti." An adept who has awakened another's Shakti also has the power to control its movement within the body and its ascent up the spine. This is why the guidance of a Shaktipat Master is so valued on the spiritual path.

One yoga that begins with the transmission of Shaktipat is called Maha Yoga, the "Great" Yoga, or Siddha Yoga, the Yoga of the "Perfected Ones." This yoga has existed since the arrival of Sanat Kumara on Lemuria and his entourage of adepts, the Sons of God. Some of the Siddha Masters in India today have received Shaktipat from gurus whose lineages extend back to the early era of Mu.

Chinese Alchemy

Chinese Alchemy came from Lemuria.

Chinese Alchemy originated thousands of years ago when China was still connected to Lemuria. At that time colonies of immortal alchemists were settled in certain areas of the country, such as the Lands of the Immortals situated in the Kun Lun Mountains, and from there they could venture out and disseminate the alchemical teachings to nascent humanity.

The first historical alchemists were based in the Shantung peninsula and around the Gulf of Chihli. From there, as the Wu Shamans, they spread down along the Yellow River.

Following the sinking of much of Mu, some of the alchemists of the continent converged along the Shantung Penninsula of China, as well as within and around the country's Gulf of Chihli. In the center of the Gulf of Chihli were a group of islands occupied by the immortals of Lemuria. Known as P'eng Lai and the Islands of the Immortals, this is where Taoist legends assert that immortal masters consumed mushrooms of immortality and drank an elixir of immortality that bubbled straight out of the ground like an artisian well. Throughout the history of China, the country's alchemists, as well as its emperors, have continually sought passage to the Islands of the Immortals, but only the most worthy seekers were able to find them.

***The Wu Shamans contributed China's first five emperors. They standard-
ized the practices of alchemy and made them part of Taoism.***

The first Dragon Emperors of China descended from the Wu Shamans and possessed a deep understanding of alchemy. Their reign began
China's Golden Age, about which it is said that the "Gods walked among
men, and all people lived in harmony with themselves and the universe."[5]
Of these incipient Dragon Kings the most important was Huang-ti, the "Yellow Emperor," who succeeded in mastering all the sciences by his teens and
all the alchemical arts by his thirties. With the help of his court officials,
many of whom were alchemists themselves, Huang-ti incorporated China's
ancient alchemical wisdom into the earliest scriptures of Taoism. These scriptures contained the first reference to Chinese herbology, massage, and the art
of acupuncture, which initially was used among the Taoist alchemists not
only for healing but to alchemically purify the etheric body and to awaken
the inner serpent fire.

***The Primal Dragon of Chinese Alchemy is known as the Tai Chi, the "Su-
preme Chi" or "Supreme Ultimate," whose polar opposite snakes or
"fishes" are united as the Tai Chi Tu symbol. The yin and yang aspects of
the Primal Dragon are referred to in Taoism as the White Tiger (yin) and
the Green Dragon (yang).***

Production of alchemical elixirs in Taoism was the art of the Feng-
shih, the "Prescriptioners," who united substances referred to as the White
Tiger (yin) and Green Dragon (yang). Some recipes called for the union of
Lead (yang) and Mercury (yin) to produce the Elixir of Immortality. The
Feng-shih also transmuted Mercuric Sulfide, or Cinnabar, into an elixir called
"Returned Cinnbar." Those alchemists who sought wealth through their ex-
periments could also use transmute Cinnabar into alchemical gold.

***Taoist Alchemy unites the polarity within the human body as fire and wa-
ter. The alchemical practices of Taoism reunite the inner polarity and resurrect the Tai Chi in a variety of ways.***

In Taoist Alchemy the male and female polarities exist as the elements of fire and water that have their seats within the Heart and Kidneys
respectively. Taoist Alchemy involves sending down the fire of the Heart to
unite with the water in the Kidneys. Kidney water, which manifests as Jing,
a liquid essence loosely translated as seminal fluids, uses the descending fire
to transmute into fiery Chi, the Chinese "Serpent Fire," that will rise up and
actualize the process of alchemy. Both controlled breathing practices and
visualizations are utilized for this purpose. Alternately, the Taoist yogi can

The Dragon and Tiger unite as the Elixir of Immortality

Emperor Hung-ti, the founder of Taoist Alchemy

wait until the time period between 11 p.m and 1 a.m. when it is said that fire naturally resides in the seat of water in the Kidney. Breathing practices performed at this time will fan the flames and bring the transmuted fluids up the Du channel, the Taoist Sushumna, to the head.

Since the Heart fire is synonymous with the mind that resides in the Heart, fire can be sent down to the Kidneys through the simple practice of focusing the mind on the Kidney region below the navel, known as the Chi-hai or "Sea of Chi." This alchemical meditation can be performed with the eyes open or closed. When closed, the alchemist need only think of the area. When the eyes are open, the Taoist will also focus on crossing the eyes while directing his or her gaze below the navel, thus further uniting the male and female polarity at the Sea of Chi.

In Taoist alchemy, the male and female polarity is also brought together by uniting the Ren and Du channels (the "twin serpents") into the Microcosmic Orbit. The two polar opposite channels can be united by a Taoist yogi by simply holding the tongue against the roof of the mouth. This will unite the male Du Meridian, which terminates at the top of the mouth, with the female Ren Channel, which ends at the bottom of the mouth. The energy in the Microcosmic Orbit can be set into motion at any time, but it is especially efficacious after the Jing is transmuted and rises up the Du Channel to the head and then sent down the front of the body in the Ren Channel to an area below the abdomen for storage. The androgynous energy then accumulates in the Sea of Chi and eventually creates an inner "fetus" or etheric Dragon Body that will serve as a vehicle for the Taoist gnostic to astral travel to other realms of the universe while still alive, and become the vehicle for them to rise to the highest dimensions of the universe at death.

The polarity is also united by Dual Cultivation, the Taoists' "Tantric Sex."

In the Tantric Sex practices of Taoist Alchemy known as Dual Cultivation, the male and female essences are passed back and forth during intercourse so that the male essence can unite with the female essence in both partners. The result is an inner alchemical fire that can initiate the process of transformation.

In Taoist Alchemy the Alchemical Trinity is known as the Three Treasures. The Three Treasures are the Jing, the Chi and the Shen. They are united at birth, separate, and are then reunited in the process of alchemy.

It is said that in the fetus, the Tai Chi or Primal Dragon is united and the Alchemical Trinity exists in its unity. However, as the human body develops the Trinity separates into Shen, Chi and Jing, the Three Treasures. Like

Air, Fire and Water, the Three Treasures are progressive condensations of each other: Shen, which denotes both Spirit and mind, contracts to become Chi, or life force, which in turn contracts to become Jing, or seminal fluids. Alchemy in the mature adult involves reuniting the Treasures and returning them to their primal state of the Supreme Ultimate.

The Three Treasures are alchemically transformed in the three Cauldrons.

The goal of Taoist Alchemy is to reverse the process of creation and transmute Jing back into Chi, Chi back into Shen, and Shen back into the "Void" or the pure consciousness of the Infinite Spirit. Through this alchemy the consciousness of the Taoist ascends and unites with the Infinite. It is achieved by moving the Three Treasures upwards to the three Cauldrons, or "Cinnabar Fields," where each is transmuted. First Jing is heated and transmuted into Chi in the Lower Cauldren; Chi then rises up in the Du Channel to the Middle Cauldren to transform into Shen; and then the refined Shen rises into the Upper Cauldren in the head to become pure consciousness.

Taoist Yoga progresses through eight stages.

Like Hindu Yoga, Taoist Yoga and the transmutation of the Three Treasures occurs through eight alchemical stages. As mentioned, the number eight unites Heaven and Earth, which in this case refers to human consciousness uniting with the Infinite Spirit:

1. **Conservation of the Jing:** Conserving the sexual fluids through abstinence or conscious retention of fluids.

2. **Restoration of the Jing:** Restoring the potency of the sexual fluids through proper diet, elixirs, exercise, Tai Chi and healthy lifestyle.

3. **Transmutation of the Jing:** Transmutation of the Jing to Chi through uniting it with fire in the Lower Cauldron.

4. **Nourishing the Chi:** Nourishing the Chi by calming the mind and emotions through detachment, Chi Kung and meditation.

5. **Transmutation of the Chi:** Transmutation of Chi to Shen in the Middle Cauldron with fire generated from Chi Kung, and muscular movements.

6. **Nourishing the Shen:** Nourishing the Shen by stilling and concentrating the mind.

7. **Transmutation of the Shen:** Transmutation of the Shen in the Upper Cauldron to pure, consciousness void of all thought through meditation and complete stillness of the mind.

8. **Transmutation of Voided Shen to Make it One with the Void:** In this final stage the individual transcends the world of name and form and completely unites with the complete "Void" of the Infinite Spirit.

Taoist Yoga is similar to Hindu Yoga in that it incorporates asanas and pranayama. The asanas of Taoist Yoga are part of the art and science of Tai Chi, while its pranayama is part of the science of Chi Kung.

Similar to the path of yoga, the eight stages of Taoist Alchemy incorporates both asanas and pranayama. The Taoist practice of Tai Chi Chuan is used to balance and stretch the body, and Chi Kung is used to control the breath and Chi. Both Tai Chi and Chi Kung were derived from alchemical practices of the early shamans, as well as from the Tantric yoga practices brought from India by Bodhidharma. In China, Bodhidharma became "Da Mo" and wrote the Chi Kung texts known as *Yi Jin Jing*, "The Muscle and Tendon Changing Classic" and *Xi Sui Jing* , "The Bone Marrow Washing Classic," which are important texts for the practitioners of Taoist Alchemy.

The adepts who achieved the greatest success in Taoist Alchemy became known as Hsien, "Immortals."

The Taoist practitioners who have succeeded in transmuting Jing, Chi and Shen back into the Tai Chi are referred to in history as Hsien, or "Immortals." The Hsien are said to have attained the highest gnostic wisdom as well as the supernatural powers of walking through fire, moving through solid rock and even flying through the air. There are many stories of prolonged inter-dimensional flights in their astral bodies, when they left their physical bodies behind for days or even weeks at a time.

The Hsien, Ko Hung, wrote the guide for the mountain hermit seeking to become a Hsien.

After achieving success in alchemy as a mountain recluse, the Hsien, Ko Hung, wrote the *Pao P'u Tzu*, which became the guide for all future hermits seeking success in alchemy. His tome included 149 secret alchemical formulas compiled into 116 volumes. To make the hermit's camp safe, Ko Hung included incantations for repelling and/or taming tigers, snakes and other wild animals. He also dedicated a section of his guide to neutralizing the effects of etheric demons that obstruct the mountain alchemist in his experiments.

The Hsien often traveled to the Paradise of Hsi Wang Mu to live out their time on Earth.

After achieving gnosis and immortality many Hsien traveled to the paradise of Hsi Wang Mu in the Kun Lun Mountains, where they remained in perpetual bliss until their inner guidance instructed them to permanently leave the Earth and ascend to a higher dimension. In Hsi Wang Mu they consumed the peaches of immortality that only appeared every three thousand years and were, therefore, immensely precious. They also co-habitated with exquisite flora and fauna and with the most ancient of Hsien who had resided there since the time of Lemuria. The most famous Hsien became known as the Eight Immortals, the images of which can be found in most Taoist temples. Legend has it that the Hsien, Lao Tzu, was on his way to Hsi Wang Mu when he was stopped by a boarder guard and requested to write down his wisdom before leaving civilization. Lao Tzu's writings were compiled into the *Tao Te Ching*, which became one of the most important philosophical treatises of Taoism.

The Immortal Lu Tang Pin
He attained the power to tame wild beasts

The Eight Immortals of Taoism

Queen Hsi Wang Mu in her Paradise

The Immortal Shou with a Peach of Immortality
Peaches grow on the Sacred Peach Tree of Hsi Wang Mu
that bears fruit only once every three thousand years.

Safe and Easy
Alchemical Practices

This chapter will present some alchemical practices that are safe, quick and easy. Like all alchemical disciplines, their goal is to unite the internal polarity or Twin Serpents, resurrect the Primal Serpent, and initiate the process alchemical transmutaton. These practices have in common the ability to generate inner fire, which is the power that drives all alchemical transformation.

The alchemical practices presented in this chapter are in three parts. Part I covers those alchemical practices that initiate inner fire by uniting the inner polarity, and Part II discusses those disciplines that stimulate internal alchemy by directly heating up the body. Part III consists of many Yogas that are alchemical paths designed to fit every temperament.

Part I:
Alchemical Practices
to Unite the Inner Polarity

Alchemical Meditation

To perform alchemical meditation, simple sitting postures and mantras that unite the inner polarity are utilized. These will be fully explained in the following pages.

Alchemical Sitting Positions

Since the right and left sides of the body correspond to the male and female polarities respectively, a very easy way to unite the polarity and stimulate inner alchemy is too unite the arms and legs through meditational sitting positions.

You can assume an alchemical sitting position either on the floor or on a chair. While sitting on a chair you can simply cross and touch your legs. On the floor, there are three different poses you can choose from. The first is the "Easy Pose," which requires you to cross your legs in the most natural and comfortable way with both feet becoming situated under your legs and touching the floor. A more advanced sitting position is the "Half Lotus," wherein the left foot and leg stay on the floor while the right leg is placed over the left leg, and the right foot is placed on top of the left thigh. The most advanced of the three sitting positions, the "Full Lotus," requires you to first place the right foot on the left thigh and then place the left foot on the right thigh. Besides uniting the polarity, the Full Lotus also locks the lower extremities so the prana cannot escape from the body as it normally does. When the prana is locked in one place for a period of time it often turns into alchemical fire, which will circulate in your system of meridians and nadis, and it may travel to the base of the spine to awaken the Kundalini serpent.

Alchemical Hand Positions

To further actuate the union of the inner polarity, you can also bring your hands together during meditation. While sitting with your legs crossed you can rest your hands in your lap, palms up, in the traditional Buddha pose, with the left hand on top of the right. Similar to the Full Lotus, which has the left leg on top of the right, this alchemical hand position requires that you place your left hand on top of your right hand. Dominance is thus given to the female principle, which governs the calming and meditative forces within you. So even though the polarity is being balanced and united, some superiority is given to the female principle.

Shiva with Alchemical Leg and Hand Positions

Shiva in Full Lotus with hands in Chin Mudra

To unite the inner polarity you can also unite your two hands in the traditional prayer position. With palms together and fingers pointing upwards, you can keep the prana from exiting your body via your hands while at the same time moving the energy in your body upwards to activate the Third Eye and Crown Chakra. This ascension of energy will assist you in communing with your deity.

Another efficacious alchemical hand position is the "Chin Mudra," which involves uniting the index finger and thumb on both hands together in little circles while the rest of your fingers are straight and your hands are placed with their palms upward on your knees. This position will help keep in your body from completely escaping through your hands, and it will also activate your Third Eye of Wisdom. It is an excellent pose for gaining guidance and intuitive answers during meditation.

Alchemical Times for Meditation

The best times for meditation are those periods when a balance of the male-female polarity exists in the world. These times include sunrise and sunset, as well as the Brahma Mahurta, the "Morning or Bhrama," between 4-6 a.m. This is recognized by the yogis of India as the best time for meditation during the 24 hour cycle because the inner male and female polarity are most balanced during those hours and most conducive to union. During the rest of the day the body breathes predominantly through the right or left nostril in 90 minute cycles, and either the male or female principles are ascendant. Every 90 minutes the prana moves through the right nostril and into the Pingala Nadi to activate the male principle, and the following 90 minutes it enters through the left nostril to activate the Ida Nadi and the female principle. Only between 4 and 6 a.m. does the body breathe evenly through both nostrils and both nadis, thus balancing the male and female principles and setting the stage for their alchemical union.

Alchemical Tools for Meditation
Technology to Alchemically Balance the Brain's Hemispheres

For those not attracted to meditating in the early morning, new meditational technologies are currently available that balance the male and female polarities in the body at any time of the day. They accomplish this by producing the same signals and frequencies in both sides of the brain so that the hemispheres work in synchronization. When the hemispheres work together brain waves in the Theta and Alpha frequency range are naturally produced, and these brain waves quickly and effortlessly transport a person into a deep meditation. These meditation technologies, which have been collectively labeled Brain Synchronization tools, include audio CDs and portable machines that unite the hemispheres by producing a variety of frequencies though the mediums of sound and light. The audio CDs work through the auricular nerves to produce meditational brain waves, while the lights do so via the optic nerves.

Alchemical Stones and Gems

Alchemical stones and gems include those minerals that when held or placed upon the body catalyze the union of the polarity and the inner process of alchemy. During meditation alchemical gems can be held in the hands, or placed on different parts of the body, to assist in stilling the mind, activating the serpent fire, and awakening gnosis. They can also be worn throughout the day as jewelry to help keep a person in gnostic consciousness.

Alchemical Meteorites

The best stones for alchemical meditation are meteorites. They include Iron Meteorites and Tektites, such as Moldavite. Meteorites were used in the Mediterranean mystery schools during initiation rites designed to unite the polarity and awaken the inner serpent fire. They were created by the union of water and fire, or the male-female polarity, and could engender a similar union within an aspirant. They were also recognized to be manifestations of the Goddess Venus, whom legends claim was similarly born from the heavens as a ball of fire that landed in the Mediterranean Sea before rising up in a cloud of steam. Thus, both Venus and her sacred meteorites were the union of water and fire, and Heaven and Earth.

Both the black and green color of meteorites stimulate inner alchemy and can awaken the Serepnt Fire. Green naturally unites the polarity, and black contributes a frequency that resonates in the Root Chakra to awaken the alchemical force. Meteorites also activate Kundalini by their strong electromagnetic field that interfaces with an individual's personal electromagnetic field. Because of the interconnected nature of a person's four increasingly subtle bodies, when their electromagnetic body is strongly stimulated, the life force in their next higher body, the etheric body, also becomes very active. If the prana pulses strong enough in the etheric body it can awaken Kundalini in the Root Chakra.

Alchemical Mercury

Alchemical Mercury can also awaken or further activate the inner alchemical force during meditation, as well as at all other times. It can be held or worn on the body as a pendant. Yogis commonly wear it in the shape of a ball around their necks, while other yogis have been known to imbibe it as a fluid or suck it into the body through the lower cavities. Some have even inserted pieces of it under the skin with excellent results.

Iron Meteorites

Moldavite Tektite

Alchemical Mercury, which is known as the "Semen of Shiva," will feed the inner Jing and catalyze the transformation of sexual energies into spiritual energy. It also has the property of disengaging the physical body from the etheric body, thus assisting a gnostic yogi in astral travel. The deity of Alchemical Mercury is the god Mercury, the guide and messenger between Heaven and Earth. By another name, Mercury is Thoth-Hermes, the Lord of Alchemy.

Black and Red Stones

All black and red stones naturally vibrate in the Root Chakra and, therefore, possess the potential to awaken the inner serpent fire that resides there. One of the best balck stones is Black Tourmaline, which contains bands or striations that both emanate a black color frequency and powerfully stimulate the bands of energy in a person's electromagnetic field. Another efficacious black mineral is Obsidian which, as volcanic glass, possesses the natural alchemical fire of a volcano. Other good black stones include Smokey Quartz and Onyx.

The darker a stone is in the red spectrum the better it is for activating the Root Chakra. In this category are the many versions of dark red garnet.

Green Stones

Green stones have a natural alchemical property by virtue of their ability to balance the inner polarity, and ultimately to unite it. Green is the middle or central color that balances the male and female principles. The most efficacious and precious green stone for alchemy is Emerald, which is why the alchemical precepts of Thoth-Hermes were engraved upon an Emerald Tablet. Of the semi-precious green stones, one of the best is Green Tourmaline because it possesses both a green color and striations to activate the electromagnetic field. Green Jade is a good alchemical stone that can lead to immortality, which is why the early Chinese alchemists would both carry it and consume it as a powder. Other efficacious green stones include Peridot, Malachite and Aventurine. Malachite, which means "Emotional Release," is one of the best minerals of alchemically transforming and releasing blocked emotions.

Quartz Crystals

In ancient times Quartz Crystals were known as "Fire Stones" because their fiery energy could stimulate internal, alchemical fire. They posssess this property because on the molecular level they are composed of tetrahedrons, and the tetrahedron is one of the five Platonic Solids associated with the element of fire. The fiery property of a Clear Quartz Crystal is also ascribed to the angle of its termination, which is often approximately that of the Great Pyramid, 51°51', thus making it a vehicle for the generation of "fire in the middle."

A six-sided Quartz Crystal unites the polarity like a six-pointed star, and it generates alchemical fire because its Star of David shape incorporates the yantra, or geometrical form body, of the fiery alchemical force itself. As solidified white light it also vibrates at the white frequency which, as the synthesis of all the colors, can balance and harmonize all the color-coded elements and chakras within the body. Thus, it is a good tool for both alchemy and healing. It is excellent for healing the human body because its atoms create a double-helix like the human DNA.

Amethyst is especially good for both meditation and alchemy. It provides the amplifying and healing power of clear quartz with the addition of iron and aluminum, which endow the stone with a violet frequency. Violet is the color at the end of an octave, and its frequency acts as a bridge for transitioning into the next higher octave. It can thus alchemically transmute or transition a person into a higher resonate frequency. The Ascended Master of Alchemy, St. Germain, is the Lord of the Violet Ray, and can be summoned when using Amethyst.

Alchemical Crystal Grids

You can design an easy and effective alchemical environment for your meditation space by simply placing crystals around you in an alchemical configuration. The two most efficacious patterns to lay your stones are the six-pointed Star of David and the eight-pointed octagon. Sit in the center and place your crystals equidistant from you in one of the configurations, and turn their terminations towards you. The alchemical stones for your grid can be Clear Quartz, Smokey Quartz or Amethyst. You can activate the crystals of your layout with sound frequencies (music or chanting), or by broadcasting light upon them that stimulates their piezoelectric property (pressure on the surface creating the movement of electrons). You can also magnify the power of the stones by a factor of three by attaching bar magnets to two of their opposing sides.

Alchemical Vortexes

You can also practice alchemy within the Earth's vortexes, which are created by the intersection of two or more energy lines or Ley Lines. Such a confluence creates a spiraling pattern similar to the whirlpool created when two rivers bisect each other. The spiral of a vortex is the etheric body of the androgynous dragon that is formed at by the Twin Serpents uniting as the polar opposite energy lines. It is for this reason that the Chinese refer to vortexes as Dragons' Lairs.

When a person enters a vortex or Dragon Lair that is created by polar opposite energy lines uniting as a spiraling serpent, their own inner polarity is sympathetically united and their inner spiraling serpent fire is awakened. It thus behooves the serious alchemist to seek out recognized vortex areas for their meditations, or find one on their own property.

The ancients located the natural vortexes within the terrestrial landscape of Earth and marked them with standing stones and stone circles. Stone circles were placed around the perimeter of the vortex to keep its spiraling energy from expanding out in a horizontal plane and thereby dissipating. The ancients discovered that when the energy was held in by a stone circle, it would increase to a critical degree that is efficacious for both healing and alchemy. For this reason the Native Americans referred to their stone circles as "Medicine Wheels." The healing of a medicine wheel can be on the physical body, but it can also heal the higher bodies by moving energy within them and helping to release emotional and mental blockages that may have been controlling a person for lifetimes.

Alchemical Pyramids

You can also create your own vortex by erecting a pyramid. Pyramids possess the same angle as a spiral created by a natural vortex, and are, therefore, solidified dragons. In ancient times pyramids were placed over vortexes to help hold in place and amplify the spiralling wave pattern of the underlying vortex. This is how they were used in Egypt, Mexico and Peru.

But even when it is not placed over a natural vortex a pyramid will conduct spiralling energy patterns through it that are conducive to alchemy. It is, therefore, a portable vortex. Similar to a natural vortex, a pyramid will perpetually unite the polarity and generate a dragon spiral. The polarity as Heaven and Earth, or fire and earth, are efficiently united in a pyramid by the singular point at the top of the pyramid (Heaven) which a pyramid's sides unite with the square at the bottom (Earth). The male-female polarity also unites in the pyramid as the tetrahedron (Spirit, fire) and cube (Earth, matter), which are synthesized in the creation of the pyramidal shape.

If you sit or lie down within a pyramid it will have the same effect on your meditation and inner alchemical process as a natural vortex does. When sitting within a pyramid, it is good to sit in the center so that the spiraling energy of the structure, which naturally flows up, can assist in the movement of your own alchemical energy and move it up to the gnostic centers in your head. When you lie down at the base of the pyramid you will be in an important alchemical zone of the pyramid known as the "Eye of Yahweh." This horizontal plane is at the center of an subtle octahedron, which results when the pyramidal energy flow continues below ground to produce a mirror image pyramid, before shooting up through the center. Thus, the Eye of Yahweh contains the polarity uniting effect of an octagon.

The best materials to make your pyramid out of are precious metals, such as gold, silver and platinum, because their conductivity will greatly assist the energy flow. The next best conduit is Venus' metal, copper which, like the Venusian meteorite, will unite the polarity and thereby enhance the alchemical effects of a pyramid. Copper will turn the color green, thus revealing its polarity uniting property and green frequency. If you intend to sleep under a pyramid, you will want to use a wood pyramid that is less stimulating than a metal one. A wood pyramid must be aligned to True North to be fully activated, while a metal pyramid must be aligned to Magnetic North. A good size for your pyramid is seven feet square at the base. Seven is the number of alchemical transformation, and it leads to the eight, the number of balance, harmony and union, of Heaven and Earth.

Pyramids and Quartz Crystals create a wonderful synergy that is much more powerful than the sum of its individual parts. Since both pyramids and crystals produce alchemical fire, their union together can engender a very dynamic alchemical effect. Sit or lie down within a pyramid and then surround yourself with a crystal layout or grid. You can also hold crystals in your hand and cover your chakras with them. Then play music and/or broadcast a colored light over you (blue, indigo, or violet is best for meditation). The results can be very dramatic.

Alchemical Labyrinths

Labyrinths, like the one covering the floor of Chartres Cathedral in France, compress the three-dimensional spiraling energy flow of a vortex into a two dimensional matrix, thus, walking a labyrinth provides a similar alchemical effect as sitting within a vortex. The alternating pathway of a labyrinth that moves right and left, back and forth is the two dimensional manifestation of the male-female polarity, or two "snakes," of a vortex, that manifest as its polar opposite right and left-handed spirals. As a person walks along the twisting path of a labyrinth, the back and forth walkway balances the inner polarity to awaken the fire serpent. It also synchronizes the left and right hemispheres of the brain to produce gnosis. When a person finally reaches the center of the labyrinth the final union of the inner polarity is accompanied by an ascension of consciousness.

Alchemical Meditation Seats

It is always good when observing still meditation to sit on a seat that has alchemical properties. Sitting on an alchemical stone, such as a flat quartz crystal, with a cushion between yourself and the mineral, is one example of an alchemical seat. Another substance that can be used in an alchemical seat is wool. Wool has been recommended for ages as a meditational seat because it captures and holds the alchemical force that the body builds up in meditation. Often referred to as the Holy Spirit, Baraka, or Kundalini Shakti, this force builds up within a church, cathedral, mosque or temple as a result of the daily worship, and it is this force that transports people entering such structures into a peaceful and meditative consciousness. If the force is regularly captured by a woolen meditative seat, then such a seat will eventually become so charged with power that within minutes of sitting upon it an alchemist will be transported into a powerful meditative state. If a meditator regularly uses a wool shawl, this will also become saturated with power.

Alchemical Altars

An alchemical altar will fill a person's meditative temple or home space with an abundance of alchemical force. To make an alchemical altar all images, photos, etc, should be placed symmetrically. When there is a balance of objects on both sides of your altar it will project a balanced energy into your room or temple. Therefore, whenever you place an image or object on the left side of an alchemical altar, you should also place one of comparable size and mass on the right side. To enhance the male-female uniting energies in your temple, it is also efficacious to place the images of female saints and deities on the left side of the altar, and those of male saints and deities on the right side.

An alchemical altar will eventually become empowered by the spiritual force the alchemist directs towards it during his or her daily worship. Regular prayers or meditation in front of an altar, along with waving lights or candles to its pictures and images, will help empower an altar. Worship of the deities resting upon an altar or within framed pictures is especially efficacious. In time the images will become alive, and blessings will then continuously emanate from them.

Alchemical Pranayama

Controlled breathing patterns are also excellent tools for uniting the inner polarity. The best time to observe these practices is just before meditation as they greatly still the mind and assist in the generation of good concentration. Because of the direct link between the mind and the breath, if you slow down or completely still one of them you will have the identical effect on the other

Alternate Nostril Breathing

Alternate Nostril Breathing is a pranayama technique that unites the polarity by balancing the left and right nostrils and the Ida and Pingala Nadis that terminate at them. This breathing exercise will also balance the brain signals being generated in both hemispheres of your brain. Your intellect will then work in tandem with your intuition to produce gnosis.

To perform Alternate Nostril Breathing, start by closing the left nostril with the index and middle fingers of the right hand. Inhale through the right nostril for a count of 4. Now close both nostrils, placing the thumb of the right hand over the right nostril. Hold you breath for a count of 8. Now open your left nostril and breathe air out of it for a count of 4. Inhale through the left nostril for a count of 4, close it, count to 8, and then open the right nostril and breathe out for a count of four. Continue in this way back and forth between the nostrils for about 2 minutes.

When you choose any form of pranayama you should initially be careful to limit the amount of time you practice it. After you have practiced the discipline for awhile you can increase the time. But keep in mind that pranayama only needs to be observed until the mind and body become still.

Alchemical Mantras

The repetition of alchemical mantras will naturally assist in both uniting the inner polarity and stilling the mind. They are helpful because they give the active mind something to focus on. They can be used during silent meditation or walking meditation, or chanted out loud to purify oneself and the surrounding environment.

OM - AUM

During meditation, and at other times when it is repeated, the mantra OM will unite the inner polarity and calm the mind. OM, which unites the polarity as O (male, Spirit) to M (female, matter), can be chanted out loud or repeated silently (mentally) to oneself. OM is the sound frequency of the Primal Serpent that resides within the Ajna Chakra, so its resonance will also activate the Divine Wisdom in the Third Eye.

OM is called the "Pranava," meaning "that which generates prana." Thus, simply by chanting this mantra you can fill both your body and temple with life force or Divine Power of the Infinite Spirit, which is the Primal Serpent. When written as AUM, this mantra denotes the three powers of creation, preservation, and destruction wielded by the Primal Serpent.

Two Syllable Mantras

The syllables that comprise two syllable mantras correspond to the male-female principles, so when these mantras are repeated they balance and unite the polarity in the body. These mantras are very calming and normally only used for deep relaxation and silent meditation. The still the breath and mind very rapidly. In practice, their repetition should be in synchronization with the breath. The first syllable is intoned on the inhale, and second syllable is repeated on the exhale.

Hamsa, So'Ham

These two mantras are mirror images of each other, and both are abbreviations of Aham Sa, meaning "I am That." During their repetition, Ham or So is repeated on the inhale and Sa or Ham is silently repeated on the exhale. It is said in the yogic scriptures that Hamsa is the most natural mantra a human can repeat because it is the sound your breath continuously makes as it moves in and out. The yogic scriptures say that each human unconsciously repeats this mantra 21,600 times each day.

If your mind and breath is very active when you begin your meditation, it is efficacious to begin with a longer mantra, such as Om Namah Shivaya. Then, when your mind slows down, you can begin using a two syllable mantra.

Ma Om

When using this two syllable mantra, the syllable Ma should be repeated on the inhale, and OM on the exhale. Ma resonates in the heart, and OM reverberates in the Third Eye, so recitation of this mantra will not only still the mind and breath it will help activate two very important centers of gnosis. The intuitive information comes from the Third Eye, your inner antennae, and the AHA and inner inspiration comes from your heart, seat of your soul.

Sixteen Syllable Mantra of the Triple Goddess

This mantra is traditionally known as the classic mantra name of Tripura Sundari, who was originally venerated as a manifestation of the Triple Goddess on Lemuria before migrating to India. This 16-syllable mantra begins with OM and the remainder of it is grouped into three parts associated with the three powers of the Goddess and Primal Serpent: creation, preservation and destruction. Thus, it is a name of the Primal Serpent and the Goddess and can be used for invoking both (they are synonymous).

The mantra: **OM Ka A E La Hrim, Ha Sa Ka Ha La Hrim, Sa Ka La Hrim.**

The A and E are repeated as a long A and E. The five syllables after the OM correspond to the number five and Creation, the middle six syllables correspond to polarity balance and Preservation (like the six-pointed star), and the last four correspond to Destruction and transformation (like the four corners and sides of the square, a form that deadens the flow of energy).

Do not worry about synchronizing a very long mantra like this one with your breath. Just keep repeating it over and over a sacred number of times (5, 7, 8, 13, 52, 108, etc.). Besides invoking the Goddess and Primal Dragon, this mantra has the power to activate the inner Primal Serpent and catapult you into a state of deep meditation.

Om Namah Shivaya

The mantra, Om Namah Shivaya, is another name of the Goddess and Primal Serpent. It incorporates within itself syllables that correspond to the five elements that the Serpent Goddess crystallizes into when creating the cosmos.

This mantra translates as "Salutations to Shiva," which means salutations to the Infinite Spirit that lives within your heart. The five syllables of Namah Shivaya

Tripura Sundari, the Lemurian Triple Goddess

are associated with the five elements and their corresponding chakras in the body. The syllable Na corresponds to the Earth Element and the Root Chakra; Ma corresponds to the Water Element and the Sacral Chakra; Shiv or Shiva is associated with the Fire Element and the Solar Plexus Chakra; Va or Vayu corresponds to the Air Element and the Heart Chakra; and Yu corresponds to the Ether Element and the Throat Chakra.

The repetition of Om Namah Shivaya will both summon the Primal Serpent as well as balance and alchemically purify the five elements of the Serpent that your body is composed of. Thus, it is both an excellent healing mantra as well as a powerful alchemical mantra for transformation. This mantra should be repeated once on the in-breath and then once on the out-breath. It is a good mantra to use for walking meditation, still meditation, and for those with a very active mind. When using it for walking meditation it is not necessay to synchronize its repetition with your breath, which may become labored and rapid. When used for still meditation, once the mind becomes still from its repetition it is good to switch to a two syllable mantra in order to travel deeper in meditation.

Long Stotra and Verse Mantras

Very long mantras, including the 108 or 1000 Names of your deity, as well as Stotra or Verse mantras, including the *Bhagavad Gita*, are comprised of all the 50 letters of the Sanscrit Alphabet and can completely empower all facets of your nature. The 50 Sanscrit letters resonate with each of the 50 petals that comprise all the lower-six chakras, so these mantras can activate all your chakras and assist in the release of their indwelling powers and wisdom. The long chants are normally done in the morning to empower and purify a yogi for the day ahead. One of the most effective is *Lalita Sahasrara,* the "Thousand Names of Lalita," who is the Triple Goddess, Tripura Sundari. All one's needs are supplied by the Goddess through the daily repetition of Her long mantra chant.

Alchemical Elixirs
White Powder Gold

For those alchemists who are drawn to consume an internal elixir to promote their inner alchemical processes, a readily available and safe elixir to use is White Power Gold. You can purchase it from many internet companies currently marketing it in either a power or dilute form, or you can produce it yourself in your own kitchen. White Powder Gold builds up the seminal fluids and supports their transformation into alchemical fire. The common complaint of most users of White Powder Gold is that they initially feel something from it and then its effects seem to wane. The initial boost occurs as the body undergoes a frequency adjustment, and the ensuing waning effect manifests after its vibration becomes consistently higher.

Alchemical Sex

An obvious way of uniting the male and female principles is through uniting the genders through sexual union. Even a simple embrace between a male and female will have its polarity-uniting and alchemical effect, albeit a subtle one. Through alchemical sex between male and female partners a most profound alchemy can be executed. Each partner exchanges his or her essence with the other, and the result is that each will manifest an androgynous essence in their sacral regions. The ensuing fire of passion between the couple, along with rythmic thrusts, will generate fire in the sacral region, and this will have the effect of transmuting the dual elixir into an alchemical fire that will ascend the spine and give rise to gnostic states of consciousness in both partners. To be successful in generating the requisite fire to transform your fluids, intercourse should continue for at least 20 minutes, and the male should continually strive to use his sacral muscles to retain his seminal fluids. This might be difficult for the male at first, but through practice he will eventually build up the strength and concentration needed for retention.

Part II:
Alchemical Practices to Heat up the Body

Besides uniting the inner polarity to generate alchemical heat, the alchemist can also introduce heat directly into the body to transform his or her sexual fluids into spiritual power. Such practices include fasting, the consumption of heating herbs, and sweat lodges, although all spiritual practices produce at least some measure of heat and therefore have an alchemical effect. It is for this reason the Hindu yogis refer to all spiritual disciplines as Tapas, meaning "burning," and "fire." Simple prayer, scriptural study, and even satsang, or "spiritual conversation," will generate some alchemical heat and assist a person in their spiritual evolvement.

Alchemical Fasting

Fasting will dry out the fluids in the body and lead to the production of inner fire. This is why this alchemical practice can be such a good tool for those initially seeking to activate the inner alchemical flame. Fasting is used in the Native American rite of the Vision Quest, which initiates a person into spiritual life by awakening their inner processes of alchemy and opening the Eye of Wisdom. Such awakening can culminate in a series of gnostic revelations or visions regarding one's spiritual name, spirit animal, and clan affiliation.

Alchemical Sweat Lodge

Another powerful Native American rite for heating the body and achieving gnostic awareness is the sweat lodge. Through sitting within a lodge that has been heated by red-hot rocks, a person's body becomes heated and the inner fluids rise up the spine as alchemical fire. When the fire reaches the higher chakras, a person can experience visions and direct communion with Spirit.

Heating Herbs

The consumption of heating and diaphoretic herbs and foods, such as ginger, cinnamon, ephedra, and salt can also be used to heat up the body and transform the inner fluids. It is, however, preferable to combine this practice with another alchemical discipline, such as mantra repetition, for best results.

Part III:
Yoga Alchemy

There are many schools of yoga, each of which is comprised of a collection of practices and study that help engender alchemical transformation in the practitioner. Each school is designed to accommodate a specific temperament. Those yogis and alchemists who are naturally more disciplined in their habits and lifestyle, for example, will gravitate to the schools of Hatha Yoga and Raja Yoga. Those who tend to be more devotional in nature will find an alignment with Bhakti Yoga, and those who are inherently more cerebral and contemplative will resonate best with the Jnana Yoga path. Of course, humans are multi-faceted, so most people will likely choose a yogic path that is a synthesis of yogic schools.

Hatha Yoga, Raja Yoga

Hatha and Raja Yoga are often united as one yoga. The asanas and pranayama of Hatha Yoga naturally prepare a yogi for the meditation practices of Raja Yoga. Both Hatha and Raja Yoga require daily discipline for their success. Once a person takes to the path of Hatha Yoga a regular regime of body stretches, known as asanas, along with pranayama, must be employed if progress is to be made on this path. Only through regular discipline can the Hatha Yoga practitioner become suitably limber and purfied for the meditation practices of Raja Yoga. Raja Yoga, which also requires regularity and great discipline for success, can take a yogi into deep states of meditation and gnosis. Both Hatha Yoga, meaning union of sun-moon or male-female, and Raja Yoga, the "Royal" Yoga, culminate in the inner union of the polarity and the activation of the serpent fire.

Bhakti Yoga

Bhakti Yoga, the path of devotion and love, incorporates many features of yogic alchemy to produce the ultimate experience, union with the object of one's devotion and meditation. The object of devotion can be one's deity or guru, or it can be the Infinite Spirit and Higher Self that is beyond all name and form.

Bhakti Yoga encourages the development of unconditional love for self, for one's guru or deity, and ultimately for all entities within the universe. The practice of unconditional love is itself alchemy because love is the magnet that balances and unites the polarity. When love unites the polarity, the center of polarity union within the body, the Heart Chakra, opens wide. Only then can one truly experience unconditional love, and only then can one know oneself as an incarnation of the Infinite Spirit.

Bhakti Yoga promotes unconditional love through its practices of devotion, service and chanting of divine names. Devotional chanting will alchemically evolve the worshipper in two ways. Chanting ascends the consciousness of a yogi and opens his or her heart through the loving thoughts and emotions that arise when contemplating the deity the chant is dedicated to. Secondly, a practitioner benefits from the alchemical sound frequencies generated by the sacred language the chant is sung in. A sacred language, such as Sanscrit or Hebrew, will both elevate consciousness and unite a worshipper with the chant's deity. This occurs because in a sacred language the name or mantra of a deity or object of devotion is very close or synonymous with its true frequency. This means that the repetition of the name of a deity or a god will fill a worshipper with the frequency of that entity, and ultimately transform the worshipper into that deity.

Jnana Yoga

Jnana is the Sanscrit term for "gnosis," and that is what a Jnana Yogi ultimately achieves on this path. A Jnana Yogi embraces the path of contemplating himself, the universe and the scriptures. As he or she contemplates meditatively the intellect of the left brain will become balanced by the intuition of the right brain and soon a flash of insight and an AHA! will take a yogi's understanding to a new level. Eventually, when the intuition has become strong enough, the yogi will become less attached to outer information for his or her contemplation and, ultimately, all wisdom will emerge within as revelation. The need to know the individual characteristics of any object will then completely dissolve, and the Jnana Yogi will intuitively comprehend the unifying spiritual essence within all things.

Karma Yoga

This form of yoga is best suited for the modern human who has too many responsibilities to find time to chant or meditate, and for those who simply want to dedicate themselves to continual service work. Karma Yoga is also for the person who loves his work so completely that he or she loses himself in it. It becomes a continual meditation for him, and there is never any thought of what fruits are being gained through the work.

Through Karma Yoga a yogi learns to make their work their principal form of alchemy by daily cultivating an attitude of service to a higher cause or power. Eventually, this attitude leads to less focus on his or her personal needs and more concern for serving a deity, a higher power, or all people. The final stage of Karma Yoga occurs when the yogi completely loses himself or herself in service and becomes solely identified with the needs of a deity or other people. He or she then becomes one with an entity, higher power, and/or with all people.

Once complete detachment for the fruits of one's labor is gained through Karma Yoga, karma ceases to be created for that person. All the fruits of his or her actions go to something or someone else. The object of service receives the karmic fruits, not the yogi. Once a yogi finally ceases to create any more karma, he or she simply needs to burn off their remaining past karma before becoming released from the karmic rounds of birth and death. Complete enlightenment can only occur through the complete dissolution and cessation of karma.

To help cultivate the right attitude towards service, the seeker on this path is encouraged to study the ancient manual of Karma Yoga known as the *Bhagavad Gita*. The *Bhagavad Gita* is a conversation that once occurred on the battlefield of Kurukshtra between Lord Krishna and his warrior and disciple Arjuna after Arjuna had become completely overcome with the grief at the thought of slaying his relatives in the opposing army. Lord Krishna taught Arjuna that, as a warrior of the Kshatriya Caste, it was his work or "dharma" to fight without any regard for the fruits of his labors, even if those fruits meant slaying those he preferred not to harm. As Krishna states, all actions and their fruits have already occurred in the Mind of God; humans are only God's instruments for their fulfillment on the physical plane. Through their long Karma Yoga dialogue Krishna ultimately teaches Arjuna the proper attitude to perform Karma Yoga and how it should extend into all work and all actions performed in life. He also reveals how the proper attitude towards service will culminate in alchemy and, finally, gnosis.

Japa or Mantra Yoga

Japa or Mantra Yoga is for the disciplined seeker who is able to commit to the continual repetition of mantras for long periods of time...and eventually throughout the day and night. Such mantras are normally the name or names of a person's deity, which are repeated either out loud or silently in a temple, or while the yogi is involved with his or her daily responsibilities. Eventually, the intensity of repetition unites the inner polarity and the serpent arises with great force from its seat at the base of the spine. The teachers of Mantra Yoga maintain that as a yogi repeats a mantra, he or she infuses power into it. Therefore, if a mantra is repeated continuously over a period of time it will acquire such power that its potential for alchemical transformation is increased exponentially. The practitioner of Mantra Yoga can also acquire a mantra from an enlightened master who has embued it with his or her own spiritual power. The repetition of such a mantra will immediately fill a person with the spiritual power of that master, and it can then have the effect of both activating the Serpent Power and leading one to gnosis.

Living Gnosis

This chapter will cover a lifestyle that will assist you in continually developing and living within gnostic consciousness. Keep in mind that the foregoing are all suggestions. A gnostic should always listen to his or her inner voice before embracing any directives. Consider this your first mandate for Living Gnosis.

Make Gnosis your Daily Priority.

All the saints and sages have made the same admonition to humanity, "Know Thyself." This was the plea of the great western gnostic Jesus Christ, who admonished his followers to "Seek first the Kingdom of Heaven, and all other things will be added unto you," while making it clear that the Kingdom of Heaven existed within them. In order to emphasize the seminal importance of self knowledge, when plied with questions from visitors at his ashram in India the great eastern gnostic Ramana Maharshi would often reply by posing another question: "Who is asking the question? Find that out first." Ramana, who was recognized to be an incarnation of the first gnostic master, Skanda-Murugan, knew that once that pivotal question was answered and the person recognized their true identity as Spirit incarnate, all other questions would be answered as well. When devotees of the gnostic sage Swami Muktananda asked him to tell them what their life's work was, rather than stating a specific profession he underlined the singular imporance of self knowledge by consistently replying, "Your work is to know the inner Self."

Study the Lives and Words of the Gnostics

To fully understand the path of gnosis, it is helpful to study the lives and teachings of the gnostics, including those currently in body as well as those who have achieved gnosis in the past. Through their life stories, both the obstacles on the path of a gnostic, as well as the gnostic state itself, can be better comprehended. The life and teachings of the Gnostic Masters Jesus and Buddha, as well as those of the Hindu gnostics, Ramana Maharshi and Sri Nisargadatta Maharaj, the author of the gnostic classic, *I AM THAT*, are helpful in this regard, as are the words of the saints of nearly all spiritual traditions.

Observe the Practice of Self-Inquiry

The principal practice that Ramana Maharshi prescribed for his devotees to achieve gnosis was the discipline of Self-Inquiry. Through the Self-Inquiry practice of mental reductionism, many his disciples achieved the ultimate goal of self identity and transcendence. It is being outlined here as a contemporary gnostic tool for both sexes, especially the intellectual males treading the Jnana Path.

The discipline of Self-Inquiry begins with the question, "Who am I?" This initial inquiry will naturally lead to a series of other questions, including: "Am I my body?" "Am I my emotions?" and "Am I my mind?" As these questions are sequentially answered one after the other your consciousness will gradually turn inwards, and at the end of your inquiry you will inevitably conclude that the only true part of you, the part that remains after all other parts of you have either died, dissolved or been transformed into something else, is the eternal witness consciousness. Then you will know, at least analytically, that your true, eternal essence is the transcendant and eternal I AM consciousness. Your body can die and your emotions and intellect can cease to function, but the witness consciousness is eternal and will never pass away. The sages say it is always functioning, even during dreams and deep sleep. Eventually, by remaining steadfast on the path of gnosis, they claim that one day you will become permanently united with it.

Besides using Self-Inquiry as a tool for self discovery, Ramana Maharshi also recommended it to his students as a practice to still their minds in preparation for meditation. You will find that the mind naturally becomes still when posed with the question of "Who am I?" Then, rather than pose a follow up question, simply dwell within that stillness.

The Stages of Gnosis
Go with your Heart!

For most people the first stage in their path to gnosis is to simply learn to "Go with your heart." By "listening" to your heart you will both feel and mentally discern specific messages emanating from your inner Spirit, and eventually you will not doubt their origin because they will be accompanied by a resounding AHA! that will reverberate throughout your entire body. Therefore, if you have not been listening to your heart, start there. That is the best place to begin your quest for gnosis.

You will find that communication from your inner Spirit will also manifest as inspiration that spontaneously arises within you. The inspiration may emerge as a feeling and/or idea for a new project, a new goal, or a new direction in life, and it will always be accompanied by an AHA!. Initially, you might not be able to identify the accompanying AHA!, so it might be confusing for you to know conclusively that you are receiving a message from Spirit; but the more you turn within for answers and inspiration the louder the AHA! will become. With practice, in time the inspiration from your heart and its accompanying AHA! will become so distinct and strong in its intensity that there will be no question it is coming directly from your inner Spirit.

Your Gnostic Development will Progress in Three Stages

As you learn to listen to your heart, the development of your gnostic consciousness will progress through three stages. During the first stage much or most of the information you use in your decision making process will come from your past experiences or from sources outside yourself (books, friends, etc). At this point in your development you are starting to activate your intuition, but you may still not be certain that the answers you are getting are coming from your own mind or from your Spirit. Consequently, at this stage it is important to rely mostly on your rational discernment when making any final decision.

In the second stage of your gnostic development you begin hearing your inner voice more clearly and become more confident that your answers are coming from within. Your attachment and need for information from external sources begins to wane and you start making decisions principally on what your inner voice tells you. You have then reached a plateau where there is a consistent union of articulation (ideas) with an AHA!; this is true gnosis.

When you progress to the third and final stage of gnostic development, the guidance coming from the inner Spirit will be so clear and direct that any external information will be secondary in your decision making. You will then know that, in every action you perform, you are being guided by Spirit, your Higher Self. Moreover, since all your actions are inspired by Spirit, you will have the reassurance and satisfaction of knowing they are in the highest good for yourself and others. The enlightened gnostics of history have all stated that after achieving this third stage of development they are so completely motivated by their inner guidance that they do not even rise out of bed in the morning unless they feel the inspiration from Spirit urging them to do so.

Strive to Daily Remain in Gnostic Consciousness

As you progress on your gnostic path you will soon be able to identify the consciousness and state of relaxation that is most conducive to receiving communication from within. You will also discover that there are many distractions in life that pull you out of that state. Therefore, in order to remain in that consciousness on a daily basis it is helpful to refresh it by observing alchemy, meditation and/or prayer at different times of the day, such as morning, afternoon and evening. Gnostics throughout the world have urged their disciples to begin each day with alchemical practices, meditation and prayer, and then to strive to maintain the consciousness they achieve in the morning by occasional periods of reflection, relaxation, and meditation throughout the day. The yogis in India begin their day with meditation between 4 and 6 a.m., because that is the time most conducive to alchemy and gnosis, and then they refresh their connection to Spirit at other strategic times of the day. Between 4-6 a.m a person breathes most equally through both nostrils during the 24 hour cycle, and this in turn makes the male and female principles in the body most balanced and gnosis forthcoming. Gnostics in other countries observe their morning meditation and prayers at sunrise, the moment when the male/female polarity as light and dark is most balanced. At 12 p.m., or at the middle of the day, many gnostics refresh their realignment with their inner Spirit through another period of meditation or prayer, and then at the third balanced time of the day, sunset, they again refresh their connection to Spirit.

Cultivate Equal Vision

At those times of the day when you are not meditating or praying there are practices you can observe to retain an even and still mind. One practice is to cultivate equal vision. Rather than letting social consciousness dictate what things you should value and admire, and those things that you should abhor, hate or reject, begin to see everything as an equal manifestation of the Goddess, and then your response to everything in your environment will be equally quiescent. Left Hand Path ideology acknowledges that all physical objects and sentient beings are contractions of pure, cosmic energy, i.e., the Goddess. Therefore, see all people and all sentient and non-sentient beings as solidified forms of the Goddess, and perceive their actions as the Goddess in motion. The cultivation of equal vision is an important Left Hand Path practice that will eventually lead to the gnostic revelation of the omni-presence of Spirit.

Cultivate Non-attachment to the Fruits of your Actions

Another recommendation that will assist you in remaining in gnostic consciousness is to become nonattached to the fruits of your actions. This is very hard for most people to initially achieve because they invest so much effort in their activities and are very focused on a specific result. If they do not achieve their sought after "pay offs" they can easily become angry and depressed. While it is good to remain focused in your activities as this helps to engender meditational consciousness (the continual flow of thought towards one object), you will not remain in meditation if you can not achieve non-atachment to their results.

One cure for attachment anxiety, contend the sages, is to dedicate the fruits of your actions to a higher power or to the greater good. You can begin by dedicating the fruits of your actions to your family or spouse. Then, it time, you can broaden your "family" to include the entire human family, and eventually you can expand it to include the universal family and its ultimate leader, God/Goddess. When you attain this final evolution you will be able to dedicate the fruits of all your actions to God/Goddess, the higher power that works through you and all humans to actualize the Divine Drama. When you reach this stage of surrender there is no attachment to the results of your actions because God/Goddess is creating exactly what it wants to through you. All your actions become inspired by the inner Spirit and you receive them as a command from God/Goddess.

The gnostic sages say it is pointless to worry about or covet the results of our actions. For the most part they are pre-determined, and secondly, we do not do anything anyway; the Goddess does it all. She has become our minds, emotions and bodies, and it is she who is the real performer of all our actions. Ask yourself who or what makes your heart beat, digests your food, replicates your cells, etc.? It is, of course, the Goddess as energy that does it all; so why should you take credit for, or covet, what your actions accomplish? The Goddess has a specific result to achieve through you, and She is *always* successful.

The right attitude that humans can cultivate in regard to action is taught within the *Bhagavad Gita,* the gospel of the alchemical path of Karma Yoga. Perhaps the most poignant line in the text, and one that perfectly summarizes it, reads: "Yoga is skill in action." This means that through being skillful in action and not getting attached to the results, you are practicing yoga and progressing on the alchemical path to gnosis.

Strive to Release Fear

One emotion that consistently works against the cultivation and distillation of a still mind is fear. Fear about self-survival in a turbulent and unpredictable world can be overwhelming. Therefore, steps must be taken to eradicate fear in the life of a gnostic so a still mind can be cultivated.

The influence of faith and surrender cannot be overstated as vehicles for transcending fear. If a gnostic truly believes that he or she is being protected by a higher power, and that everything always happens for the greatest good, then fear will evaporate and the mind can become still. Fear for one's physical safety can also cause perturbations in the mind, but this can be overcome by learning some basic self-defense techniques and/or by repeating protecting mantras. It is not necessary to master a martial art, only to learn enough so that you feel secure in being able to defend yourself and those relying upon you.

Some feelings of fear are hard to understand and release because they are the result of past traumatic experiences, from this life or another, that are buried deep within the unconscious. To resolve this fear some form of energy release work and/or psychotherapy is useful to bring up the past trauma and release it. Many traumas will remain within our energy bodies as blockages and control us until they are removed by pranayama and healing modalities designed to move energy. They can also be transmutted by the awakened Serpent Fire.

Consume food and drink that support gnosis.

To remain in gnostic consciousness the kinds of food and drink you consume are immensely important. The kind of food and drink that supports alchemy and gnosis is easy to digest, natural, and provides plenty of sustained nutrition to the body. It has been said that your mind is as pure as the food you eat, and your life force is as pure as the liquids you drink. Without a pure mind and life force, alchemy and the cultivation of gnostic consciousness is very difficult. The importance of pure food and liquids is at the root of the viscious cycle many of us revolve upon. When you consume food that does not supply ample nutrition and is hard to digest you will weaken your body; when your body is weak, your mind will quickly become agitated and resort to negative thinking; and when your mind looses its stillness, the guidance coming for the inner Spirit is obscured and lost.

In India, it is said that there are three categories of food and drink: Sattva, Rajas and Tamas. Sattvic food and drink, which make a person peaceful and supports meditation and gnosis, includes natural fruits, vegetables, and grains. Rajasic food and drink, such as red meat, rich or dense foods, and power drinks, make a person's body and mind very active. Tamasic food and drink, such as old or overcooked food, or processed products and excess alcohol, make a person feel dull, lazy, uninspired and negative. Thus, a gnostic should strive to consume Sattvic foods and drinks whenever possible.

Excess Food, Sex, or other Activity make Gnosis Difficult

The sages typically admonish us to observe "Moderation in everything." When you consume too much food or indulge in too much sex or other activity, you drain your life force. When the life force is drained the mind becomes overactive and one's gnostic connection to Spirit is lost. If excessive behavior is indulged in for a long period of time, the inner source of life force, the Jing or sexual fluids, become consumed and serious problems can set in. You will become weak, depressed, constantly ill, and your gnostic progress will come to a grinding halt.

Always Strive to Live in Balance!

Gnostic consciousness is supported by the inner balance of the male and female polarity. Therefore, strive to cultivate an inner balance of the male and female qualities. Balance aggressiveness with softness, intellect with intuition, self focus with service for others. Tukaram Maharaj, the great gnostic saint of Maharashtra, India, once described his own inner balance by proclaiming: "I am so tough I could break a thunderbolt over my knee, but I am also so soft I would get bruised in a bed of rose petals."

Begin each day by establishing an inner balance through the observance of any of the meditational alchemical practices mentioned in the previous chapter. Besides meditation and prayer, certain morning exercises, including Hatha Yoga and Tai Chi, can greatly assist you in finding balance. The stretching postures of Hatha Yoga can be practiced before meditation to loosen up the body so that the alchemical sitting postures can be held comfortably for long periods of time. The balancing movements of Tai Chi will also help you achieve physical flexibility, as well as discover both an inner and outer balance in all areas of your daily life.

Take a Day or Two once in awhile to Reactivate Gnosis

After your life has been out of balance for a while, or when a major event seriously upsets you, such as a death or a divorce, it is always good to take a few days off to reopen the channels of gnostic awareness and reconnect with Spirit. This can be achieved through the alchemical meditation practices mentioned previously and/or through traveling to a serene environment that promotes a sense of peace and well-being. You might be inspired to observe some variation of the Native American rite of the Vision Quest, or you might be drawn to a specific vortex area. Again, let you inner gnosis direct you, and you will naturally gravitate to the right place.

Make your Home a Gnostic Temple

It is often difficult to remain in gnostic consciousness during the day while in a work environment, and you may not have the power to change or influence such an environment. You do, however, have the power to make your home into a temple that promotes peace and gnostic awareness. Your house can become a temple by building it in a vortex area, near water, in a forest or within an area with a very peaceful ambiance. Its construction should optimally be conducive to the flow of the life force and built as a dome, pyramid, sphere, hexagon, octagon or some other sacred geometrical structure. If you live in a square building you can make it more energy conductive through placing pyramids and/or crystal grids in the corners of your rooms. Within each of your rooms a balance of the male and female principles can be achieved by simply placing objects equally on both the left and right sides. You will know when the proper balance is achieved because the room or altar will generate an energy of harmony and peace, and you will feel comfortable and relaxed residing there. Adhering to the rules of Feng Shui, the Chinese art of placement, can also assist you in creating a balanced environment in your home.

Balance the Influences of the Planets, the Archons

Another directive to remain in a gnostic consciousness comes from the ancient gnostics, who understood that the Archons, the planetary spirits, have a perceptible effect on human consciousness. The gnostics believed that the Archons intentionally worked to keep humans from achieving gnosis and knowing their divine nature, so they used mantras, gems, and talismans to ward off and neutralize their inhibiting influences.

Today, astrologers recognize that some planets are efficacious in cultivating gnostic consciousness and some are not. Which planets will support a person on their gnostic path depends on their birth chart. After careful study of their birthchart, an astrologer can recommend certain mantras and gems to offset the negative influences of certain planets in the chart, as well as gems to enhance its positive, planetary influences. The information in a natal chart is also supportive of a gnostic in other ways. By understanding your destiny from your birthchart you are better able to witness life and not get too caught up and worried by events. This will help to still the mind and assist you in remaining in gnostic consciousness. Moreover, by following the transits of planets and how they interact with your chart you will know what days and times are most supportive for gnostic or alchemical practices. You can then plan to be in alchemical environments during the most powerful and auspicious of these transits. Some astrological prognostications also give some important clues as to when you might achieve full and permanent gnosis

To Intensify Gnosis, Perform more Alchemy

At some point you will feel inspired to deepen your gnostic practice. You might be getting close to a gnostic breakthough at that time and Spirit is directing you to intensify your alchemical disciplines. Increase of such practices should be done slowly and with caution. An intensification of alchemical practices can over-tax the body with alchemical fire, and it can also dredge up fearful and over-whelming emotions that are difficult to process. Over a period of time such intense reactions will drain the body of its life force and precious essence, and then it will be nearly impossible to maintain a still mind or continue on the path to gnosis.

Contacting your Inner Witness

In some predetermined time you will spontaneously unite with the inner witness consciousness. This breakthrough in your gnostic progress that will offer many future opportunities for slipping into a transcendant state of witness con-sciousness that feels like home, and where you can simply "be." The more time you spend in this consciousness, the more you will identify it as being the true you. In time, you will recognize that your physical, emotional and mental bodies are the vehicles you function out of, but the true you transcends them all. Finally, the inner revelation of I am That I am will powerfully emerge inside of you, and you will know conclusively that your true essence is the pure witness consciousness.

Eventually you will Merge with your Inner Witness

At your appointed time, you will complete your gnostic journey. You will transcend into witness consciousness and remain there permanently. Nothing will be able to take you out of it. You will then be established in Turiya, the fourth state of consciousness that underlies the other three states of waking, dream and deep sleep. Even when you are involved in an activity, you will remain immersed in Turiya, and then you will experience the divine paradox. You will react without reacting, eat without eating, and walk without walking. You will perpetually have a foot in two worlds, although you will be rooted in the transcendental world.

Your Path to Gnosis will Culminate in Transcendence

The enlightened gnostics who have achieved complete and permanent witness consciousness maintain that they are never again at the mercy of their minds and emotions. They have the option of whether or not to experience thoughts and emotions, or to just remain the witness. They calmly watch as the Goddess dictates all activity both in their inner and outer world. In the gnostic classic *I AM THAT,* the great gnostic sage Sri Nisargadatta Maharaj describes his personal experience of this transcendant witness consciousness. He states:

"Nothing is done by me; everything just happens. I do not expect; I do not plan. I just watch events happening…. The three states rotate as usual - there is waking and sleeping and walking again, but they do not happen to me. They just happen. To me nothing ever happens. There is something changeless, motionless, immovable, rock-like, unassailable; a solid mass of pure being-consciousness-bliss. I am never out of it. Nothing can take me out of it, no torture, no calamity."

The Gnostic Master Sri Nisargadatta Maharaj

The Gnostic Master Ramana Maharshi
Incarnation of Skanda-Murugan

Footnotes

Chapter 1

1. *The Secret Books of the Egyptian Gnostics*, Jean Doresse, Inner Traditions International, Rochester, Vermont, 1986
2. *Children of the Rainbow: The Religions, Legends, and Gods of Pre-Christian Hawaii,* Leinani Melville, Quest Books, 1969
3. *The Secret Books of the Egyptian Gnostics*, Jean Doresse, Inner Traditions International, Vermont, 1986
4. *The Mandeans of Iraq and Iran*, E.S. Drower,Gorgias Press, 2002
5. *The Ancient Atlantic*, L. Taylor Hansen, Amherst Press, 1969
6. Ibid
7. Ibid
8. *At the Edge of History and Passages About Earth,* William Irwin Thompson, Doubleday, 1989

Chapter 2

1. *Gnosis: The Nature and History of Gnosticism*, Kurt Rudolph, HarperSanFrancisco, 1987
2. Ibid
3. *The Secret Books of the Egyptian Gnostics*, Jean Doresse, Inner Traditions International, Rochester, Vermont, 1986
4. Ibid
5. Ibid
6. *Gnosis: The Nature and History of Gnosticism*, Kurt Rudloph, HarperSanFrancisco, 1987
7. *The Gnostic Scriptures: Ancient Wisdom for the New Age*, Bentley Layton, Doubleday, 1987
8. *Gnosis: The Nature and History of Gnosticism*, Kurt Rudloph, HarperSanFrancisco, 1987
9. *The Secret Books of the Egyptian Gnostics*, Jean Doresse, Inner Traditions International, Rochester, Vermont, 1986
10. *The Sumerians*, Samuel Kramer, University of Chivago Press, 1963
11. *Ponder on This*, Alice A. Bailey, Lucis Publishing, 1980
12. Ibid

Chapter 3

1. *Mysteries of the Dark Moon: The Healing Power of the Dark Goddess*, Demetra George, HarperOne, 1992
2. *The Life of Ramamskrisna,* Romain Rolland, Vedanta Press, 1929

Chapter 4

1. *The Mandeans of Iraq and Iran*, E.S. Drower, Gorgias Press, 2002
2. Ibid
3. Ibid
4. *Anacalypsis*, Godfrey Higgins, A&B Books Publishers, 1992
5. Ibid
6. *The Gnostic John the Baptizer: Selections from the Mandaean John-Book,* G.R.S. Mead, Kessinger Publishng
7. *The Templar Revelation: Secret Gaurdians of the True Identity of Christ*, Lynn Picknett & Clive Prince, Touchstone Books, NYC, 1998
8. *The Complete Dead Sea Scrolls in English,* Geza Vermes, Penguin Books, 1998.
9. *The Gnostic John the Baptizer: Selections from the Mandaean John-Book,* G.R.S. Mead, Kessinger Publishng
10. *The Gnostic Scriptures: Ancient Wisdom for the New Age*, Bentley Layton, Doubleday, 1987
11. *The Templar Revelation: Secret Gaurdians of the True Identity of Christ*, Lynn Picknett & Clive Prince, Touchstone Books, NYC, 1998
12. *The Secret Books of the Egyptian Gnostics*, Jean Doresse, Inner Traditions International, Rochester, Vermont, 1986
13. *The Templar Revelation: Secret Gaurdians of the True Identity of Christ*, Lynn Picknett & Clive Prince, Touchstone Books, NYC, 1998
14. Mary Magadelen Picknett
15. *The Secret Books of the Egyptian Gnostics*, Jean Doresse, Inner Traditions International, Rochester, Vermont, 1986
16. Ibid
17. *Gnosticism: Fragments of a Faith Forgotten*, G. R.S. Mead, Forgotten Books, 2008
18. *Pistis Sophia: A Gnostic Gospel*, G.R.S. Meade, The Book Tree, San Diego, 2003
19. *The Gospels of Mary*, Marvin Meyer, HarperSanFrancisco, 2004
20. *Secret Societies & Subversive Movements*, Nesta H. Webster, A & B Publishers Group, NYC, 1998

21.   *Royal Masonic Cyclopaedia*, Part 1, Kenneth R. H. Mackenzie, Kessinger Publishing
22.   *Secret Societies & Subversive Movements*, Nesta H. Webster, A & B Publishers Group, NYC, 1998
23.   *The History of Magic*, Eliphas Levi, Translated by A.E. Waite, Weiser Books, 2001
24.   *The Templar Revelation: Secret Gaurdians of the True Identity of Christ*, Lynn Picknett & Clive Prince, Touchstone Books, NYC, 1998
25.   *Royal Masonic Cyclopaedia, Part 1*, Kenneth R. H. Mackenzie, Kessinger Publishing

Chapter 5

1.   *The Templar Revelation: Secret Gaurdians of the True Identity of Christ*, Lynn Picknett & Clive Prince, Touchstone Books, NYC, 1998
2.   *Fulcanneli Master Alchemist, Le Mystere des Cathedrales*, translated from the French by Mary Sworder, Brotherhood of Life, 1990
3.   Ibid
4.   Ibid
5.   *Les Illumines de Baviere et la Franc-Maconnerie Allemonde,* Rene Le Forestier
6.   *The Hidden Church of the Holy Grail: Its Legends and Symbolism* A.E.Waite, Rebman, London, 1909
7.   *The Guilt of the Templars*, G. Legman, Basic Books Inc. Publishers, NYC, 1966
8.   *Secret Societies & Subversive Movements*, Nesta H. Webster, A & B Publishers Group, NYC, 1998
9.   Ibid

Chapter 6

1.   *The Brotherhood of the Rosy Cross*, A.E. Waite, Barnes and Noble Books, 1993
2.   Ibid
3.   Ibid
4.   Ibid
5.   *The Rosicrucian Enlightenment,* Frances A. Yates, Routledge, 2004
6.   *The Dragon Legacy: The History of an Ancient Bloodline*, Nicholas deVere, The Book Tree, 2004
7.   *The Sufis*, Idries Shah, Doubleday, 1964

8. Ibid
9. *A New Enclyclopaedia of Freemasonry*, A.E. Waite, Wings Books, NYC, 1996
10. Ibid
11. *An Encyclopedic Outline of Masonic, Hermetic, Qabbalistic, and Rosicrucian Philosophy*, Manly P. Hall, The Philosophical Research, Society, L.A., 1979
12. *The Count of Saint- Germain*, Isabel Cooper-Oakley, Rudolph Steiner Publications, 1970
13. *The History of Magic*, Eliphas Levi, Translated by A.E. Waite, Weiser Books, 2001
14. Ibid
15. *The Count of Saint- Germain*, Isabel Cooper-Oakley, Rudolph Steiner Publications, 1970
16. *Secret Societies & Subversive Movements*, Nesta H. Webster, A & B Publishers Group, NYC, 1998
17. Ibid
18. *The Tarot of the Bohemians*, Papus, Senate, 1994
19. *Twenty-First Century GRAIL: The Quest for a Legend*, Andrew Collins, Virgin Books, 2004
20. *Secret Societies & Subversive Movements*, Nesta H. Webster, A & B Publishers Group, NYC, 1998

Chapter 7

1. *The Rosicrucian Enlightenment,* Frances A. Yates, Routledge, 2004
2. Ibid
3. *Secret Societies & Subversive Movements*, Nesta H. Webster, A & B Publishers Group, NYC, 1998
4. Ibid
5. *A History of Secret Societies*, Arkon Daraul, Citadel Press, NYC, 1989
6. Ibid
7. *Secret Societies & Subversive Movements*, Nesta H. Webster, A & B Publishers Group, NYC, 1998
8. Ibid
9. *World Revolution: The Plot Against Civilization*, Nesta Webster, Veritas Publishing, 1994
10. Ibid

Chapter 8

1. *The Rays and The Initiations*, Alice A. Bailey, Lucis Publishing, NYC, 1993
2. *Initiation Human and Solar,* Alice A. Bailey, Lucis Publishing, NYC, 1992

Chapter 9

1. *Children of the Rainbow: The Religions, Legends, and Gods of Pre-Christian Hawaii,* Leinani Melville, Quest Books, 1969
2. Ibid
3. *Ponder on This,* Alice A. Bailey, Lucis Publishing, 1980
4. *The Way to Shambhala,* Edwin Bernbaum, Shambhala, 2001
5. *Shamanism: Archaic Techniques of Ecstasy,* Mircea Eliade, Pinceton University Press, 1972
6. *Burning Water: Thought and Relgion in Ancient Mexico*, Laurette Sejourne, Grove Press, NYC
7. *The Mayan Factor,* Joes Arguelles, Bear and Co, 1987
8. *The Yezidis,* Eszter Spat, Saqi Books, London, 2005
9. Ibid
10. *The Mandeans of Iraq and Iran,* E.S. Drower, Gorgias Press, 2002
11. Ibid
12. Ibid
13. Ibid
14. Ibid
15. *The White Goddess,* Robert Graves, Farrar, Straus, and Giroux, NYC, 1948
16. *An Encyclopedic Outline of Masonic, Hermetic, Qabbalistic, and Rosicrucian Philosophy*, Manly P. Hall, The Philosophical Research, Society, L.A., 1979
17. *The Complete Dead Sea Scrolls in English,* Geza Vermes, Penguin Books, 1998.
18. *Gnosis: The Nature and History of Gnosticism,* Kurt Rudloph, HarperSanFrancisco, 1987
19. *Religions of the Silk Road: Overland Trade and Cultural Exchange from Antiquity to the Fifteenth Century,* Richard Foltz, Plagrave Macmillan, 2000
20. *Montsegur and the Mystery of the Cathars,* Jean Markale, Inner Traditions, Rochester, Vermont, 1986

Chapter 10

1. *World Revolution: The Plot Against Civilization*, Nesta Webster, Veritas Publishing, 1994
2. *The Sacred Geometry of Washington D.C.*, Nicholas Mann, Green Magic Publishing, 2006

Chapter 11

1. *Lost Secrets of the Sacred Ark,* Laurence Gardner, Element, 2003
2. *An Encyclopedic Outline of Masonic, Hermetic, Qabbalistic, and Rosicrucian Philosophy*, Manly P. Hall, The Philosophical Research, Society, L.A., 1979
3. Ibid
4. Ibid
5. *Taoism, The Road to Immortality*, John Blofied, Shambhala, 1978

The Author

Mark Amaru Pinkham KGCTpl is Grand Prior of The International Order of Gnostic Templars which is dedicated to reviving the Divine Feminine and the gnostic rites and teachings of the original Knights Templar. Mark is the author of a series of books on the esoteric history of the ancient Goddess Tradition and the gnostic, alchemical, and mystical sects that emerged out of it. Mark lives in Sedona, Arizona, where he conducts vortex tours and oversees St. John's Knight Templar Commandery and Preceptory. Mark often travels to countries around the globe to lead Knight Templar and gnostic pilgrimages for Sacred Sites Journeys (www.SacredSitesJourneys.com) and to teach the wisdom of the Gnostic Templars. Mark is Co-Director of The World Alliance for Planetary Enlightenment and currently hosts the popular internet show *The Guardians of the Holy Grail* on BBS Radio (www.BBSRadio.com). Mark is also the Director of the Seven Rays of Healing School and an Astrologer of both the Western and Vedic (Hindu) Systems. Please visit www.GnosticTemplars.org to learn more.

The International Order of Gnostic Templars

A division of the Scottish Knight Templars

Spiritual Warriors

Dedicated to the Revival of Gnostic Wisdom & the Goddess Tradition of the Original Templars

Statue of Prince
Henry Sinclair
by Shawn Wilkerson

www.GnosticTemplars.org

The International Order of Gnostic Templars (IOGT) is a diverse group of men and women who are committed to assisting in the revival of both the Goddess Tradition (The Path of the Divine Feminine) and the Gnostic path of knowing one's Self fully by experiencing Inner Gnostic Wisdom.

The IOGT seeks to complete the mission of the original Knights Templar by revealing the common links uniting the spiritual traditions of the East and West.

The members of the IOGT are dedicated to living in accordance with the ideal of the spiritual warrior, i.e., one who is able to effectively, and without fear, meet any and all challenges that life places in his/her path.

The IOGT Five-Point Plan
For a One-World Spirituality

1. First we reveal the common threads that unite all religions, thereby creating more peace, love, tolerance and understanding between the world's religions, along with a sense of kinship and knowing that we are all One.

2. We also reveal that many of the world's religions also have the same heritage and even originated in the same places, such as the Motherlands of Atlantis and Lemuria. We also reveal that many religions began as pure gnostic spirituality before dispersing around the globe and becoming clouded over by regional and hierarchal dogmatic teachings.

3. We then define for our brothers and sisters what the path of pure spirituality is unclouded by dogma. This is the evolutionary path involving purification and transformation through alchemy that culminates in gnosis.

4. We also teach that there are many alchemical paths involving purification and transformation that are designed for people of all temperaments. And as a person evolves he or she can pick and choose from a multitude of alchemical practices.

5. Finally, when enough people have opened to gnosis, all dogmas can dissolve, and a one-world spiritual tradition will become a reality.

Yezidi Genocide!

The Yezidis are urgently in need of your help!

The Yezidis of northern Iraq are a people with a very ancient gnostic heritage who have been under attack by fanatical Moslems since the inception of Islam. Many millions have died over the centuries for refusing to convert to Islam, and the genocide continues. Many thousands have fled from their homeland to other countries, while those left behind are often without food or pure water. Many are not even able to leave their homes to work or visit relatives out of fear of being tortured and possibly murdered. Humanity can not sit back and allow this inhuman treatment to continue.

Find out what you can do to help!
visit:
www.YezidiTruth.org

411

ORDER FORM

10% Discount When You Order 3 or More Items

One Adventure Place
P.O. Box 74
Kempton, Illinois 60946
United States of America
Tel.: 815-253-6390 • Fax: 815-253-6300
Email: auphq@frontiernet.net
http://www.adventuresunlimitedpress.com

ORDERING INSTRUCTIONS

✓ Remit by USD$ Check, Money Order or Credit Card
✓ Visa, Master Card, Discover & AmEx Accepted
✓ Paypal Payments Can Be Made To:
    info@wexclub.com
✓ Prices May Change Without Notice
✓ 10% Discount for 3 or more Items

SHIPPING CHARGES

United States
✓ Postal Book Rate { $4.00 First Item / 50¢ Each Additional Item
✓ POSTAL BOOK RATE Cannot Be Tracked!
✓ Priority Mail { $5.00 First Item / $2.00 Each Additional Item
✓ UPS { $6.00 First Item / $1.50 Each Additional Item
NOTE: UPS Delivery Available to Mainland USA Only

Canada
✓ Postal Air Mail { $10.00 First Item / $2.50 Each Additional Item
✓ Personal Checks or Bank Drafts MUST BE
   US$ and Drawn on a US Bank
✓ Canadian Postal Money Orders OK
✓ Payment MUST BE US$

All Other Countries
✓ Sorry, No Surface Delivery!
✓ Postal Air Mail { $16.00 First Item / $6.00 Each Additional Item
✓ Checks and Money Orders MUST BE US$
   and Drawn on a US Bank or branch.
✓ Paypal Payments Can Be Made in US$ To:
   info@wexclub.com

SPECIAL NOTES
✓ RETAILERS: Standard Discounts Available
✓ BACKORDERS: We Backorder all Out-of-
   Stock Items Unless Otherwise Requested
✓ PRO FORMA INVOICES: Available on Request

ORDER ONLINE AT: www.adventuresunlimitedpress.com

Please check: ✓

☐ This is my first order   ☐ I have ordered before

Name			
Address			
City			
State/Province		Postal Code	
Country			
Phone day		Evening	
Fax	Email		

Item Code	Item Description	Qty	Total

Please check: ✓

Subtotal ▶	
Less Discount-10% for 3 or more items ▶	
☐ Postal-Surface — Balance ▶	
☐ Postal-Air Mail — Illinois Residents 6.25% Sales Tax ▶	
(Priority in USA) — Previous Credit ▶	
☐ UPS — Shipping ▶	
(Mainland USA only) — Total (check/MO in USD$ only) ▶	

☐ Visa/MasterCard/Discover/American Express

Card Number

Expiration Date

10% Discount When You Order 3 or More Items!